The Psychology of Aging

PRENTICE-HALL INTERNATIONAL, INC., *London*
PRENTICE-HALL OF AUSTRALIA, PTY., LTD., *Sydney*
PRENTICE-HALL OF CANADA, LTD., *Toronto*
PRENTICE-HALL OF INDIA (PRIVATE) LTD., *New Delhi*
PRENTICE-HALL OF JAPAN, INC., *Tokyo*

The Psychology of Aging

James E. Birren

NATIONAL INSTITUTES OF HEALTH

Prentice-Hall, Inc., *Englewood Cliffs, New Jersey*

Copyright © 1964 by PRENTICE-HALL, INC.,
Englewood Cliffs, N.J.

All rights reserved. No part of this book
may be reproduced in any form, by mimeograph or any other means, without
permission in writing from the publisher.

Library of Congress Catalog Card Number: 64-14540

Current printing (last digit):
12   11   10

Printed in the United States of America
73342-C

Preface

The purpose of this book is to provide a text on the psychology of adult life. The psychology of aging is a part of the broader subject of general psychology and, more specifically, a part of developmental psychology, which is no longer concerned only with the child. Perspectives have broadened, and it is recognized that the goal of developmental processes is the fully mature adult. This book is concerned with the changes in the young adult as he grows older and undergoes many psychological, social, and physiological transformations.

The book was kept small so that the reader can grasp the subject matter as a whole. It should be useful as a supplemental text in developmental psychology courses, in courses in the social and biological sciences, or as a basic text when the subject matter of the psychology of the adult is taught.

A broad range of professional services is being organized to deal with the requirements of aging adults. If such services are to rest upon a rational basis, a grasp of the basic psychological characteristics of advancing age is necessary. Both experimental scientists and professional personnel should be expected to have at least a minimum knowledge of the changes in the human organism as it advances from the neonate to old age. The present book may serve as an introduction to their studies.

In the past, there has not been much confidence in the applicability of the scientific method to the psychology of aging. Perhaps this arose because of a certain feeling of inevitability about aging. However, from the history of science we have been able to learn that what is unmodifiable in one generation is often found to be modifiable in the next. The obligation of any generation would seem to be to face the available facts with discerning and inquiring minds. Objectivity aided by research will, over time, improve the conditions of human life.

The psychology of aging touches upon more preconceptions and personal values than do most sciences. This implies an initial slowness in sorting out facts and evolving experiments leading to new discoveries and principles in the pursuit of a scientific psychology of aging. It is a difficult subject for one to comprehend at first. Man's behavior over a lifetime both determines and is determined by his environment. It would be highly convenient but overly optimistic to expect that experimental studies will soon indicate that man's aging can be explained by a few simple principles and that, by the application of such principles, man might control the main events of his life span. Not all individuals are fortunate in being provided with good environmental raw materials for their growth and development. However, the attractive prospect before us is that, as we gain more knowledge, we can bring about a society with optimum opportunity for individuals of all ages.

Acknowledgments

Dr. Bernice Neugarten read the entire manuscript and Dr. Asser Stenbäck read the major portion of it. I am most grateful for their thoughtful comments and suggestions. I am grateful also to my wife Betty. Without her collaboration and assistance I could not have completed the book.

J. E. B.

Table of Contents

1. Dynamics of the Life Cycle   1

Change over the life span, 1   Childhood and adulthood, 3   Problems and developmental tasks, 3   Phases of the life cycle, 5   The life cycle, 5   Role uncertainty, 7   Drives, 7   Point of view, 8   Irreversibility, 8   History of subject, 9   Psychology of aging defined, 10   Three kinds of aging, 10   Theories of aging, 10   Aging and nature of time, 11   Periodic and sequential phenomena, 12   Subsystems of the organism, 12   Manifest age, 13   Changes in appearance, 16   Differences in rates of change, 16   Individual differences, 16   Changes in maturation, 17   Emergent features, 19

2. The Social and Cultural Determinants of Aging   25

Selective Service data, 27   Socioeconomic status and mental illness, 28   Correlates of mobility, 31   Decision and behavior, 32   Dynamics of social class, 34   Income, 39   Medical expenditures, 41   Economics of widowhood, 43   Ethnicity, region, and religion, 44

3. Biological Influences   51

Aging of cells, 52   Species differences, 56   Within-species differences, 59   *Potentialities of the organism, 62*   Studies

viii   Table of Contents

of twins, 64 Parental age, 65 Health, 65 Mortality rates, 67 Major causes of death, 68 Biological clocks, 68 *A general biological theory of aging, 72 A counterpart theory, 73* Behavior and survival, 75

4. The Special Senses and Perception   81

Sensory functioning and behavior, 84 Sensory acuity, 86 Stimulus complexity, 87 Irrelevant stimulus elements, 87 *Vision, 88 Dark adaptation, 89* Critical flicker fusion, 94 Pupillary response, 96 *Audition, 96* Vestibular apparatus, 98 *Taste sensitivity, 99 Olfaction, 100 Pain, 100 Touch, 101* Vibration sense, 101 *Complex perception and judgments of stimuli, 104* Lifted weights, 104 Visual form perception, 105 Implications of sensory changes, 107

5. Speed and Timing in Development and Aging   111

Speed and timing, 112 Major conditions influencing speed of behavior, 113 Response conditions, 113 Reaction time in development and aging, 114 *Movement time, 117 Speed and complexity, 120 Expectancy or set, 125* Organism condition, 126 *Importance of slowed reactions, 127* Change of viewpoint, 128

6. Psychomotor Skills   133

Definition, 134 *Personal skills, 135 Automobile drivers and transportation problems, 137 Occupational skills, 140* Airplane pilots, 141 Athletic skills, 143 Experimental studies of skill, 145

7. Learning   151

Definitions, 152 Modifying conditions, 153 Conditioning, 154 Animal studies, 156 Speed in learning, 158 Interference effects, 158 Set or expectancy, 160 Studies of occupational learning, 161 Incidental learning, 168

8. Thinking and Intelligence   171

Elements of problem solving, 172 Some studies of thinking, 173 Inflexibility of approach and low objectivity, 175 The nature of intelligence tests, 177 Test results, 177 Criteria of adult intelligence, 182 Mental-physical correlations in aging, 183 Age, brain damage, and mental abilities, 187 Sex differences, 188 Rigidity and problem orientation, 189 Abstract-concrete orientation, 191 Behavioral load, 192

9. Employment, Productivity, and Achievement 199

Productivity, 200 Age, sex, and employment, 204 The uses of time, 205 *Scientific productivity and achievement, 206* Athletic achievements, 212 Age and income, 214 Values, employment, and leisure, 214 Continuing productivity in the aged, 217

10. Personality and Aging 223

Personality types, 224 Theoretical issues, 225 Hunger and thirst, 227 Sexual behavior, 229 Differentiation of the adult personality, 230 *Personality development in young adults, 231* Intelligence and personality change, 232 *The Berkeley studies of personality, 233 The University of Chicago studies of personality and adjustment, 235* Criteria of successful aging, 237 Personality processes, 238 Interests, 240 Attitudes, 243 Sex differences in attitudes, 245 Beliefs about the aged, 246

11. Aging, Maladjustment, and Psychopathology 253

Age and maladjustment, 254 Suicide and sex differences, 258 Mode of suicide, 259 Classes of mental illness, 260 Brain syndromes, 262 Circulatory disorders, 263 Senile brain disease, 264 Studies of psychopathology in the population, 266 Elements of geriatric psychiatry, 267

12. Life Review, Reconciliation, and Termination 273

Futurity, 275 Content of the review, 276 *Terminal decline, 279* Terminal cognitive change, 280 *Grief and the task of dying, 280* The normal psychology of the end of life, 286

The Psychology of Aging

1. Dynamics of the Life Cycle

Change Over the Life Span. As man grows older, he is said to become "more like himself." This is meant to imply that the individual increasingly shows a pattern of appearance and behavior that is characteristic of him. He is, of course, always moving forward in time and is in a dynamic transformation from his past to his future.

The general viewpoint being presented in this book is that the individual is a biological, psychological, and social constellation moving forward in time. The dynamics of the transformation of the individual from childhood through adulthood are such that mixtures of stability and change, persistence and adaptation, and emergence of new features are seen in the wide range of human characteristics.

Metaphorically, man's development over the life span might be likened to the growth and branching of a tree. Once branching has occurred, the pattern is somewhat determined, and growth proceeds on previous growth. Behavior also develops by branching and selection at choice points. Unlike the tree, however, man is both the result of and a determiner of his environment. His choices of behavior lead to further differentiation and to a more efficient ensemble of behaviors.

Trees, like animals, have characteristic lengths of life and show forms typical of their species. Trees may be distinguished not only by their appearance, but also by their lengths of life; there are short-lived, fast-growing trees (poplars) and long-lived, slow-growing ones (redwoods). Soil and climate conditions result in individual variations in the general characteristics. Registration of varying environmental conditions is seen in the width of the annual rings of the cross section of tree trunks. In man, registration of the thousands of daily stimuli and the consequences of reactions to them are the special function of the nervous system and memory. Adults retain the quality of "openness" of behavior by combining previous elements of behavior and organized stimuli into larger units. Thus the gradual transition of the individual over the life span is accompanied by the emergence of new patterns of behavior representing adaptations to his past history as well as to present physical and social circumstances.

A gap between the attempted explanations of aging from the viewpoint of molecular biology and those of psychology hinges upon the fact that the nervous system is organized to a significant extent as a result of interactions with the environment. The fact that the individual is also involved in the selective choice of experience which is cumulated in memory has no analogy in the isolated, molecular biological system. While much information is needed about the more elementary molecular processes, it should not be assumed that it will provide a sufficient explanation of age changes in behavior, particularly behavior of a communicative nature involving abstract processes and arbitrary symbols, such as in language, art, mathematics, and science.

At the psychological level, there is an "I," ego, which has an awareness of continuity from childhood and of a unique existence, so that each person can distinguish his personal history from those of others. A strong subjective impression of continuity can minimize the fact that we also show high replacement of the constituent parts of our bodies. We continue to develop new cells in body tissues and to replace chemical components. Chemically and cellularly we are high turnover systems, although both *stability* and *change* mark our biological organization just as they do our psychological and social organization.

Human development refers to the series of changes that individuals characteristically show as they progress in time toward maturity (growth and maturation) and through adult phases toward old age (aging). Aging may be regarded as beginning when the forces of growth bring the organism to a relative equilibrium. Terms like "maturation" and "aging" imply direction to events, direction that is controlled by psychological, social, and physical environmental forces as well as by genetic forces common to the species and unique to a particular individual. Organisms appear to differentiate continually in time and do not show "degrowth";

there are no reported instances of individuals retracing their course of development.

Childhood and Adulthood. There are many events in adult life that are of great importance to the individual and that seem to be without directly equivalent events in childhood; e.g., marriage, childbirth, change of occupation, and retirement. Some biological phenomena, like menopause and chronic illness, have consequences that are in part predictable in terms of the individual's constitution, background, and personality, and in part in terms of the immediate context of the adult. It is a truism that one cannot know the child in detail unless one knows the parents. It might be added that one cannot know the parents without knowing something of the grandparents. However, one can see not only the effects of the parents upon the development of their children, but also the effect of children upon parental development. Such interactions between the biological and psychological nature of individuals with the characteristics of their environments comprise a comprehensive developmental psychology, of which the adult phase is the longest and is the goal of the growing child *(Kagan and Moss, 1962)*.

Problems and Developmental Tasks. In describing the life span, it is rather difficult to avoid giving attention to the problems and crises of various periods of life. Thus the life span may appear, from technical descriptions, to be filled with a collection of unpleasant hurdles, resulting in a stumbling, bruising journey for the individual. This is obviously not a balanced picture, since there are many problems that are successfully met and solved and satisfactions gained that are not readily apparent. In a sense, the rewards of adult life take care of themselves; it is only the problems that demand attention. Because of rising standards, family life is often thought to have degenerated from a more blissful, earlier period of history; evidence suggests rather that the individual and the family have advanced not only economically, but also psychologically, medically, and socially *(von Mering and Weniger, 1959)*.

In the absence of records of the conditions of family life in preindustrial society, there is a tendency to romanticize life as it then was. One objective description of the period has been found in the records of the rector of the church in Clayworth, England, for the years 1676-1701 *(Laslett and Harrison, 1963)*. There were 412 persons in the population, and the average household ranged between four and four and one-half persons. This is small by present standards and suggests what further study of the records bears out—that three generations did not commonly live together. Rarely did a mother live with a married daughter, although quite commonly the household contained resident servants in addition to man, wife, and children. The pattern seemed to be one of the older adult's having to provide living arrangements independent of the other members of the family. In one instance, when the father died and the son became head of the household, the son installed his wife and two children in the house and turned out his mother and unmarried sister to live on alms. Orphans seemed to have been the only ones living with relations, and since mortality was high, about 28 per cent of children were from homes broken by death. One surprising fact is the high turnover in the population. Over a twelve-year period nearly two-thirds of the originally registered people were no longer in the village. Of these, 37 per cent were recorded as having died. From many aspects, life in a pre-industrial village does not appear to have been stable or problem-free.

Situations arise at characteristic ages that require the attention and capacities of the individual. The child's first steps, his learning to read and write, his first dance are absorbing events of growing up, as are finding a job and learning its skills, marriage, childbirth, job advancement, and retirement. All these situations not only challenge the individual, but also tax him. Throughout the life span, the capacity of the individual to adapt will be challenged by situations that may be novel to him but that are characteristic of an age level. Adequate adaptation or resolution of the problems and dominant concerns of an age level helps the individual become an increasingly more differentiated and competent person.

Not all of the stressful situations that tax the adult's capacity to adapt arise from negative influences. Making a choice between two positive, or attractive, alternatives can also be very difficult. A middle-aged man may be offered two jobs, either of which might be superior to his present one. His vacillation because of the inability to choose between two equally attractive alternatives can be a most unpleasant experience for him.

Achievement may bring with it unexpected problems for the adult, and he may be unable to handle success. This implies competence in the struggle for achievement, but a lack of adaptation in coping with success. Some men drink heavily at the very peak of their careers and thus ruin the success they were so bent on achieving. Marriages of young adults often work out well during the early years of struggle, but just when the goal of a stable family and home has been achieved and they can relax about financial matters, the marriage breaks up. Other examples of adult problem solving crises are easily cited: the stress of the marriageable girl in deciding among several equally attractive men, or the perplexity surrounding the choice between the attractions of marriage and a career.

The principal point being emphasized is that adult life, like that of the child, is always evolving. Furthermore, phase relationships can be important in evolving relationships. If the wife begins a job in middle age, after the children leave home, her husband, who may be experiencing the feeling of being passed over for a promotion, may see her horizons as expanding while his remain stationary. Because of his own middle-age job plateau, the husband may resent the new freedom and competence shown by his wife.

Some adults find that the death of a parent or sibling evokes old family issues and relationships in unpredictable ways. Since losses of close relatives and friends occur more frequently with advancing age, coping with grief and bereavement is one of the more significant of the psychological tasks of aging.

These brief examples are used to suggest that at every point of the life span there are challenges to the capacity to adapt. Many of the problems or tasks are characteristic of specific age levels.

Phases of the Life Cycle. The human life cycle may be divided in many ways, including the ages at which most individuals are presented by society with particular demands. Thus some human phases have no counterpart in animals and reflect cultural determination or age grading. Development, maturity, and senescence will be divided differently depending upon the use of anatomical, physiological, psychological, or social criteria. Behavioral criteria of maturity further differ depending on whether they are mostly concerned with motor skills, verbal learning, thinking and problem solving, or social behavior. Table 1-1 is based upon arbitrary phases of the life span and takes into account not only the phases used by social institutions, but also psychological capacities, always recognizing that there are differences in individuals of the same age.

TABLE 1-1. DURATION OF PHASES OF THE LIFE SPAN

Phase	Age
Infancy	2
Preschool	2-5
Childhood	5-12
Adolescence	12-17
Early maturity	17-25
Maturity	25-50
Later maturity	50-75
Old age	75

The Life Cycle. From the previous discussion it may be inferred that no single curve illustrating the life cycle in all its phases and rates of change is possible. The rate of change in a line graph depicting human maturation and senescence varies—be the measurements biological, psychological, or social. In addition to physical features of growth, the social group expects, and perhaps encourages, certain behavior and attitudes and interests at about the same time in life. An impulsiveness in the young child, or a compelling assertiveness of the young adult for independence and ascendance, is expected. The mature man is expected to show less impulsiveness in solving problems and a greater disposition to counsel and to a review of alternatives.

Analyses of biographical material have suggested a tempo or rhythm to adult life. *Frenkel (1936)* examined biographies for three kinds of information: (1) activities and events, (2) internal reactions to these events, and (3) accomplishments and productions. Her results led her to the opinion that there were rather clearly demarcated phases through which every individual passes; corresponding to these phases were sets of behavioral characteristics. In general, the phases corresponded to the notions of (a) construction, (b) culmination, and (c) reduction. Her observations were based upon biographies of Europeans in a relatively stable period of history. For this reason perhaps, one should not expect more than a general agreement between her study and the evolution of the personal life of individuals in America during this period of change and emphasis on early sexual gratification and marriage. Nonetheless, the work has been useful in pointing to a psychological rhythm to adult life, with a phase of expanding activities followed by a plateau, then a little unrest, and later by a withdrawal from previous activities.

The phase of change from striving to withdrawing has also been described as one of disengagement (*Cumming and Henry, 1961*). Late life for most people is characterized by a reduction in physical activities and social interaction. There is a constriction of life space—physically, socially, and psychologically. Given a reduction in energy, aged individuals will be willing accomplices in the process of separation from active society. They will be more content with this "disengaged" position in society than if their former, more active position had to be maintained. Aged individuals with different temperaments and experience, however, may resist retirement and changes toward a less active position.

The extent to which the older person anticipates losses or retrenchments by withdrawing himself emotionally, or affectively, is not certain. It is probable that some part of the affective withdrawal from life by the aged is a normal developmental process of the later years. The age grading of activities by society contrives to keep the individual in step. But inner drives and needs for gratification also accelerate or retard our response to the activities available to us within an age level.

In the process of late-life disengagement, both the stimulation value of the environment and the internal level of arousal or drive are relevant. Biopsychological and social factors influence the pattern of late-life change or development, and the values of the individual determine the acceptability of the changes.

During early life, the healthy organism provokes a high level of interaction with the environment. The general high energy output of young organisms may be contrasted to the more systematized behavior of the older adult, in whom specific patterns of behavior are evoked by the environment.

The rhythm of the life span is influenced by the selective reinforcement of behavior. What is appropriate behavior for a child in the eyes of his parents at one age will not be viewed as appropriate at another age. Behavior is thus selectively encouraged and discouraged according to a concept of what is correct for the age. Later "shaping up" of behavior according to age is influenced by the school, friends, relatives, and social groups, and it results in an awareness of the behavior expected according to one's age and situation. Also influential in the changes in adult behavior are the persons implicitly or explicitly being used as a standard to be copied (*Erickson, 1959*). Identification with other persons and ideas leads to selectivity in behavior. For example, childhood heroes are often seen clearly in the way children speak, dress, or act. In adult life, the "heroes" may be less obvious but nonetheless active in the selection of behavior appropriate for an age level and situation.

Role Uncertainty. As the individual advances from one age level to the next, as from home to school, he is uncertain of what to expect and how to behave. Similarly, graduation from college and transition to a career is an age-related change in role. Marriage and retirement can also be looked at from the viewpoint of role uncertainty. Crisis points in the life span can be looked at as phases of social role uncertainty. The uncertainty (and possible stress and anxiety) tends to be minimized when the individual has social contacts that result in high input of information. A youngster asks others: "What was it like?" even as adults inquire about the new and uncertain.

There is evidence that marriage requires different role changes of the man and woman and that during the course of marriage a man's role becomes defined more rigidly and the woman's more flexibly (*Tharp, 1963*). Presumably this role differentiation has some advantage for the marriage. However, it does suggest that the pattern of adult development can be quite different for men and women. At retirement the man may need to have an adaptiveness for which he has not been well prepared as a result of his specialized role as a worker.

Drives. Influencing the activities of the adult are the biological drives and appetites. The general impression of biological drives is of an early-life increase in drives and appetites, followed by a middle-age plateau and a later-life decline. Even if such a simple description were correct, the habits acquired during learning would in late life be expected to have some autonomy of function. This is to say that habits may acquire the character of drives, and a diminution in the strength of the original biological drive need not lead directly to a change in behavior. Certain forms of behavior may thus persist after the drives are diminished (e.g., sex and food).

In describing the selectivity of adult behavior, changes in strengths of motivations should be noted. A girl with a strong need for achievement and a high level of vocational aspiration may not show much social interaction, but if she achieves sufficient rewards, she may find these motives satiated by middle age and might then show a relative rise in affiliative tendencies and seek a middle-age marriage. Not all motives or secondary drives are easily satiated, and some, if highly generalized, may resist extinction or satiation and persist. Thus an aggressive young man may develop into a successful and continuing high income producer throughout his life span with the "drive" toward the acquisition of money unsatiated. Such a man, however, may turn into an active philanthropist late in life when he becomes concerned with the image he will leave behind.

Point of View. A description of the life span either in terms of biological drives alone or in terms of socially learned drives alone is unsatisfying from a psychological point of view. A large number of words relate to aversions and goals suggesting a mixed biological and learned basis as well as gradations in intensity: interest, aspiration, wish, desire, liking, hunger, thirst, lust, yearning, loathing, fear, phobia, shunning, avoiding. It might be remotely possible that all the positive and negative motivations and drives of an individual could be satiated in adulthood and the "ennui of a crushing satiety" experienced. Rather more common, however, is a continuous transmutation of interests and goals over the life span, so that one is aware of change and has a sense of becoming.

Some genetically determined traits can be said to be buffered against change and appear as invariant characteristics of the species. The number and placement of limbs and sense organs are highly rigid characteristics of the species. Other traits, such as learning, provide for plasticity in behavior; learning also has survival value. In comparison with other animals, man's behavior is remarkably plastic in response to changes in his environment. Plasticity in behavior is itself genetically determined, although the environment must evoke the trait and, within limits, permit modification of structure and function. The limits of man's plasticity of behavior in youth and in old age are only vaguely known in contrast to knowledge about the physiological limits of his survival, as in extremes of temperature or oxygen lack.

Irreversibility. Several terms and concepts are useful in discussing aging and development. The term used to name the property of events moving in only one direction, like the little ratchet and cogwheel in a watch or clock, is "irreversibility." If events flow only in one direction, then the related property of "cumulation" of consequences may also be observed.

New personal experiences are built on the past. The properties of irreversibility and cumulation are useful, but they do not in themselves lead to a definition of aging.

The term "aging" refers to something closely related to chronological age but not identical with it. By itself, chronological age is one of the most useful single items of information to know about an individual. Knowing an individual's chronological age, one can make a number of predictions about his most likely anatomical, physiological, psychological, and social characteristics. Age is a useful and powerful index in classifying large amounts of information; but "aging" is used in a broader sense. It is a very broad term and one should take care in using it. Some of its meanings antedate modern science.

History of Subject. Aging is a natural phenomenon with not only broad scientific implications for all living forms, but also with profound personal implications for each individual. Man has long been reflective about changes occuring in behavior and temperament with advancing age, and the record of his subjective reactions to aging are well recorded in sculpture, painting, prose, and poetry. Despite a long prescientific history, an empirically based psychology of aging did not appear until about 1835 with the work of Quetelet, and it showed a very slow growth in factual information until after World War II *(Birren, 1961)*.

It may seem rather strange that the psychology of aging began so recently when there is such a long history of the awareness of differences between young and old adults; e.g., as shown in the Bible. However, an objective psychology of aging had to wait until there were methods of gathering data systematically and of using controls to minimize biases in point of view, which, in the case of something as personal as aging, are difficult to impose. Self-deception can obscure the truth, and opinionated self-observation has passed with the credence of scientific generalizations. One view of ancient origin is that old age is the result of disease. This view has supported the pursuit of the most enthusiastic cures for old age and attempts at rejuvenation, like that of inhaling the breath of young girls *(Burstein, 1955)*. Reflection about the characteristic life spans of other animals might have suggested that man's life span is also a natural phenomenon. Yet such a view would have been a weak opponent to the more subjective need for a belief in personal immortality, and the belief that aging was disease dominated. This latter idea was to some extent supported by the obvious fact that many lives are shortened due to preventable accidents and disease.

Among the more objective observers of aging was Leonardo da Vinci. Because of his interest in anatomy and his consequent dissections, he saw in an objective context a wider sample of persons of different age than did most who pronounced on the subject of aging. Among other descriptions, he presented in detail the anatomy of a centenarian (*Belt, 1956*). As a result of his knowledge of the anatomical changes of aging, he was able to formulate rules for artists for representing persons of different ages that might suggest a regularity in the changes in appearance.

Psychology of Aging Defined. Description and explanation of the evolution of adult behavior over the life span is the subject matter of the psychology of aging. This includes the study of capacities, skills, feelings, emotions, and social behavior as they differentiate in the adult with age.

Three Kinds of Aging. It is useful to distinguish three kinds of aging: *biological, psychological,* and *social.* The central feature of *biological aging* is how long the individual or species will live. Thus the biological age of a person is his present position relative to his potential life span. Biological age thus defined is closely related to chronological age but is not identical with it, since it is derived from a different set of measurements.

Psychological age refers to the adaptive capacities of individuals as observed from their behavior, but it may also refer to subjective reactions or self-awareness. Psychological age is related both to chronological and to biological age, but it is not fully described by their combination.

Social age refers to the social habits and roles of the individual relative to the expectations of his group and society. Again, an individual's social age is related to, but not completely defined by, his chronological, biological, and psychological age. Age is an important factor in determining how individuals behave in relation to one another, and within societies there are often elaborate age-status systems. The age grading of expected behavior is a long-evolving process in society, and it is only partly related to the biological and psychological characteristics of individuals at a given age.

Theories of Aging. Theories about aging are attempts to describe or explain the changes that occur in individuals with advancing age. Theories can generally be divided into three groups: *genetic* theories; *counterpart* theories, in which adult changes are regarded as counterparts of earlier development and are thus related or traced to early life origins; *accident* or "wear-and-tear" theories in which adult characteristics are related to an accumulation of the effects of random events or accidents. Examples can be found of biological, psychological, and social theories in all three categories. A personality theory relating a late-life trait to early-life experience is essentially a counterpart theory in that aging is regarded as a counterpart of some early events. A biological theory that views aging as resulting from increased stress is an accident theory. It should not be expected that one science or one theory can explain all the changes that occur in individuals. Thus no one theory should be expected to be universally serviceable to the biologists, psychologists, and social scientists.

A *behavioral* theory of aging is concerned with systematic explanation of age differences in behavior and capacities of adult organisms. What are to be explained are the many age differences in sensory and perceptual function, psychomotor skills, learning and memory, thinking and problem solving, motivation and emotion, and, for man, that complex area identified as personality.

For those aspects of behavior that show change with age, it is important to establish the timing or regularity of events with advancing age. The accumulation of experiences or consequences, as in learning, need not imply regularity in the antecedent events. Memory is probably the irreversible property of the organism that, for behavior, gives the system direction in time, but it does not in itself imply an orderly accumulation of registered events.

The accumulation of consequences can eventually result in large individual differences, even though the day-to-day dynamic differences are small. Consider two children, one of whom spends 1 per cent of his waking time reading history and the other, 1 per cent of his time reading about sports. At the end of a several-year period, a large difference would exist between them in achievement or storage of information, leading to further definition of interests. An observer watching individuals on any single day might easily miss the small biases in their selective experience. This is to say that people will differ more in achievement or in storage of information than they will in the rate of gain of experience. There is a circularity involved, in that having achieved or learned more, individuals are also in a position to learn still more; but the point should nonetheless be made that individuals are probably not so different in their capacities or in the dynamics of daily functioning as long-term accumulation effects might lead us to suppose.

Aging and Nature of Time. One cannot discuss aging without becoming concerned with the nature of time and its measurement. The measurement of time involves a unit and a reference standard. In previous sections it was pointed out that psychological, biological, and social time need not be identical. Awareness of the passage of time or our feelings about how old we are would hardly be accepted as a measure of elapsed time. Nor would the age at puberty or marriage provide a standard unit of time for regulating commerce. Elapsed time is probably not registered at the same rate in all organs or subsystems of the body. *Reichenbach (1959)* has indicated that time may even have different directions in different portions of the physical universe. From this it might be inferred that parts of the body occasionally have different directions in time, that a function or structure may for an interval reverse its trend in time and grow younger, as during regeneration. Whole individuals move in the direction of the majority of the component systems. By analogy to the physical universe, the individual is viewed as a complex system moving irreversibly forward in time (increased entropy), with subsystems in which rate of change and even the direction of time may not be the same. The model of the physical universe suggests that the biological, psychological, and social functions of the individual, while part of a total complex system, need not be related on a one-to-one or moment-to-moment basis.

Periodic and Sequential Phenomena. Cyclical, or periodic, behavior is seen in many of the systems of the body: heartbeat, contractions of the intestines, brain waves, and menstruation. Such rhythms range from less than a second to many days in cycle length. Although the human organism may display complex cyclical behavior, the individual organism does not return to precisely the same state it was in at the beginning of the cycle. While the essential feature of such systems is a periodic return to a characteristic state in a fixed time, the organism of which they are a part has moved forward in time. By contrast, growth is a sequential phenomenon with prior stages being prerequisite to later ones. When the sequential order is broken, growth abnormalities result. For example, if bone growth is induced in the older animal, a disadvantageous state results. Growth at the wrong time or the wrong rate may have serious consequences for the animal's survival.

Subsystems of the Organism. It was suggested earlier that not all subsystems of the body are constantly interacting. For example, the cardiovascular system in the young adult usually functions within a safe range where the amount of blood flow does not influence behavior. Variations in blood flow may be tolerated over a moderate range without an effect on behavioral output, although some minimum blood flow is a necessary condition for the existence of the individual. Similarly, many vitamins and enzymes must be present in the body in order for normal life to exist, but once present in minimum amounts, they are no longer variable determinants of the changing states of the organism. Relationships may be said to be quantity-bounded; e.g., thirst above some threshold level of water deprivation becomes the dominating stimulus for directing the behavior of the whole organism for a limited period of time. Individuals may show characteristic behavior at particular times of the day. Thus, rather than viewing the behavior of the individual as showing continuous interaction between all parts of his biological and social system at all times, it is more correct to regard interactions among the subsystems as time-limited and quantity-bounded. For the healthy person under normal conditions, most of the organic functions of the body might be said to lie within a range called *maintenance biology;* i.e., the organic processes occur in ranges wherein they provide a safe existence for the individual but do not directly influence his behavior. With advancing age, relationships may change between behavior and the biological subsystems (e.g., circulation, glandular secretion, and respiration), as their activity begins to fall outside the normal physiological limits. In this way, new biological influences on behavior may appear that have no analogy in the young adult or child. The adaptive organism, almost by definition, must show discontinuity in behavior in order to give a novel response to environmental change. Were behavior not free of most internal states, adaptation would be seriously limited. Adaptation implies new behavior, which may not necessarily be wholly predictable from past behavior; it may even be unique for the individual and for the species as well. By contrast, lack of adaptation, as displayed in the rigid or repetitive behavior of individuals with brain damage, is more characteristic of pathological states. Rigidity implies that the individual can operate under only one set or a few very limited sets of instructions.

Manifest Age. Social and psychological characteristics date the individual as much as do physical characteristics. In language, words are in a constant state of flux—as to both meaning and pronunciation. Use of a slang expression, therefore, or a formerly acceptable word, gives the listener information about the probable age of the speaker. Cultural turnover is involved in the sense that word choice, rather than the speaker's ability to use words, tends to become obsolete. Clothing style is often an indication of age, as are uses of certain polite, social forms of speech or certain actions. Personal and social values develop over the life span and also evolve in society, and they thus date the person expressing them.

There is an analogy of obsolete social forms of the very aged to the obsolescence of automobiles, clothing, or hair styling. Certain functional features of the antiquated form (e.g., ability of the automobile to transport) may remain intact, but obviously other features of the car are involved as a reflection of the owner's position in his social group. Occupational skills, as well as social roles and personal concerns, manifest the individual's age and the society in which he has lived.

Some activities and concerns are a result of factors in family life, such as age of marriage and child bearing. Still other behavior relates to the individual's position in social organizations. Often with increasing age there is increased power in social organizations, until some point where the linkage between the individual and the organization begins to change to a pattern of dissociation. Societies and organizations have some properties resembling individuals; they have differential survival, productivity, and morale. The purposes, age, and status gradings of a social organization are not necessarily identical with those of the individual member. Therefore the individual only partially identifies with the group, his morale being dependent upon the extent to which his personal

FIGURE 1-1A. One-egg twins at the ages of 5, 20, 55, and 86 years.

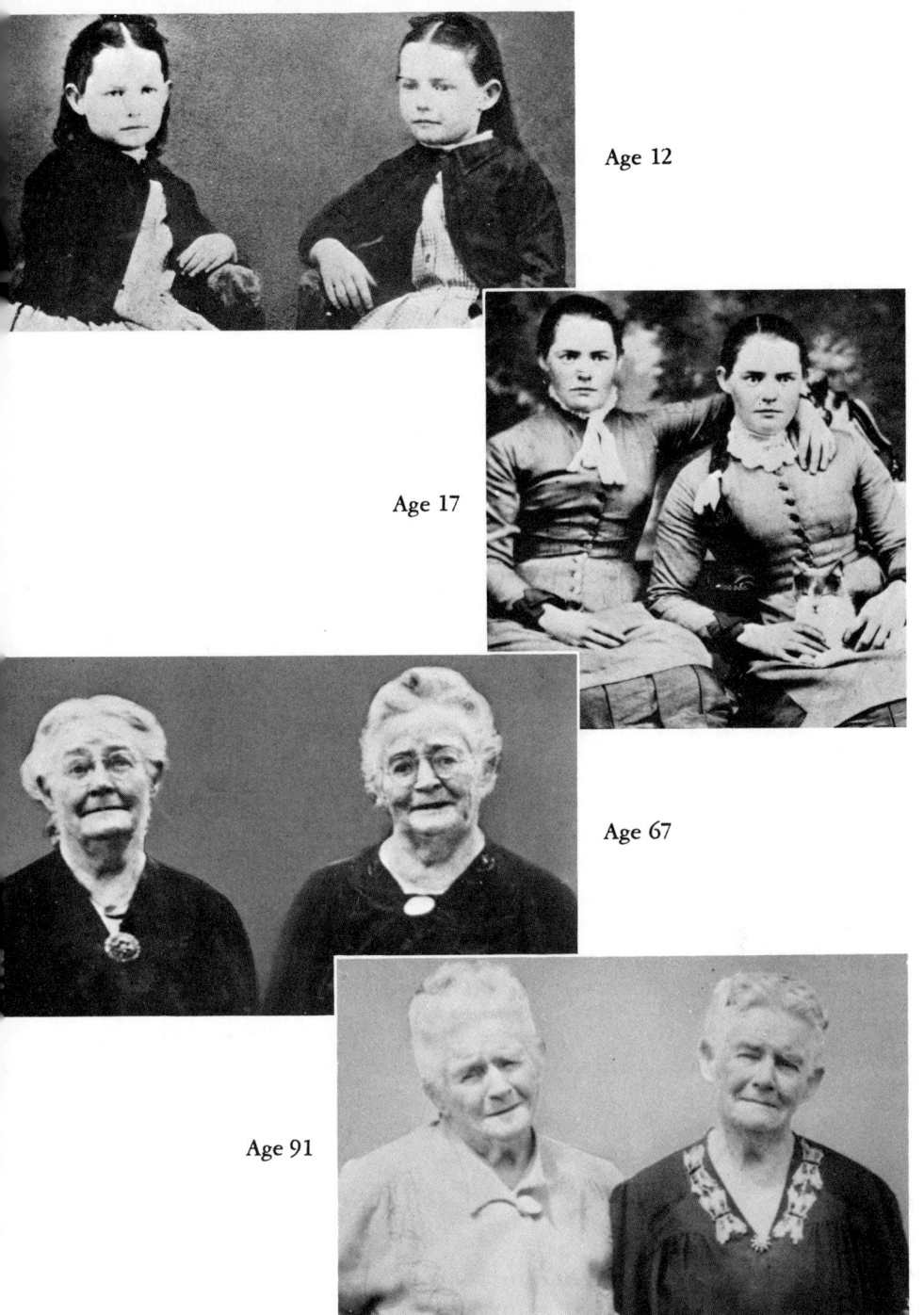

FIGURE 1-1B. One-egg twins before and after long separations (between the ages of 18 and 65).
Source: Franz J. Kallmann and Lissy F. Jarvik. Individual differences in constitution and genetic background. In J. E. Birren (ed.), *Handbook of Aging and the Individual* (Chicago: University of Chicago Press, 1959), pp. 216-263.

goals are served by his activities within the group. The goals of the group tend to remain more stable than those of the individual. Havighurst has pointed out that, for work situations, the meaning of work to an individual changes with age *(Friedmann and Havighurst, 1954)*. Importance to the individual of participation in decision making, of guarding protocol and customs, and of companionship or social involvement in work situations, as well as monetary return, are a complex function of the psychological, social, and biological forces of aging.

Changes in Appearance. Facial appearance shows developmental changes characteristic of the species, so that few would mistake the appearance of an old person with that of a young adult, and certainly not with that of a child. Judgments about age based upon appearance influence behavior between strangers. Similarities in the pictures of one-egg twins over the life span suggest that, within the progression of age changes in appearance, there are stable familial resemblances, or hereditary factors.

Changes in appearance over the life span are also influenced by the marks of accidents and results of diet and physical environment. If literature is a good indicator, the sailor, farmer, craftsman, and city-living gentleman in the past more clearly showed in their appearance the nature of their occupations than do men today.

Differences in Rates of Change. Different functions and structures of the body show different rates of change over the life span. Biological characteristics of the body organs, such as the brain, heart, and liver, show quite varied rates of change in development and aging. In a general way, it would appear that many biological or physical characteristics show earliest maturation and decline, that psychological capacities mature and decline later, and that social processes are slowest to reach full development and plateau and show least late-life decline.

Individual Differences. Whatever aspect of man is observed, it is found that, in addition to similarities, there are individual differences. Mental abilities, strength, height, longevity—in fact, all psychological, physiological, and anatomical measurements show individual differences around the average-age trend. Species differences also exist. In comparative science one species is compared with another for some particular trait. Both longevity and ability to learn (among other traits) show a wide range of differences *between* and *within* a species. Confusion can arise if it is not realized that the zoologist, psychologist, and sociologist may each be trying to explain a different kind of variation, individual or species.

While there are individual differences at every age, it is most likely that, if he lives long enough, each individual will show age changes characteristic of his species. However, most wild animals rarely attain old age, since the hazards of their environment usually truncate their lives

Dynamics of the Life Cycle 17

at or near the age of peak fertility. The fact that such animals will show a pattern of senescence under the favored conditions of the laboratory indicates that the species has an inborn *potential for senescence*. The origin of the potential for senescence will be discussed in Chapter 3.

Changes in Maturation. In humans, the forward thrust of physical growth results in most individuals' attaining adult size and form by the late teens, and by age twenty certainly all but the exceptionally slow have reached full height. Most girls have reached their maximum height by age sixteen, and boys by age eighteen, or slightly over. In terms of present

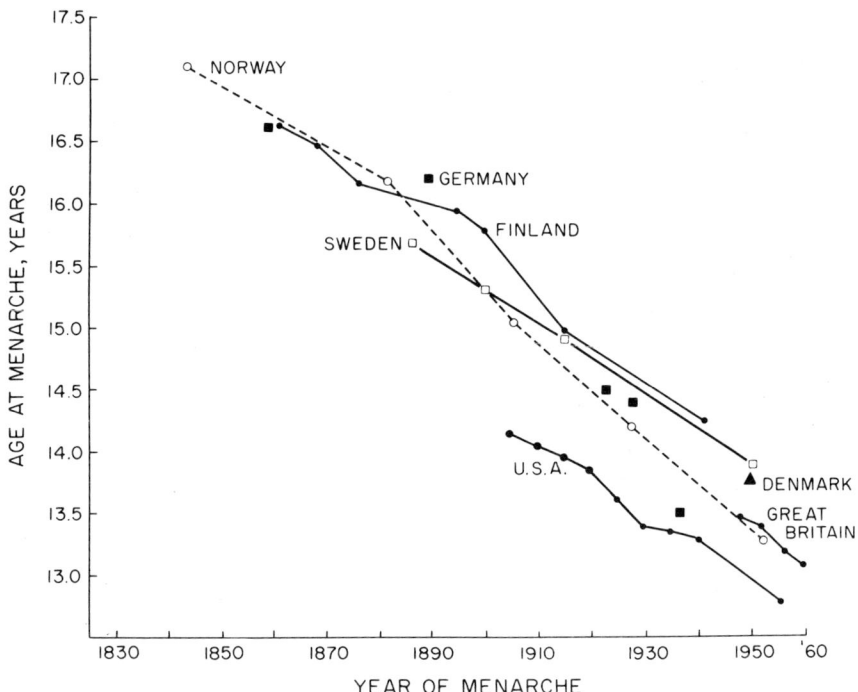

FIGURE 1-2. Trend toward earlier age at menarche 1830-1960.
Source: J. M. Tanner, *Growth at Adolescence,* 2nd. ed. (London: Oxford University Press, 1961), p. 153.

life expectancy, this means that most individuals will spend 25 per cent of their life span attaining adult size. Since women live longer than men and also mature about two years earlier, they are "adults" a somewhat greater proportion of their life span. Physical growth, of course, is not the only—nor necessarily the best—criterion of the adult state, but it is a useful index to structural maturity. By contrast with height, maximum muscular strength is attained somewhat later. Muscular strength depends not only upon structural maturity to bring it to maximum function, but also upon use.

Perhaps the figure 75 per cent may be taken as the duration of the adult phase of the life span in contemporary western cultures, recognizing that this proportion differs somewhat for the sexes as well as for the particular features of the organism considered.

Along with a trend toward a longer average life, there also appears to be a trend toward earlier puberty and physical maturity in western societies that leads to a further shortening of the proportion of growth phase of the life span. There may be, however, some late-life consequences of accelerated development, but there is not much information yet on the late-life outcomes and longevity of early- and late-developing individuals.

In the United States, associated with the trend to earlier puberty, though not necessarily related to it, is the trend toward early marriage and child bearing. Contrary to a widespread belief, "grandmother" did not, on the average, marry earlier than do women in the present generation. The trend toward early marriage has been going on for seventy years at least, with the age of both husband and wife becoming younger. In 1960, the median age at first marriage was 20.3 for the wife and 22.8 for the husband; in contrast, in 1890, the husband's age was twenty-six years and the wife's age was twenty-two years. It has been put this way:

> The average married couple of 1890 could expect only thirty-one years of married life together, and they could not look forward to any time spent alone without children. Their marriage would have been terminated by the death of one or the other on the average of two years before the marriage of the last child. On the other hand, the married couple of 1950 could expect to live a total of 40.3 years together, of which 13.9 years are spent together after the marriage of the last child (*von Mering and Weniger, 1959, p. 295*).

Early maturity, early marriage, and longer survival have psychological and social consequences. For one thing, longer parental survival has resulted in fewer orphans, with a resulting reduction in orphans as a major problem of social dependency. Furthermore, most men and women in this generation survive beyond the age when their last child leaves home. Thus the contemporary married couple will have a significant period of late-life marriage, involving new psychological and social elements.

Many of our concepts of family life have come from periods when mere survival beyond childhood was a feat. Also, our attitudes and concepts of the life cycle and family life have been greatly influenced by what has been written by members of the upper classes (the only literate people of

TABLE 1-2. MEDIAN AGE OF HUSBAND AND WIFE
AT SUCCESSIVE EVENTS IN THE FAMILY CYCLE

STAGE	1890	1940	1950	1959	1980
Median age of wife at:					19.5-20.4
First marriage	22.0	21.5	20.1	20.2	27-28
Birth of last child	31.9	27.1	26.1	25.8	48-49
Marriage of last child	55.3	50.0	47.6	47.1	65-66
Death of husband	53.3	60.9	61.4	63.6	
Median age of husband at:					
First marriage	26.1	24.3	22.8	22.3	22-23
Birth of last child	36.0	29.9	28.8	27.9	29-30
Marriage of last child	59.4	52.8	50.3	49.2	51-52
Death of wife	57.4	63.6	64.1	65.7	68-69

Source: Paul C. Glick, David M. Heer, and John C. Beresford, "Family Formation and Family Composition: Trends and Prospects," paper read at annual meeting of the American Association for the Advancement of Science (Chicago, December, 1959), 12.

their day) in past centuries. One can infer from the figures of child mortality and illegitimacy in the eighteenth century that family life in western societies was not a state of ideally organized bliss for most people, but a preoccupying struggle for survival (*Quetelet, 1835*). Sentimentally, the historical family tends to be looked upon as a model from which the contemporary family deteriorated; but there is little reason to believe that individuals and families were physically, mentally, or emotionally stronger in the past.

Emergent Features. With an increase in the average length of life, new features of adult life are emerging. Interest is shifting from the period of growth toward the adult, the "center of gravity" of the life span. The individual life cycle and the family as we know it today have some features not easily compared with those of the past, and changes are still in process. For example, as the average life span increases, women tend to gain more than men in the additional length of life, and, as both live longer, there may be a further widening of the differential life expectancy of men and women. This has already resulted in the psychological and social problem of longer and more frequent widowhood. The sex difference in life expectancy is amplified by the fact that women tend to be younger than their husbands at marriage. This is reflected in the fact that in 1956, 55 per cent of older women were widows, while only 22 per cent of the men were widowers.

Automation of production is another factor in a changing environment. The trend since World War II has been toward automated production, and some of the features of this trend are now becoming apparent. There is primarily a greater stress upon man's ability as a thinker-

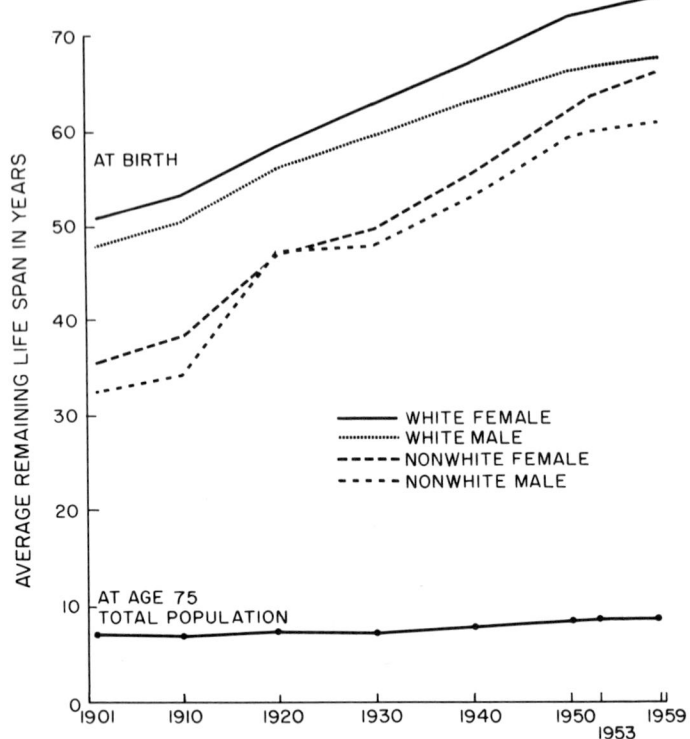

FIGURE 1-3. Expectation of life at birth in the United States at various periods for males and females, whites and nonwhites.

Source: P. L. Altman and Dorothy S. Dittmer (eds.), *Growth* (Washington, D.C.: Federation of American Societies for Experimental Biology, 1962), pp. 442-444.

integrator than upon his psychomotor skills. The early craftsman had to have intimate knowledge of his raw materials and tools, and he had to develop high coordination of the "hand and eye." Not only did the craftsman have to have fine skills, he often needed physical strength and endurance as well. The modern worker is more a controller of production than an actual producer. He takes in information (often from remote sources) and organizes it, or he forms concepts that are used as the basis for actions that have long-term consequences for the output in quality and quantity. Maintenance workers are still needed, but even here higher levels of skills are required. In the maintenance of modern industry, abstract mental skills, rather than manual skills, are usually critical.

It has been said that a good set of ideas used to last a man a lifetime; now they last merely a generation—or perhaps only a decade. As the

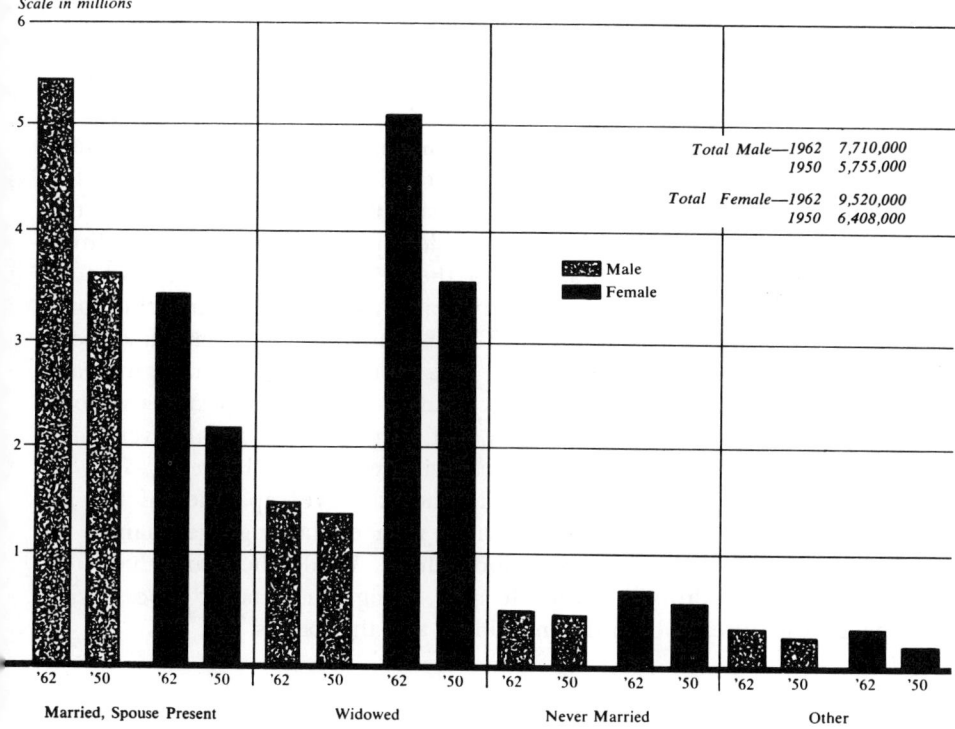

FIGURE 1-4. Marital status of persons over the age of 65 in 1950 and 1962.
Source: U.S. President's Council on Aging, *The Older American* (Washington, D.C.: Government Printing Office, 1963), p. 60.

dominant emphases of society rapidly change, so will the expression of human motivations. Changes in length of life and our greater mastery of the physical environment result in differences between generations in patterns of thought, attitudes and values, feelings and social behavior. It is thus apparent that the psychology of aging is jointly a biological and social science.

Summary

Several concepts have thus far been introduced that will help the reader in organizing his thoughts about the facts to come in later chapters. In addition, a limited description of changes in society was given in order to establish the fact that individuals are adapting throughout their life span to a changing environment. The psychological capacities of the individual are continually involved in adapting. Some problems or tasks face the individual at characteristic phases of the life span. These age-level tasks and the underlying changes in drives and motivations give adult life a characteristic rhythm or tempo. Individual differences, however, are always apparent in aging, just as in development. We have presented the concept of the individual as a complex system moving forward in time to further differentiation. Memory is the likely element that, for behavior, provides an irreversible forward direction to experience. Not all aspects of the organism are regarded as constantly interacting; rather, autonomy exists within subsystems, thus providing for novelty in adaptation. Three kinds of aging were described: biological, psychological, and social. The nature of theories of aging vary with the kind of variation to be explained. It is not expected that one theory will explain all the changes that occur in individuals over time. *Biological* theories of aging try to deal with facts about longevity. *Psychological* theories deal with changes in the adaptive capacities of the individual. Social theories are concerned with explaining age changes in the social roles and activities of individuals. While there are characteristic changes in adults over the life span, aging is a dynamic process with emergent features in both the individual and the species.

References

*Anderson, J. E. Dynamics of development. In D. B. Harris (ed.), *The Concept of Development,* pp. 25-46. Minneapolis: University of Minnesota Press, 1957.

Belt, E. Leonardo da Vinci on "The hard teeth of the years." *General Practice,* 1956, **19**, Nos. 4 and 11.

Birren, J. E. A brief history of the psychology of aging. *The Gerontologist,* 1961, **1**, 69-77, 127-134.

Burstein, Sona R. Papers on the historical background of gerontology. *Geriatrics,* 1955, **10**, 189-193, 328-332, 536-540.

*Cumming, Elaine and W. E. Henry. *Growing Old.* New York: Basic Books, Inc., 1961.

Erikson, E. H. Identity and the life cycle: selected papers. *Psychol. Issues,* Monogr. No. 1, 1959.

Frenkel, Else. Studies in biographical psychology. *Character and Personality,* 1936, **5**, 1-34.

Friedmann, E. A. and R. J. Havighurst. *The Meaning of Work and Retirement.* Chicago: University of Chicago Press, 1954.

*Kagan, J. and H. A. Moss. *Birth to Maturity.* New York: John Wiley & Sons, Inc., 1962.

---

* Suggested additional reading.

Laslett, P. and J. Harrison. Clayworth and Cogenhoe. In H. E. Bell and R. L. Ollard (eds.), *Historical Essays 1600-1750,* pp. 157-184. London: Adam & Charles Black, Ltd., 1963.

Quetelet, A. Sur l'homme et le développement de ses facultés. Paris: Bachelier, Imprimeur-Libraire, 2 vols., 1835.

Reichenbach, Maria and Ruth A. Mathers. The place of time and aging in the natural sciences and scientific philosophy. In J. E. Birren (ed.), *Handbook of Aging and the Individual,* pp. 43-80. Chicago: University of Chicago Press, 1959.

Tharp, R. G. Psychological patterning in marriage. *Psychol. Bull.,* 1963, **60,** 97-117.

* von Mering, O. and F. L. Weniger. Social-cultural background of the aging individual. In Birren, 1959, *op. cit.,* pp. 279-335.

2. The Social and Cultural Determinants of Aging

An individual's early social class and his social mobility influence not only his behavior as he grows older, but also his length of life. Although each individual is unique, with particular genetic, psychological, and social characteristics, the accumulated effects of social class have an impact upon the way in which humans age. The conditions under which individuals are conceived, born, develop, work, and die, are functions of socioeconomic forces. Man can be looked upon as a register of events since the nervous system records the consequences of social experience and projects their influence into the future. Since the consequences of biological, psychological, and social forces are registered over time, in the fullest sense an individual cannot start "all over again" at any age. Rather he may become further differentiated with new experiences being built upon the past. Past experience determines responsiveness to new elements over the life span, and it influences moods, feelings of life satisfaction, and the undertaking of new directions in activities.

Just as there are in the speech of an individual the elements or traces of his origin in a distant community, so are there embedded in his expectations about growing older his early family and regional influences. Influenced by ethnic and class differences are child-rearing practices, dietary patterns, recreation and work patterns, exposure to toxic and infectious agents, exposure to information and to systematic education, values, and religious practices. The kinds of experiences and traumas to which individuals are exposed, the manner of adapting, and the conditions that support recovery from handicapping conditions vary with their environments.

Membership in the middle class tends to bring with it a relatively high level of educational attainment, and associated with this a greater awareness of good personal hygiene and a grasp of principles of health maintenance. High incomes, coupled with more education and greater access to information, also provide more opportunity for adequate dietary practices and better housing—all of which tends to facilitate good mental and physical health habits. Generally speaking, the higher the social class of the individual, the higher are his expectations for personal services, the greater is his recognition of his individual needs, and the greater is his awareness of his own initiative and power in decision-making functions.

Some of these issues can be seen in a study made in the city of New York of 500 noninstitutionalized persons over the age of sixty (*Kutner, et al., 1956*). Four problems were of interest in this study: (1) personal adjustment, (2) factors affecting or related to health, (3) use of community health services, and (4) attitudes toward health and social centers. Because Kutner and his associates also gathered information on the socioeconomic status of their subjects, some interesting information on class differences is available. Contrary to the view that lower class people are "happy but poor," the study showed that high economic status was related, in general, to high morale. "Morale" as here used refers to the relative balance of happiness and unhappiness and satisfaction and dissatisfaction with life. The authors pointed out that low income is generally related to a relatively less respected social position and to increased drudgery. It follows that high morale tends to be associated with high economic status (Table 2-1).

If one now examines these results with regard to health, morale, and high and low socioeconomic status, an interesting fact appears: Poor health appeared to influence the morale of the high socioeconomic group less than it did the low group. In fact, the results shown in Table 2-1 indicate no difference in morale between those reported to be in good health or in poor health among individuals in the high socioeconomic group. What seems to be reflected in the data is the fact that poor health and low economic status are amplifying or interacting factors in a negative direction. That is, while high economic status gives the individual some advantages that offset consequences of poor health, an individual who has both low economic status and poor health is disproportionately reduced in level of morale. "Low status alone acts as a depressant, but

TABLE 2-1. MORALE ACCORDING TO HEALTH
FOR HIGH AND LOW SOCIOECONOMIC STATUS

MORALE	High status		Low status		Number of cases
	Good health	Poor health	Good health	Poor health	
	(Percentages)				
High	50	44	39	20	*185*
Medium	28	30	31	30	*150*
Low	22	26	30	50	*165*
Total	100	100	100	100	
Number of cases	*137*	*66*	*147*	*150*	*500*

Source: B. Kutner, D. Fanshel, Alice M. Togo, and T. S. Langner, *Five Hundred over Sixty* (New York: Russell Sage Foundation, 1956), p. 53.

when coupled with poor health the outlook becomes still more grim" (*Kutner, et al., 1956, p. 54*). A factor like social status is never simple in its influence. In fact, the New York study by Kutner and his associates suggests that relative social isolation is an important concomitant of low economic status. In their study, nearly two out of three persons in the lowest economic group could be regarded as relatively isolated. What seems to be crucial is a combination of poor health, low economic status, and social isolation. One senses that a complex of negative factors exists which precludes the utilization of community health services by the individuals who may most need them. For example, widows who tend to be isolated and have low incomes might well profit from medical attention, but those who maintain social contacts seem to be more likely to utilize the services of a medical center.

Selective Service Data. Large numbers of men were called by the Selective Service for physical examinations before entrance into the armed services during World War II. The age limits for inductees never went above forty-four years and never under eighteen years. Nearly 18,000,000 men were given physical examinations during the period from 1940 to 1945. Caution must be used, however, in interpreting the data, since there were fluctuations in standards for service depending upon changing military needs; men who had been rejected in one period were often re-examined and accepted for service later. Also, healthy men were often deferred for occupational reasons. The data show, however, that age was closely related to rates of rejection. If the total number of disqualified men and the men with limited or remedial defects are added together, the total percentage of rejected men aged eighteen to twenty was 29.3 per cent, whereas for men of thirty-eight to forty-four the rejection rate was 64.7 per cent. However, a few causes for rejection were actually higher in the younger age group; e.g., educational and mental deficiency. Mental illness and defects of the eyes and ears tended to be somewhat higher in the youngest groups (*Gold-*

stein, 1951). The likely influences of social and economic differences associated with the rejection rates for military service are shown by the fact that rejection rates were higher for agricultural than for nonagricultural workers. The total rejection rate for farmers was 48 per cent and for nonfarmers 41.5 per cent. This relationship held true for both the white and Negro populations. The rejection rate for white farmers was 44.7 per cent and for Negro farmers, 60.2 per cent; for white nonfarmers, 39.4 per cent and for Negro nonfarmers, 50.9 per cent. Regional differences in rejection rates also suggest socioeconomic influences. For example, New Jersey had a rejection rate of 23 per cent for all registrants eighteen to thirty-seven years, in comparison with South Carolina, which had a rejection rate of 42.9 per cent. This nearly twofold difference between the proportion of rejectees in various states undoubtedly reflects to a considerable degree the influence of educational opportunity. Of all causes for rejection, illiteracy and mental deficiency differed most markedly between agricultural and nonagricultural workers. For example, in the number of defects per 1000 white registrants examined, about ninety-seven agricultural workers were rejected for illiteracy and mental deficiency in contrast to about twenty-three nonagricultural workers. Illiteracy was a heavy contributor to rejection and should be regarded as a preventable defect.

Certainly not all of the defects leading to rejection for military service in World War II were preventable or remediable through early attention. There was a tendency, however, to neglect earlier noted defects. For example: "Studies of school health records of young men rejected in Hagerstown, Maryland, because of defective dentition and vision showed that the same defects had been noted fifteen years earlier in school examinations of these same individuals" (*Goldstein, 1951, p. 607*).

It might be assumed from the marked regional differences in the data of military service rejections that climatic factors were also involved in producing defects. In a study of the relation of diseases of the cardiovascular system to climatic and socioeconomic factors, it was found that ". . . the social economic group of factors accounts for approximately 72 per cent of the total variation in diseases of the circulatory system and in chronic nephritis, while the climatic group of variables takes care of only 28 per cent of the total variation" (*Moriyama and Herrington, 1938, p. 427*). Socioeconomic factors and the degree of urbanization obviously have a significant effect on mortality rates for circulatory diseases as well as on other somatic and mental defects.

Socioeconomic Status and Mental Illness. A close relationship between socioeconomic level and mental illness was reflected in Selective Service rejections. The data suggest that the lowest socioeconomic groups have the greatest prevalence of mental illnesses. Persistent mental and physical illness may result in the individual's downward mobility in society to a lower socioeconomic level. Position in the lowest group would then be the result rather than the cause of mental illness. In addition, low social class membership of parents brings with it less interest in the growing child's health habits, less attention to health deficiencies, school progress, and the general psychosocial development of the individual. The more one examines relationships between physical and mental well-being and socioeconomic class, the more one is impressed with reciprocal relationships. Low social class position tends to exacerbation of previously existing defects as well as to an intrinsically greater likelihood of initial health defects. The survey of *Midtown Mental Health* tried to control for this reciprocal relationship between socioeconomic class and mental health by considering the socioeconomic status of the parents of the persons surveyed. When the respondents were classified according to their parental socioeconomic status, the number of mentally ill persons varied twofold between the upper and lower classes; i.e., approximately 9.9 per cent of the high social group were respondents classified as psychiatrically impaired, compared to 19.8 per cent of the lower group. Investigators of the survey made this clear proposition, which seems to have been borne out: ". . . successively lower parental SES (social economic status) tends to carry for the child progressively smaller chances of achieving the well state during adulthood" (*Srole, et al., 1962, p. 215*).

While social aspirations and upward mobility have been criticized for placing excessive pressures on individuals, the results of the New York survey showed that groups that were regarded as upwardly mobile have a somewhat higher percentage of psychiatrically well persons. Partly, of course, contemporary society stresses upward mobility, and to be downwardly mobile is to be socially deviant from the norm. Regarding the consequences in adolescence of parental class mobility, the authors' comments are most interesting:

> . . . on the whole healthier adolescents tend to be more heavily into the traffic of upward-moving adults, whereas more disturbed adolescents tend to be shunted into the downward traffic. We suggest the further hypothesis that on the whole those in the ascending traffic stream are subsequently less likely to show exogenous deterioration in mental health than those in the descending stream (*Srole, et al., 1962, p. 228*).

Apparently, upward mobility is psychologically as well as financially more rewarding than downward mobility. Social and economic status differences clearly represent a very persistent constellation of relations that go back in their influences to early childhood.

In the lowest socioeconomic group there are to be found particularly vulnerable people in a most unsupporting environment. Families that are upwardly mobile are more likely to intervene in problems of mental and physical health and social maladjustment than those that are downwardly mobile. The lack of intervention compounds the effects of multiple unfortunate circumstances that are more likely to occur. The above results were confirmed in a study of social class and mental illness (*Hollingshead and Redlich, 1958*). It was also found that a definite association exists between social class position and psychiatric illness, with a higher proportion of patients in the lowest social class. For psychotic disorders, an increasing prevalence was noted with lower class status, whereas for neurotic disorders, there is a small but real decline in the prevalence from the upper to the lower social classes. An important inference from this study is that there are very powerful social factors that determine what individuals in particular age ranges are treated for mental illness and where, how, and for how long they are treated.

In a second study of the urban area of New Haven, the relationship between mental illness and social mobility was analyzed (*Myers and Roberts, 1959*). In patients from the middle class, there is a correlation between the amount of achievement and upward mobility and the severity of psychiatric illness. Lower class patients do not show striving for respectibility and high status. The results should probably be interpreted less in terms of mobility's being a cause of mental illness than in terms of the kinds of behavior deviations produced in relation to social class, given extreme representatives of parents, family constellations, and susceptible individuals.

Because among upward mobile persons there are highly visible "strainers" who push toward higher class status without having redeeming personal qualities, it might be assumed that upward mobility is wholly a negative characteristic. Actually, high achievement seemed to come in the natural course of events to many of the gifted children studied originally by Terman in 1921. He gathered data on 1500 intellectually superior children; follow-up data in 1955 showed the group to be high scholastic and vocational achievers. In their mid-forties, 86 per cent of the men were found to be in the professions, semi-professions, and higher business occupations. Nearly 70 per cent of the total group graduated from college, and many more than would be expected by chance were listed in biographical directories of distinguished persons in the country. If such conspicuous (for many)—and certainly higher than average over-all achievement—came at undue personal cost, there should be evidence of higher than average personal maladjustment. However, the data as a whole suggest no such effect. The authors concluded:

> Physically the gifted subjects continue to be above average as shown in their lower mortality record and in the health ratings. While personal adjustment and emotional stability are more difficult to evaluate, the indications

are that the group does not differ greatly from the generality in the extent of personality and adjustment problems as shown by mental breakdowns, suicide, and marital failures. The incidence of such other problems as excessive use of liquor (alcoholism) and homosexuality is below that found in the total population, and the delinquency rate is but a small fraction of that in the generality. Clearly, desirable traits tend to go together. No negative correlations were found between intelligence and size, strength, physical well-being, or emotional stability. Rather, where correlations occur, they tend to be positive (*Terman and Oden, 1959*).

At a minimum it can be concluded that in the intellectually gifted, high achievement and the upward social mobility that accompanies it are not marked by signs of mental distress or social maladjustment. Perhaps in mental illness, when upward mobility and achievement appear to be contributing causes, the relations between ability and high motivational level produce continuing unresolved tensions.

Correlates of Mobility. As the standard of living has risen for successive generations, children have tended to rise above the social class of their parents. This is accentuated in the parts of the country where recent immigration and rapid social development of new areas have led to dramatic changes in the social class membership of successive generations. In the middle west, a study of Kansas City has indicated that individuals are not necessarily in the same social class at middle age as they were at birth: 37 per cent were upwardly mobile, 13 per cent downwardly mobile, and 50 per cent stable (*Havighurst and Neugarten, 1962*). In contemporary America, the downwardly mobile individual is more deviant than the upwardly mobile individual, and he has quite different personal and social characteristics.

Individuals from the lowest classes tend to show more direct aggressive behavior and to act out their conflicts in overt behavior. They pass from childhood more directly into adulthood, and in so doing miss the establishment of many of the behavior controls found in the middle class person.

> Lower class patients express their instinct-demands more directly and with less restraint, whereas higher class patients are more likely to check their aggressive and sex drives or express them by way of compromise. The higher classes are also, generally speaking, the ones who either sublimate their unconscious needs or express their conflicts in neurotic reactions (*Hollingshead and Redlich, 1958, p. 366*).

Perhaps more attention should be directed to downward mobile persons. While no studies have analyzed their characteristics in detail, it might be suspected that, unlike gifted children, downward mobile persons will have many limiting traits or defects, not all of which need be highly interrelated. The joint presence of relatively low mental ability, poor health, low drive, and family problems would be apt to result in the excessively passive person with a "chip on his shoulder." Upward mobility is associated with expanding social competence, and it is to be expected that upwardly mobile persons will in old age show a more manipulative attitude and approach toward their environment than the downwardly mobile.

One of the important implications is that late in life the reactions of individuals to death of spouse, retirement, reduced income, and loss of social role and physical prowess will be in terms of long-developing values, values that have their roots in class differences and in particular family constellations. It might be expected from this that aged lower class individuals would prove to be antagonistic but passive in the face of age changes. Middle class individuals would be expected to be more "hurt" by the psychological implications of the changes. To this extent social class origins and mobility influence the way in which an individual ages, the way in which he reacts to the characteristic changes of later life and to particular age-related problems; i.e., whether he is highly controlled or aggressively impulsive. In addition, there are individuals who have constitutional weaknesses (intellectual, temperamental and somatic) who cannot adapt even to commonplace stresses. This is quite apart from those environments whose elements are so inconsistent and conflicting that they may be pathogenic even for the normally equipped.

Failure to reach early goals would be a psychological problem for the aspiring middle class man about to retire, but not for the lower class man who would probably blame his employers or others for what he might consider a "bad deal."

The above statements imply that to a great extent personal characteristics of the young adult lead to mobility over the life span rather than mobility's leading to personal characteristics. This is said in general, for there is a reinforcing quality about social behavior, and "success leads to success." In social and occupational achievement the individual's decisions at choice points are critical: does he stay in school or drop out, does he join a club or not? Having at an earlier point made a choice that has led to acceptable results, he is more likely to make a similar choice on the next occasion. The individual starts initially with some traits that lead to his exposure to the choice situations and to subsequent social development.

Decision and Behavior. Different cultural emphases influence the individual's selection of forms of behavior at choice points and in crisis situations throughout the life span. Thus statistics from various countries show different rates of socially disapproved behavior: alcoholism, suicide, divorce, and murder. Socially approved characteristics of work, art, drama, and religion also vary. All things being equal, individuals choose that form of behavior for their age group which is most reinforced by the culture and subgroup in which they live. An adult has an image of the culture in which he lives and has learned the kinds of behavior expected of him in various situations. Also, he has an image of himself in relation to the culture that gives rise to notions of ingroup and outgroup attitudes.

From the analyses by Hollingshead and Redlich of family patterns in the lower and middle classes, it is obvious that the parental identifications of children vary with social class. Middle class individuals are prone to overidentify with, or be bound by, the aspirations of their parents, and their life pattern can be one of a continuing aspiration and striving for mobility. In contrast, lower class persons show less striving for stated goals and concentrate on day-to-day subsistence. The roles of the father and mother differ with class, as do the relationships of siblings. The lower class person is motivated by material needs in the aggressive world he views. The upper class person is inwardly driven as a result of the internalization of parental and group values.

Studies of activities and social roles have generally shown that high social participation is related to good personal and social adjustment. Furthermore, individuals who maintain employment tend to have better attitudes about their lives. Gainful employment, however, is not a simple factor, for it presumes adequate health and also the ability to get along effectively in the culture and with employed peers. Thus attempting to improve life satisfaction by re-employing many older persons would probably not be universally satisfactory, since employment itself is a selective variable in society, and over the life span a variety of factors have led to selection of individuals who remain in the labor force. Some of these factors have to do with personal qualities of the individual, such as temperament, health, and stamina. One of the crucial issues is the system of values the individual uses in arriving at his choices.

Studies that have been done on development and aging indicate that the mere occurrence of adverse environmental characteristics or isolated unfortunate experiences during the life span are not sufficient in themselves to lead to highly deviant personal and social adjustment. Vulnerability of the individual to crises rarely arises from one variable. In the lives of successful aged individuals there have often been phases involving poverty, orphanhood, divorce, cruelty, and criminal victimization, which otherwise might be regarded as overwhelming events. If, however, the consequences of such events are woven into a pattern of behavioral organization, they generate what might be called a "downward spiral of behavioral organization," and the individual proceeds over his adult years through successive states of decreasing adaptive capacity. The opposite trend is one in which there is an upward spiral of positive contributing factors seen in the individual who has increased successes and is exposed to increasing opportunities for learning the social roles of the culture. The timing and sequence of critical events during the life span and the sensitivity of the individual at the time of occurrence help form generalized involuting or evolving patterns of behavior. There are probably nonlinear combinations of both negative and positive factors in the lives of individuals that place them in an expanding or contracting state with regard to their adaptive capacity.

Chronic frustration may play a pervasive role in motivational changes of aging (*Kuhlen, 1963*). Five sources of frustration that are age-related in society and that may also vary with social class are: (1) an age status system that idealizes youth, (2) pressures of time and money that lead to a restriction of former interests, (3) physiological changes that demand, or usurp, attention, (4) technological changes that increasingly outdate the skills of aging persons, and (5) with age, individuals become more "locked in" in being less able to move out of a frustrating situation. Thus viewed, chronic frustration can deflect the individual from earlier goals and impart an unduly low level of motivation. Frustration is regarded as antagonistic to the need for "growth-expansion": growth-expansion is postulated as a life-long need and is related to feelings of life satisfaction and positive self-assessment.

Dynamics of Social Class. It has been pointed out that in aging, social class and cultural differences appear to influence the likelihood of adverse events and the registration of their consequences. Some of these relationships will be discussed further in this section. The lower class, poorly educated individual, particularly an aged person with such a background, generally lacks a sufficient grasp of physiology to appreciate the significance of health measures, such as reducing sugar or salt intake, even when given some apparently reasonable explanation for doing so. This is in contrast to the middle class individual, who, through reading and conversation, has probably developed a more rational picture of the way the body functions. Gains in knowledge are more quickly transmitted to the middle classes, and furthermore, much of the activity of these classes can be characterized as "information seeking." Individuals who have high exposure to information and are high in information-seeking behavior, have a greater probability of avoiding adverse events and reducing their consequences. Aged and young persons, upper and lower class persons, live in different streams of information that influence their willingness to seek information and initiate constructive behavior. Greater constriction of the psychological life space occurs with age in the lowest social classes (*Williams, 1960*). Presumably, this reflects a greater likelihood of joint adverse factors involving physical and mental health, income, and marital and family relationships.

Among the current changes in western societies is the trend toward increasing divorce. Of those who divorce, only about one-half remarry. This leaves a large number of older individuals socially isolated, and undoubtedly affects the nature of their relations with their children. It has been pointed out that there is no religious commandment that enjoins us to take care of our children, but on the other hand, there is a commandment that directs children to honor parents. Upon reflection it would seem that the acceptance of the dependency of children by the parents is a very primitive and primary role, whereas the dependency of a parent upon the children in late life is a less clearly defined role (*Streib and Thompson, 1960*). In cultures in which people survive to late life, the evolution of the individual's affective life from childhood onward is such that he displaces his ties with his parents with affective investments in others. In turn, his relations with spouse, close friends, and children, are a differentiation of, and to a considerable extent supplant, early childhood ties. It seems important to emphasize that the affective relationships between children and their dependent parents are not the inverse of the affective relationships between parents and their dependent young children.

In urban areas, there are few functions that an aging individual can meaningfully perform for himself or his family. This is in contrast to the rural setting, in which there are many significant roles for aging persons and for their maintenance as contributing, rather than dependent, members of the family. Families are usually better able to provide for the social and psychological dependency of the children than for that of older adults.

The expectations a community has for the behavior of older persons and for the distribution of its services are in part dependent upon its age structure and the social class and mobility of its population. A city such as St. Petersburg, Florida, which has much in-migration and has over one-third of its residents above the age of sixty-five, tends to give more attention to the needs of older persons. Some of these facilities are obvious, like the ramps over its street curbs for less agile older people and the many benches near street intersections. In a community having a high proportion of persons over the age of sixty-five, greater emphasis is placed upon recreational and social services for older persons than would be found in a suburban area having many children.

One of the most general measures of variations in health that may be examined in relation to environmental differences is the mortality rate. For example, unskilled workers have a mortality rate about twice that of professional workers. The higher mortality rate in unskilled jobs has to do partly with adverse conditions of work; other related factors have to do with the income from the job and the things that a higher income buy; e.g., better housing, nutrition, medical care, and education. Since the Negro tends to be in unskilled jobs, his mortality rates are relatively higher than the white population's (*Goldstein, 1954*). In past years, infectious diseases were understandably high among Negroes because of crowded housing. However, cardiovascular renal disease, the largest cause of death among whites, has even a higher death rate among nonwhites. In the late 1940's, when the Negro was making many social gains, his average income was still only 50 to 60 per cent that of the average white male. On a low income, the Negro would tend to buy less medical service—and less would be available.

Perhaps of greatest significance is the fact that comparisons of health statistics between the white and non-white populations show small differences, if any, when the data are adjusted for environmental factors such as income, occupation, and place of residence (*Goldstein, 1954*).

Much of the preceeding discussion was to the effect that adverse environmental conditions vary with social class. If this is true, then there ought to be a relationship between social class and disability due to accidents. Using income as an index to class, this relationship seems to be true. One general index of adverse environmental circumstances is the number of days of disability per person per year associated with illness or injury (Table 2-2). As the family income rises, the number of days of disability diminishes. Public Health surveys show that for families with incomes under $2000 per year, the number of days of restricted activity is 29.8, compared with only 13.0 days per year for persons of families having incomes of $7000 or more. Thus disability is 2-1/3 higher in lower income families. Number of hospital days also tends to be higher in low income groups. (*National Center for Health Statistics, 1963, Series 10, Number 2*). The number of hospital days may underestimate disability in the aged and in lower class persons, since they would tend to avoid hospitalization for financial reasons. Older persons are disproportionately represented in the low income group, thus tending to inflate the low income disability rates. However, even when age is held constant, the lowest income groups have highest rates for restricted activity, bed disability, and work loss.

An interesting reversal is that low income males have a higher number of hospital days than low income females, but that high income females spend more time in hospitals than comparable males. This probably reflects to some extent occupational hazards for the male that vary with type of occupation and correlated income. This interpretation is supported by data on days lost from work in relation to family income. As income increases, the days lost from work due to injuries decreases. Lower income males appear to be exposed to more adverse working

TABLE 2-2 (A). NUMBER OF DISABILITY DAYS PER PERSON PER YEAR, BY FAMILY INCOME AND SEX: UNITED STATES, JULY, 1960-JUNE, 1961

SEX AND DISABILITY DAYS	Family Income					
	All Incomes	Under $2,000	$2,000-3,999	$4,000-6,999	$7,000+	Unknown
Both sexes:	(Number of disability days per person per year)					
Restricted activity	16.5	29.8	17.7	13.8	13.0	14.7
Bed disability	5.8	10.4	6.2	4.9	4.6	5.4
Hospital	0.9	1.0	1.0	0.8	0.8	1.0
Work loss[1]	5.4	8.0	5.9	5.1	4.7	5.3
School loss[2]	4.8	5.2	4.9	4.8	4.8	3.5
Male:						
Restricted activity	14.6	27.5	17.3	12.0	11.0	10.9
Bed disability	5.0	9.8	5.9	4.0	3.8	3.8
Hospital	0.9	1.3	1.1	0.7	0.7	1.1
Work loss[1]	5.3	8.8	6.2	4.9	4.4	5.6
School loss[2]	4.8	5.0	5.2	4.7	4.9	3.7
Female:						
Restricted activity	18.3	31.7	18.0	15.5	15.0	18.2
Bed disability	6.6	10.8	6.5	5.8	5.5	6.7
Hospital	0.9	0.8	0.8	0.9	0.9	1.0
Work loss[1]	5.6	7.0	5.5	5.6	5.3	4.6
School loss[2]	4.7	5.3	4.5	4.8	4.8	3.2

[1] For currently employed persons.
[2] For children 6-16 years of age.

TABLE 2-2 (B). PERCENTAGE DISTRIBUTION OF POPULATION, BY AGE AND FAMILY INCOME: UNITED STATES, JULY, 1960-JUNE, 1961

AGE	Family Income					
	All Incomes	Under $2,000	$2,000-3,999	$4,000-6,999	$7,000+	Unknown
	(Percentage distribution)					
All ages	100.0	100.0	100.0	100.0	100.0	100.0
Under 15 years	32.1	24.8	32.0	36.5	31.5	26.2
15-24 years	13.2	14.6	14.7	12.3	12.7	13.9
25-44 years	25.5	15.2	21.9	29.3	29.1	22.0
45-64 years	20.4	21.5	20.3	17.7	22.4	25.0
65+ years	8.7	23.9	11.1	4.3	4.3	12.9

Source: National Center for Health Statistics Series 10, No. 2. (Washington, D.C.: USDHEW, PHS, July, 1963).

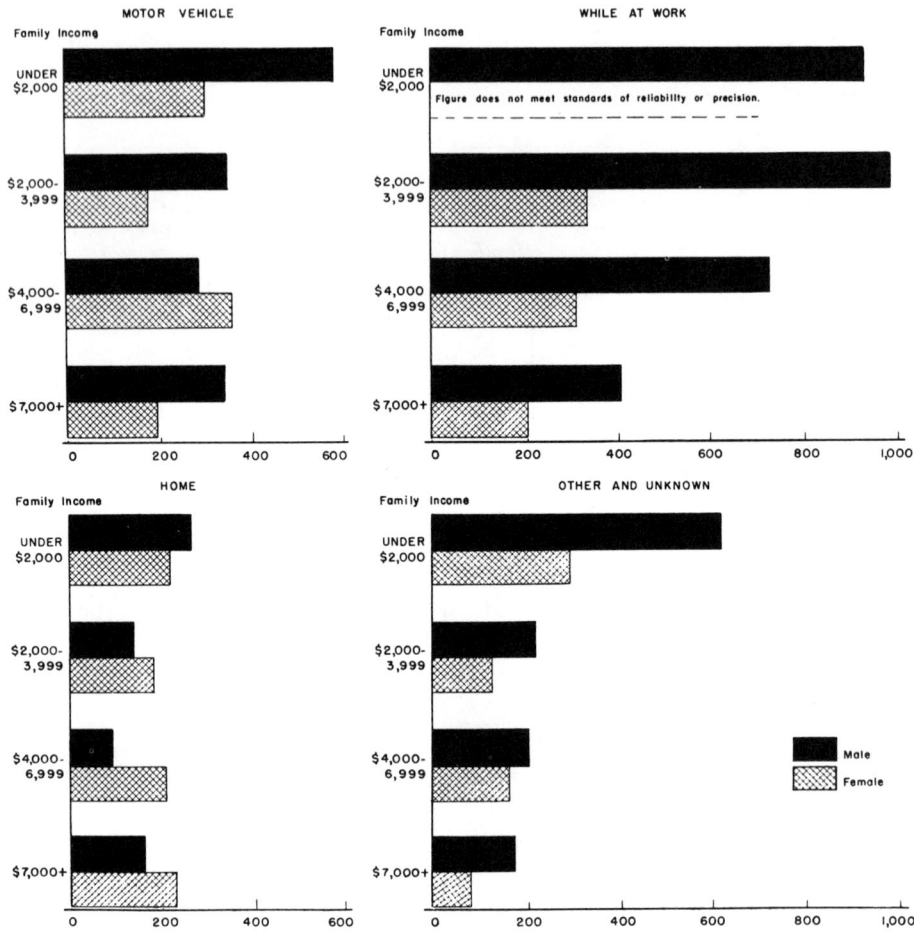

FIGURE 2-1. Average annual work-loss days due to injuries per 1000 currently employed persons, by sex and family income.

Source: USDHEW, *Vital and Health Statistics* (Washington, D.C.: Public Health Service, 1963), Series 10, No. 2.

conditions, using days, lost due to injuries as the criterion. Figure 2-1 shows the variations with sex and the place where injuries occurred.

The importance of exposure to accidents can be appreciated from the large number of injuries that each year require medical attention or lead to a restriction of activities for a day or more. In a survey by the Public Health Service, it was found that on the average, 45,000,000 persons per year sustained injuries. The annual rate of 255 per 1000 population, or about one out of four persons, is sufficiently high to be a significant contributor to accumulating disability with age, particularly if the injuries do not receive proper attention. Surprisingly, there appeared to be a low rate of medically attended injuries among retired persons. Since retired persons have low incomes, they may avoid medical attention and neglect injuries because of medical costs and lack of insurance.

Except for home accidents, injuries do not appear to increase with advancing age. The reason for this probably lies in decreasing exposure to work injuries and vehicle and recreation accidents, to which younger persons are more frequently exposed.

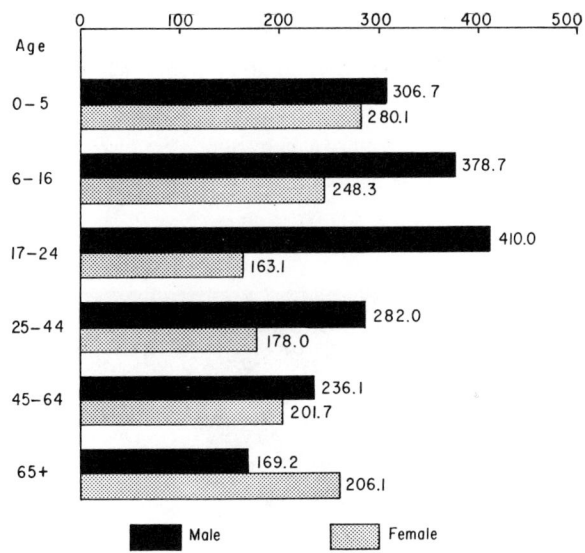

FIGURE 2-2. Numbers of persons injured per 1000 population per year, by sex and age.

Source: USDHEW, *Health Statistics* (Washington, D.C.: Public Health Service, 1962), Series B-37.

Injuries from falls rise with age, but again there may be an age difference in exposure, since retired persons usually spend more time at home. Despite the explanation of the data, falls represent a serious hazard for the older population.

Income. The previous section indicated that income is related to health and to recovery from injury. The income of the aged is usually reduced after retirement (*McConnell, 1960*). For example, half of the persons

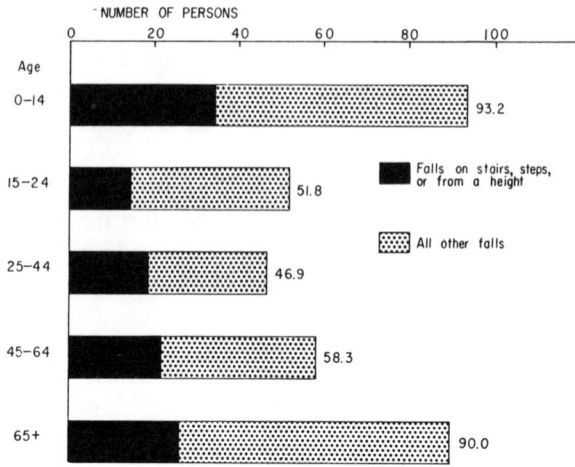

FIGURE 2-3. Number of persons injured in falls per 1000 population per year, by age.

Source: Ibid.

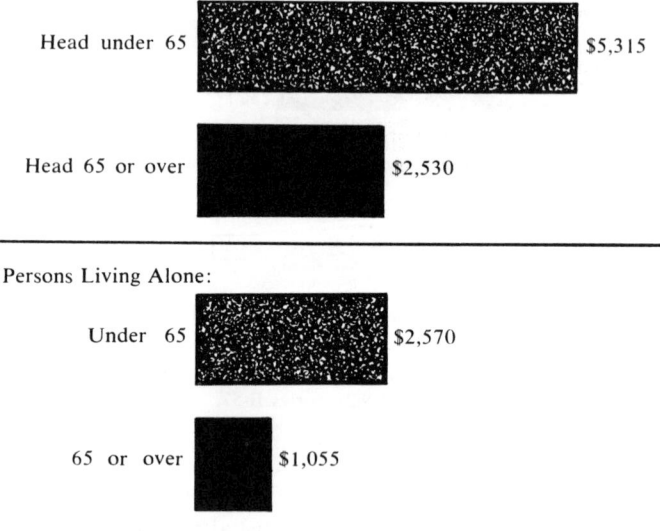

FIGURE 2-4. Income of two-person families and persons living alone, median income in 1960.

Source: U.S. President's Council on Aging, *The Older American* (Washington, D.C.: Government Printing Office, 1963), p. 9.

The Social and Cultural Determinants of Aging 41

over sixty-five living alone had annual incomes of $1000 or less. Four per cent of men over sixty-five had no cash income. Figure 2-4 shows the median incomes of persons over and under age sixty-five.

Most people over sixty-five derive their incomes from other than current employment. There is a continuing trend toward persons over sixty-five being dependent on nonearned income. In 1900, about 65 per cent of men over sixty-five were in the labor force; today only about 35 per cent are. Women over sixty-five have never been in the labor force. There is no reason to expect that in the near future earned income will help to relieve the low income position of persons over sixty-five.

Medical Expenditures. Since people over sixty-five tend to have limited incomes, individuals must make compromises with their previous patterns and standards of living. Faced with difficult choices of spending a limited income, for example, the aged individual, hoping that he will be able to avoid costly medical care, may not buy health insurance.

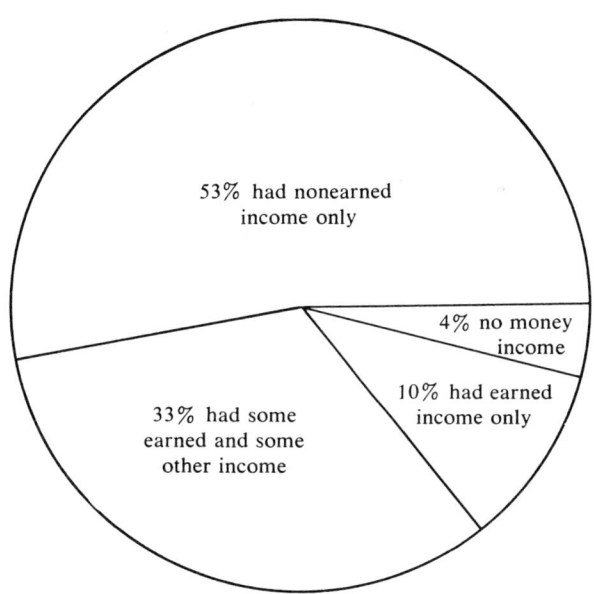

FIGURE 2-5. Income sources in men over the age of 65.

Source: U.S. President's Council on Aging, *The Older American* (Washington, D.C.: Government Printing Office, 1963), p. 8.

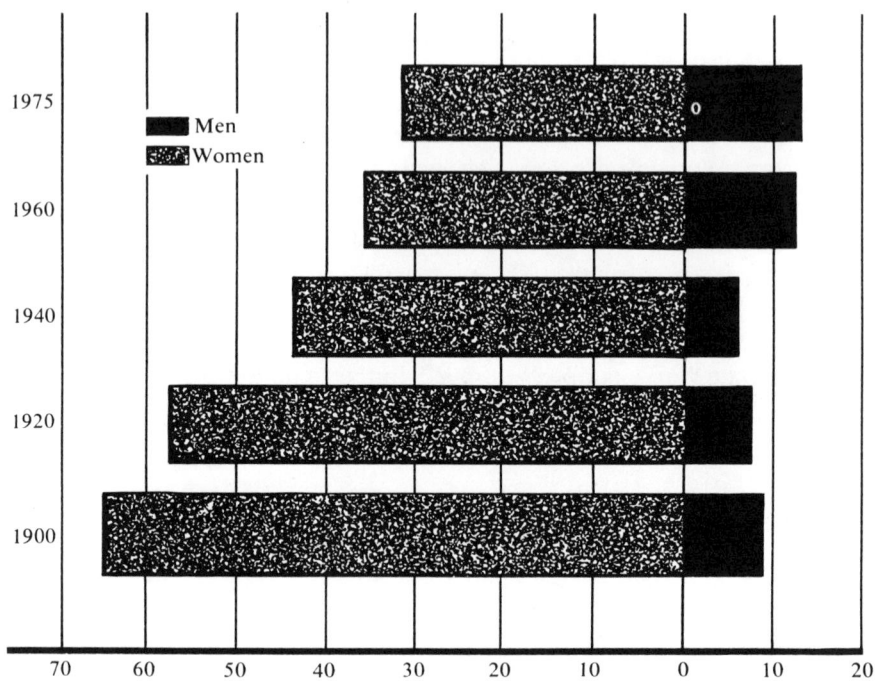

FIGURE 2-6. Percentage of persons over the age of 65 in the labor force.
Source: U.S. President's Council on Aging, *The Older American* (Washington, D.C.: Government Printing Office, 1963), p. 21.

While most of the younger population can afford adequate health insurance, the older person often finds it difficult, or impossible, to pay the costs. Thus the older person frequently takes a chance that he will not be ill for long periods and spends his income for current needs. In taking this chance, however, he is betting against strong odds.

About one out of six older persons will enter a hospital during any one year, and will have an average stay of two weeks, which is about twice as long a stay as that of a younger person.

In 1961, average medical expenses were $226 for older persons and $103 for younger persons. Health expenditures not only are more than double for the aged than for the young, but they are also increasing at a higher rate. Advances in medical treatment may further accentuate the differences in costs of care for the young and aged because of the types of illnesses found among older persons and the complex medical tech-

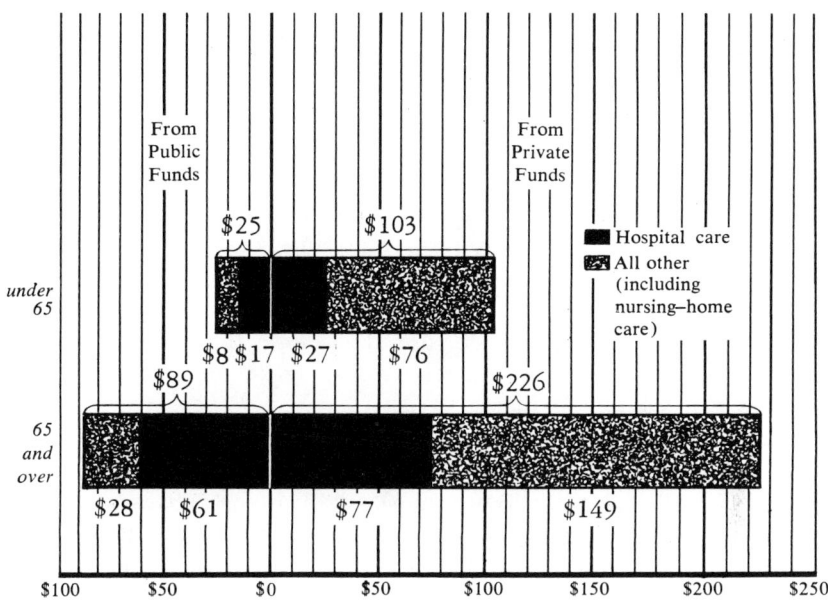

FIGURE 2-7. Per capita expenditures for medical care for persons over and under age 65, in 1961.

Source: U.S. President's Council on Aging, *The Older American* (Washington, D.C.: Government Printing Office, 1963), p. 14.

nology required in treatment. The average *hospital bill*, not including the doctors' fees, was about $525 for the average older person entering a hospital. Nearly half of the aged persons are unable to meet these expenses from health insurance, assets, and income.

Economics of Widowhood. It was pointed out that the average cost of hospitalization for the older person is over $500 and that families rarely have a sufficient financial cushion to absorb such costs. Most older persons do not, for example, have $1000 in liquid assets. Serious illness, and particularly a terminal illness, often wipes out all the resources of the family. Thus, in addition to the psychological and social consequences of widowhood and the physiological effects of bereavement, there are direct economic consequences. The terminal illness of the spouse usually costs much more for hospitalization, physician's fees, medicines, transportation, and other ancillary costs than is provided for by insurance. Burial expenses are also taken from the assets of the family and tend to represent a large proportion of the total assets. Furthermore, following the death of the spouse there is often the cost of relocating residency. Thus the death of the spouse is accompanied by a large reduction in the financial resources of the survivor. This places the survivor in the position of having to make more choices and take action based upon smaller resources.

Because of the number of related issues, widowhood after a long married life is probably the greatest role change experienced over the life span. The economic pressures are such as to accentuate the problems of psychological and social adjustment. Since women tend to survive their husbands, the financial status of the unrelated female defines one of the largest single groups of economically deprived persons. Older women may not have had previous work experience, or have had it so long ago as to be of little current use. Therefore, there is little expectation that significant numbers of widows can enter or re-enter the labor force for gainful employment.

For the man, some elements of retirement are analogous to widowhood for the women; e.g., loss of primary role and reduced income. Both the retired man and the widow can re-establish themselves with meaningful personal relationships and activities, but this must be done with the handicap of reduced income and resulting reduced mobility. Reduced income often makes it difficult for the individual to maintain or replace the relationships that have had special importance.

Widowhood has been given special attention here because of the social problem being created in contemporary society by the large—and rising—proportion of widows. Women tend to live longer than men and marry men who are older than they. In the older population there are over 5,000,000 women who are widowed and about 1,500,000 widowed men. Facing depleted resources and little or no income is thus a much more common problem for the aged woman than for the man.

In addition to the things money will buy and the social mobility it encourages, the reduced income of widowhood can have an important secondary meaning to the man or woman whose life's values have been primarily expressed in terms of the common denominator of cash income. For such persons, reduced income can be reacted to as though it were a loss of status and potency, thus creating an impediment to the individual's re-establishing or maintaining effective interpersonal relationships.

Ethnicity, Region, and Religion. The general point of view of this chapter is that the expression of an individual's biological potential for longevity or senescence is modified by his way of life as determined by his social class and other environmental influences. Rural-urban and regional differences influence variations in health. Other regional differences also appear; e.g., injuries from all causes are more common in the far west than in the northeast. Public Health statistics showed that in the west there were 308.5 injuries per 1000 population in contrast to 232.5 per 1000 in the northeast. For reasons largely unknown, motor vehicle, work, home, and miscellaneous injuries were all higher in the west. Deaths due to accidents may vary as much as twofold between a low in an eastern state and a high in a mountain or Pacific coast state.

Public Health statistics show that chances of survival at birth vary with region. Infant mortality rates may vary between states from a low of about twenty deaths of children up to one year old per 1000 live births to a high of slightly more than thirty-five deaths. Total death rates per 1000 population also vary among the states, but these data are more difficult to interpret, since the populations of states vary in average age.

There are differences in death rates for white and nonwhite populations, with significantly better survival for whites up to about age sixty-five to seventy. Thereafter there is a slightly better survival rate for the nonwhite population. Since the nonwhite population tends to be concentrated in the low income groups, it is not surprising that the nonwhite population has somewhat higher death rates for most of the life span. The reasons for the late-life reversal of the death rates for white and nonwhite are not known at present.

The nonwhite population is mostly Negro, about 19,000,000 according to census figures. There are, however, other groups, such as the American Indian, which while small proportionately in the total population are nevertheless appreciable in number; Indians number somewhat over 500,000. There are other groups also, such as the Japanese, with over 450,000. These data imply a cultural diversity in the population that is often overlooked in analyses of national trends, and these groups have many cultural differences that influence their life patterns.

The emphases of different religions with regard to features of family life certainly vary (*Maves, 1960*). In the United States there are over eighty-five religious groups each with over 50,000 members. To categorize these as simply Protestant, Catholic, Jewish, or other is to minimize important diversity among them. There are in Pennsylvania, for example, religious groups that strongly emphasize farm life, do not use gasoline power, and do not wear buttons on their clothes. To call them simply "Protestants" obscures the fact that they live in an almost separate culture from most urban Protestant congregations. Some of the early religious groups in America have practically disappeared, such as the Harmonists or the Shakers, who had celibate communal societies. Although these and other groups are rarely thought of as contemporary influences, their religious beliefs were very strong in many immigrant groups, and vestiges of their beliefs are still reflected in society and provide the basis for diverse activity patterns over the life span.

While urbanization has minimized much diversity, contemporary differences exist among people in eating, drinking, and smoking habits, fondness for exercise, interest in study and education, and proneness to gambling and high risk behavior. These differences, which result from the ethnic diversity of the population, are still important in behavior, though they are perhaps less obvious than in days of high immigration, when language and dress were immediate signs of the origin of the individual. Choices in behavior over the life span are influenced by remote cultural factors, not all of which are known to the individual.

Family cohesion and parental and filial responsibility over the life span are conditioned by social background. Many state laws governing the responsibilities of adults show regional influences, such as those coming from the Puritan tradition, in the nature of provisions requiring adult children to support aged parents (*Schorr, 1960*). The expression of care for aged parents is, of course, modified by the income of the adult children. Most aged adults live independently of their children, although the likelihood of three-generation families is influenced by health and income. Middle class families tend to make cash contributions for the care of parents. In lower class families, faced with a shortage of cash, the aged parent is more likely to live with the children. Whether three generations can live together congenially, other things being equal, depends upon the traditions of the family and past interpersonal relationships. Old and young adults appear to prefer living independently, and it is questionable whether many aged adults would live in the households of their children if reasons of inadequate health and subsistence were not present. As in the biology of late life, personal relations will show emergent features as more and more people survive to late life with financial security and good health.

Summary

In this chapter, the large-scale variables of social class, ethnicity, and income have been discussed. These factors influence how long individuals live and the patterning of their lives. The likelihood of exposure to adverse environmental conditions, such as work hazards and disability due to injury, varies with income. In addition to the social class variations in exposure to injury and noxious conditions, there are variations in conditions that favor recovery from injury. The individual of low income and low education, lacking a grasp of elementary principles of human physiology, may not understand the significance of an illness or injury or the importance of medical treatment, or of following a diet and adhering to a prescribed regime. Rather, he will hope that he can save the cost of medical care and that the "inconvenience" will pass away with time. He tends to ignore minor and major symptoms of potential danger. The older person with reduced income may avoid medical care because of the costs involved.

Because of the diverse ethnic origins of people in America, there is probably greater heterogeneity among older people here than in most western cultures. It seems justified to assume that older persons in such countries as the Netherlands, Sweden, and Great Britain have a greater homogeneity of culture and life patterns than do Americans, who come from a wide range of national and religious backgrounds, with many different attitudes toward education, work and achievement, health practices, and diet. Thus the biologist may not assume that the sociocultural influences operating on individuals are constant, and the social scientist may not assume that heredity and physiological status are constant for all members of society.

Interpersonal relationships also influence the way in which individuals evolve over the life span. Interpersonal relationships of the family are particularly significant in influencing what choices are made at critical branching points in the life span. The models of interpersonal relationships that have become part of the individual's personal standards will affect his relationship to his aged parents as well as to his peers and to his own children. In general, lower class behavior is influenced by a struggle for simple subsistence. Behavior tends to be direct and aggressive, but at the same time passive in the sense that general or remote goals are not worked toward. Middle class behavior, not being preoccupied with the struggle for simple subsistence, is more involved in working toward abstract goals and tends to be achievement-oriented.

Class differences influence not only the way in which individuals grow older, but also the types of mental illnesses individuals develop as adults. Generally, the lowest class is found to have the highest incidence of mental illness. Social mobility is a common feature of life today; perhaps half of the population end their life in a different social class than they were in at birth. Upward mobility is associated with more positive features of personal and social adjustment than is the less common downward mobility. Constellations of factors, some unrelated, contribute to the upward or downward mobility of individuals. One characteristic problem for the older person is to adapt to reduced social roles, status, and income associated with retirement. For women, the greatest role change of all is the change to widowhood.

The organization of life-long behavior patterns determines the way individuals adapt to the characteristic problems that face them over the life span. Over time, a style of adaptation develops that is characteristic of the individual. Young and old adults, upper and lower class persons, all live in different contemporary streams of information that influence their perception of the physical and social world and their willingness to seek information and initiate action. While aging and behavior have been viewed as being dependent upon social cultural influences, nevertheless the individual is also a determining factor in his own evolution and in the differentiation of motives and choices of action over the life span.

References

*Burgess, E. W. (ed.). *Aging in Western Societies*. Chicago: University of Chicago Press, 1960.

Cavan, Ruth S., E. W. Burgess, R. J. Havighurst, and H. Goldhamer. *Personal Adjustment in Old Age*. Chicago: Science Research Associates, Inc., 1949.

* Cumming, Elaine and W. E. Henry. *Growing Old*. New York: Basic Books, Inc., 1961.

Goldstein, M. S., Longevity and health status of whites and nonwhites in the United States. *J. National Med. Assoc.*, 1954, **46**, 38-104.

———. Physical status of men examined through Selective Service in World War II. *Public Health Reports*, 1951, **66**, 587-609.

Gordon, Margaret S. Aging and income security. In C. Tibbitts (ed.), *Handbook of Social Gerontology*, pp. 208-260. Chicago: University of Chicago Press, 1960.

*Havighurst, R. J. and Ruth Albrecht. *Older People*. New York: David McKay Company, Inc., 1954.

———, and Bernice L. Neugarten. *Society and Education*. Boston: Allyn and Bacon, Inc., 1962.

Hollingshead, A. B. and F. C. Redlich. *Social Class and Mental Illness*. New York: John Wiley & Sons, Inc., 1958.

Kuhlen, R. G. Motivational changes during the adult years. In R. G. Kuhlen (ed.), *Psychological Backgrounds of Adult Education*, pp. 77-113. Chicago: Center for the Study of Liberal Education for Adults, 1963.

*Kutner, B., D. Fanshel, Alice M. Togo, and T. S. Langner. *Five Hundred over Sixty*. New York: Russell Sage Foundation, 1956.

Maves, P. B. Aging, religion and the church. In Tibbitts (ed.), *op. cit.*, pp. 698-749.

McConnell, J. W. Aging and the economy. In *ibid.*, pp. 489-520.

Moriyama, I. M. and L. P. Herrington. The relation of disease of the cardiovascular and renal systems to climatic and socio-economic factors. *Amer. J. of Hygiene*, 1938, **28**, 423-436.

Myers, J. K. and B. H. Roberts. *Family and Class Dynamics in Mental Health*. New York: John Wiley & Sons, Inc., 1959.

Schorr, A. L. *Filial Responsibility in the Modern American Family*. Washington, D.C.: U.S. Department of Health, Education and Welfare, 1960.

*Simmons, L. W. *The Role of the Aged in Primitive Society*. New Haven: Yale University Press, 1945.

---

* Suggested additional reading.

Srole, L., T. S. Langner, S. T. Michael, M. K. Opler, and T. A. C. Rennie. *Mental Health in the Metropolis.* New York: McGraw-Hill Inc., 1962.

Streib, G. F. and W. E. Thompson. The older person in family context. In Tibbitts (ed.), *op. cit.,* pp. 447-488.

Terman, L. M. and Melita H. Oden. *The Gifted Group at Mid-Life.* Stanford, Calif.: Stanford University Press, 1959.

*Tibbitts, C. (ed.). *Handbook of Social Gerontology.* Chicago: University of Chicago Press, 1960.

*Townsend, P. *The Family Life of Old People.* London: Routledge and Kegan Paul, Ltd., 1957.

U.S. Department of Health, Education and Welfare. *Health Statistics.* Washington, D.C.: Government Printing Office, Series B, No. 8, 1959; Series B, No. 9, 1959; Series C., No. 4, 1960; Series B, No. 37, 1962; Series 10, No. 2, 1963.

U.S. President's Council on Aging. *The Older American.* Washington, D.C.: Government Printing Office, 1963.

von Mering, O. and F. L. Weniger. Social-cultural background of the aging individual. In J. E. Birren (ed.), *Handbook of Aging and the Individual,* pp. 279-335. Chicago: University of Chicago Press, 1959.

Williams, R. H. Changing status, roles, and relationships. In Tibbitts (ed.), *op. cit.,* pp. 261-297.

3. Biological Influences

Unlike inanimate objects or physical systems, living organisms have the capacity for self-repair. In fact, not only do organisms repair the effects of an infection, for example, but the same infection may be resisted on subsequent exposures. With advancing age, organisms appear to grow more susceptible to deleterious conditions, and self-repair does not return the organism quite so near to its previous level of functioning. It was previously pointed out that the various organ systems may age at their own rate. They also vary in their capacity for self-repair. Some tissues, like the skin, are able to repair themselves quite well at any age and form new cells by division of existing ones. Other tissues, like those of the adult nervous system, are relatively stable and cannot readily, if at all, produce new cells when damaged.

One biologist has defined aging as follows:

Aging is the deterioration of a mature organism resulting from time-dependent, essentially irreversible changes intrinsic to all members of a species, such that, with the passage of time, they become increasingly unable to cope with the stresses of the environment, thereby increasing the probability of death (Handler, 1960, p. 200).

This excellent definition of aging from a restricted biological point of view takes as the fundamental dependent variable the probability of death. For reasons that will become apparent, it seems efficient for the student of psychology to regard the biological changes of aging to be of a multifactor nature. (Shock, 1960; Verzár, 1963).

Aging of Cells. It has been quite well established by experimental biologists that cells die with age in many of the critical organs of the body. Thus counts of the number of cells in the brain or kidney will show a reduction in the number by advanced age (Strehler, 1962). In addition to the "spontaneous death" of cells, those remaining may or may not be at peak efficiency. The picture is one of important body organs having a lessened functional capacity because of cell loss. Under critical conditions, the loss in functional capacity may lead to the death of the individual. Rather than stress itself being the variable, the changing characteristic is the resistance of the host. The task of the biologist is to explain why cells die with advancing age. To say that there is an inborn disposition to lose cells with age does not in itself suggest a sequence of steps. These steps are now beginning to be outlined by biologists. Before describing them, it is well to emphasize that cell death is not the same as death of the organism. The organism can tolerate and, with time, adapt to the loss of many cells. In aging, then, the critical cells would seem to be those that are so highly developed or differentiated that they can no longer divide.

The favored explanation of cell death is that with time, damage or accidents occur to the nucleic acids of the cell chromosomes, which are the ultimate controls over the structure and function of the cell. With damage to the desoxyribonucleic acids (DNA) of the chromosome, (or extra chromosomal genes) defective messenger molecules (ribonucleic acids, or RNA) are produced that may be unable to synthesize the necessary enzymes for maintaining cell function. Such cells would presumably die. Not all of the DNA is utilized in the functioning cell, but is called into action at the time of cell division. Thus, for cells that can continue to divide, death of the cell may occur at the time of attempted cell division, or mitosis.

Radiation, such as X-rays, produces a variety of mutations by damage to the genetic DNA. It has been proposed that "radiation mimics aging." Whether radiation actually produces damage characteristic of aging is not known. It is very likely that aging results in characteristic nuclear damage; i.e., some portions of the chromosome are more vulnerable than others in the processes of normal cell activity. The idea of deleterious, spontaneous mutations in somatic cells over time is perhaps the most plausible of current theories of cell aging.

Although it has been pointed out that organs may lose cells with advancing age, to date there have been no convincing demonstrations of universal age changes in individual cells. A precise localization of intrinsic age changes in the isolated cell has yet to be made. From the viewpoint of the organism, of course, aging may be largely a phenomenon of aggregates of cells, particularly manifest in systems wherein certain cells are fixed; i.e., have lost their capacity for division. Morphologists have long believed that cells which can continue to divide are able somehow to renew themselves; what happens to the cells that cannot divide is yet to be determined.

There is a strong intimation that aging may be a special characteristic of highly differentiated cells, those that have lost their potential for further division and remain fixed post-mitotic cells. The organizations of such cells as should epitomize aging are the nervous, vascular, muscular, and, perhaps, the immunological systems. The reader may be surprised because no mention is made of endocrine tissue, but endocrine cells are fairly primitive cells, which retain the capacity for mitotic division if stimulated. Thus if aging is manifested by the endocrines, it is probably a reflection of changes in their stimulation via other endocrines, particularly the pituitary, and ultimately from the hypothalamus and higher brain centers. The distinction here is one of primary and secondary aging. Cells of the endocrine glands (of epithelial origin) retain their potential for division and thus, due to lack of stimulation, show aging as a secondary factor.

With age, heart muscle and brain cells show an increased accumulation of particles known as pigments (*Bondareff, 1959; Strehler* et al., *1959*). To some morphologists, the persistence of these particles suggests that they are insoluble compounds which begin to interfere with vital cell functions. Other than their frequent presence in old cells, little more is known about the chemical composition or the mode of formation of the pigments.

Because of its integrative role in the physiology of the organism and in behavior, the nervous system is in a particularly crucial position to pass on influences of aging. As in all aspects of aging, the question of whether the nervous system changes with age invokes the issue of the pathogenic versus normal physiological bases of the changes seen in older brains. The psychopathology of aging will be considered in a later chapter; here the point is only that there is a distinction between those changes in structure and function of the nervous system that result from disease (hence, pathogenetic) and those presumed normal physiological processes of senescence. Since the brain is so very sensitive to the lack of oxygen, any temporary interference with blood supply would result in death of neurons. Furthermore, since in advanced years, there commonly occurs interference with circulation in the brain, there is reason to suspect that a common cause of changes in older brains is circulation. Such changes, however, are likely to be limited to localized regions; i.e.,

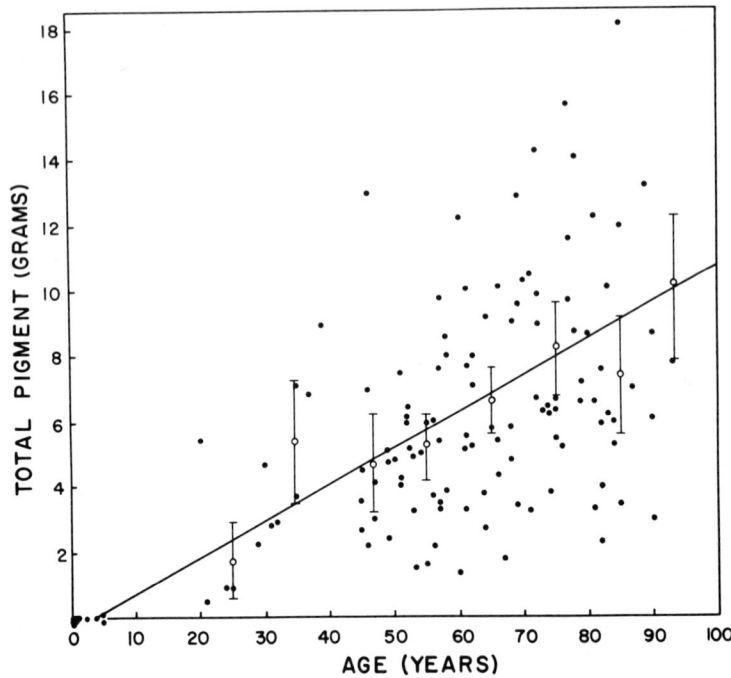

FIGURE 3-1. Pigment accumulation in the human myocardium in relation to age. Data obtained from heart muscle at autopsy for 156 individuals.

Source: B. L. Streheler, D. D. Mark, A. S. Mildvan, and M. V. Gee. Rate and magnitude of age pigment accumulation in the human myocardium. *J. Geront.* (1959), **14**, 433.

have specific foci rather than being diffuse. Most older persons do not show behavior typical of focal brain damage. Consideration of some comparative evidence also reduces the emphasis on blood flow. For example, the rat, in most environmental conditions, shows little gross change in its vascular system with advancing age—and it is certainly free of arteriosclerosis. However, the rat brain has also been studied in relation to age, and it shows a diminution of cells and a slowing in psychomotor behavior. These are also to be noticed in aging humans. Since there is in at least one other species a diffuse loss of cells in the brain with advancing age and a tendency toward slowness of behavior, one suspects that there may be a primary pattern of brain change with age.

Simply put, the question is: If one could observe the brains of aging humans in the living state, would they be found to be indistinguishable from those of young adults? The tentative answer is that it is not likely that the brain of any aged individual would be indistinguishable from that of a young adult. Descriptions obtained from both gross and microscopic examinations of brains of individuals of different ages are all suggestive of changes with age. However, not all of these observed changes should be presumed to have a direct consequence for functioning, and, indeed, none of the anatomical changes can, at the present time, be linked with specific functional alteration (*Birren, Imus, and Windle, 1959*). The older brain is often found to be somewhat lighter in weight than the young brain, although in many instances this change could very well be associated with the conditions leading to death rather than being due to aging. Extensive studies indicate that with advancing age there is a diffuse loss of cells from the human cerebral cortex (*Brody, 1955*). This is suggestive of a physiogenic basis for the changes in the nervous system. If cells have different thresholds of survival, it might be expected that they would die in a diffuse pattern. This is in contrast to their being damaged by a disease that would affect a limited region and result in a highly characteristic loss of, rather than in a diminution of, function. Unlike many organs of the body, the nervous system cannot regenerate cells once they die. The apparent reason for this lies in the fact that the nerve cell is highly differentiated and far removed from its more primitive precursor. Thus differentiated, it can no longer divide itself, and if a neuron dies, its neighbor cannot undergo mitotic division to replace the missing cell. The basic number of neurons in the brain appears fixed at a relatively early age, and while the brain may expand somewhat in volume, it does not expand in the number of neurons. One possible qualification of this lies in the fact that the interstitial cells of the brain, the glial cells, may divide and, in fact, do multiply, or proliferate, under some circumstances. Thus even if brain weight were unchanged with age, there might be a gradual loss of neurons and an increase in glial cells. The evidence rather strongly suggests that there is a diminution in brain weight with advancing age, although the more grossly shrunken brain is probably characteristic of a pathological process rather than of normal senescence (*Bondareff, 1959*).

The loss of cells in the nervous system with advancing age occurs in the frontal lobes, the temporal and occipital cortex, as well as in the cerebellum. Other commonly found changes in the brain are the so-called "senile plaques," due perhaps to a pathological process, and the previously mentioned pigment substances found within cells, the "lipofuscin." These pigment granules have been found in neurons of both animals and humans. Unlike artifacts produced in nervous tissue by fixation and preparation for microscopic examination, the pigments can be observed in living cells and tissue cultures. The nerve cells, although fixed and undividing over the adult life span, do show continual turnover of their chemical constituents. At least some parts of nuclear proteins appear to be different in their absorption characteristics with advancing age. Since oxygen lack also tends to increase the amount of pigment substance in neurons, one should have reservations about this being a wholly normal process of senescence. However, merely because there is an alternate pathway to the production of the pigment need not preclude its being a by-product of a normal process of senescence. The foregoing underscores the necessity for being cautious about accepting a simple explanation of the age differences in the morphology of the nervous system (*Bondareff, 1959*).

The preceding discussion was largely based upon anatomical findings, both macroscopic and microscopic. Functional changes could well exist within the nervous system yet be unobserved by either the light or the electron microscope. Small changes at the synapse could result in such alterations as are seen in the psychomotor slowness of many organisms with advancing age, yet the basis for such a change might be unobservable at the microscopic level at the present time. Until one can with surety examine both function and structure in the nervous system as a function of age, one cannot hold very definitive ideas as to the course of events. However, the diffuse changes, particularly the loss of cells in the nervous system with advancing age, would seem to characterize a physiogenic, or normal, senescent process, which the individual is privileged to show if he survives the more insidious pathologic processes. Because of the slow course of aging, the nervous system can compensate and maintain adequate function even in the centenarian.

The suggestion has been made from time to time that the later-evolved portions of the nervous system are more vulnerable to noxious conditions—and perhaps to aging as well. Partly, of course, this can arise from the fact that if pathogenetic influences affect the lower vegetative centers of the nervous system, the individual will not survive to show other effects, such as changes in the cerebrum. The individual can survive if he has suffered gross cortical damage, but not if he has suffered gross damage to the vegetative centers in the brain stem. The reasonable possibility exists that there is a gradient of aging effects according to an evolutionary sequence. The more primitive organs (those that evolved early) would necessarily have resulted in successful adaptation in order to permit the evolution of more differentiated structures. For the species to survive, ova and sperm would have to be least susceptible to aging.

Species Differences. Animals tend to live a span of life that is characteristic of their species, implying genetic control over the length of life. Also, the behavioral characteristics of mammals tend to remain with the individual animal throughout the life span, the tortoise remaining slow-moving and the hare fast. Since under most naturally occurring life circumstances the environment is never identical or constant, longevity and behavior are results of both genetic and environmental influences. Furthermore, within a species, the individual members do not commonly have identical genetic backgrounds; hence *individual differences* result from genetic, as well as from environmental, differences (*Medawar, 1957*). Notwithstanding some amount of naturally occurring environmental variation, *species differences* in longevity appear to be largely determined by biological controls that are within the animals at birth. Table 3-1 lists some of the generally accepted maximum lengths of life for many animals.

It is most improbable that the length of life of a rat or housefly could be extended to equal that of man. Perhaps forced hibernation, through

TABLE 3-1. LENGTH OF LIFE OF MAMMALS AND BIRDS

Common Name	Scientific Name	Period of Gestation (Mammals) or Incubation (Birds) (in days)	Usual Length of Life (in years)	Maximum Length of Life (in years)
Man	Homo sapiens	280	70-80	110?
Chimpanzee	Troglodytes niger	260	15-20	> 30
Monkey	Macacus sinicus	160 (210)	12-14	—
Cat	Felis domestica	56	9-10	—
Lion	Felis leo	105	20-25	40
Dog	Canis familiaris	60	10-12	34
Bear	Ursus maritimus (arctus)	240	40-50	—
Mouse	Mus musculus	21 (23)	3-3½	—
Rat	Epimys decumanus	21	2½	—
Beaver	Castor fiber	42	20-25	50?
Rabbit	Lepus cuniculus	30	5-7	—
Guinea pig	Cavia cobaia	63	4-5	—
Cow	Bos taurus	285	20-25	30
Sheep	Ovis aries	150	10-15	20
Goat	Capra hircus	150	12-15	19
Reindeer	Rangifer tarandus	240	16	—
Camel	Camelus (dromedarius)	360-400	25-45	50
Pig	Sus scrofa	120	Ca. 16	27
Hippopotamus	Hippopotamus amphibius	210-250	40	—
Rhinoceros	Rhinoceros (unicornis)	510-550	40-45	—
Horse	Equus caballus	330-350	40-50	62
Elephant	Elephas indicus	628 (615)	70	98
Fin whale	Balaena mysticetus	360?	Several hundred?	—
Vulture	Gyps fulvus	—	118	—
Eagle	Aquila chrysaetes	—	104	—
Canary	Fringilla canaria	—	24	—
Pigeon	Columba livia	17-19	50	—
Chicken	Gallus domesticus	20-22	20	—
Duck	Anas boschas	26-30	50	—
Goose	Anser cinereus	28-31	80	—
Ostrich	Struthio camelus	—	50	—
Owl	Bubo bubo	—	—	68

Source: A. I. Lansing, General biology of senescence. In J. E. Birren (ed.), *Handbook of Aging and the Individual* (Chicago: University of Chicago Press, 1959), p. 121.

very low temperature, would significantly extend the life span of short-lived animals; however, this would not contradict the point that relative differences of longevity of species are more a function of genetic differences than of the naturally occurring environmental differences. The life span of the rat, for example, has a distinct upper limit that is, on the average, one thirty-fifth as long as that of man. Control of diet by underfeeding, temperature, and other laboratory conditions may double the usual length of life of a small animal like the rat. While a doubling of the life span is indeed dramatic, it should be compared with the fortyfold differences in life span that may be found among

TABLE 3-2. LENGTH OF LIFE OF COLD-BLOODED METAZOAN ANIMALS

Group and Common Name	Scientific Name	Maximum Length of Life (in years)*
Reptilia:		
Crocodile	*Crocodilus niloticus*	40 (+?)
Alligator	*Alligator mississippiensis*	40
Lizard (skink)	*Scincus officinalis*	> 9½
Lizard	*Anguis fragilis*	> 33
Giant turtle	*Testudo sumeiri*	152
Amphibia:		
Toad	*Bufo (vulgaris?)*	> 40
Tree frog	*Hyla arborea*	11
Giant salamander	*Megalobairachus japonicus*	55
Salamander	*Salamandra maculosa*	11
Salamander	*Triton alpestris*	15
Salamander (axolotl)	*Amblystoma mexicanum*	12
Fish:		
Herring	*Clupeus harengus*	2
Goldfish	*Cyprinus carassius auratus*	Usually 6-7; max. 10
Pike	*Esox lucius*	70-80
Sturgeon	*Huso dauricus*	50-55
Catfish	*Silurus glanus*	80
Mollusca:		
Snail	*Helix pomatia*	18
Marine Snail	*Natica heros*	> 30
Marine Snail	*Littorina littorea*	20
Other snails	—	1, 2, 5, 10
Giant clam	*Tridacno tridacna*	100?
Oyster	*Ostrea edulis*	10
Fresh-water clam	*Anodonta fluviatilis*	10
Fresh-water clam	*Unio rassus*	12
Fresh-water clam	*Margaritana margaratifera*	100 (150?)
Other clams	—	1-4
Arthropoda:		
Housefly	*Musca domestica*	76 days
Fruit fly	*Drosophila melanogaster*	37 days
Bee (queen)	*Apis mellifica*	5

Table 3-2 continued

Group and Common Name	Scientific Name	Maximum Length of Life (in years)*
Ant (worker)	*Formica sanguinea*	5
Ant (female)	*F. fusca*	7
Other ants	—	Up to 15
Beetles	*Carabus auratus* and others	7-11
Earwig	*Forficula auricularia*	5
Spider	*Atypes piceus*	7
Spider	*Mygale avicularis*	15
Lobster	*Homarus europaeus*	33
Crayfish	*Astacus fluviatilis*	30
Copepods	*Cyclops calanus, Diaptomus*	1, 1½
Annelida:		
Leech	*Hirudo officinalis*	27
Earthworm	*Lumbricus terrestris*	10
Rotifera:		
Rotifer	*Rotifer vulgaris*	42 days
Nematoda:		
Trichina and other encapsulated parasitic worms	—	30
Trematoda:		
Flatworm	*Planaria torva*	1⅙
Polyclad	*Yungia aurantiaca*	1
Coelenterata:		
Sea anemone	*Actinia equina*	> 15
Sea anemone	*Sagartia troglodytes*	50?
Sea anemone	*Actinia mesembryanthemum*	66 +
Hydra	*Hydra grisea*	1 (almost)
Sponge	*Axinella* sp.	> 4

*Unless otherwise noted.
Source: Ibid., p. 122.

mammalian species (Table 3-1). If cold-blooded vertebrates and insects are also included in the comparison, the range of species differences in life span is many hundredfold (Table 3-2).

Within-species Differences. Individual members of a species show a dispersion of life spans about an average characteristic of the species. Some part of the difference in longevity is due to differences in heredity. For man, several studies have shown that having long-lived parents and grandparents is associated with greater than average length of life. Identical, or one-egg, twins tend to live more similar lengths of life than two-egg twins or siblings (*Kallmann and Jarvik, 1959*). In comparison with the effects of environmental influences, it would seem that at present the congenital determiners of individual differences in man's longevity are relatively small. This is to say that, on the average, the potential life spans of children are currently more a function of the characteristics of the environments in which they will live and of their habits than of their hereditary backgrounds. It has been estimated that rural living gives an average of five years greater life expectancy than

Table 3-3. Physiological Age and Life-Span Differences

REVERSIBLE		PERMANENT	
Comparison	Years	Comparison	Years
Country versus city dwelling	+ 5	Female versus male sex	+ 3
Married status versus single, widowed, divorced	+ 5	Familial constitutions:** 2 grandparents lived to 80 yr.	+ 2
Overweight		4 grandparents lived to 80 yr.	+ 4
25 per cent overweight group	− 3.6	Mother lived to age 90 yr.	+ 3
35 per cent overweight group	− 4.3	Father lived to age 90 yr.	+ 4.4
45 per cent overweight group	− 6.6	Both mother and father lived	
55 per cent overweight group	− 11.4	to age 90 yr.	+ 7.4
67 per cent overweight group	− 15.1	Mother lived to age 80 yr.	+ 1.5
Or: an average effect of 1 per		Father lived to age 80 yr.	+ 2.2
cent overweight	− 0.17	Both mother and father lived to	
Smoking		age 80 yr.	+ 3.7
1 package cigarettes per day	− 7	Mother died at 60 yr.	− 0.7
2 packages cigarettes per day	− 12	Father died at 60 yr.	− 1.1
Atherosclerosis		Both mother and father died	
Fat metabolism		at age 60 yr.	− 1.8
In 25th percentile of population having "ideal" lipoprotein concentrations	+ 10	Recession of childhood and infectious disease over past century in Western countries	+ 15
Having average lipoprotein concentrations	0	Life Insurance *Impairment Study* Rheumatic heart disease, evidenced by:	
In 25th percentile of population having elevated lipoproteins	− 7	Heart murmur Heart murmur + tonsillitis	− 11 − 18
In 5th percentile of population having highest elevation of lipoproteins	− 15*	Heart murmur + streptococcal infection Rapid pulse	− 13 − 3.5
Diabetes		Phlebitis	− 3.5
Uncontrolled, before insulin, 1900	− 35	Varicose veins Epilepsy	− 0.2 − 20.0
Controlled with insulin		Skull fracture	− 2.9
1920 Joslin Clinic record	− 20	Tuberculosis	− 1.8
1940 Joslin Clinic record	− 15	Nephrectomy	− 2.0
1950 Joslin Clinic record	− 10	Trace of albumin in urine	− 5.0
		Moderate albumin in urine	− 13.5

*This 70 per cent difference in distribution of lipoproteins, between 25 per cent versus 5 per cent highest, is equivalent to a total of 25 years in relative displacement of physiologic age.

**As measured in 1900. These effects may be measurably less now, as environment is changing to produce greater differences between parents and progeny.

Source: H. B. Jones, The relation of human health to age, place, and timing. *Ibid.*, p. 354.

does city residence (*Jones, 1959*). By comparison, having four grandparents surviving to eighty years gives four years greater than average life expectancy. This comparison is made only for the purpose of illustrating relative contemporary influences and does not exclude the possibility of considerable interaction of hereditary and environmental factors in individuals. The above are relative statements, since environments change. If man can evolve a constant, optimal environment, individual differences in longevity will become increasingly due to genetics and to congenital influences. This implies that aging must be viewed from an evolutionary viewpoint, both biologically and socially. As society may gain insight into and control over the characteristics of optimum environments, new aspects of aging or longevity will emerge, for within species there are latent potentials that will emerge as the environment changes. Thus any statement about the importance of environmental or biological influence is relative to the period of time when the data are recorded.

An exclusively physical-chemical explanation of aging in living organisms is severely limited in that it ignores the fact that living organisms are clearly distinguished by their history. Physical concepts do not readily lend themselves to the description of those properties that seem most related to the aliveness of the organism, particularly their historical character. A chemist may rather satisfactorily describe a chemical reaction without resorting to the history of the molecules involved, whereas in the biological sciences, experimentation must include some control of the history of the organism, if not of the molecular complexes involved. *Development* and *aging* are clearly concepts that emphasize the historical character of the organism. The place where individuals develop and the conditions under which they live have consequences for the kinds of diseases they will have in later life. Psychology is even more concerned with the historical properties of the organism than is classical physiology. However, beginning with the work of Pavlov, it was apparent in physiology that the history of the animal was relevant. If by bringing close together in time an electric shock and the ringing of a bell, one can condition a dog to give a fear response to the bell, time is demonstrated as an independent variable. That is, the time interval between events, rather than the heredity of the animal, becomes the determining element in what future response is associated with what stimulus. A further logical step leads to the assumption that chronic effects of conditioning will influence subsequent health as well as subsequent behavior. Research on conditioning indicates that conditioned patterns of physiological arousal can last over much of the life span of animals; e.g., sheep and goats. While one approach to experimental biology is that of working as much as possible toward the exclusion of historical material in the description of living organisms, an equally valid approach is that of attempting to study and identify those mechanisms that give the organism the character of an historical system; i.e., mechanisms that register events.

Potentialities of the Organism

An interesting example of variation in the potentialities of organisms for longevity comes from the honey bee, which has a long-lived winter brood and a short-lived summer brood from the same genetic line (*Maurizio, 1959*). Summer bees live from a minimum of twenty-five to thirty-five days to a maximum of sixty to seventy days. Winter bees live six to eight months. The difference appears to be related to the consumption of protein-containing pollen and to nursery activity that is high in summer and low in winter. Winter bees have pharyngeal glands, which remain in the nursing state for many months. The difference in life spans of summer and winter bees does not seem to reflect physical activity or metabolism in response to heat or cold, since summer bees may increase their life span fourfold if placed in a queenless colony. A study of the number of neurons in the brains of honey bees indicated that, with age, the loss in neurons was about the same in hive bees as in a queenless indoor colony (*Rockstein, 1959*).

The large difference in longevity of summer and winter bees occurs in an inbred organism and is clear evidence of the relativity of longevity to the environment when there is genetic constancy. The summer-winter difference in life span is large when viewed in relation to the species itself; compared with life spans of other organisms, this species variation, while appreciable, may even be regarded as small.

The existence of general limits of life span for species plus variations dependent upon environment presents a conceptual problem. There would appear to be a "state of being" toward which the organism organizes and reorganizes its functions and structures. For all organisms, evolution appears to have resulted in an end or goal state of development. Interference with development may reveal alternative or latent paths by which the same end may be realized. A proper grasp of the nature of development and aging would thus seem to be best served by observing phenomena more complex than the molecular. In this sense, psychology and the study of behavior may well contribute to more integrated research in such fields as zoology and physiology. One statement about development is very appropriate to aging and the importance of behavior as a general regulator of the organism:

> It is difficult to make a sharp separation between these more strictly biological processes of embryology and physiology and those psychological ones called behavior. All these are manifestations of the regulatory action of protoplasm:

embryology, in the orderly construction and repair of the bodily organism, moving toward a specific norm; physiology, the control of processes taking place within the organism in conformity to a functional norm; and behavior, the regulatory activities of the organism as a whole *(Sinnott, 1959, p. 2).*

Much of what has been said leads to the impression that the organism has a purpose. The word "purpose" has a teleological connotation of a naive vitalism or spirit, yet words like "development," "senescence," "program," and "mutation" implicitly accept the fact that the organism is directed toward normative states of existence. Genetic control of development and aging reflects successful survival and reproduction of past generations and imparts "purpose" to the individual, but it is a purpose that is both plastic for the individual and still evolving for the species. Within organisms at the time of birth there exists some determination of how long the individual will survive. Hence one cannot regard survival in the population wholly as a matter of random mortality, like the disintegration of radioisotopes. The hereditary basis of longevity may certainly be called a long-term program, since in the human its consequences will not be seen for eighty or ninety years in the very long-lived.

Genetic control over longevity implies an invariant transformation toward some end state, a process that is irreversible for the individual. This statement does not deny the important potentiating effects of genetic control by manipulation of the environment. To the irreversible transformation under genetic control must be added the accumulation of irreversible damage incurred during the life span. These processes, while irreversible for the individual, may not be irreversible for the species; i.e., it is quite conceivable that if humans mated selectively according to ancestral longevity, a generally longer human life span would evolve. Similarly, control of toxic processes in society would reverse the longevity trends of the populations, but not necessarily reverse the consequences in individuals.

The fact that there is a tendency for children to have lengths of lives similar to their parents may obscure the fact that there is much genetic diversity among individuals. Cytoplasmic influences should not be minimized either. Each egg and each sperm not only has a unique combination of genes, but the egg also has cytoplasm that can influence the egg's development after fertilization. Thus with advancing age, alterations in the cytoplasm may result in an interaction with the genes. For cells such as neurons that have such long lives, there is good opportunity for a changing cytoplasm to influence cellular, and thus tissue and organ, functions. The variable would thus be a matter of total cellular environment rather than of genetic change; i.e., not a mutation. Since overfeeding accelerates mortality, it seems possible that the amount of food ingested may affect the rate of cell activity, and hence the rate of cellular damage.

Studies of Twins. Perhaps more revealing than the early studies of the life span in relation to ancestral longevity are the studies of aging in twins (*Kallmann and Jarvik, 1959*). Causes of death were found to be more similar in one-egg than in two-egg twins. Furthermore, in studies of senescent twins (those dying over the age of sixty) the difference in life span was smaller for one-egg than for two-egg twins. Regardless of the qualifications that may be introduced, the results do point to a partial genetic basis for longevity. Equally as important as the twin correlation in length of life is the finding of positive correlations in intellectual characteristics. Correlations between scores on intelligence tests are higher in senescence between one-egg than between two-egg twins. The authors conclude: "On the whole, the data revealed that gene-specific intellectual variations persist into a well-advanced age" (*Kallmann and Jarvik, 1959, p. 251*). Thus not only has genetic control of longevity been demonstrated, but also some degree of genetic control over the intellectual characteristics of late life.

The theory has been proposed that individuals are born with a variable amount of genetic damage, upon which is superimposed additional random damage that is in time accumulated to a lethal level (*Szilard, 1959*). When the individual has accrued sufficient genetic damage, he dies. There are several important aspects of this theory; one is the assumption of a variable initial genetic damage which implies that no one is born genetically perfect. In this regard, the theory is not designed to shed light on how the limits of the life span for the genetically perfect individual would be established or on how the initial damage is incurred. Presumably the genetic limits on the life span would have to have been established in the process of evolution. The random somatic insults that individuals receive over time, "hits," would presumably not be in the germ plasm, otherwise successive generations of individuals would show much more variation in aging than they do. In fact, however, Kallmann's one-egg twins show remarkable similarity of appearance in later life, suggesting that the process of aging is not wholly random. It strongly suggests that there is a genetic basis to such changes as skin elasticity and body proportions.

Szilard's point about random damage has to do with the single fact of time of death. Others have made the point that, to some extent, death is always an accident. But the point of interest is the readiness of the aged host for the accident; in the very aged, the somatic readiness often seems to be of greater importance than the magnitude or character of the accident that precipitates the death. In the aged, less would seem to hinge upon the force of the trauma or virulence of the agent than upon the state of the host.

Parental Age. There appears to be some evidence of a relationship between longevity of offspring and the age of the parents. That is, the last born will tend to live less long than will the first born of a series of offspring. The parental age effect would seem to be theoretically important, for it indicates that an influence may be transmitted in the absence of genetic variation. Cytoplasmic transmission at the time of conception would seem to be the most likely manner of transmitting the effects of parental age to the offspring, although maternal age may also be of significance during gestation. Evidence of the effect of parental age on offspring longevity in humans is neither large nor well established, possibly because the environmental differences are at present so much more important. Small animals offer the opportunity of controlling both genetic and environmental variations (*Johnson and Strong, 1963*). Lansing studied aging in a small marine animal, the rotifer, which has about 1000 cells. Since it reproduces asexually, the experimenter was able to gather eggs laid on successive days of life. Under these circumstances, "mean life span of offspring of older mothers have still shorter life spans and so on until extinction of the line" (*Lansing, 1959, p. 127*). Parental age effects in the common housefly have been studied, and although the results are not exactly parallel with those of previous work on other species, an effect of parental age is seen on offspring longevity (*Rockstein, 1957*). The over-all conclusion may be drawn that there are influences of parental age upon the offspring that are cumulative but also reversible in successive generations, although not necessarily in the first generation. It is thus proper to regard development and aging of organisms as being under genetic, cytoplasmic, and also extracellular controls.

Health. While health is presumably a state of the organism that varies in degrees, it is most frequently measured in the negative sense in terms of the number of physical defects or observable diseases. There is thus an unmeasured zone between complete physical and mental well-being and manifest illness. Practically, the health of a community and country tends to be indexed by the number of persons ill of specific diseases, or by mortality rates for various diseases and groups in the population. These show a decline in health with advancing age.

Another aspect of health is physical fitness for various activities, such as sports or occupations. The Selective Training and Service Act of 1940 was designed to select physically fit men for the armed forces of World War II. While the data are subject to many qualifications, they do supplement information about national health from mortality statistics.

Rejection rates were higher for the older age groups. "If the class 1-A remediable and limited-service men are included with the disqualified group, since most of the former were also deferred, the total percentage of rejected men aged eighteen to twenty was 29.3 and of men aged thirty-eight to forty-four, 64.7" (Goldstein, 1951, p. 598). Since by ordinary standards, the age range thirty-eight to forty-four is not old, the finding of so close a relation between age and physical fitness is startling.

An indication of the importance of remedial attention is shown in the following statement: "For example, of white children reared in five large North Carolina orphanages, only 1.4 per cent were rejected by Selective Service in contrast to a white rejection rate of 44.6 per cent for the State as a whole, a difference attributed largely to the better pediatric and surgical care received in the orphanage compared with that available to other children in the State" (Goldstein, 1951, p. 607). This suggests that availability of preventive and remedial measures was far more important than aging in the physical fitness of men for military service. This is particularly pertinent to the high rate of rejection for illiteracy and mental deficiency and the even higher rate for mental illness. These two categories were the top two causes of rejection, and they accounted for almost one-third of the total rejected registrants.

While not all of the limitations of physical fitness associated with age are preventable or remediable, the effects of aging during the working life are most likely of less significance than are the availability and utilization of medical services and public health and educational facilities. In recent years, children in Great Britain have been given physical and dental examinations in the schools each year beginning at the age of five, with direct referrals to family physicians and discussions with parents when necessary. It is too early, however, to determine the effect of the program on the health and fitness of the adult population.

Physical fitness has two common meanings: (1) the capacity to engage in a particular activity and (2) the consequences to the individual of engaging in an activity or the ease of recovery of physiological equilibrium. Physical fitness may be defined as the "capacities of individuals for psychomotor activities"; it is in this sense that the term is used in connection with sports or military service. The dimensions of physical activity are *speed, timing, precision* (or *accuracy*), *endurance,* and *complexity.* "Psychomotor fitness" or "behavioral capacity" would be better terms than the more generally used "physical fitness" when discussing the ability of the individual to engage in an activity. "Physical fitness" should be used to refer to the strain or consequences to the individual of engaging in an activity; e.g., shoveling, smoking, or climbing stairs, the consequences of which rise as a result of aging and of disease that limit the functional capacities of various organs of the body. Generally, there appears to be some reduction in muscular strength and in recovery from exertion with age (*Shock, 1960*).

A survey was made by the Public Health Service of the relationship between chronic illness and socioeconomic status. The original results and a twenty-year follow-up both showed that there was a progressive increase in the prevalence of chronic disease from the "well-to-do" to the "very poor," (*Lawrence, 1948*). The relationship seems to be twofold: (1) chronic disease results in a reduced socioeconomic status of individuals and families and (2) low economic status is related to conditions that predispose to illness and magnify the consequences. From these results one might conclude that both individuals and families register the effects of illness. Particularly if the major wage earner in a family is incapacitated, the consequences of the reduced income and the direct economic costs of the illness have deleterious effects on the other family members over a long time.

Mortality Rates. It has been previously stated that, at the present time, individual differences in human longevity are determined more by environmental than by hereditary factors. This relationship may be viewed as changing, in the sense that as the environments of modern man tend to become similar and thus restricted in variance, hereditary factors will emerge as larger in influence.

After childhood, the percentage of people dying accelerates with age. The death rate is usually expressed as the number of deaths per 1000 persons of an age group alive at the beginning of a given interval, such as one year or ten years. The rate of increase in the death rate is often called the "force of mortality." It is the fact that the mortality rate of man and other organisms changes with age that is of such basic importance to biologists. Were the mortality rate the same in each age group, it could be validly argued that nothing in the individual changes, but that some random process(es) exist(s) in the environment that is (are) distributed through the population. Also, a constant mortality rate would result in a few dramatically long-lived individuals, whereas in fact the upper limit of life has been quite stable. Thus from the evidence of the mortality rate's increasing with age, the biologist makes the inference that there is a "force of mortality" that leads to the decreasing probability of survival with increasing age.

Disease is usually thought of as being like an infection that depends upon the circumstances of exposure. Not all disease is readily distinguished from the normal state of the organism. However, one can point to the interaction of disease with the age of the host as demonstrating a changing characteristic of the host. The increased mortality with age due to cancer is a statistical demonstration that the host ages. At the present time, much of our biological information about aging is inferred from the interaction of disease states with the age of the host. It seems likely from the literature that at autopsy no aged individual will be free from abnormalities (*Simms, 1959*); however, these pathological processes cannot be assumed to be free of the effects of aging in the host. A distinction between physiological and pathological aging is not one that can be easily made.

Major Causes of Death. Currently, the four leading causes of death are, in order: cardiovascular diseases, cancer, accidents, and influenza and pneumonia. If cerebral hemorrhages are separated from cardiovascular diseases, they become the third largest cause of death.

There seems to be a cyclical, or seasonal, change in deaths from cardiovascular disease that is not seen in cancer (Figure 3-2).

Seasonal variations in deaths from accidents of certain types may also occur. However, collectively the seasonal variations are small (Figure 3-3). That most accidents occur in the home suggests little seasonal variation in exposure.

At the beginning of the twentieth century, the three major causes of death were tuberculosis, pneumonia, and diarrhea and enteritis. Today, heart diseases take many more lives than did any of the single previously important infectious diseases. In addition to fatal age-related diseases, there are diseases that debilitate but do not cause early death. Arthritis and senile dementia often have such protracted consequences for the individuals affected. Both diseases become more common with advancing age.

Because of its functions as a regulator of bodily processes, the nervous system should be considered as influencing the occurrence and course of diseases associated with age. In a related manner, the individual's attitudes and habitual patterns of reactions over long portions of the life span can influence the regulation of bodily processes. This leads to the anticipation that future research on age-related diseases will show correlates in temperament and behavior.

Biological Clocks. A clock analogy to aging would imply that the regulator of events over the life span and the energy released by these events would be independent of the energy of the clock. The adequacy of a clock as an accurate timing mechanism is a different consideration than that of its efficiency as a mechanical device. The clock analogy to the nervous system seems rather apt in some respects. The energy utilized by the nervous system is trivial compared with that of the systems of the organism it regulates; the nervous system, surprisingly, uses about the same amount of energy whether the organism is active or inactive (*Himwich and Himwich, 1959*).

Without a periodic system the organism would not "know" how much time had elapsed and therefore could not initiate its next phase at the proper moment. Periodic changes are clearly established for female reproductive cycles; for lower animals, changes of color and behavior may follow an apparent cyclical pattern. If the process is periodic, the char-

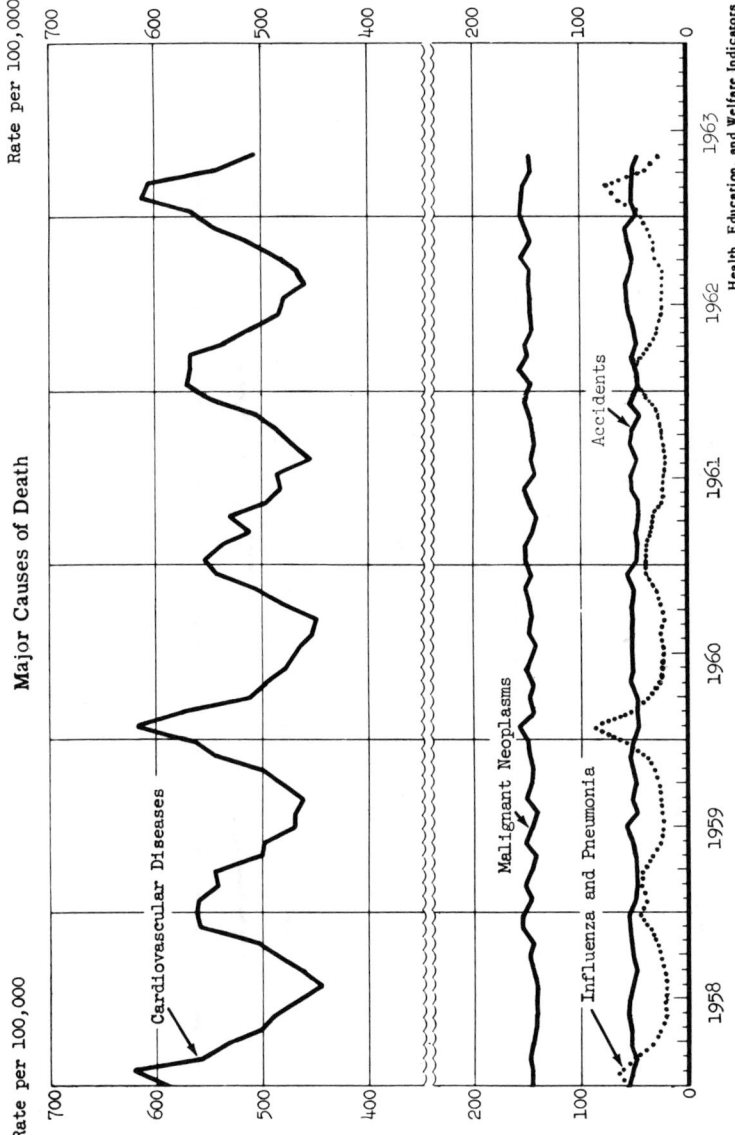

FIGURE 3-2. Major causes of death for a five-year period. Deaths from cardiovascular diseases show a seasonal variation. *Source:* USDHEW, *Health, Education, and Welfare Indicators* (Washington, D.C.: Government Printing Office, December, 1963), p. 5.

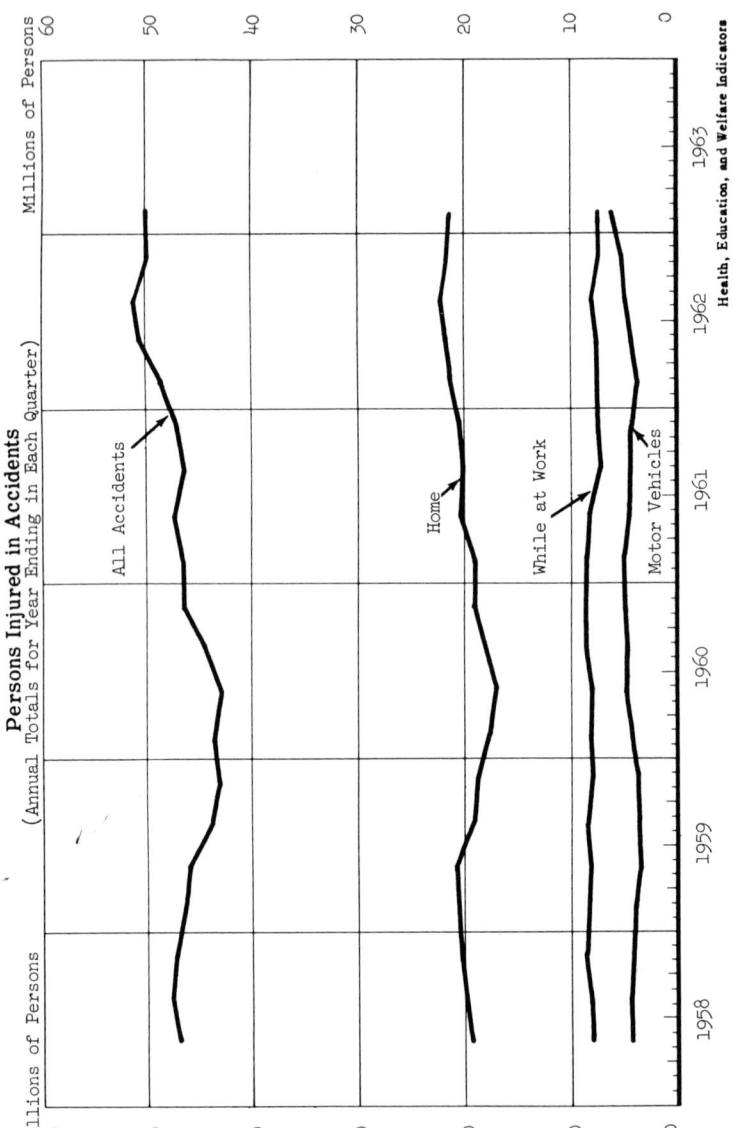

FIGURE 3-3. Annual rates for persons injured in accidents. *Source*: USDHEW, *Health, Education, and Welfare Indicators* (Washington, D.C.: Government Printing Office, December, 1963), p. 9.

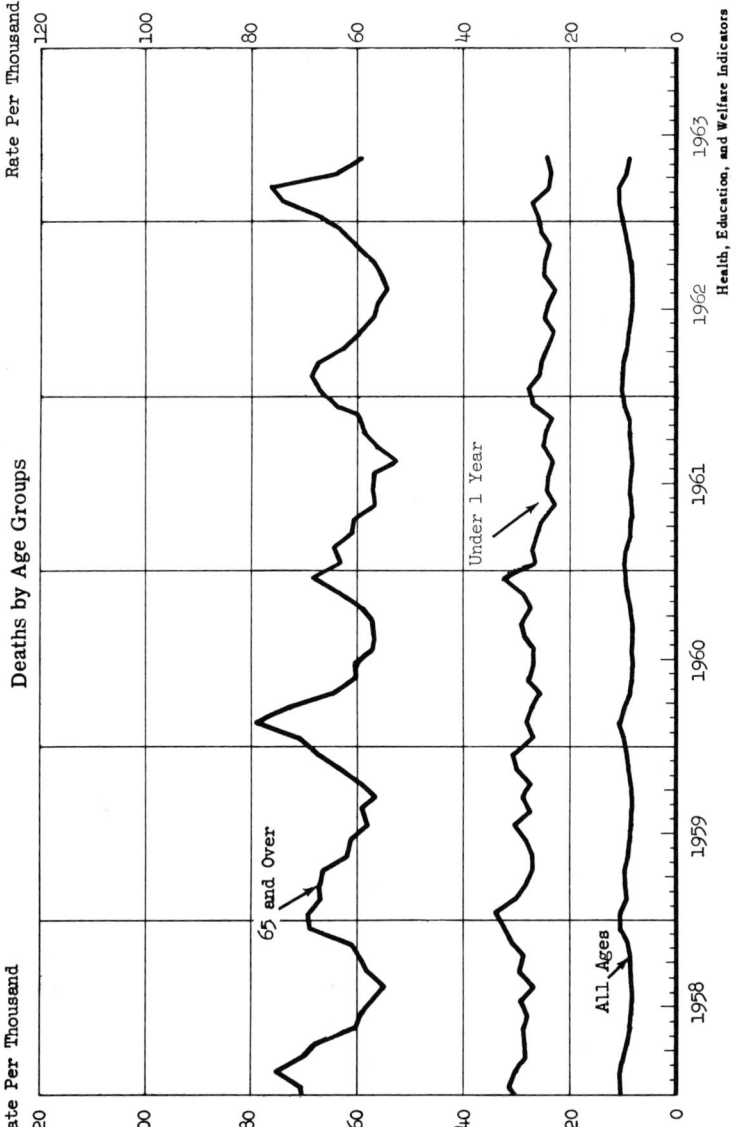

FIGURE 3-4. Major causes of death by age groups. Death rates are highest and most variable in the group 65 and over.

Source: USDHEW, *Health, Education, and Welfare Indicators* (Washington, D.C.: Government Printing Office, March, 1963), p. 4.

acteristic interval of recurrence is called the "period." "Some of these processes, such as the survival times of the individuals of certain species under constant conditions, show a rather narrow distribution over time. The death of a single such individual could serve fairly satisfactorily as a timing device to mark off an interval of time" (*Landahl, 1959, p. 81*). Many summer insects emerge and die in characteristic intervals. In contrast, the survival times of certain reptiles, amphibians, and fish are broadly distributed over time and show a closer resemblance to the probability of survival of a radioactive isotope or of dissipative processes.

Even if the individual survival times are extremely erratic, the average survival time from a large population may serve quite satisfactorily as a "clock" to mark off a constant interval of time. While a dissipative process may serve as a clock in the sense of measuring a time interval, its nature is different from a periodic clock, such as the menstrual rhythm or sleep cycle.

It is important to note that while some cycles, such as the chirping of a cricket, change with temperature, others are little influenced by temperature and may be regarded as "compensated clocks." Landahl cites the example in which the daily color change in the fiddler crab persists, even in the absence of light intensity and temperature changes. Physiological systems of the human are organized to compensate for changes in temperature, and homeostatic mechanisms keep the brain in a particularly constant chemical and physical state despite fluctuations in the temperature of the environment.

Concepts about clocks of different types are abstract, and the question may be raised about the usefulness of the clock model or its correspondence with factual information about aging. Since we do not know the mechanism underlying the lower probability of survival with adult age, concepts about compensated, periodic, and dissipative nonperiodic clocks should be kept in mind as models for at least some of the phenomena of aging. Such notions are to be contrasted with those ideas earlier described in relation to cellular mechanisms of aging.

Contrary to the idea of a single, central, controlling clock of aging—e.g., the cells of the central nervous system—is the idea of the increasing disorganization with age of the vital subsystems of the body. In other words: "The organism ultimately dies of old age because it is now an unstable system which is provided with no further sequence of operational instructions, and in which divergent processes are no longer coordinated to maintain functions" (*Comfort, 1956, p. 189*).

A General Biological Theory of Aging

The previous discussion should lead to the impression that it is not possible at present to advance with any degree of confidence a synthesizing or general biological theory of aging. Even if a theory were limited to the one dependent variable of how long organisms live, the biological mechanisms governing length of life might well vary from species to species. Furthermore, to be useful, theories of aging should not be limited to explaining the single fact of length of life. This leaves out too many observations of apparently regular changes in the behavior, appearance, and physiological functioning of organisms, as well as their altered probability of survival with advancing age.

An earlier discussion stated that many biologists are beginning to accept the view that at the most elementary level of the cell, defects occur with time in the nucleic acids, the genetic material. These defects presumably lead to impaired function and eventually to cell death. Within the cell it is unlikely that there is a single gene or group of genes that controls nothing but the length of life. Therefore, those genes that are important in aging and cell death have other functions in earlier development.

Evolutionary selection has undoubtedly led to an organized sequence of early life changes, a progression of developmental changes toward limits of size, form, and function. There could well be unexpected late-life outcomes of early-life selection. Such outcomes would appear only if the species lived long enough; e.g., escaped predation. Surviving an early phase allows a later trait to appear, one that was latent in the evolved developmental characteristics of a species. Consider, for example, what might be seen if farm animals, bred for early-life marketing characteristics, were allowed to live their full life spans. Most likely, such old animals would have characteristics quite different from the less selected wild stock. Entering into considerations of domesticated animals is behavior, since selection is often made for temperamental or other behavioral characteristics as well as for tissue characteristics. For complex animals in the wild state, it is, in fact, selection for behavior that has probably been most important in evolutionary selection, with the complex successful behavior having selective dominance over necessary, but more elementary, biological processes.

A Counterpart Theory

It seems plausible to accept the fact that in the evolution of a species, selective pressures eventuate in a characteristic developmental pattern. Even for complex organisms there is a remarkable following of the developmental pattern of the species by each individual. Such a simple picture cannot be evoked for old animals, since naturally occurring variations cannot be selected for characteristics that appear after the age of reproduction. The basic issue is how an orderly sequence of events could have evolved for the old, or post-reproductive, animal. A counterpart theory of aging holds that post-reproductive characteristics for a species cannot have been directly subject to natural selection. Hence any biologically based order in the changes of late life must arise in association from counterpart characteristics of development that were subject to pressures of selection. Genes important in aging are likely to be important in development.

If aging could in no way have been selected for, late-life characteristics would remain a matter of individual uniqueness or natural variation, and aging would have to be viewed as random changes. It is suggested that the order in aging arises from genetic selection for some counterpart in development. This view appears to be testable, in that animals selected for longevity should show changes in developmental characteristics. Some relevant research in this area has already been made, although for other purposes. One study has reviewed the evidence that organisms bred from strains varying parental age show different life spans (*Lansing, 1959*). Important in the present context is that the long- and short-lived lines had different ages of maturity; e.g., egg laying. Lansing has also shown that parental age affects the longevity of offspring, and that the effect is cumulative, transmissible, and reversible in subsequent generations. One might argue that experimental manipulation of parental age varies the extent to which the individual organisms can express the genetic limit or potential of the species. This avoids the point, however, of how the late-life limits were established.

If cross-breeding of two inbred laboratory strains of animals produces a strain of greater longevity than either inbred line, this can be regarded as a release of the species potential that was reduced as a consequence of inbreeding. How did the species potential for longevity come to be established? A clue seems to come from the abovementioned study, which shows that variations in life span produced by manipulation of parental age are associated with developmental changes, such as in age of egg laying. This interdependence of developmental and late-life characteristics suggests the avenue by which order is introduced into late-life phenomena, phenomena that otherwise would escape the ordering of natural selection.

Although the counterpart theory of the origin of control over aging gives emphasis to irreversible changes from limits set on individual development, it does not follow that aging could not evolve for the species. The natural or induced limits of development can evolve or be changed by selective breeding, and if counterparts exist, the length of life of a species may also change over successive generations. The counterpart theory does not require that all characteristics of the postreproductive animal be controlled as a counterpart of some developmental characteristic. It describes a pathway through which order could have been introduced into the changes in the old, or postreproductive, animal. Obviously, beyond the order implied by a counterpart theory, events occur that superimpose their consequences on organisms that in the above view have some long-term programing.

Behavior and Survival. For complex organisms living in the wild state, capacity for effective behavior governs survival. Also, the adaptive organism in future, similar events incurs fewer consequences because of memory. The nervous system not only has the property of memory, but it also possesses the property of anticipation. It might be said that the immunological system learns and has a memory, since potential future infections from the same disease will be met more effectively. However, it seems to lack the additional property of anticipation, by means of which the organism could have appropriate responses, to varying degrees, organized in expectation of the moment of infection.

Although genetics determines our development, successful behavior in complex animals has resulted in the selection of particular genetic lines; in this sense, behavior has determined genetics. Mammals that have survived to old age have been able to learn, act quickly, and engage in complex behavior over long intervals of time. For man, survival has come to depend upon the central nervous system rather than upon a protective secretion, protective armor, or muscular strength. In particular, speed and timing of components of complex behavior seem to have high survival value. It seems not unreasonable that aging in man might be particularly noticeable in changes of speed and timing of behavior.

It has been suggested that there has been some pressure of selection of lines according to parental longevity. That is to say, due to social reasons, children whose parents have lived longest have tended to survive better. Longevity under tribal conditions may also contribute to amassing wealth and thus possibly to improved living conditions for children of long-lived parents. This idea of a sociological influence on survival of family lines, in the direction of favoring long-lived parental lines, may have some validity, but it is difficult to obtain evidence to evaluate it. When the average length of life was short, the longest-lived parents tended to produce the most children, thus resulting in selection for longevity. However, for man this effect of selection for longevity does not seem to have been important in the recent past, when the largest gains in average length of life have been made.

In considering aging as a genetic counterpart process of development, it should not be assumed that early life advantages are necessarily advantageous in later life. It has been pointed out that high blood pressure is related to age and to a shorter life expectancy *(Smith, 1957)*. Smith neatly separates early- and late-life effects in his remarks:

> A high blood pressure may contribute to death from cardiac disease in old age, but cannot have consistently adverse effects on fitness, since if a high blood pressure were uniformly disadvantageous, natural selection would reduce the

mean level in the population. It is, therefore, probable that the deleterious effects of high blood pressure in old age are counter-balanced by advantages, perhaps earlier in life, natural selection maintaining the mean arterial pressure in the population at an optimal value *(Smith, 1957, p. 121).*

Insofar as a trait like high blood pressure may be polygenically determined, it may be related to temperamental differences. In turn, this leads to the suggestion that there will be psychological correlates of individual differences both in longevity and in cause of death, as well as in early-life physiological characteristics.

Summary

To summarize the biological aspects of aging is difficult, since they include a wide range of topics, including the comparative longevity of different species, organs, and cells, as well as the associations of health, physical fitness, and mortality with age for human populations. Several biological principles can be stated, however, which, while they do not explain all biological phenomena of aging, are generally useful in understanding the subject.

The biology of aging is concerned with explaining why organisms tend to live characteristic lengths of life. Although the average life span for man has been dramatically lengthened, the proportion of persons in the population reaching such an advanced age as eighty has not changed much. Evidence indicates that individuals tend to have relatively fixed upper limits of length of life characteristic of their species, assuming a relatively constant environment. Hence individuals at birth have an inborn potential to live a certain length of life, a *potential for senescence.* It has been shown that identical, or one-egg, twins tend to live closer lengths of life than two-egg twins.

As individuals age, they change in appearance. Biologists can "date" individuals to some extent from the number of cells lost from body organs with age by examining the changes (thickening) in the connective tissue fibers that lie between the cells of the body or by the disappearance of elastic fibers from skin and blood vessels. These changes reduce the adaptability of the organism to withstand environmental changes and to engage in self-repair. Thus advancing age brings with it greater susceptibility to disease and to consequences of accidental damage. The expression of the basic changes of aging is the increased mortality rates with age shown for the common causes of death.

Consideration of the evidence indicates that there must be time-dependent processes that limit the capacity of older organisms and cells to sustain themselves. Time-dependent processes give rise to concepts of biological clocks in which, with the passage of time, critical substances are dissipated or characteristic damage occurs. One of the currently favored explanations for the occurrence of cellular death is that time brings with it the likelihood of damage to the critical genetic material of the cell. This substance, desoxyribonucleic acid (DNA), leads to the formation of ribonucleic acids (RNA), which in turn synthesize the enzymes necessary for cellular functions. Given either a lack of, or defective, enzymes, the cell could not survive. This idea of genetic damage, or mutation effect, has tended to gain credence through observations that radiation seems to accelerate aging. As yet, however, there is no evidence that radiation causes the same types of cellular damage as are associated with aging. What seems likely is that in the cells of the body there are characteristic sites on the chromosomes that are susceptible to damage with time. It is most unlikely that there is a single gene or group of genes that does nothing except limit the length of life.

Why there are built-in liabilities to cellular death with age poses a problem of explanation for evolution, since the trait of longevity does not appear until after the age of reproduction. Since animals, including humans, could not have selectively bred for longevity, hereditary control over longevity must arise in association with some characteristic of development that was favorable for survival. This explanation is known as the counterpart theory; i.e., that the mechanisms for aging evolved in association with characteristics of development that were favorable to survival.

Cells that do not or cannot divide seem to show aging more than do cells that divide. In the process of dividing, cells seem to discard accumulated damage. In man, several important cells do not divide: neurons of the nervous system and muscle cells. These cells, as old as the individual, thus appear to be critical in the expression of the potential for senescence. The nervous system in particular is able, through its role in integrating the functions of the body, to diffuse the effects of age changes to remote systems and cells. It is thus not unreasonable to assume that there are common behavioral and tissue changes of aging in the same individual.

Not all persons are able to realize their full potential for senescence, for many are cut short in their potential life span by pathogenetic, or disease, processes. In fact, at the present time, individual differences in longevity are more a function of environmental differences than of inborn potential. With improved control over environmental factors, including early- and mid-life disease, the genetic determiners of the life span will emerge to greater importance. One interesting emergent characteristic is already seen in the greater gain of life span in women than in men; i.e., as both sexes live longer, women tend to gain in life span more than do men. At present, women have a life expectancy at birth that is about six to seven years longer than men's.

Biological Influences

The mechanisms of aging are said to lead to irreversible changes with the passage of time. This does not imply that variations in the environment cannot modify the expression of aging, or that aging cannot evolve for the species. As understanding is gained through research on the biology of aging, the conditions that lead to molecular damage in the cell will likely be discovered along with ways of minimizing the damage.

References

Birren, J. E., H. A. Imus, and W. F. Windle (eds.). *The Process of Aging in the Nervous System.* Springfield, Ill.: Charles C. Thomas, Publisher, 1959.

Bondareff, W. Morphology of the aging nervous system. In J. E. Birren (ed.), *Handbook of Aging and the Individual,* pp. 136-172. Chicago: University of Chicago Press, 1959.

Brody, H. Organization of the cerebral cortex. III: A study of aging in the human cerebral cortex. *J. Comp. Neurol.,* 1955, **102**, 511-556.

*Comfort, A. *The Biology of Senescence.* London: Routledge & Kegan Paul, Ltd., 1956.

Goldstein, M. S. Physical status of men examined through Selective Service in World War II. *Public Health Reports,* 1951, **66**, 587-609.

Handler, P. Radiation and aging. In N. W. Shock (ed.), *Aging,* pp. 199-223. Washington, D.C.: American Association for the Advancement of Science, Publ. No. 65, 1960.

Himwich, Williamina A. and H. E. Himwich. Neurochemistry of aging. In Birren (ed.), 1959, *op. cit.,* pp. 187-215.

Johnson, F. and L. C. Strong. The effect of maternal age on time of first litters in inbred mice. *J. Geront.,* 1963, **18**, 246-249.

Jones, H. B. The relation of human health to age, place, and time. In Birren (ed.), 1959, *op. cit.,* pp. 336-363.

Kallmann, F. J. and Lissy F. Jarvik. Individual differences in constitution and genetic background. In *ibid.,* pp. 216-263.

Landahl, H. D. Biological periodicities, mathematical biology, and aging. In *ibid.,* pp. 81-115.

*Lansing, A. I. General biology of senescence. In *ibid.,* pp. 119-135.

Lawrence, P. S. Chronic illness and socio-economic status. *Public Health Reports,* 1948, **63**, 1507-1521.

Maurizio, Anna. Factors influencing the life span of bees. In G. E. W. Wolstenholme and Maeve O'Connor (eds.), *Ciba Foundation Colloquia on Ageing,* V, pp. 231-246. Boston: Little, Brown & Co., 1959.

*Medawar, P. B. *The Uniqueness of the Individual.* London: Methuen & Co., Ltd., 1957.

Rockstein, M. The biology of ageing in insects. In Wolstenholme *et al.* (eds.), *op. cit.,* pp. 247-264.

─────. Longevity of male and female houseflies. *J. Geront.,* 1957, **12**, 253-256.

* Suggested additional reading.

Scheinfeld, A. The mortality of men and women. *Sc. Amer.*, 1958, **198**, 22-27.

Shock, N. W. Some of the facts of aging. In Shock (ed.), *op. cit.*, pp. 241-360.

Simms, H. S., B. N. Berg, and D. F. Davies. Onset of disease and the longevity of rat and man. In Wolstenholme *et al.* (eds.), *op. cit.*, V, pp. 72-89.

Sinnott, E. W. A common basis for development and behavior in organisms. In A. D. Bass (ed.), *Evolution of Nervous Control from Primitive Organisms to Man*, pp. 1-5. Washington, D.C.: American Association for the Advancement of Science, Publ. No. 52, 1959.

Smith, J. Maynard. Genetic variations in ageing. In W. B. Yapp and G. H. Bourne (eds.), *The Biology of Aging*. London: Institute of Biology, 1957, pp. 115-122.

*Strehler, B. L. *Time, Cells, and Aging*. New York: Academic Press, Inc., 1962.

———, D. D. Mark, A. S. Mildvan, and M. V. Gee. Rate and magnitude of age pigment accumulation in the human myocardium. *J. Geront.*, 1959, **14**, 430-439.

Szilard, L. On the nature of the aging process. *Proc. National Acad. Sc.*, 1959, **45**, 30-45.

*Verzár, F. *Lectures in Experimental Gerontology*. Springfield, Ill.: Charles C. Thomas, Publisher, 1963.

4. The Special Senses and Perception

Man's capacity for complex skills and even his ability to survive depend upon the reception and integration of information from specialized nerve endings, such as those in the eye, ear, skin, and muscles. However, there is not necessarily a direct relation between the sensitivity of sensory receptors and the adequacy of behavior. Some amount of reduced acuity can be tolerated without obvious impairment of behavior. There are usually wide safety margins in that there is more sensory input than is necessary for detection or discrimination of signals. Also, the individual may be able to adapt by using the information available from other sense organs. Furthermore, some sense information may be less critical than some other; reduced taste and smell would usually be less important to an individual than reduced hearing or vision. The consequences to the individual of reduced sensory acuity depend upon how critical the particular sensory system is to his activities. Thus the principle should be kept in mind that acuity has to be interpreted in the context of the individual and how he adapts. Generally with advancing age there is a reduction in sensory acuity, as a consequence of injury, disease, and changes in the structures and functions of neural tissues

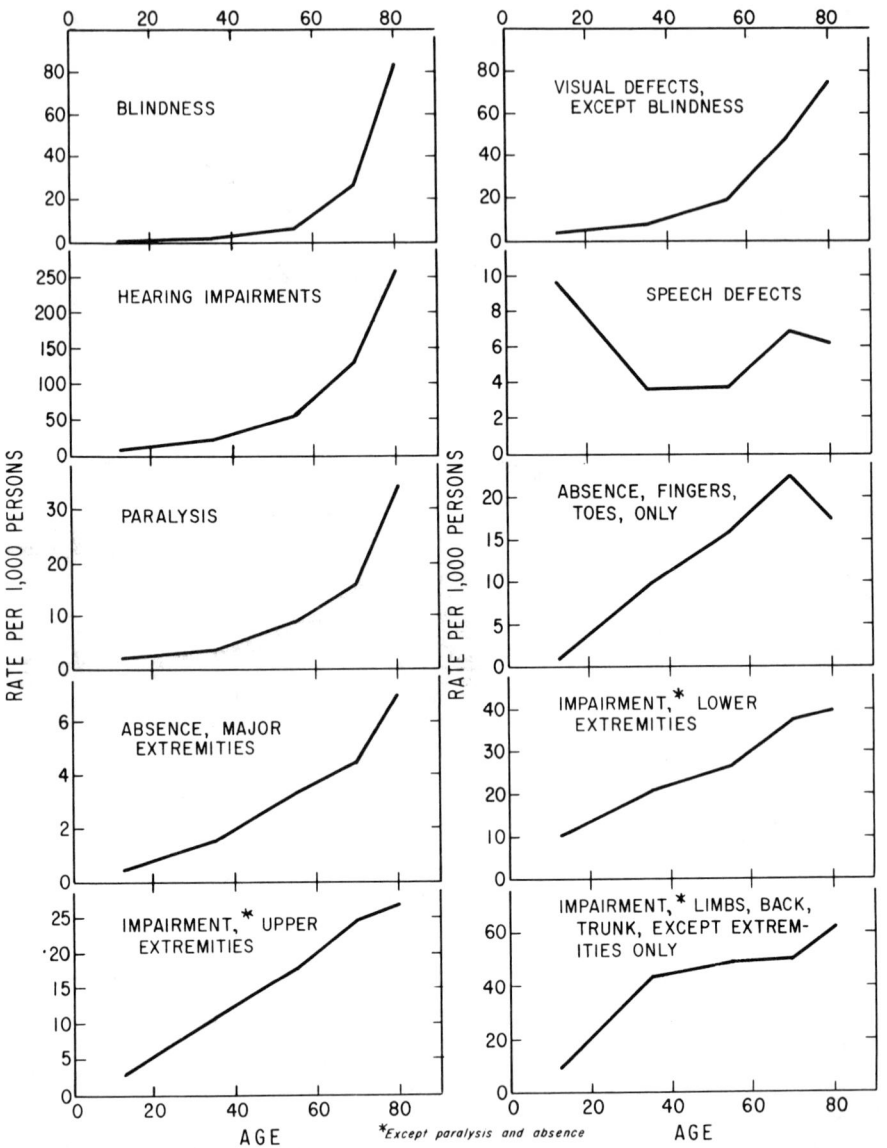

FIGURE 4-1. Age and various sensory motor impairments. Impairments are given as the rates per 1000 persons of given ages.

Source: USDHEW, *Health Statistics* (Washington, D.C.: Public Health Service, 1959), Series B-9.

that are probably due to primary aging. The number of impairments in vision and hearing per 1000 persons can be seen in relation to other types of impairments in Figure 4-1.

The curves for sensory impairments and paralysis show an accelerating increase in the number of impairments with age compared with impairments of limbs. The latter more readily reflect injuries related to occupation and activity and, therefore, decline in occurrence after retirement.

Considerable information has been collected on age changes in sensory functions. While there are indications of common aging effects among the sensory systems, most of the data have been collected with reference to only a single system, and not with regard to the interaction among sensory inputs that is typically the background for behavior. A few statements of principles will prove useful before considering evidence about age changes in sensory functions.

The information received from the receptors in the viscera, the interoceptors, and in the muscles and tendons, the proprioceptors, is usually less apparent than that from the exteroceptors: seeing, hearing, touch, smell, and taste. The proprioceptors give information concerning the movements and positions of the body, information that is usually reacted to automatically and without awareness. This is also true of information received from the vestibular apparatus of the inner ear. These sources of information are important, however, and failure to receive information from the proprioceptors would, for example, result in an inability to stand upright with closed eyes.

The individual can be considered as existing in a sea of sensory stimulation from both within and without. The individual's sensitivity to such stimulation, his ability to integrate it and to attend selectively to it is a continuing dynamic process. The development of effective perceptual habits of handling masses of sensory information in large units enhances the ability to cope with the environment with speed and with a minimum of error. Generally, the terms *sensory acuity, sensation,* or *sensory processes* are used when referring to the ability to be aware of simple stimuli like noise, light and dark, touch, taste, odor, or vibration. When stimuli are more complex, their recognition is called *perception*. Perception refers more to the interpretation of, or meaning attached to, the pattern of sensation than to the mere awareness of sensations.

Each of the sensory organs has its own *threshold*. The "threshold" is defined as the magnitude of a stimulus that is just at the level of awareness or, in other words, the stimulus of smallest magnitude that produces a sensation. The minimal loudness of a tone that can just be heard would be called the "loudness threshold." Since the background conditions under which the threshold is measured are important, usually just specifying the loudness of a tone in decibels is not quite sufficient to define the threshold. It is necessary to control the frequency of the stimulus tone and the surrounding noise level. The lowest magnitude of a stimulus that can be perceived is known as the *absolute threshold*. There is an absolute threshold for taste that can be defined in terms of the dilution of a substance—salt, for example—in water. Background stimulation even in taste is not often at absolute zero, and the magnitude of the stimulus is relative to the background stimulation. The ambient stimulation in the visual environment requires that a light be proportionately brighter than the environment in order to be perceived. The *difference threshold* is that increment in the magnitude of the stimulus that is necessary for the difference to be perceived.

In addition to relatively small changes in the absolute and difference thresholds of the special senses of some individuals, there are more gross sensory impairments that are frequently found with advancing age. Thus in the age range over sixty-five years, more persons are classified as blind and deaf than are young adults. For example, one survey shows about 25.9 per 1000 persons aged sixty-five to seventy-four classified as blind, in contrast to 1.3 per 1000 in the age range of twenty to forty-four years (*U.S.D.H.E.W., 1959*). Studies of hearing or auditory acuity have also shown large numbers of persons with auditory impairment in the older age group. For example, 54.7 per 1000 persons aged sixty-five to seventy-four were found to be functionally deaf, compared with 5.0 per 1000 in the age range twenty-five to thirty-four years (*Beasley, 1940*).

Sensory Functioning and Behavior

In addition to simply being aware of sounds, the ability to interpret the auditory stimuli is of considerable importance. Mere acuteness of hearing in terms of absolute thresholds is no criterion of the ability to interpret speech. Some mammals have more acute sense organs than man and can detect much weaker stimuli. But these mammals have not the range of perceptual capacity that would enable them to perceive complex relationships among signals such as those involved in speech perception.

There is no direct relationship between changes with age in sensory thresholds and their consequences in behavior. For one thing, the level of stimulation that must ordinarily be responded to is considerably higher than man's sensory thresholds. In a group of older men, it was found that only about one-half of them with speech reception thresholds in excess of forty decibels considered themselves hard of hearing (*Kleemeier and Justiss, 1955*). Of a group of forty-five men in the same age range with speech reception thresholds under forty decibels, only one indicated that he was hard of hearing. Partly these results may reflect a reluctance of men to admit sensory limitations. They may also reflect the fact that there may be a considerable reduction in sensitivity in speech reception without its seriously interfering with normal communication. Furthermore, to some extent individuals may *compensate* for changes in sensory acuity. Reduced vision may be compensated for by wearing glasses, raising the level of illumination in the environment, and reading material of larger type size. The question of how much compensation can be achieved for sensory acuity changes is difficult to answer. Few studies have been done on the minor adjustments that people make to compensate for acuity changes. Also, little is known about the interrelationship of changes in the sensory system. Most of the sensory phenomena have been studied for their own sake, without regard to their possible interrelationships with or compensations for other changes. For example, if changes in hearing usually were correlated with changes in visual acuity, an older person could not compensate by emphasizing one system were the other to begin to fail. A major kind of compensation for reduction in sensory acuity is for the individual to attend more carefully to stimuli and to review the stimulus input over a longer period of time. This, of course, reduces the scope of potential attention to the environment, but it maintains performance relative to some especially important sensory input. Driving an automobile at night is an example of the kind of activity needing careful attention, because the stimulus input is near threshold; the glare resulting from oncoming headlights demands particularly close attention so that vision can be resumed as soon as the glare has passed. It has been noted that older drivers do not usually drive at night. This may be an unconscious adaptation to the fact that their night vision is not as good as that of young adults and also that they are more troubled by glare. Thus to some extent the reduction in night driving is compensation, although it may also be a reflection of a changing daily habit pattern; i.e., older people tend to go out less at night than do younger people.

Before discussing some of the specific age changes in receptors, it is worthwhile to point out that the habits of adults are based upon previous sensory capacities. If these capacities change in late life, there may be emotional reactions to them in which the individual either denies or masks the changes, such as in vision, or furiously rejects an activity he previously took pride in, such as hunting or marksmanship. If the changes take place slowly enough, the individual may unconsciously compensate; e.g., with reduced auditory acuity, he may, without awareness, begin to attend to lip movements.

Certain of the peripheral structures of the sensory receptors are sufficiently specialized—e.g., lens of the eye and tympanum of the ear—as to suggest that there would be no common process of aging involved in some of the structures. Furthermore, changes in touch or taste sensitivity would very likely follow a somewhat different pattern than would vision, since there is lacking a structure analogous to the specialized cornea and lens of the eye. Aside from these unique changes in the specialized peripheral structures, there remains a strong likelihood that there are common processes involved. This likelihood rests upon the fact that sensory receptors are nerve endings derived from nervous tissue. Thus diffuse changes in the nervous system could to some extent influence all sensory processes.

Sensory Acuity

In general, it may be said that the organs of special sense have higher thresholds with advancing age. This means that stimuli must be of greater magnitude or have higher energy in order to produce a sensation. This has been particularly well demonstrated for hearing and vision, for which stimuli can be controlled and measured accurately. In order to be perceived, the minimum loudness of a tone must be greater for an older than for a younger person. Similarly, the minimum brightness of a light that is just perceptible has to be of higher brightness for the older person than for the young. Some part of the minimum energy required to stimulate a sense organ is absorbed in structures prior to reaching the nerve endings themselves. For the sense of touch, some of the energy is absorbed in the skin, and for the eye, the cornea, lens, and vitreous in front of the retina absorb or diffuse some of the entering light. Similarly, with the ear, changes in the tympanic membrane and the small bones of the inner ear absorb energy. These changes may occur independently of the sensitivity of the nerve endings in the receptor. This might be described by the term "dark glasses effect." If one were to put on a pair of dark glasses, the interference with visual perception that one would experience would be that of diminishing the amount of light reaching the retina. Under these circumstances, the threshold level of vision would be raised; i.e., the minimum amount of light necessary to be perceived would be higher in order to make up for that absorbed by the dark glasses. All other functional relations would presumably be the same once the threshold level were reached. However, if in addition to the elevated threshold, other changes in the sensitivity of the receptor system existed, then the amount of light that would have to be added to the stimulus in order for it to be perceived as an increment would have to be greater. The ratio between a stimulus and an increment that must be added to it in order for the difference to be perceived is known as the "Weber ratio" *(Stevens, 1951)*. By gradually raising the intensity of a stimulus, the number of discriminable steps that can be perceived by a subject from minimum to maximum intensity can be determined. Application of this principle is seen in a study of absolute pitch discrimination as a function of age *(König, 1957)*. The results make it apparent that the difference threshold does rise with age and rises disproportionately at the higher frequencies. This implies that the average older person can make fewer discriminations in pitch; i.e., can detect fewer just noticeable differences.

Stimulus Complexity

As indicated earlier, age changes, such as the one just cited concerning a reduction in the number of discriminable steps in pitch, do not lead directly to predictions of the consequence for effective behavior of the individual in daily life. Since stimuli in daily life are always complex, the significance of sensory changes must always be carefully demonstrated. Indeed, any stimulus, however simple it may seem, is always complex. In looking at what appears to be only a light stimulus, an individual may be paying particular attention to its brightness, its hue, or its area. Similarly, in attending to a simple tone, an individual may be concentrating primarily on its pitch, although its loudness is simultaneously a factor. A stimulus can be regarded as simple only if there is some common agreement concerning what aspects of it are to be ignored and what aspects are to be attended to. A stimulus is unitary, in the information sense of being a "bit" only if there is an agreed upon coding system. The amount of information in a stimulus would appear to be in direct proportion to the number of possible ways in which people can respond to it or the number of ways in which it can be classified. In other words, since there are always a great many ways of looking at or perceiving a stimulus, the amount of information in the stimulus depends upon the attentive set or coding the subject is using at the time he is considering it. What could be a rather complex stimulus might indeed be a simple one if the subject has a concept of a rather high level abstraction that embraces all the elements of the stimulus at once. Said in another way, how simple or complex a stimulus is depends upon the purpose or set the subject has when he attends to it.

Irrelevant Stimulus Elements. The foregoing suggests that a stimulus always has some aspects that a subject is ignoring when he considers or reacts to it. Discrimination learning is as much a process of beginning to know what aspects of the stimulus to concentrate upon as it is of learning to know what aspects to ignore. In comparing stimuli, there are always one or a few aspects on which crucial judgments are to be made— and other elements that are irrelevant for judgments. The task a subject has in making complex discriminations or judgments is to be able to attend to certain elements of the stimulus while excluding certain other stimulus dimensions. Implied is the fact that as the number of relevant and irrelevant elements in a situation or stimulus increases, the subject's ability to ignore irrelevant and distracting aspects may be overtaxed (*Rabbitt, 1961*). It was pointed out earlier that what a subject "sees" in a situation depends upon his purpose or plan at the time he views it. To this must be added his capacity for handling a large number of relevant and irrelevant aspects. It should not be assumed from these remarks that as individuals develop from childhood to adulthood they acquire a more accurate or true interpretation of the environment. With increasing age, children may in fact become more rather than less susceptible to visual illusions (*Wapner* et al., *1960*). Over the years of development and early adulthood, there is a tendency to acquire a uniform perception of stimulus situations in terms of their meaning or usefulness, although this view may be a less literal or accurate reproduction of the physical stimulus conditions. An increasing tendency to illusions or preference for certain proportions reflects adaptation to the environment (*Nienstedt and Ross, 1951*). Fixation of perceptual habits generally makes for greater efficiency in a stable or familiar environment.

Vision

One general measurement that reflects the efficiency of vision is the measurement of acuity. Acuity is defined in terms of the smallest object that can be discriminated; it is usually expressed as the visual angle subtended by the smallest object that the subject can perceive. In visual testing, familiar letters of the alphabet or direction arrows are usually used as the test object. The distance at which a subject can see letters of a given size usually seen by persons with normal vision at twenty feet expresses his visual acuity. Twenty/twenty vision means that the person examined is able to perceive letters as small as the average normal person can at twenty feet. Visual acuity is relatively poor in young children and improves up to young adulthood. Thus children need large type in their primers not only because they are unfamiliar with the letters, but also because their visual acuity is not fully developed. From about the midtwenties to the fifties, there is a slight decline in visual acuity, and for many persons there is an accelerated decline thereafter. This pattern of findings has been demonstrated in many studies carried out over the past hundred years. One was a study of visual acuity and color vision in a group of 574 individuals from age five to seventy-nine (*Chapanis, 1950*). In general, visual acuity would appear to vary little between the ages of fifteen and fifty. Expressed as a curvilinear correlation, the relation between age and visual acuity was found by Chapanis to be about .50.

The pupil size of the eye tends to diminish with age, thus reducing the amount of light reaching the retina. Figure 4-2 shows the relationship between age and the diameter of the pupil. From this it may be gathered

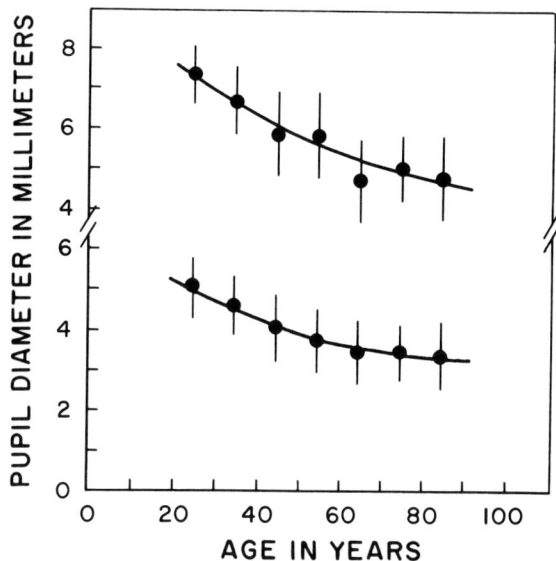

FIGURE 4-2. Mean pupil diameter (mm.) of the eye in relation to age. The upper curve was derived from measurements of pupil size in the dark; the lower curve from pupil size under 1.0 millilambert brightness. Vertical lines represent ± 1 standard deviation.

Source: J. E. Birren, R. C. Casperson, and J. Botwinick. Age changes in pupil size. *J. Geront.* (1950), **5**, 216-221.

that the older person's vision will improve relatively more than the younger person's when the general illumination is raised.

Another change shown by the eye with age is in the ability to accommodate or focus on objects at varying distances. The eye accommodates or adjusts its focus to nearby objects by shortening the focal distance of the lens. With age, however, the muscular system may change, and perhaps the rigidity of the lens itself may increase. Thus the older lens tends to have a more fixed focus, with less ability to adjust to objects close to the eye. Figure 4-3 shows the changes in accommodation with age.

Perhaps the most sensitive indicator of the efficiency of the visual system is shown by the minimum light threshold of the fully dark-adapted eye.

Dark Adaptation

Dark adaptation is the process whereby increased visual sensitivity is gained by remaining for an interval in the dark. If one remains in the

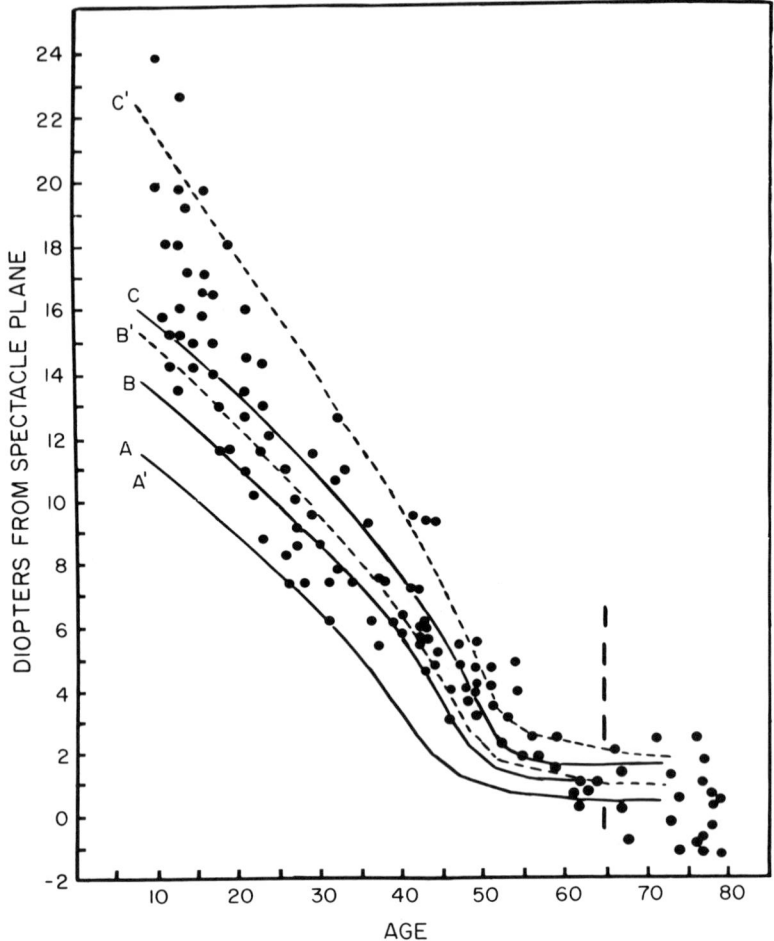

FIGURE 4-3. A comparison of the trend of the amplitude of accommodation according to Donders (dots) and according to Duane (curves). All specifications are made with respect to an assumed spectacle plane 14 mm. anterior to the cornea. *A, B,* and *C* represent Duane's minimum, mean and maximum monocular values respectively. *A', B',* and *C'* represent Duane's minimum, mean, and maximum binocular values respectively. The scattering of Donders' findings above the age of sixty-five is exaggerated by the computation method employed in transcribing the original data.

Source: A. D. Weiss. Sensory Functions. In J. E. Birren (ed.), *Handbook of Aging and the Individual* (Chicago: University of Chicago Press, 1959), p. 506.

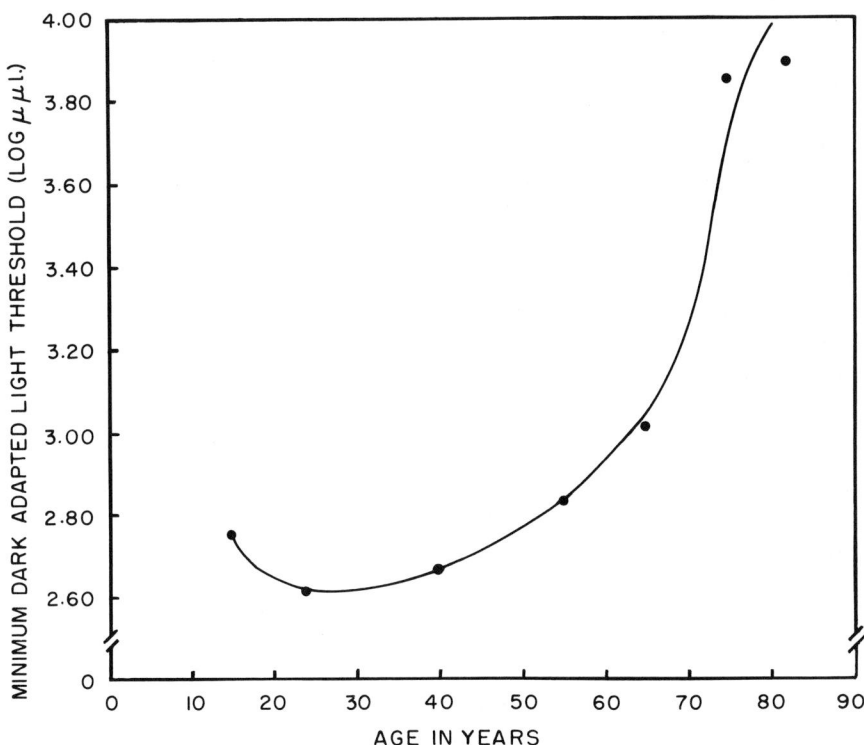

FIGURE 4-4. The minimum light threshold of the dark-adapted eye in relation to age.

Source: J. E. Birren, M. W. Bick, and Charlotte Fox. Age changes in the light threshold of the dark adapted eye. *J. Geront.* (1948), 3, 267-271.

dark for about half an hour, vision becomes increasingly sensitive. The threshold, or minimum perceptible light, decreases as the function of time in the dark (up to a minimum arrived at between thirty and forty-five minutes). Figure 4-4 shows the change in the minimum light threshold as the function of time in the dark. In ordinary situations, such as entering a semi-dark room, one observes that it takes a few minutes of adaptation in order to perceive the objects in the room. This is also seen in the increasing number of stars that can be observed in a few minutes after leaving a highly illuminated house.

At the minimum light threshold, as at higher levels of brightness, ability to distinguish the presence of an object from the kind of object it is depends upon the size and contours of the object and the contrast it offers to the background. A considerable increase in contrast and brightness is necessary for an object to emerge from being just visible to being easily and accurately recognized.

Figure 4-5 shows age differences in the light threshold of the dark-adapted eye. These data have been controlled for normal reduction in pupil size with age. Generally speaking, the rate of adaptation, or the change in the threshold as a function of time in the dark, is not closely related to age. In contrast, however, the light threshold itself is highly age-related.

These data have important practical implications. They suggest that driving an automobile in the dark would be difficult for a person with a high light threshold. The length of time taken for the eye to recover its sensitivity after passing an oncoming car with bright lights would seriously lengthen the period of nonseeing for the driver with poor night

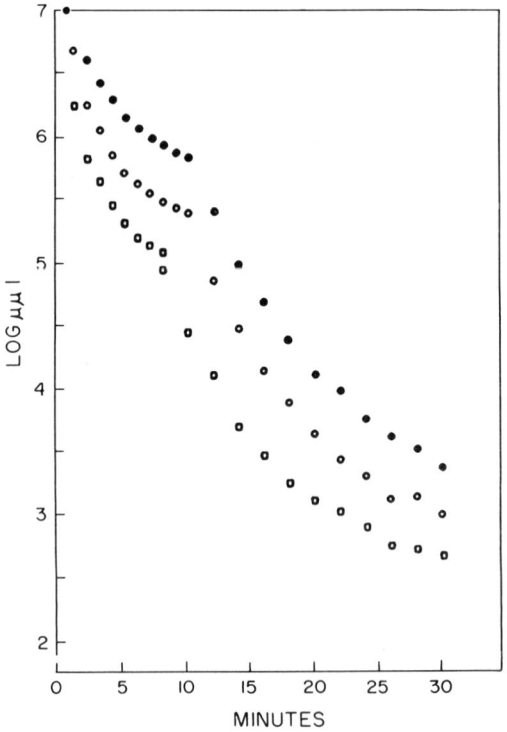

FIGURE 4-5. Dark adaptation curves for three age groups. Mean values are based on individual thresholds: age 40-59, $N = 22$; age 60-69, $N = 28$; age 70-83, $N = 41$.

Source: J. E. Birren, and N. W. Shock. Age changes in rate and level of visual dark adaptation. *J. Appl. Physiol.* (1950), 2, 407-411.

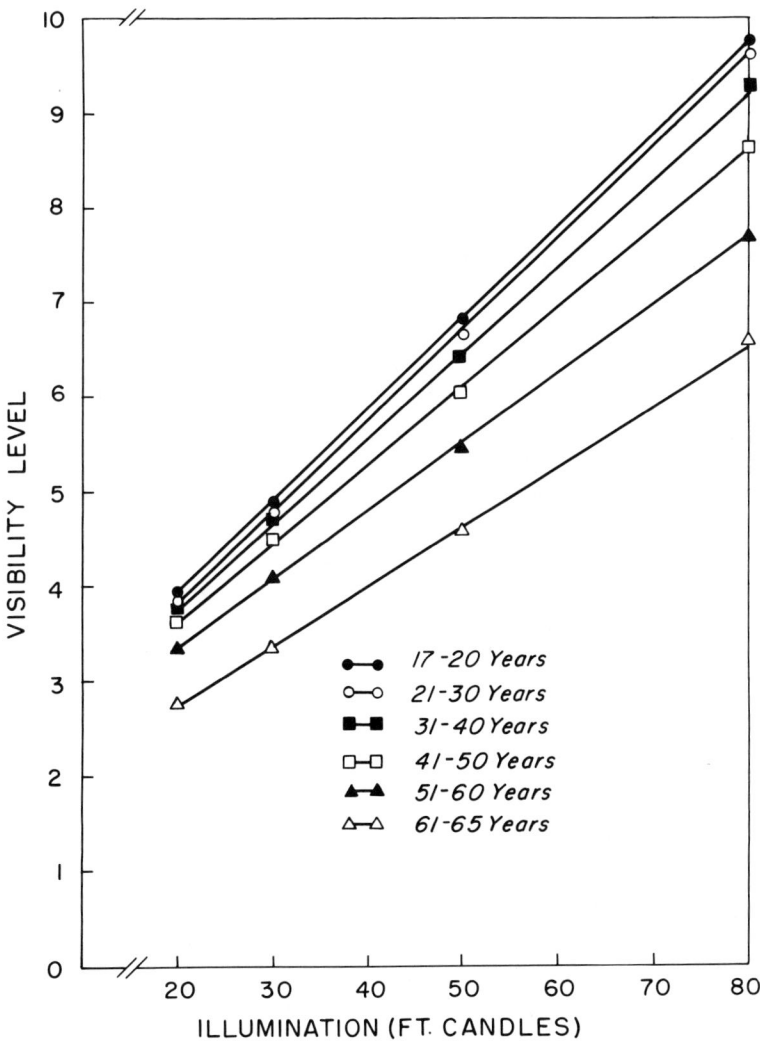

FIGURE 4-6. The relationship between illumination and visibility level for different age groups.

Source: S. K. Guth, A. A. Eastman, and J. F. McNelis. Lighting requirements for older workers. *Illuminating Engineering* (1956), **51,** 656-660.

vision. Visibility is thus a function of visual acuity and the changes from one level of illumination to another. A study was made of the lighting requirements for older persons, using a group of subjects whose eyes were corrected for refractive errors (*Guth, et al., 1956*). In this study, each subject attempted to read ten seven-letter words under different conditions of illumination. Figure 4-6 shows that with advancing age there is a tendency toward requiring higher illumination to attain equal visual recognition. This is a demonstration of the tendency of older subjects to gain somewhat more benefit by increasing environmental levels of illumination.

In an unselected sample of older persons, a high proportion of eye pathology contributes to lowered visual efficiency. Not all of the change in visual sensitivity with age, however, can be attributed to pathological change in the eye itself (*Birren, Bick, and Yiengst, 1950*). In studies of selected populations of institutionalized aged persons, the frequency of ocular pathology is surprisingly high. In a study of over 1000 aged persons in a home for the aged in New York, about 86 per cent of the sample could be regarded as having good to adequate vision. Some evidence of cataract formation was found in 61 per cent of the entire group; retinal disease was found in 29 per cent (*Kornzweig, et al., 1957*). These figures are slightly higher than those from a survey in California of the extent and causes of blindness in persons age sixty-five and over who were receiving public assistance (*Belloc, 1956*). It was found that in over 1500 individuals about 3 per cent were functionally blind. It is not surprising that a slightly higher number of blind older persons would enter a home for the aged than might be found in a community at large on public assistance. It is of interest that the proportion of blindness rates tended to increase in the lowest income levels. Individuals having family income levels of under $2000 a year tended to have the highest percentage of blindness (*Belloc, 1956*). Considering the age of onset of impaired vision, the California study revealed that over one half of the cases of blindness had their onset after the age of sixty-five, with another 30 per cent occurring between age forty-five and sixty-four. Thus about 85 per cent of the blindness had its onset after the age of forty-five, clearly implying age-related processes.

Critical Flicker Fusion. Critical flicker fusion refers to the perception of a flashing light's becoming fused and perceived as a constantly glowing light source. With a bright light, a subject can perceive flickering up to about forty cycles per second; after this frequency of flashing, the light tends to be seen as a constantly glowing source. There are individual differences, of course, in the threshold for fusion. Several investigators have found a decrease in the critical flicker threshold with age; i.e., a tendency with advancing age for the frequency of fusion to decline (*Brozek and Keys, 1945; Misiak, 1947*). Figure 4-7 shows the mean frequency at which fusion occurs for different age groups over the range of seven to ninety-one years. It might be assumed, as with the minimum light threshold of the dark-adapted eye, that the smaller pupil of the older eye limits the amount of light entering. It is true that in general the smaller pupil of the older person means that he is taking most visual tests at a lower level of illumination. Two investigators studied the fusion threshold in relation to age with the pupils of the eye dilated and not dilated (*Weekers and Roussel, 1946*). In the undilated eye, the mean threshold for subjects twenty to thirty years was 40.2 cycles per second, in comparison with 31.6 in subjects aged sixty-one to seventy. For the same subjects with pupils dilated, the mean frequencies were 42.8 and 38.4, respectively. These data suggest that the smaller pupil does contribute significantly to the lower threshold of the older person, but they by no means explain all of the change with age in the fusion threshold.

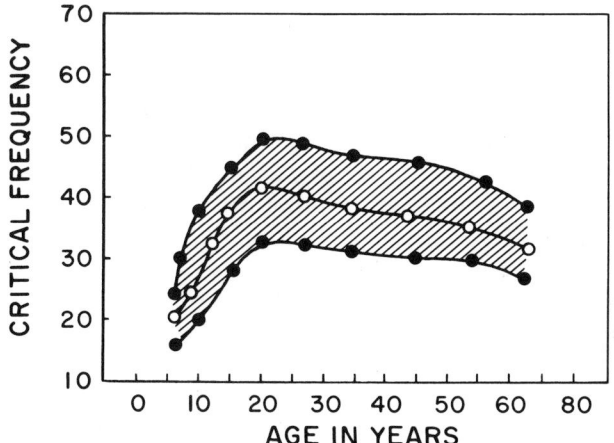

FIGURE 4-7. Critical frequency of electrical phosphene disappearance of the visual system as a function of age.

Source: E. N. Semenovskaia and A. I. Verkhutina. [Age-related changes in the functional mobility (lability) of the visual analyzer.] *Prob. fiziol. Optiki* (1949), 7, 34-38.

The flicker fusion threshold varies with the percentage of the cycle time that the light is on as well as with the brightness of the light source. Thus a light flashing at forty cycles per second might be dark one half of the time and illuminated one half of the time. This would be described as having a light-dark ratio of one, or a light phase of 50 per cent. It has been shown that younger subjects tend to have relatively higher thresholds when the light is off a longer proportion of the time than do older subjects; i.e., subjects in the age range of thirteen to twenty-nine years tend to have their highest fusion threshold at about 10 per cent light time in the flickering source, while those in the age range of seventy to eighty-nine years show their highest threshold at about a 50 per cent light time. (*McFarland, et al., 1958*). The explanation for this finding has not been established. It may be that the older visual system takes a longer time to integrate the energy received from a light flash and thus gains relatively more in excitation from a longer on-phase.

Pupillary Response. The pupil of the eye dilates and constricts in accordance with the amount of light entering the eye. It was previously pointed out that generally the older eye has a smaller resting pupil. The older pupil does, however, constrict and dilate proportionately, so that while it admits less light, its relative control over the amount of light entering the eye compares favorably with that of a young person. Several other aspects of the pupil have been studied in relation to age. These are the *latency* of the response—i.e., the length of time before there is some perceptible movement of the pupil in response to stimulation, either in dilation or constriction—and the *velocity* of this change. A further aspect studied was the so-called "psychosensory restitution" phenomenon. This phenomenon was studied by having sixty light stimuli presented to the subject for one second each, one every four seconds (*Kumnick, 1954*). This repetitive stimulation tends to fatigue the pupil. When a sudden noise is presented, the fatigue "disappears." The relationship between the fatigued and noise-restituted pupil size changes with age. The differential effects of age on pupillary response are seen by the fact that while the latency of the constriction of the pupil did not seem to be related to age, the latency of pupil dilation was significantly so; i.e., the older pupil tended to have a longer latency in response to the exposure to dark. Whether these differential effects in the pupil with age are a consequence of different changes in control by the sympathetic (constriction) and parasympathetic (dilation) nervous systems, or whether they might reflect changes in the iris itself, is unknown. The fact that the psychosensory restitution effect of a sudden loud sound on the fatigued pupil occurs with age suggests that a neurophysiological rather than a muscular or mechanical factor is involved.

Audition

The tendency in older persons for poorer hearing of high tones has been known for many years. Individuals over the age of sixty-five generally have difficulty in perceiving frequencies higher than 10,000 cycles per second. Figure 4-8 shows a relationship between age and the level of hearing at different frequencies. The level expected for normal young adults is at zero decibels for all frequencies. It appears as though most individuals above the age of forty will show some loss of high tone perception. Also, there is a somewhat greater tendency for men to show

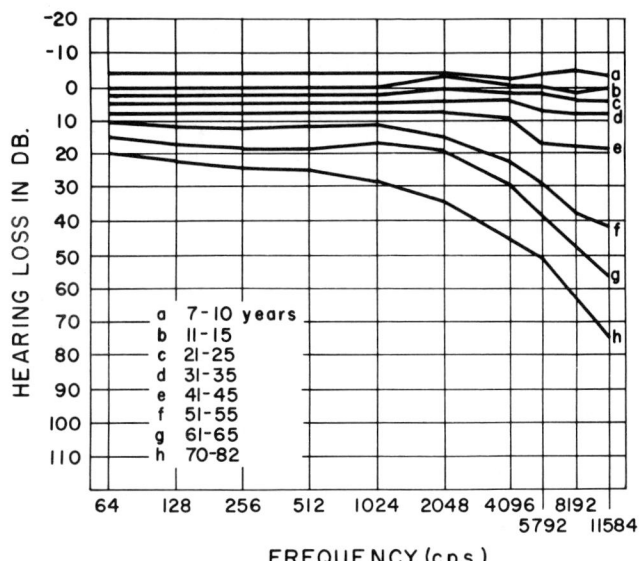

FIGURE 4-8. Mean hearing loss over the audiometric frequency spectrum for different age groups.

Source: B. Graf de la Rosée. Untersuchungen über das normale Hörvermögen in den verschiedenen Lebensaltern unter besonderer Berücksichtigung der Prüfung mit dem Audiometer. *Ztschr. Laryng. Rhin. Otol.* (1953), 32, 414-420.

impaired hearing than for women. The cause of this is uncertain. One contributing factor may be that men are more often exposed to high noise levels in their occupations. Occupational noise may result in hearing impairment, particularly in older individuals. One study found that five years of high occupational noise resulted in greater impairment in older than in younger workers with an equivalent initial level of hearing (*Pell, 1957*).

While it is generally agreed that hearing at higher frequencies shows loss with age, it is not commonly recognized that differences in hearing may appear at the lower frequencies as well. A study was made of pitch discrimination and age (*König, 1957*). A level of stimulation was adopted that began forty decibels above the individual's threshold for a particular frequency. König then determined the absolute difference above this level that was required in order for the change in frequency to be perceived. With this method he was able to show that for the very low frequencies—e.g., 125 cycles per second—age differences were found, although they were not nearly so marked as those that appeared above 1000 cycles per second. König thought that the loss in pitch discrimination with age was probably a result of a loss in the number of neurons and their associated conducting fibers in the auditory nerve. It is worth noting that a study of threshold changes in hearing found reduced acuity for a group of men and women over the age of sixty-four who had no history of acoustic disease or trauma. Thus the loss in hearing sensitivity with advanced age cannot be explained wholly by the occurrence of exogenous damage to the hearing apparatus.

The level at which a hearing impairment becomes socially handicapping is uncertain, for individuals vary in their intellectual level and perhaps in their listening habits as well. Research suggests that more intelligent listeners tend to be maximally efficient at the very onset of an auditory test, so that less intelligent subjects may initially appear to have poorer hearing; i.e., a higher threshold *(Farrimond, 1962)*. However, in the ability to hear speech, a relatively greater contribution of the central, or intellective, factors is made. It is not unexpected, therefore, that investigators frequently find a disparity between the pure tone thresholds of an individual and his ability to perceive speech. This discrepancy is important in the gain that an individual will achieve through the use of a hearing aid. While sensitivity of the aging hearing organ itself places a limit on the ability to hear, intellective factors and the integrity of the higher brain centers also contribute to the ability to interpret complex sounds.

Vestibular Apparatus. Anatomically close to the cochlea, which is responsible for hearing functions, is the vestibular apparatus. This is a labyrinthine structure that contains receptors sensitive to changes in body position and orientation in space. Measurement of the sensitivity of the sense of balance is not a simple matter. Ordinarily, individuals are not aware of sensations arising from the vestibular apparatus, although it is important in regulating our upright stance. Indirect evidence may be obtained about the sensitivity of vestibular receptors by rotating a person in a revolving chair and suddenly stopping him. The sudden stop instigates a series of rapid eye movements from side to side, called "nystagmus." The duration of the nystagmus can be measured. With advancing age, a slight decline is seen in the duration of nystagmic eye movements after vestibular stimulation. Similarly, side effects to the stimulation, such as feeling sick, tend to decrease somewhat with age. Another way of testing the vestibular apparatus is by the introduction of cold water into the ear. This also induces the characteristic eye movements. Collectively, the data on rotational induction of nystagmus and the use of water of different temperature would seem to show that the vestibular apparatus is most responsive between the ages of about forty to fifty years. This is a later age than is found for maximum sensitivity of other sensory organs.

The role of the vestibular apparatus in the high incidence of falls among older persons needs to be explored more fully. Perhaps pathological changes, including that of reduced or irregular blood supply to the labyrinth and brain centers, may result in irritation and the falls result from the false initiation of postural reflexes. One report states that body sway tends to increase with age (*Sheldon, 1963*). Dizziness is also a factor in falls. In a study of one hundred and three patients complaining of postural dizziness, thirty-one suffered from positional nystagmus; i.e., eye movements associated with a particular position of the body—horizontal, vertical, or lying on the side (*Koskenoja and Orma, 1956*). Only eight of sixty-two control patients showed positional nystagmus. The findings were interpreted as indicating that the nystagmus had a central etiology; i.e., an origin within the central nervous system. What may change with age is the relative control over the sensory input from the labyrinth to the nervous system. With advancing age, one may have a slightly less sensitive labyrinth, yet show a greater appearance of labyrinthine induced reflexes because of reduced control by the central nervous system itself. Thus the appearance of nystagmus after rotation may be more a matter of central nervous system inhibition than a reflection of the sensitivity of the peripheral sense organs. A study in the U.S. Naval School of Aviation Medicine at Pensacola, Florida, compared a group of subjects aged nineteen and twenty-one with a group aged thirty to fifty-three; the younger subjects had a mean post-rotational nystagmus of 24.7 seconds, while in the older group the nystagmus was 31.1 seconds in duration (*Guedry, 1950*). Since the nervous system is already mature at age thirty, it seems rather unlikely that it would become increasingly sensitive thereafter. It is more plausible that older individuals have less central nervous system control over vestibular reflexes. Whether this arises by processes of adaptation, disuse, or deterioration cannot be said. Older adults rarely engage in the highly varied accelerated and decelerated body movements of acrobatics, so it is quite possible that some of the changes with age are a result of adaptation to normal activities. Perhaps a study ought to be made of older acrobats in comparison with young and old control subjects.

Taste Sensitivity

Studies have been made of the threshold of taste for salty, sweet, bitter, and sour substances. One study found a sex difference in taste sensitivity, with men having less sensitivity than women at all ages (*Bourlière,* et al., *1958*) It was also found that in men salty taste increased in threshold with age. A more extensive study was done on one hundred subjects (*Cooper,* et al., *1959*). Cooper and his associates used the four different qualities of taste in different dilutions in distilled water. By tasting each solution in comparison with only distilled water, the subject was able to report when the substance began to taste different from the other and then the point in concentration at which it arrived at a definite taste quality. This point was taken as the threshold value. Generally, not much change was seen in taste thresholds up to age fifty. After the late fifties, however, a decline in sensitivity was noted for all four taste qualities. Unlike the previous results of Bourlière, no differences were found associated with sex in the Cooper study.

Studies of the taste receptors on the tongue have shown a slight decline in the number of taste buds up to age seventy and a greater reduction thereafter. One study indicates that the taste buds, or papillae, become fully developed around pubescence and remain relatively unchanged until the mid-forties, when they show some signs of atrophy (*Allara, 1939*). However, large changes in taste sensitivity would appear to be a relatively late phenomenon in life; i.e., after age seventy.

Olfaction

Since the senses of smell and taste are so commonly interacting, as in eating, in daily life it might be expected that losses in one might to some extent be compensated for by greater attention to the other. However, because of the difficulties of studying the sense of smell quantitatively, there is little evidence to indicate precisely how the sense of smell changes with age. Evidence from anatomical studies of the nasal epithelium and the olfactory bulb suggest that in both man and lower animals there is a trend from early life onward toward a decrease in the number of fibers in the olfactory nerve. Almost more than with other sense organs, occupational conditions of odors and airborne toxic substances could influence the trends with age in olfactory sensitivity. Also relevant here is the amount of tobacco used as snuff or in smoking. Valuable evidence on this point might be obtained by studies of olfactory sensitivity of nonsmoking rural-living persons in comparison with smoking and nonsmoking city dwellers.

Pain

Unlike the other sensory receptors, which are normally used for continual monitoring of the environment, pain is an emergency, or alarm, system. Pain should alert the body to emergency states associated with noxious conditions and trauma. Since it *is* an alarm system, the precise level of pain sensitivity does not have the same implications as the thresholds of vision or hearing.

One method of studying pain sensitivity is to paint a small area of the skin with India ink and then expose it to a controlled high light source. The radiant energy from the light is absorbed by the black spot on the skin, and at some intensity a pricking sensation is felt that can be identified as pain. The level at which a subject reports pain can be calibrated in terms of calories delivered per second. Several studies using the radiant heat method of determining the threshold found little or no change with age in the pain threshold. It should be pointed out that these studies of pain in the skin may show different results from pain arising in the deeper organs; e.g., the viscera. A more recent study of pain sensitivity using the radiant heat method studied three different ethnic groups in the Montreal area (French, Anglo-Saxon, Jewish). Within these three ethnic groups there was a difference between subjects aged twenty to thirty years and those aged sixty-five to ninety-seven years, with both young and old men having somewhat higher thresholds than women of the corresponding ages (*Sherman and Robillard, 1960*). In this study it was noted that about an 18 per cent difference occurred between the first awareness of pain; i.e., the perception of it and an overt reaction to the pain. The difference in pain sensitivity between the old and the young was about 20 per cent. It should be noted that young and old here represent a difference between twenty- and thirty-year-olds and those above age sixty-five. Very likely, the individuals between sixty-five and seventy-five would show less difference than would still older persons. If this is subsequently found to be so, the results would be similar to other data showing that sensory changes begin to be particularly striking after the age of seventy. One study indicates that coal miners show a hyposensitivity to pain, suggesting that the conditions of heavy and hazardous work over a long period of years may result in a rising threshold of pain (*Sherman, 1943*).

Touch

The sense of touch may be examined by using hairs of different rigidity or weights of different amounts placed so as to deform or rest on the skin in a limited area. Using the technique of calibrated hairs, touch sensitivities have been determined on a number of areas of the body: the cornea of the eye, limbus of the eye, upper and lower limbi, and tip of the nose (*Zobel, 1938*). These results are presented in Figure 4-9. Generally, touch sensitivity remains unchanged from early adulthood through about age fifty to fifty-five, with a rise in threshold thereafter.

Vibration Sense. Closely related to the sense of touch is the ability to detect vibration. If a tuning fork vibrating with sufficient amplitude is

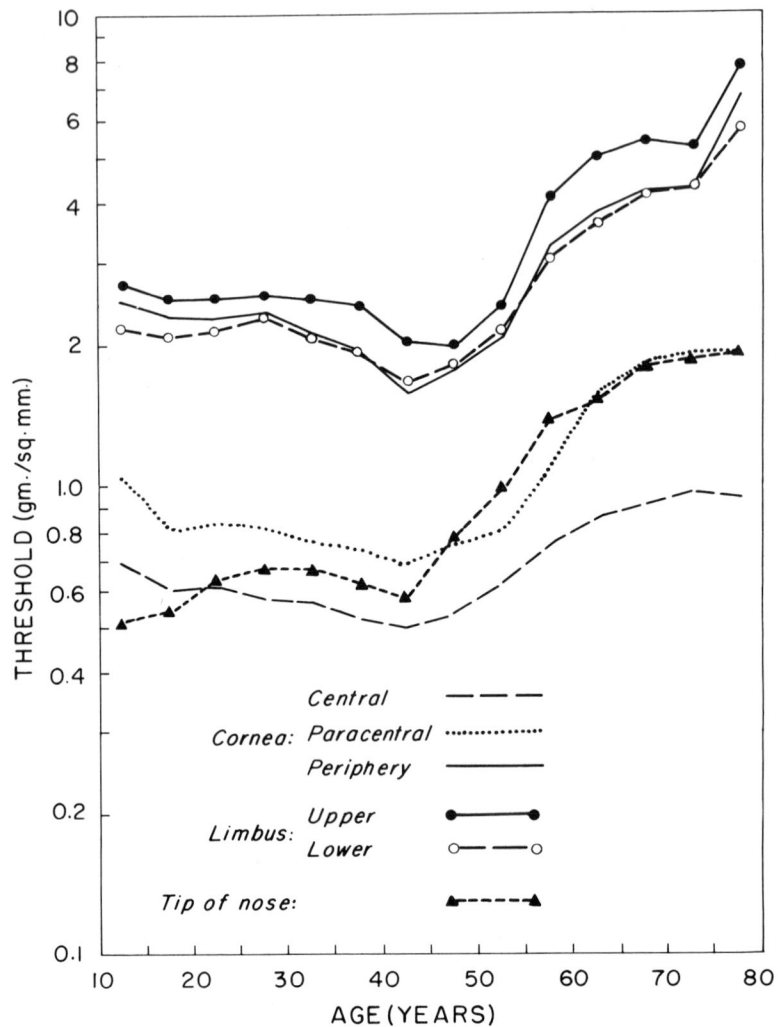

FIGURE 4-9. Sensitivity of different areas of the cornea of the eye, of the upper and lower limbi of the eye, and of the tip of the nose in relation to age.

Source: H. Zobel. Die Sensibilität der Hornhaut in den verschiedenen Lebensaltern. *von Graefes Arch. Ophth.* (1938), **139**, 668-676.

put on a part of the body, vibration is perceived. One study used the vibrating tip of a phonograph record-cutter head, permitting variation in the amplitude of the oscillation while controlling the frequency

(*Cosh, 1958*). Using a frequency of one hundred vibrations per second, Cosh found the results in vibration thresholds with age as shown in Figure 4-10. The vibration sensitivity in the finger was found to be relatively constant for the whole adult age range, whereas the great toe showed a rather continuous and accelerating loss of sensitivity to vibration with age. These results refer to vibration sensitivity in soft tissue. If a tuning fork is placed on a bony protuberance, such as the wrist or elbow, receptors deeper than the skin are stimulated. Using a clinical

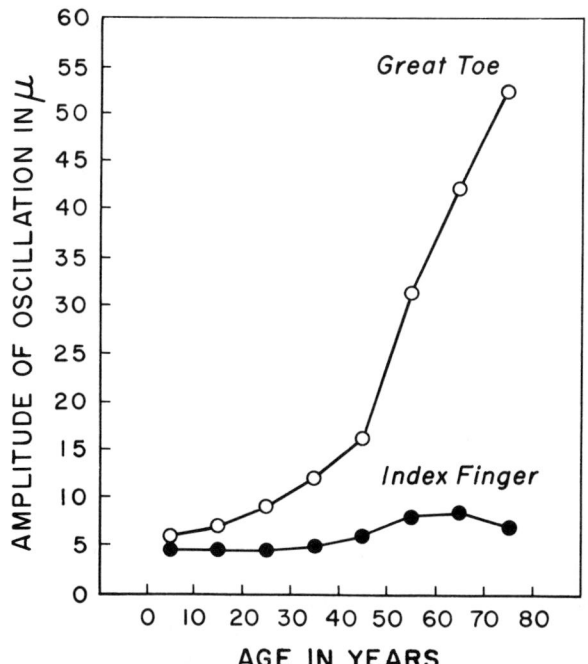

FIGURE 4-10. Vibration thresholds of the index finger and great toe in relation to age.

Source: J. A. Cosh. Studies on the nature of vibration sense. *Clin. Sc.* (1958), 12, 131-151

criterion of the percentage of persons registering vibration sense, one study reported that a greater proportion of older subjects failed to have vibration sense in the legs than in the upper extremities (*Howell, 1949*). Table 4-1 indicates that about 99 per cent of Howell's subjects had perception of vibration in the wrists and elbows, compared with about 70

The Special Senses and Perception

TABLE 4-1. PERCENTAGE REGISTERING VIBRATION SENSE

AGE	Number of Subjects	Wrists		Elbows		Shoulders		Ankles		Shins		Knees		Sacrum
		R	L	R	L	R	L	R	L	R	L	R	L	
65-69	16	100	100	100	100	80	94	87	87	94	87	50	56	12
70-74	57	100	100	100	100	98	98	88	84	81	79	61	67	18
75-79	72	100	100	100	100	90	89	76	73	73	74	51	53	15
80-84	32	97	97	94	97	94	94	62	56	62	44	31	34	10
85-91	9	100	100	100	100	100	100	89	89	67	78	67	78	11
Mean		99	99	98	99	94	94	79	76	75	72	52	56	15

Source: T. H. Howell, Senile deterioration of the central nervous system, *Brit. Med. J.* (1949), **1**, 56-58.

to 75 per cent in the shins and 50 to 56 per cent in the knees. These data suggest an age gradient of loss of sensitivity, with the hands retaining sensitivity to touch and vibration longer than the feet.

Complex Perception and Judgments of Stimuli

Lifted Weights. Previously it was mentioned that the touch threshold could be investigated as a function of the minimum perceptible weight per some unit area of the skin. Generally, touch did not appear to change much before the late fifties. A more complex kind of perception, depending upon an integration of input from peripheral receptors, is the judgment of lifted weights. In one study, subjects were required to compare lifted weights (*Landahl and Birren, 1959*). A standard weight of one hundred grams was used that was compared with four other weights of one hundred, one hundred five, one hundred ten, and one hundred fifteen grams. When the standard weight was presented in one hand and the variable weight in the other, the subjects were required to say which was heavier. In comparing young subjects eighteen to thirty-two years with older subjects fifty-eight to eighty-five years, it was found that the discrimination performance of the older subjects was about 60 to 70 per cent that of the young. However, when the two weights were presented successively in the same hand, the elderly subjects did nearly as well as the younger ones. There is the implication that older persons may have more difficulty in comparing information received contralaterally than ipsilaterally. Apparently the way in which stimuli are presented to subjects determines whether there will be a small or large difference in discrimination ability.

In the previous experiment, the response time of the subjects indicating their judgments was also recorded. Generally, the older subjects took about one-half second longer than did the younger ones. It is of interest, however, that neither the young nor the old group took more time when the weights being discriminated were closer together; i.e., when the task was more difficult. This contrasts with previous work on other kinds of perceptual judgments. One study showed a variation in the time taken to compare two line lengths; i.e., when the lines were more nearly alike in length (hence more difficult to judge), both young and old subjects took more time to make their judgments *(Birren and Botwinick, 1955)*. Perhaps in visual perception subjects can benefit from the additional time and make more comparisons, whereas with lifted weights, additional time may not result in an appreciable increase in the clarity of the subject's perception.

Visual Form Perception. It was just pointed out that a longer view of a visual stimulus may improve the accuracy of judgment. Due to older subjects' lower light sensitivity, and perhaps contrast discrimination as well, they in particular will gain more from a somewhat longer view of the stimulus. A study was done on age and form perception in which the subjects were required to recognize visual forms *(Crook, et al., 1958)*. Given optimum viewing conditions and long exposure time, little or no age difference was found between the ages of twenty and fifty. However, with short exposures, reduced contrast, and other interfering visual stimuli, age differences appeared and increased in amount as conditions were made more rigorous. As might be expected from previous studies, reduction in luminance produced a marked age effect. It is doubtful if the peripheral changes in the eye and the limitations induced by rapid exposures under low conditions of illumination could explain all the age differences in the perception of form in these complex tasks. In the age range of twenty to fifty years, apparently under optimum conditions of illumination and exposure, there is no age difference in the ability to discriminate between two-dimensional, visually presented forms. What is somewhat surprising about these results is the fact that the conditions of presentation were so critical. Many other studies of sensory functions have shown that sensitivity does not decline significantly until after the age of fifty. Perhaps there is an interaction between the difficulty of the stimulus and the conditions under which it is presented, so that a one-variable description of the sensory process in relation to age is hardly adequate.

Another study of age differences in perception of complex figures used the recognition of the Gottschaldt concealed figures—in which subjects are required to isolate a smaller figure in a more complex context—and Gestalt Completion Tests—in which subjects are required to identify the figures in drawings parts of which have been obliterated *(Basowitz and Korchin, 1957)*. It was found that the older subjects, mean age seventy-eight years, were significantly poorer in performance than were younger subjects, mean age twenty-six years. Related findings were interpreted as resulting from differences in cognitive controls; i.e., from overly rigid cognitive functioning rather than from the more literal influences of the content of the materials used (*Korchin and Basowitz, 1956*). In another study bearing upon cognitive control of perception, the subjects were presented with an ambiguous picture that could be seen either as a young or an old woman (*Botwinick*, et al., *1959*). In addition to the picture of the ambiguous figure that contained the elements of both the young and old woman, there were two separate pictures, one of a single figure of a young woman and the other of a single figure of an old woman. Seventy-four male subjects were divided into two age groups, sixty-five to eighty-one and nineteen to thirty-four. When the ambiguous figure was first presented, if the subject identified it or re-

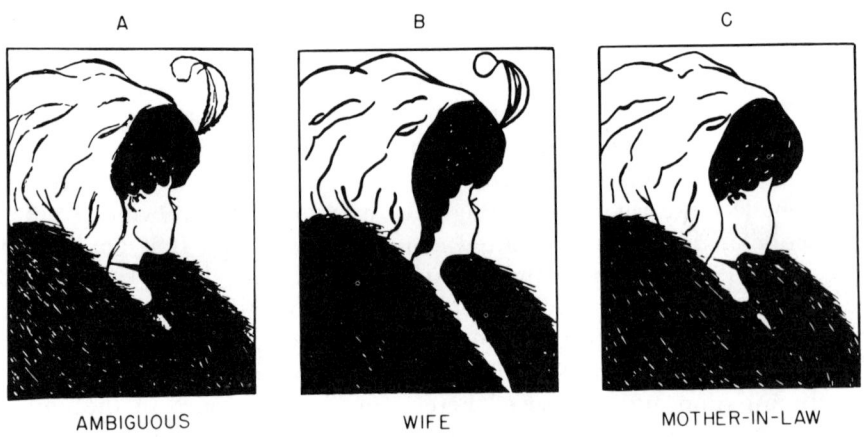

FIGURE 4-11. A. Ambiguous figure of "my wife and my mother-in-law." B. Unambiguous figure of "Wife." C. Unambiguous figure of "mother-in-law."

Source: E. G. Boring. A new ambiguous figure. *Amer. J. Psychol.* (1930), **42**, 444-445.

plied within ninety seconds, he was informed that another figure could be seen in it and was asked what it was. If the subject did not perceive the second picture in another ninety seconds, then either the unambiguous "mother-in-law" or "wife," whichever was appropriate, was shown for an additional nine seconds. If he did not perceive the alternative picture, the features were pointed out to him. The ambiguous figure was then re-presented to the subject, and he was asked what he saw. The older men usually did not reorganize their perception of the figure; i.e., they saw only one figure in it and clung to this original percept. There was also some evidence that subjects with low education had a greater tendency not to reorganize their perception. If older subjects tend to cling more rigidly to an initial perception of a figure and to resist reorganization, then the phenomenon may in part have to do with an age difference in discriminability of the elements of the figure. Poor discriminability itself may lead to rigidity, although it should be kept in mind that cognitive rigidity may exist independently, as a personality characteristic of the subject.

Implications of Sensory Changes. It is obvious from the foregoing that sensory and perceptual changes in older persons have important consequences for the effectiveness of their functioning in their environments. While there is not necessarily a direct relation between sensory acuity and effective behavior, there are circumstances that are particularly embarrassing for the older person; e.g., night driving may be difficult because of relatively poor light sensitivity and a greater sensitivity to glare. Generally speaking, older people perform relatively better under conditions of high illumination, for limited periods of exposure, and with enlarged figures of high contrast to the background.

With advancing age, individuals accumulate the consequences of occupational injuries and other traumas that cause injury to the sensory receptors and accessory apparatus. Several anatomical studies of sensory systems have shown a gradual diminution with age in the number of fibers and neurons responsible for mediating sensory impressions. However, not all the changes in sensation and perception can be explained on the basis of loss of sensory elements. The interpretation of sensory input is a function of the brain: intelligence and the level of education influence the extent to which an individual is a careful observer and interpreter of sensory information. However, anatomical changes in the sensory receptors associated with aging reduce the amount of information that can be imparted to the nervous system per unit time. At what age this becomes important or limiting for behavior is difficult to tell. For many of the sensory systems, it would appear that age seventy is the age at which sensory processes *per se* are frequently a serious limiting factor in the behavior of the individual. Until that time, disease and other unique circumstances would appear to be more relevant than an intrinsic age-related change would be. One difference in the perceptual performance of older and younger subjects that has been carefully considered is that of speed, to be discussed in more detail in the next chapter. Older subjects generally are slow to respond to most sources of stimulation. Two interpretations have been widely advanced to explain this. One is that with age, subjects become more cautious and, therefore, wish to review the stimulus longer before responding. Another position is that because of the inability to impart to the central nervous system the same amount of excitation per unit time via the receptor system, more time is required to achieve clear discrimination of the stimulus. Probably the older subject both requires more time to view stimuli and wants more time to be certain of his response. Of particular importance in relation to aging is the necessity not to regard the perception of sensory input as resulting only from peripheral alterations in the sensory receptors. The role of the central nervous system in integrating sensory input must always be kept in mind. In aging, the central nervous system itself is very likely undergoing some process of primary cellular changes, perhaps somewhat in phase with changes in the peripheral perceptors.

Summary

In summary, it should be said that sensory receptors have in common their essential nature as neural structures or extensions of the nervous system. Thus the tendency toward reduced numbers of receptors with age may have a common basis in the ability of cells of the nervous system to survive and function. In addition to having a common or primary process of neural aging, receptors have specialized structures, such as the lens of the eye, which tends to become opaque (cataract) in many older individuals. These specialized structures, while influencing sensory function with age, are aging in a very unique manner.

The changes in the central nervous system, in the peripheral sensory receptors, and in their specialized structures result in a reduced sensory input with age. Thus, compared with young adults, the older person is, in general, making discriminations among stimuli of lower intensity. Another effect of the reduced sensory input may be the lowering of the total level of excitation imparted to the nervous system and the affecting thereby of the level of activity of the individual.

References

Allara, E. [Investigation on the human taste organ. I: The structure of the taste papillae at various ages.] *Arch. Ital. Anat. Embriol.,* 1939, **42,** 506-564.

Basowitz, H. and S. J. Korchin. Age differences in the perception of closure. *J. Abnorm. Soc. Psychol.,* 1957, **54,** 93-97.

Beasley, W. C. The general problem of deafness in the population. *Laryngoscope,* 1940, **50,** 856-905.

Belloc, Nedra B. Blindness among the aged. *Public Health Reports,* 1956, **71,** 1221-1225.

Birren, J. E., M. W. Bick, and Charlotte Fox. Age changes in the light threshold of the dark adapted eye. *J. Geront.,* 1948, 3, 267-271.

———, ———, and M. Yiengst. The relation of structural changes of the eye and vitamin A to elevation of the light threshold in later life. *J. Exp. Psychol.,* 1950, **40,** 260-266.

―――― and J. Botwinick. Speed of response as a function of perceptual difficulty and age. *J. Geront.*, 1955, **10**, 433-436.

――――, R. C. Casperson, and J. Botwinick. Age changes in pupil size. *J. Geront.*, 1950, **5**, 216-221.

―――― and N. W. Shock. Age changes in rate and level of visual dark adaptation. *J. Appl. Physiol.*, 1950, **2**, 407-411.

Botwinick, J., J. S. Robbin, and J. F. Brinley. Reorganization of perceptions with age. *J. Geront.*, 1959, **14**, 85-88.

Bourlière, F., H. Cendron, and A. Rapaport. Modification avec l'âge des seuils gustatifs de perception et de reconnaissance aux saveurs salée et sucrée chez l'homme. *Gerontologia*, 1958, **2**, 104-112.

*Braun, H. W. Perceptual processes. In J. E. Birren (ed.), *Handbook of Aging and the Individual*, pp. 543-561. Chicago: University of Chicago Press, 1959.

Brozek, J. and A. Keyes. Changes in flicker-fusion frequency with age. *J. Consult. Psychol.*, 1945, **9**, 87-90.

Chapanis, A. Relationships between age, visual acuity and color vision. *Human Biol.*, 1950, **22**, 1-31.

Cooper, R. M., I. Bilash, and J. P. Zubek. The effect of age on taste sensitivity. *J. Geront.*, 1959, **14**, 56-58.

Cosh, J. A. Studies on the nature of vibration sense. *Clin. Sc.*, 1953, **12**, 131-151.

Crook, M. N., Edith A. Alexander, Edythe M. S. Anderson, J. Coules, J. A. Hanson, and N. T. Jeffries, Jr. *Age and Form Perception*. USAF School of Aviation Medicine, Randolph AFB, Texas, 1958, Report No. 57-124.

Farrimond, T. Factors influencing auditory perception of pure tones and speech. *J. Speech Hearing Res.*, 1962, **5**, 194-204.

Geudry, F. E., Jr. *Age as a Variable in Post Rotational Phenomena*. USN School of Aviation Medicine, Naval Air Station, Pensacola, Florida, 1950, NM-001-063.01.19, Report No. 19.

Guth, S. K., A. A. Eastman, and J. F. McNellis. Lighting requirements for older workers. *Illuminating Engineering*, 1956, **51**, 656-660.

Howell, T. H. Senile deterioration of the central nervous system. *Brit. Med. J.*, 1949, **1**, 56-58.

Kleemeier, R. W. and W. A. Justiss. Adjustment to hearing loss and to hearing aids in old age. In I. L. Webber (ed.), *Aging and Retirement*, pp. 34-48. Gainesville: University of Florida Press, 1955.

König, E. Pitch discrimination and age. *Acta-oto-laryng.*, 1957, **48**, 475-489.

Korchin, S. J., and H. Basowitz. The judgment of ambiguous stimuli as an index of cognitive functioning in aging. *J. Person.*, 1956, **25**, 81-95.

Kornzweig, A. L., M. Feldstein, and J. Schneider. The eye in old age. *Amer. J. Ophthal.*, 1957, **44**, 29-37.

Koskenoja, M. and E. J. Orma. Positional nystagmus in elderly patients with postural dizziness. *Annals Otol. Rhin. Laryng.*, 1956, **65**, 707-713.

Kumnick, Lillian S. Pupillary psychosensory restitution and aging. *J. Optical Soc.*, 1954, **44**, 735-741.

Landahl, H. D. and J. E. Birren. Effects of age on the discrimination of lifted weights. *J. Geront.*, 1959, **14**, 48-55.

McFarland, R. A., B. Warren, and C. Karis. Alterations in critical flicker fre-

―――――
* Suggested additional reading.

quency as a function of age and light: dark ratio. *J. Exp. Psychol.*, 1958, **56**, 529-538.

Misiak, H. Age and sex differences in critical flicker frequency. *J. Exp. Psychol.*, 1947, **37**, 318-332.

Nienstedt, C. W., Jr., and S. Ross. Preferences for rectangular proportions in college students and the aged. *J. Genetic Psychol.*, 1951, **78**, 153-158.

Pell, S. The relation of occupational noise exposure to loss of hearing acuity. *A.M.A. Arch. Otolaryng.*, 1957, **66**, 79-92.

Rabbitt, P. M. A. *Perceptual Discrimination and the Choice of Responses.* Cambridge: Cambridge University Library, Ph.D. dissertation, 1961.

Sheldon, J. H. The effect of age on the control of sway. *Geront. Clin.*, 1963, **5**, 129-130.

Sherman, E. D. Sensitivity to pain. *Canadian Med. Assn. J.*, 1943, **48**, 437-441.

——— and E. Robillard. Sensitivity to pain in the aged. *Canadian Med. Assn. J.*, 1960, **83**, 944-947.

Stevens, S. S. Mathematics, Measurement, and Psychophysics. In S. S. Stevens (ed.), *Handbook of Experimental Psychology*, pp. 1-49. New York: John Wiley & Sons, Inc., 1951.

U.S. Department of Health, Education and Welfare. *Impairments by Type, Sex and Age.* Washington, D.C.: Government Printing Office, Series B-9, Pub. No. 584-B9, 1959.

Wapner, S., H. Werner, and P. E. Comalli, Jr. Perception of part-whole relationships in middle and old age. *J. Geront.*, 1960, **15**, 413-418.

Weekers, R. and F. Roussel. Introduction à l'étude de la fréquencé de fusion en clinique. *Ophthalmologica*, 1946, **112**, 305-319.

*Weiss, A. D. Sensory functions. In Birren (ed.), 1959, *op. cit.*, pp. 503-542.

Zobel, H. Die Sensibilität der Hornhaut in den verschiedenen Lebensaltern. *von Graefes Arch. Ophthal.*, 1938, **139**, 668-676.

5. Speed and Timing in Development and Aging

One of the generally observed changes after middle age is a tendency to slowness of behavior. Among the most reliable facts shown through research on human aging is the trend toward psychomotor slowness. The slowness can be examined in relation to its underlying causes or for its consequences in effective behavior, as in complex skills. In the preceding chapter it was pointed out that older persons show a reduction in the speed of perception or recognition of stimuli. One of the contributory factors to over-all speed of behavior is a reduction in sensory input due to weak or difficult stimuli or to lower sensory acuity. Were this the only factor, then older adults would show quickness in self-initiated responses. Actually, the evidence indicates that all behavior mediated by the central nervous system tends to be slow in the aging organism. Hence, while reduced sensory input may contribute to slowing, it is not the only or necessarily the largest factor in the generalized slowing of old age. The reduced sensory input may itself be a manifestation of primary neural aging, in which transmission in the nervous system tends to be reduced because of the loss of cells and age changes in the physiological properties of nerve cells and fibers. In the view favored here, slowness of behavior is the principal manifestation of a primary process of aging in the nervous system.

Modifying the changing limits of speed of behavior with age are the effects of practice. Individuals of all ages tend to be slow when dealing with unfamiliar or ambiguous stimuli. Slowness is apparent in recognizing relatively unfamiliar words or figures. Generally, the young adult, who has a great capacity for the rapid intake of information, is limited largely by differential familiarity or practice. He is fast or slow depending upon the difficulty of the material he is dealing with. With advancing age, however, a general quality of slowness is evidenced apart from the speed of behavior related to differential practice or familiarity.

In the early years of childhood, the nervous system is undergoing anatomical and physiological development and thus determines the upper limit on the differential effects due to the behavior that the child is practicing. In later adulthood, changes in the nervous system due to aging again limit the speed of transmission or the linkage of sensory input and behavioral output. Thus the total number of units of behavior that can be effected in a unit of time is reduced with advancing age. The precise limitation that changing speed may impose on the effectiveness of the individual depends upon his capacity to compensate, to be motivated to additional effort, to concentrate his effort or practice, or to so change the nature of his activities that experience rather than rapidity of action is of primary importance.

Speed and Timing. One should distinguish between speed in doing a task and timing in performance. "Speed" refers to the fastest time in which a task can be performed. It may range from the speed with which a finger is raised in response to a simple sound signal to the speed of running the one hundred yard dash. In contrast to speed, "timing" refers to the sequential relationships between parts of a task. What may distinguish the highest levels of skill may not be so much the minimum time in elements of performance as it is in the timing of the various task components. When new skills, such as playing a musical instrument or learning to write, are learned, first attempts are slow, halting, full of errors. The integration of the task elements into a smooth performance is poor. After practice, errors of content, or commission, disappear, and performance is essentially correct, although still slow. With further practice, speed and timing both improve, providing a measure of quality of performance at the advanced level of skill where errors are rarely seen. This does not suggest that errors are unrelated to speed but that the probability of making an error is so small near the top level of performance that it is not a useful measurement. Accuracy, or the probability of errors, is a more useful measure of the quality of performance in the early stages of development of a skill, whereas speed and timing of responses tend to reflect gradations in well-developed skills.

Since the young child increases speed with increased practice, it is easy to suspect that changes in psychomotor speed often seen in older persons are a consequence of the lack of practice, a matter of the reverse process of early learning and development. While there have been no sustained-practice studies in older persons, what argues against this hypothesis is the fact that even in such highly overlearned skills as handwriting there is a trend toward slowing in older persons. Also, slowing tends to have a general characteristic, that is, speed of writing shows a relationship with the speed of performing a great range of activities.

Major Conditions Influencing Speed of Behavior. The major factors governing psychomotor speed are the complexity and strength of the stimulus; familiarity with the stimulus; expectancy, or set, for the stimulus; the complexity of the response; and the age and condition of the individual organism. In other words, a quick response is made to a stimulus if the stimulus is expected, familiar, strong, and unambiguous, and the response is simple. A fast response is made to a bright light or a loud sound. "Complexity" refers to the number of elements in a stimulus and its context that have to be discriminated before a differential response can be made. A stimulus is difficult if there are a large number of elements to consider simultaneously, if the elements are quite similar to one another, and if there are many irrelevant items that have to be ignored. The context of the stimulus is important insofar as it focuses attention on important details at about the time the stimulus is to be presented. If the stimulus elements are presented too rapidly, an individual may not be able to perceive them. If there are delays in presenting the task or stimulus elements to be integrated, then short-term memory may be overtaxed.

A useful distinction has been added with regard to stimulus conditions (*Rabbitt, 1961*). In his research, Rabbitt not only varied the number of stimulus elements on cards to be sorted (letters of the alphabet), but he also added varying numbers of irrelevant stimuli. Generally, the older person is more affected than the young adult by the introduction of irrelevant stimuli. For example, the performance of the older subject on a two-choice task with irrelevant stimuli appears equivalent to that of the young subject performing an eight-choice task. Irrelevant aspects of a situation that have particularly strong or idiosyncratic meaning are distracting to a subject of any age.

Response Conditions. The complexities of the response must also be taken into account in discussing speed and timing. An individual may have to make a relatively simple response to a very complex set of stimulus conditions; e.g., raise his right hand in response to a long and complicated chain of events. However, in driving an automobile, for example, the driver may have to make several different sequential movements of hand and foot to turn and stop or to accelerate the car. Thus in contrast to a simple response to a complex stimulus, there may also be a highly complicated response to a relatively simple stimulus. In part, response time varies with the amount of monitoring necessary to maintain high quality of task performance.

Reaction Time in Development and Aging. A laboratory for gathering anthropometric and psychological measurements was established in London by Francis Galton in the nineteenth century. Over a period of several years, the laboratory gathered measurements on more than 9000 persons of both sexes and of all ages. Among the measurements were

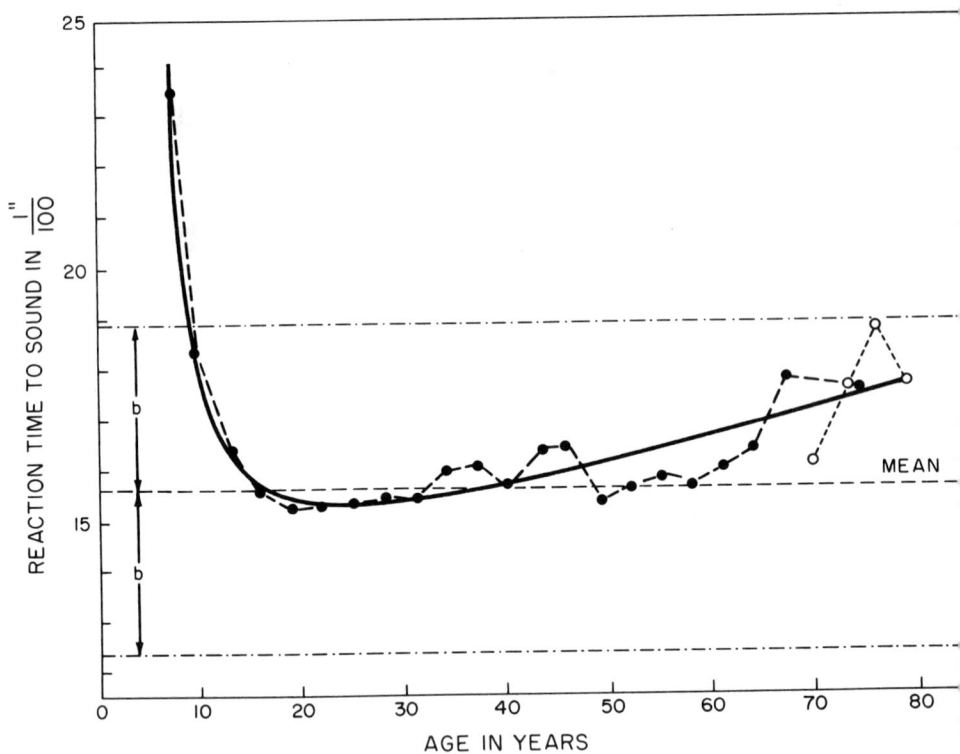

FIGURE 5-1. Reaction time to auditory signals in relation to age.

Source: Y. Koga and G. M. Morant. On the degree of association between reaction times in the case of different senses. *Biometrika* (1923), 15, 355-359.

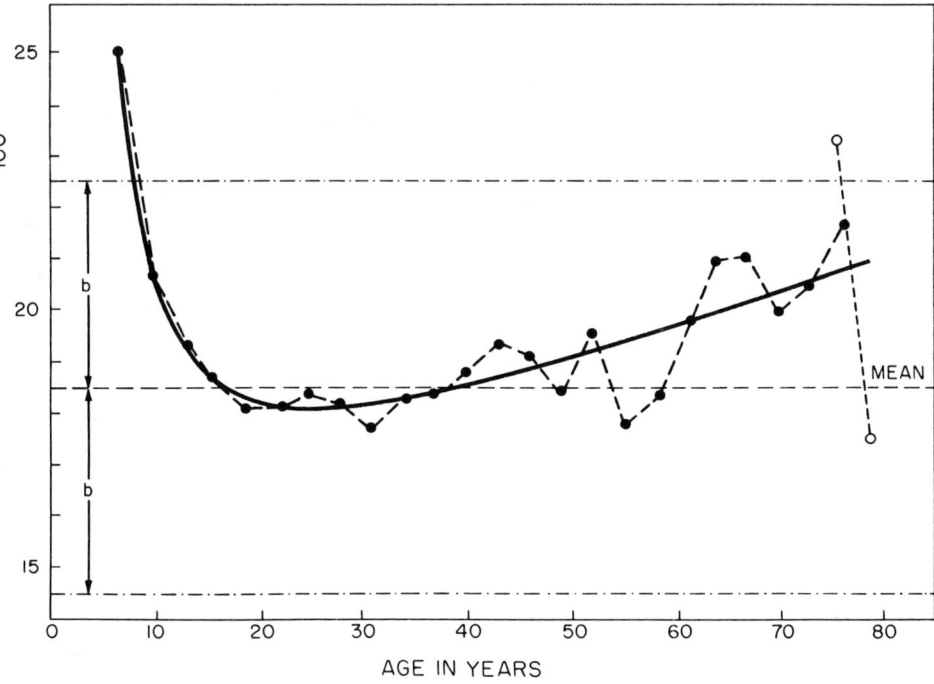

FIGURE 5-2. Reaction time to visual signals in relation to age.
Source: Ibid.

those of reaction time to sudden sound or light stimuli. The data on male subjects were analyzed in detail and are still among the most valuable data on reaction time (*Koga and Morant, 1923*). Figures 5-1 and 5-2 show the increase in speed of reaction during childhood and the gradual slowing of reaction time after the age of forty. The fact that visual reaction time is slightly slower than auditory reaction time has been verified in other studies.

Relative to other skills, rapid reaction time appears to mature early. The figures suggest that reaction time reaches its minimum around age eighteen. The question raised in the previous discussion about the contribution of sensory acuity to reaction time can be answered from these data, since on the same subjects on which reaction time was measured, visual and auditory acuity were also measured. The investigators found that auditory and visual reaction times were more closely correlated in their subjects than were the measurements of auditory and visual acuity. While they found evidence that sensory acuity influences the rapidity of response, more important was their finding of a central factor of response time. The authors concluded: "The association between reaction times involving different senses is very much closer than the relation between the acuteness of those senses. It would thus appear that reaction time depends very little on the fineness of the organs of sense." (*Koga and Morant, 1923, p. 372*).

The question may be raised whether the trend toward slowing of reaction time with age is true only of humans. To answer such a question, a study was made of age differences in reaction time of rats to electric

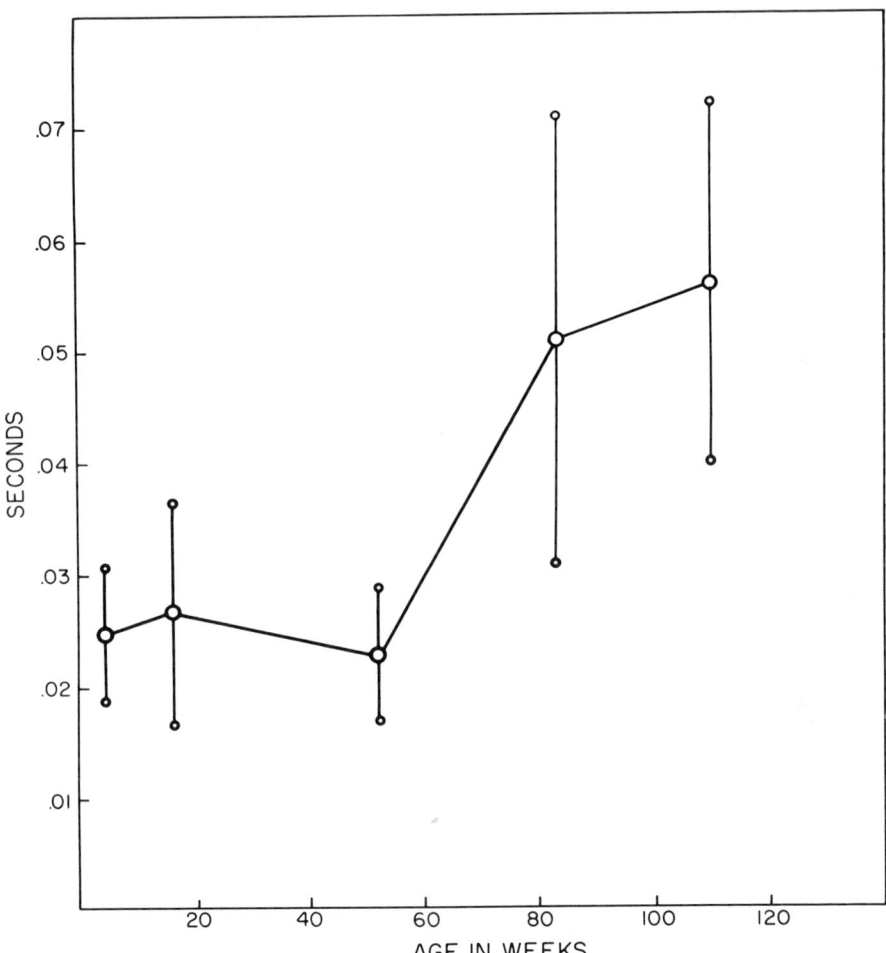

FIGURE 5-3. Startle reaction time of the rat to sudden stimuli in relation to age.

Source: J. E. Birren. Age differences in startle reaction time of the rat to noise and electric shock. *J. Geront.* (1955), **10**, 437-440.

shock. It was found that reaction time decreased from birth to about one hundred days, remained relatively constant up to about 500 days, and then increased (*Brody, 1940*). Generally, rats older than about twenty months or two years are regarded as "old." Another study of startle reaction time in rats used both electric shock and a loud noise as stimuli. Both sources of stimulation showed a slowness of response in old animals (*Birren, 1955*).

Since the excitation resulting from a stimulus has to be conducted to the central nervous system and also from the spinal cord to the responding muscles, the question can be asked whether the slowness of aging is not due in part to a reduced conduction velocity of peripheral nerves in old animals. This question was answered in a study of the conduction velocity of the sciatic nerve of rats of different ages (*Birren and Wall, 1956*). Results showed that conduction velocity increases in the rat up to about 300 days and thereafter remains constant. Thus development in the rat is marked by an increase in the velocity of peripheral nerve conduction. No evidence was found after maturity that conduction velocity decreased in late life paralleling the observed slowing in reaction time. This is strongly suggestive that the basis for the slowing of response speed with age is a function of processes within the central nervous system.

Early development in children is similarly marked by a decrease in reflex time, but after the age of about six years, a reflex such as the knee jerk (patellar reflex) may increase in time. "Time" here means the amount of time that elapses between the moment the knee tendon is struck until there is movement of the leg. Growth of the leg may be contributing to the additional reflex time in the growing child. Since reaction time in children is decreasing over the same period of years when reflex time is increasing, one is led to conclude that peripheral factors, even additional nerve conduction time associated with limb growth, are not important in determining individual differences in reaction times (*Knowlton and Britt, 1949*). Studies of nerve conduction velocities in humans give evidence of a slight trend toward lower velocities in old adults, but the trend is so small as to be of little contribution to age changes in reaction time (*Norris, et al., 1953; Wagman and Lesse, 1952*).

Movement Time

The previous discussion does not take into account the possibility that muscular movements may be slowed with age. One of the distinctions made in speed of response is between *movement* time and *reaction* time. "Movement time" refers to the interval needed for a free muscular move-

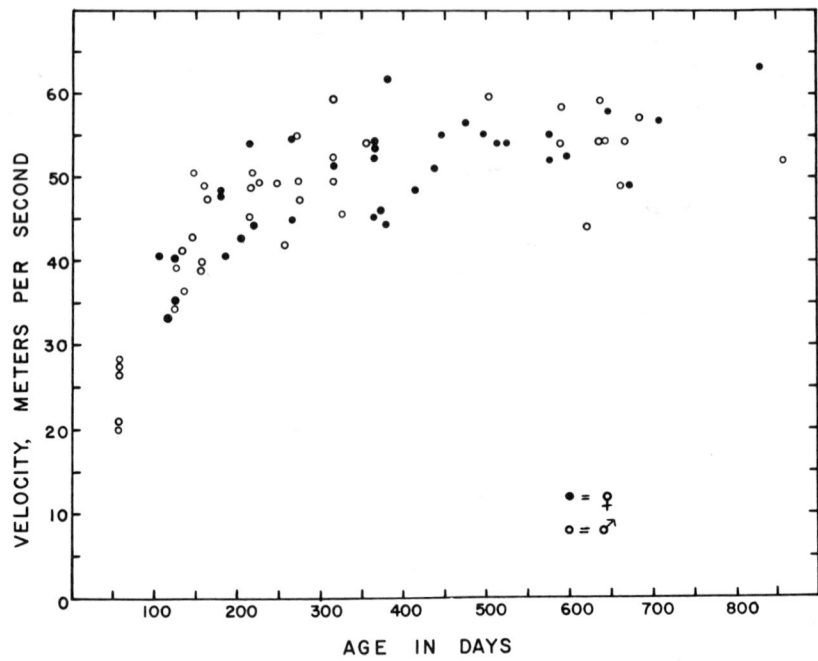

FIGURE 5-4. Age and the conduction velocity of rat sciatic nerve.
Source: J. E. Birren and P. D. Wall. Age changes in conduction velocity, refractory period, number of fibers, connective tissue space, and blood vessels in sciatic nerve of rats. *J. Comp. Neurol.* (1956), **104**, 1-16.

ment of a part (finger, arm) or all of the body. In its simplest form it consists of the length of time necessary to swing an arm in a free movement. While simple movement, or motility, times may change slightly with age, a number of experiments suggest that by far the largest portion of the increased time with age is in the reaction time—i.e., the time from the appearance of a signal to the beginning of the movement—rather than in the movement time. The change with age in movement time is clearly of a lesser magnitude than the central lengthening of reaction time *(Singleton, 1955)*.

Experiments that show different results appear to differ because of experimental conditions. Early studies of reaction time showed that the different speeds of response might be due to whether the subject was concentrating on when the stimulus was going to be presented or on the movement he was supposed to make. In some experiments in which movement times were measured, the subject first raised his finger from a key when he heard or saw a sudden signal, then he had to move his arm to a distant position. Apart from watching for the stimulus, he thus was expected to do two different things—lift his finger and move it to some distant place. Such an experiment involves a complex set or expectance on the part of the subject and tends to make all components slow. Reaction times are known to be susceptible to set or expectancy effects; i.e., the subject is slower when several different expectancies are involved. Therefore, what might often seem to be independent measurements of movement time and reaction time in relation to age really reflect a joint expectancy in a complex situation.

Finger tapping time comes close to being a repetitive movement independent of any extraneous choices or expectancies. Thus the number of times per minute a person can tap the surface of a table with his finger is a reasonably good measure of his movement time. Tapping time has been observed to be little changed up to the late seventies (*Fieandt,* et al., *1956*). While the tapping rates reported were not necessarily the fastest for the subjects, they do suggest that speed of such simple repetitive movements are not much changed with age.

Speed of repetitive movement was studied in the rat by using a task in which rats were required to swim eleven and one-half feet. The differences between mature young and old rats for fastest swimming time was 12 per cent for females and 14 per cent for males (*Birren and Kay, 1958*). This difference in swimming time is less than half that in startle reaction time previously discussed (*Birren, 1955*). Thus the largest component in slowing does not appear to be in repetitive movement *per se,* but rather in the central nervous system control over behavior, particularly involving the processes of discrimination and choice.

Another difference in the results of the two rat studies is that the reaction time study did not find a sex difference, whereas in the swimming study, females were found to be faster. Swimming time, however, may be influenced by the fact that male rats tend to be about one third heavier in body weight than females. A further study of swimming speed in the rat gave the animals practice for twelve days, with fifteen swimming trials in the tank per day. Practice did not essentially change the fastest time the individual rats swam the tank, although it markedly reduced susceptibility to fatigue, particularly in the old males (*Kay and Birren, 1958*). This suggests that the fatigue was a reversible phenomenon, whereas the age difference in speed was a relatively fixed characteristic, probably involving neural control over movements.

One attempt was made to study the length of time taken for a single synaptic reflex (a reflex arc involving one juncture between nerve cells) in the spinal cord of a rat (*Wayner and Emmers, 1958*). Results showed an increase with age in the so-called spinal synaptic delay time. The additional time was small, on the order of thousandths of a second. This raises the possibility that in the central nervous system, where many synapses must be involved in complex behavior, the additional time taken in a single aged synapse can be cumulated over many thousands of such synapses, thus yielding a large over-all time difference with age.

It is useful at this point to return to the consideration of the speed of simple reflexes in humans. Evidence is found that relatively simple reflexes in humans change slightly in speed with advancing age. One study has indicated that the latencies of foot (plantar) reflexes and abdominal reflexes are somewhat longer in the aged (*Magladery, 1959*). It is pointed out, however, that such delays may result from influences from higher centers, which diminish potentiation of simple reflexes. Such effects would presumably be cumulative when the reflex processes extend over multiple spinal reflex arcs. The longer the pathway within the nervous system in terms of number of neural junctions, the more there is found an influence of a slowing of psychomotor processes with advancing age. The picture is thus one of a small amount of additional time taken by some elementary neurophysiological process, such as synaptic transmission. Generally from this reasoning it would be expected that old and young individuals will differ more in the speed of complex than of simple tasks.

Speed and Complexity

The question should now be examined whether the age difference in simple visual or auditory reaction times is larger or smaller than choice reactions. From certain data it can be seen that complex choice reactions are somewhat longer with advancing age than simple reactions (*Goldfarb, 1941*). The experimenter found an increase in simple reaction time between the ages of eighteen to twenty-four and fifty-five to sixty-four of .011 seconds. For a two-choice reaction time, the age difference was .057 seconds; and for a five-choice reaction time, .066 seconds. Were slowing only a matter involving the overt response, it would be expected that older persons would become more like younger persons when the stimulus conditions are made more complex. The results do not bear this out, and whatever the ultimate neurophysiological nature of slowing with age involved in simple reaction time, it seems to become increasingly involved in complex choices and associative processes.

The previous point has been further tested in an experiment involving association times to many kinds of stimuli: simple lights, numbers, letters, words, syllables, colors, and symbols (*Birren, Riegel, and Morrison, 1962*). The results showed a higher intercorrelation among the response times of older persons, leading to the conclusion that older persons show a general change in speed of behavior. Young subjects tend to be task specific in their speed of performance—i.e., they are fast or slow depending upon the demands of the task—and one may not readily predict from the speed of a simple reaction in young persons their speed of doing rather complex tasks. By contrast, older persons tend to perform at a slow rate characteristic of them as individuals. If they are slow in simple tasks, they tend to be even more slow in complex tasks.

Handwriting is a complex skill that is learned over many years. For the adult, little attention is given to the physical movements of handwriting itself; rather is attention devoted to the content of what is to be written. Maximum speed of handwriting appears to slow down somewhat with advancing age (*Birren and Botwinick, 1951*).

Figure 5-5 indicates a wide range of measurements for older adults that may reflect individual differences in practice and also personal tempo. To some extent, the speed of writing may be viewed as being adaptive in that the individual learns at what speed to write in order to insure legibility and yet save time. After many years, the speed of writing may become relatively fixed for an individual in that he will rarely write much faster or slower than his characteristic speed. This seems to be supported in a study in which subjects had to write a standard phrase ("New Jersey Chamber of Commerce") under three different sets of instructions (*Botwinick, et al., 1959*). Each subject was required to write at (a) normal speed, (b) as fast as possible, and (c) as slowly as possible. The younger subjects of the study wrote both faster and more slowly than did the elderly. The results suggest that older subjects perform in a narrower range of possible response speeds than do young subjects.

Slowing of writing speed with age involves more than the time taken in movements of muscles and joints; as in previously discussed instances of slowing, the central nervous system is implicated. If a subject were adding columns of digits and writing down the answers, he might be slow in completing many problems merely because it took a long time to record the answers. However, as the list of digits to be added became longer, the proportion of time spent in writing answers would become less and less, and accordingly the subject in whom writing speed was a limiting factor would become relatively faster in completing addition problems. A study has indicated that there is in fact a correlation between writing speed and addition speed in older subjects, but very little correlation in young subjects. Although the reasoning was indirect, the implication is clear that the older subjects were found to be slow not merely because they could not record their answers quickly, but because of some process that affects both writing speed and mental addition.

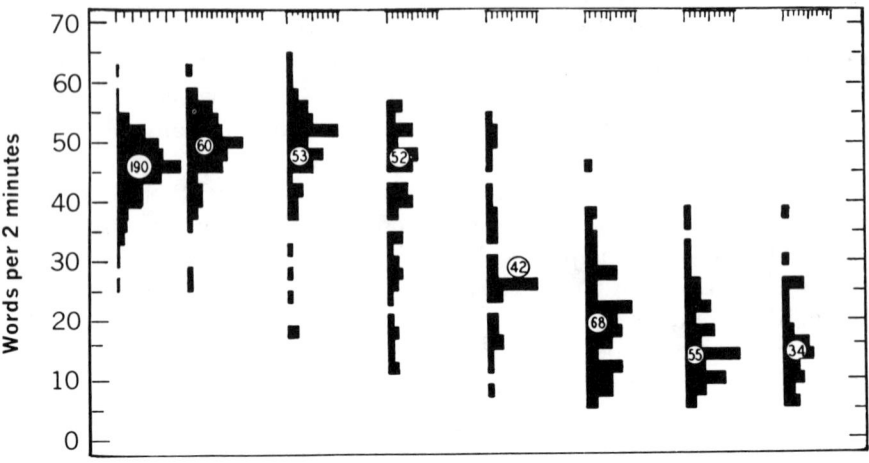
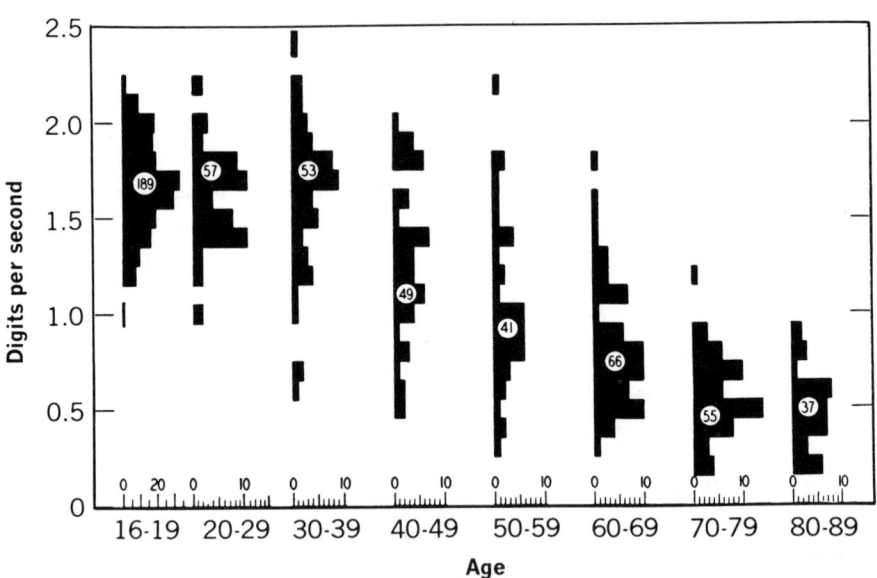

FIGURE 5-5. Age differences in writing speed. Frequency polygons are shown for each age group. The number of individuals in each group is indicated on the distributions.

Source: J. E. Birren and J. Botwinick. The relation of writing speed to age and to the senile psychoses. *J. Consult. Psychol.* (1951), **16**, 399-405.

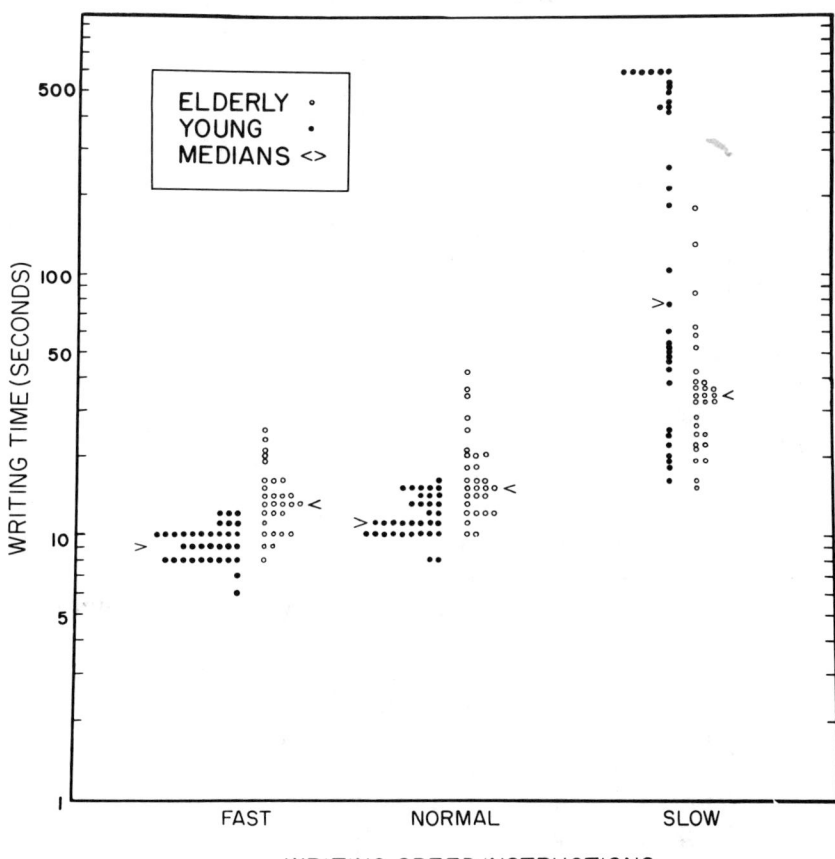

FIGURE 5-6. Age differences in writing time under three sets of instructions. Subjects were told to write the phrase "New Jersey Chamber of Commerce" (a) as fast as possible, (b) at a usual or normal speed, and (c) as slowly as possible. Each point represents a subject. Values are given as the logarithm of the time in seconds with a maximum cut-off of 600 seconds.

Source: J. Botwinick, J. F. Brinley, and J. S. Robbin. Modulation of speed of response with age. *J. Genet. Psychol.* (1959), **95**, 137-144.

Another demonstration that slowness of aging is not dependent upon some particular form of overt response was made using word associations (*Birren, Riegel, and Robbin, 1962*). In this study, subjects reported aloud words that came to mind in association with some instruction. Thus a subject might be told to give all the names of vegetables or of friends as quickly as possible. In this manner, it was found that older persons tend to be slower in associating words than are young adults. Although the content of some verbal associations may lead to temporary blocking, in general the flow of associations would appear to be slower with advancing age. One might question whether the overt response, or speech itself, is not slower with advancing age. Evidence suggests that spontaneous speech is a little slower in old persons, but hardly sufficient to account for the magnitude of difference obtained in word association studies. Age differences in speaking time may also reflect an individual's adaptation over the life span; it is, however, interesting that the impromptu speaking and oral reading rate was found to be rather high, about 137 words per minute in subjects over the age of sixty-five (*Mysak and Hanley, 1958*).

Differences in speed of behavior between young and old individuals seem least when dealing with a flow of familiar or repetitive events, as in speaking, handwriting, or tapping, and largest when the subject has to assimilate complex information to which he must make novel associations and appropriate responses. What is suggested by the evidence is that there is a change with age in the minimum time the nervous system requires even for very familiar operations. As the operations become complex and unfamiliar, the limitation imposed by the minimum operations time becomes more apparent. With some subjects, if the task cannot be completed in a minimum time, the instructions held in short-term memory may disintegrate, and the task cannot be completed; i.e., if an unfamiliar or complex task is too long in the doing, the purpose of the task is lost from memory. The rapid apprehending of information from the environment and the forming of interrelationships so that behavior can be planned according to some goal or instruction touches upon the concept of intelligence. One of the widely used tests of adult intelligence, the Wechsler Adult Intelligence Scale, includes a subtest that requires decoding of digits. Decoding is done according to associated geometric figures by means of a decoding chart. This particular test shows one of the highest correlations with age of any widely used test. The Digit-Symbol test also shows a very high correlation with response time in older subjects (*Birren and Spieth, 1962*). In general, the older the subject, the fewer the decoding operations carried out per unit time. It is questionable whether or not memory is involved; i.e., whether the subject may have difficulty in holding in mind one element while he is hunting for the decoding symbol. In the process of hunting, he may lose the memory trace of what he was trying to decode. Should the processes of perception and decoding take long, it may well be that elements begin to slip from memory and have to be reinstated. This does not preclude the possibility that there may not be a primary memory change, but merely suggests that speed, memory, perception, and decoding may be rather intimately entangled in a joint relation to chronological age.

Expectancy or Set

A review of research on reaction time showed the importance of the subject's expectancy of a stimulus on the time taken to respond (*Botwinick, 1959*). The data suggest that older subjects do best when the stimulus is likely to occur at a regular interval following a warning signal, in contrast to when the stimulus follows a warning signal at random intervals. It follows that older persons develop a less intense set and maintain it less well over long intervals. With progressive loss of stimulus input with age, the organism tends to become less "keyed up," or set, to respond. A general tendency to slowness of response could in part be a function of diminution of sensory input and level of stimulation. Thus any stimulus context that tends to arouse and focus expectancy or attention will result in considerable gain for the older person. Whether the change in alerting or expectancy is independent of a change in speed of response is open to question. At the present time it may be best to regard the age change in expectancy as somewhat independent of a general speed factor.

An illustration of the effect of set is seen in the runner who, by training, is able to minimize the delay between the firing of the starting gun and his start. At times the runner's expectancy may be so great that he will "jump the gun" and start to run at some irrelevant sound or movement. From one study of reaction times, it may be concluded that older individuals have difficulty in responding quickly to stimuli for which they have little time to prepare; i.e., about 0.5 seconds (*Brinley and Botwinick, 1959*). Older subjects improve with practice, so it may be concluded that older persons can to some extent improve their reaction times by learning to prepare for a stimulus. The question may be raised whether there is a difference with age in the maximum degree of set, or attentiveness, that may be developed. Future research must answer this; practically, however, aging must be viewed as resulting in lowered set, or expectancy, to initiate behavior in response to stimuli. Stimuli are always presented to an individual in some context that to a varying degree prepares or alerts him. The older person may use fewer context cues to direct his attention or prepare himself for the arrival of critical signals.

The effects of set may be looked at in another way by studying the speed with which individuals can alternate types of tasks. The point is the contrast between the speed of doing a single task and the speed of doing mixed tasks. Consider, for example, doing separate series of addition and subtraction problems and then a series of mixed, or alternating, addition and subtraction problems. If it is difficult for a subject to shift set rapidly, then doing mixed problems will take more time than doing an equivalent number of a single type of problem. A study was done using this type of material to determine if older adults have more difficulty in alternating tasks than young adults (*Botwinick, Brinley, and Robbin, 1958*). An alternation index was computed in which the speed of doing series of addition and subtraction problems was compared with the speed of doing mixed problems. Generally, the older subjects (over sixty-five) took more time in alternating tasks than did the young (eighteen to thirty-two), and the alternation was slower with more difficult problems. While these results seem to indicate that adults over the age of sixty-five show less facility in alternating tasks rapidly, the age difference in speed of alternating was less than the difference in speed associated with task difficulty (in this case, problem length).

Organism Condition. In addition to the nature of stimulus and response, the state of the organism must be considered in psychomotor speed and timing. Individuals differ not only in their familiarity with a task, but also in their physiological status, which influences the amount of data they can perceive, integrate, and respond to in a given unit of time. Various kinds of patients—cardiovascular, depressed, schizophrenic—respond slowly to stimuli. One interpretation of age changes in speed and timing is that the loss in speed results from damage to the central nervous system from diseases, particularly vascular, that are common in later life. Though not definitely refuted, such an argument must certainly be qualified in view of the observation that laboratory rats, which tend to be relatively free of vascular disease, show a slowing in startle responses to sudden stimuli (*Birren, 1955*).

However, it is also true that individuals with vascular disease may show slowness of response. In particular, individuals with elevated blood pressure tend to have slow reaction times. Furthermore, subjects with stabilized cardiac disease tend to have slowed reaction times. Such slowness might be viewed as a consequence of damage in the central nervous system resulting from impaired circulation and diminished oxygen supply to brain tissues. It should be noted, however, that the correlation between age and reaction time is higher than the correlation between age and elevation in blood cholesterol or blood pressure (*Birren and Spieth, 1962*). Thus the speed change would appear to be more universal than the vascular changes. Older subjects suffering from depression also tend to show psychomotor retardation, or slowing of behavior (*Birren, et al., 1963*). Such depressions may be accompanied by elevation in blood pressure. The psychophysiological pattern of depression somewhat resembles the pattern seen in aroused or angry persons. In aging, however, it may be that there is a pattern of psychophysiological changes which predisposes the individual to a depressive reaction to environmental stimulation. Recent research has shown that there are moment-to-moment variations in response speed to signals depending upon when during the heart cycle or phase of the brain waves the signal is presented. Individual differences in the moment-to-moment variation in response speed may have correlates in temperamental qualities, qualities that over the adult life span may have a relation to the personality characteristics of the individual and the likelihood of his developing cardiovascular disease.

While the slowing of psychomotor behavior with age seems to fit a concept of a normal psychophysiological change, and not the exclusive result of adventitious events like disease or trauma, precisely what has been changed in the older nervous system that leads to the slowing cannot yet be said with confidence. There is no reason to believe that, once the process is understood, psychomotor slowing cannot be modified in the time and rate of appearance in the individual, even if the underlying changes have a genetic basis.

Importance of Slowed Reactions

A number of studies of age changes in simple auditory or visual reaction time show approximately a 10 to 20 per cent slowing between twenty-year-olds and sixty-year-olds. It might well be pointed out that a difference of 10 per cent in simple reaction time may amount to as little as .02 seconds. Thus reaction time to a simple visual signal by twenty-year-olds might be carried out in .20 seconds. In sixty-year-olds, this would be about .22 seconds or a little longer. For most daily life situations, differences in response time of .02 seconds would hardly be regarded as important.

Actually, the results obtained under laboratory situations such as those mentioned above cannot be translated directly into terms related to daily behavior. Much of daily behavior is carried out under conditions that do not present simple stimuli, but complex ones that are often not easily discriminable or expected. The conditions under which the older person would be slowest would involve weak stimuli with many irrelevant aspects to which the individual would have to respond by making choices of complex motor sequences that had to be monitered by him. The execution of behavior sometimes pre-empts attention from the environment. For example, if one has to watch one's feet in stepping off a curb, then attention to oncoming traffic will be lessened and the rapidity of evasive movements slowed. Behavior sequences in daily life require of the older person additional time in the processes of perception, choice of behavior, and the control of the resulting body movements. Situations may maximize or minimize the differences in speed of behavior in young and old adults.

Probably the greatest practical implications of research on psychomotor speed for the well-being of the older person are for accidents, since older persons tend to have high rates of fatalities from all common forms of accidents. Indications are that, being more influenced by irrelevant stimuli and less set "to go" at the proper time, the older person, as a motorist or pedestrian, may initiate activities that are out of proper phase. This is particularly true if the older person must conform to the pace of younger persons, as he would have to in most traffic conditions. The role of psychomotor speed in home accidents and falls is not clear, although distraction and speed of initiation of evasive movement may be involved. Since the older person may have to monitor his physical movements more closely than does the young adult, he is less attentive to environmental stimuli, and thus more vulnerable to the unexpected.

Change of Viewpoint. In early thinking about age changes in speed of timing, there was a tendency to regard the slowing as limited primarily to the overt response or to effector mechanisms. This view placed greater emphasis on speed of movement and less on premovement functions. One subjective reason for this view's being favored was that it implied that speed of response was merely a function of motor rapidity, with the central nervous system itself in no way involved. Another interpretation of slowing with age has been the view that slowing is an adaptive characteristic of the organism; i.e., the organism, in becoming more conservative with advancing age, achieves a higher level of certitude by viewing stimulus conditions for a longer time before responding. A cautious attitude protects the organism against making serious errors, but it requires more time. Although caution and adaptation may indeed add to slowing with advancing age, a convincing body of evidence clearly indicates that the major portion of the slowness is due to a change in the nervous system beyond the voluntary or adaptive control of the individual.

Some physiologists have assumed that the slowness of the aging reflects a lack of "liveliness" of neural processes. Their initial research suggested that both establishing and extinguishing a conditioned response are more difficult with aged subjects. (The relationship of this evidence to learning will be discussed in Chapter 7.) They concluded that the cortex of the older person cannot receive a maximum degree of excitation at any specific point, but that excitation is irradiated over a large area (*Marinesco and Kreindler, 1934*). In this view, maximum excitation and concentration are precluded in an older person.

Clearly, it is overreaching at present to force all the facts of age changes in behavior into a single explanation involving the speed of a primary neural event. However, there is an indication that many of the facts may be attributable to an age change in speed of neural activity. This change is epitomized by the slowness of reaction time in older individuals. Its consequence may be modified by differential experience or previous learning and by the current physiological state of the organism.

Summary

One of the most distinguishing features about aging persons is their tendency to slowness of behavior. Whereas young adults are quick or slow in their behavior in accordance with the demands of the situation, older adults have a general slowness of behavior. Slowness in the young adult can be thought of as nonspecific; i.e., a great many factors can lead to slowness of behavior. These factors include: stimuli that are weak or of low intensity, stimuli that are ambiguous or unfamiliar, stimuli that are unexpected, stimuli that tend to evoke conflicting responses, and difficult or complex stimuli. Responses that must be made in a sequential manner or responses in which the consequences may be inordinately great may be studiously delayed until the individual feels the conditions are optimum. These factors affect the differential speed of response in older persons as well as in the young, but they represent time in addition to a generalized tendency to slowness in the aged.

The generalized slowness of behavior in older persons is looked upon as being most probably an expression of a primary process of aging in the nervous system, the precise localization or basis of which is not known. The most likely explanations involve the loss of nerve cells with advancing age, reduced neural excitability, physical-chemical changes at the synapse that limit transmission speed, and a lowering of subliminal excitation of the nervous system resulting from changes in subcortical centers.

Although much has been learned about psychomotor speed and aging, not much is known about the modifying conditions that maintain an alert organism with a potential for precise and rapid response. Thus whether continuous high-level stimulation in later life will retard or advance psychomotor slowing is not known. Also, the role of fatigue is unknown in its effect on, or relation to, psychomotor slowness.

Slowness can be looked upon as a change dependent upon more elementary processes in the nervous system, or it can be examined with regard to its consequences for behavior. In the latter view, the slowness of advancing age comes as close as any identifiable process to being an independent aging variable; i.e., slowness defined as a minimum operations time in the nervous system can be used to explain other psychological phenomena of aging. One consequence of the slowing is that the individual is limited in the amount of activity or the number of behaviors he can emit in some unit of time. The slowness may also have other consequences or concomitants in mood and energy.

To some extent, the psychomotor slowness of older persons may be affected by a depressive mood. However, a heavy, lethargic mood is probably superimposed on a pre-existing slowness and may in fact be more likely to develop in the aged. Depression of affect is not an adequate explanation for the slowness of advancing age, although it can be a factor that expands its consequences.

The older person adapts to his slowness of response by avoiding situations with unusual time pressures. Slowness itself can be in part a manifestation of adaptation. As the individual becomes less sure of himself in walking, fearing the consequences of a fall, he may tend to slow down his movements considerably. Also, with a reduction of activities in later life, to some extent forced upon the individual, slowness may accompany adaptation to the level of stimulation of the environment. While it is unreasonable to expect that all of the slowing can be attributed to adaptation to the stimulation value of the environment, some part of it may arise from this source. Long-term adaptation to a characteristic level of activity may result in the speed of response becoming fixed so that increased stimulation will not reinstate the previous limits of behavior. The view that the organism is reacting to a changing environment must be balanced with the view that the organism is also a self-activated system that may change over time and show a reduction in the numbers of behaviors emitted per unit time. Limiting the number of behaviors that can be emitted per unit time is the minimum operations time of the central nervous system, a basic process that appears to change with age.

References

Birren, J. E. Age differences in startle reaction time of the rat to noise and electric shock. *J. Geront.*, 1955, **10**, 437-440.

——— and J. Botwinick. The relation of writing speed to age and to the senile psychoses. *J. Consult. Psychol.*, 1951, **15**, 243-249.

———, R. N. Butler, S. W. Greenhouse, L. Sokoloff, and Marian R. Yarrow, (eds.), *Human Aging*. Washington, D.C.: Government Printing Office, Public Health Publication No. 986, 1963.

——— and H. Kay. Swimming speed of the albino rat: age and sex differences. *J. Geront.*, 1958, **13**, 374-377.

———, K. F. Riegel, and D. F. Morrison. Age differences in response speed as a function of controlled variations of stimulus conditions: evidence of a general speed factor. *Gerontologia*, 1962, **6**, 1-18.

———, ——— and J. S. Robbin. Age differences in continuous word associations measured by speed recordings. *J. Geront.*, 1962, **17**, 95-96.

——— and W. Spieth. Age, response speed, and cardiovascular functions. *J. Geront.*, 1962, **17**, 390-391.

——— and P. D. Wall. Age changes in conduction velocity, refractory period, number of fibers, connective tissue space and blood vessels in sciatic nerve of rats. *J. Comp. Neurol.*, 1956, **104**, 1-16.

*Botwinick, J. Drives, expectancies, and emotions. In J. E. Birren (ed.), *Handbook of Aging and the Individual*, pp. 739-768. Chicago: University of Chicago Press, 1959.

———, J. F. Brinley, and J. S. Robbin. Modulation of speed of response with age. *J. Genetic Psychol.*, 1959, **95**, 137-144.

———, ———, ———. Task alternation time in relation to problem difficulty and age. *J. Geront.*, 1958, **13**, 414-417.

Brinley, J. F. and J. Botwinick. Preparation time and choice in relation to age differences in response speed. *J. Geront.*, 1959, **14**, 226-228.

Brody, E. B. The influence of age, hypophysectomy, thyroidectomy, and thyroxin injection on simple reaction time in the rat. *J. Gen. Physiol.*, 1941, **24**, 433-436.

Fieandt, K. von, A. Huhtala, P. Kullberg, and K. Saari. *Personal Tempo and Phenomenal Time at Different Age Levels.* Psychological Institute, University of Helsinki, 1956, Report No. 2.

Goldfarb, W. *An Investigation of Reaction Time in Older Adults.* New York: Teachers College, Columbia University, 1941, Contributions to Education, No. 831.

Kay, H. and J. E. Birren. Swimming speed of the albino rate. II: Fatigue, practice, and drug effects on age and sex differences. *J. Geront.*, 1958, **13**, 378-385.

Knowleton, G. C. and L. P. Britt. Relation of height and age to reflex time. *Amer. J. Physiol.*, 1949, **159**, 576 (abstract).

Koga, Y. and G. M. Morant. On the degree of association between reaction times in the case of different senses. *Biometrika*, 1923, **15**, 346-372.

*Magladery, J. W. Neurophysiology of aging. In Birren (ed.), 1959, *op. cit.*, pp. 173-186.

Marinesco, G. and A. Kreindler. Des réflexes conditionnels, troisième partie: application des réflexes conditionnels à certains problèmes cliniques. *J. Psychol.*, 1934, **31**, 722-791.

Mysak, E. D. and T. D. Hanley. Aging processes in speech: pitch and duration characteristics. *J. Geront.*, 1958, **13**, 309-313.

Norris, A. H., N. W. Shock, and I. H. Wagman. Age changes in the maximum conduction velocity of motor fibers of human ulnar nerves. *J. Appl. Physiol.*, 1953, **5**, 589-593.

Rabbitt, P. M. A. *Perceptual Discrimination and Choice of Response.* Cambridge: Cambridge University Library, Ph.D. dissertation, 1961.

Singleton, W. T. Age and performance timing on simple skills. In *Old Age and the Modern World*, pp. 221-231. London: E. & S. Livingstone, Ltd., 1955.

Wagman, I. H. and H. Lesse. Maximum conduction velocities of motor fibers of

---

* Suggested additional reading.

ulnar nerves in human subjects of various ages and sizes. *J. Neurophysiol.,* 1952, **15,** 235-244.

Wayner, M. J., Jr., and R. Emmers. Spinal synaptic delay in young and aged rats. *Amer. J. Physiol.,* 1958, **194,** 403-405.

*Welford, A. T. Psychomotor performance. In Birren (ed.), 1959, *op. cit.,* pp. 562-613.

6. Psychomotor Skills

The previous chapter discussed the implications of age changes for the speed of the nervous system in processes of perception, choice, and motor control. With advancing age, the individual becomes limited to some extent in the speed with which he can modify his behavior in response to environmental conditions. Compensations exist, however, so there is no simple or direct relation between the extent to which slowness limits the effectiveness of an individual's behavior. *Compensation* is meant to imply that with a little extra effort or attention to particular features of a task, the performance may be maintained or even improved in the presence of physical limitations. Usually the individual has some control over the context of his performance, and by manipulating the conditions he maximizes his performance. With experience, individuals acquire work methods or methods of approach to familiar tasks so that a high quality of performance may be sustained; in contrast, the inexperienced person who does things the "hard way" puts the physical and physiological limits of his capacity more to the test. Consideration only of the internal capacities of the individual would neglect the fact that skilled performance over a lifetime is a continuing process of adaptation in which the individual develops work methods and tempo in relation to his particular limitations or capacities. Measurements of physical and psychological capacities, while essential, do not lead directly to estimations of how well individuals, given a period of learning and adaptation, will perform at tasks.

Definition. "Psychomotor skills" is a term of convenience used to refer to those activities in which dexterity is shown. A skill is an acquired pattern of finely coordinated voluntary movements of the body or body parts. The word "dexterity" comes from the Latin *dexter,* referring to the "right," which is for many persons more skillful than the left hand. "Skill" implies that practice will lead to improvements in the execution of a particular type of performance. The notion of capacity to develop the skill is also important. For example, while most persons can learn the psychomotor skill of typewriting, there are individual differences in the rate of acquisition of this skill, as well as in the final level of competence; there are individual differences in the limits of perception, speed, and potential refinement of neural control resulting in dexterity.

Coordinated locomotor movements of the body can occur without the control of the cerebral cortex. These movements are coordinated and complex and reflect an inborn pattern. Lacking higher control, the movements always appear in the same pattern; they are stereotyped and lack originality. The skilled movements displayed in daily life are the result of an interaction between congenital and learned controls. How complex the control must be is shown by the fact that thirty muscles are employed in the movement of the joints of the hand *(Paillard, 1960).* A particular pattern of movement depends upon the initial position of the body muscles and the resistance it meets. The ordering of the muscular actions in space and time is a subtle combination of facilitative and inhibitory neural influences in the spinal cord under the direction of the motor cortex and its pathway, the "pyramidal system." Optimum preparation and releasing of movements at the appropriate moment are special issues in aging because of the possibility of reduced sensory input and of a basic change in the speed of neural events. In some movements, the earliest contractions need not be seen in the muscle primarily responsible, but rather in some participating muscle whose action gives the movement its precision. Movement is thus not an instantaneous matter, but rather a distribution over time of graded activities in many muscles. The pattern of movement shows influences of many elements— not only the level of activity of the muscles and of the cells in the spinal cord, but also the intent of the movement, past learning, and the individual's mood. There are no examples of movements involving only one muscle, and for man, the influence of the higher centers of the nervous system are to be expected even on the simplest spinal reflex.

Conversely, any "higher" command to lower centers is to some extent modified on the basis of local conditions; e.g., position of limb.

It has been pointed out that skills have the following characteristics:

> (A) They consist essentially of the building of an organized and coordinated activity in relation to an object, stimulus, or situation and thus involve the whole chain of sensory, central, and motor mechanisms which underlie performance. (B) They are learned in that the understanding of the object or situation and the form of the action are built up gradually in the course of repeated experience. (C) They are serial in the sense that within the over-all pattern of the skill many different processes or actions are ordered and coordinated in a temporal sequence (*Welford, 1958, p. 18*).

Psychomotor skills vary as to whether the critical factors lie in the sensory processes or in the recognition and integration of incoming signals from the environment and body parts and the critical nature of the motor response. Perhaps the important feature to emphasize about a psychomotor skill is its unitary character. In learning to typewrite, the novice advances from the perception and typing of individual letters to seeing words as entities and typing whole words without being aware of the individual letters. Similarly, in learning the Morse code, the learner advances from individual letter perception to a perceptual span of entire words or phrases. Reading skill also advances from the perception of small units to larger words and phrases. In the development of a skill, the unit of organization becomes progressively larger. This is not unlike the concept of a word that is learned and subsequently enlarged in associations through verbal learning. Once a concept is formed, many more unitary processes become simple. As a psychomotor skill develops, the elements that were once individually perceived, integrated, and responded to become organized into a larger unit with overlapping elements, with one element quickly becoming the cue for the next in a sequence of actions. For the mature child and adult, walking is largely an automatic process, since each element or movement of walking is a signal or a stimulus for the next response. If walking becomes difficult because of poor lighting or rough ground, an individual may have to look at his feet, and his attention is thus diverted from other aspects of the environment.

Personal Skills

When the word "skill" is used, very complicated or dramatic actions frequently come to mind. Rarely thought of are the many simple skills important in daily life that are slowly mastered during early development but that may change in later life. The following list may suggest many areas for consideration.

PARTIAL LIST OF PERSONAL SKILLS

1. *Locomotion skills:*
   walking, running, stepping, jumping
2. *Personal maintenance skills:*
   eating, dressing, washing, shaving, hairdressing
3. *Communication skills:*
   reading, writing, speaking, typing
4. *Household skills:*
   cleaning, washing, cooking, sewing, shopping
5. *Musical skills*
6. *Free-time skills:*
   sports, gardening, handcrafts

Latent limitations in a simple skill may be seen under emergency conditions. A situation in which it is necessary to escape from a fire by strenuous effort, perhaps involving climbing or jumping, may suddenly reveal limitations of movement not previously suspected. The agility and strength of adults of different ages must be considered in defining standards, such as the size of signs or notices, the pressure required to open escape doors, or the size of the opening through which it will be necessary to escape, which may require bending of the body or a simultaneous step and bend.

Changes in basic motor skills in persons over sixty-five contribute to their high accident rate. Accidents are the sixth largest cause of death in persons over sixty-five, and of these, deaths due to falls account for more than all others combined. Since over half of the total fatal accidents in persons over sixty-five occur at home, unusual precipitating factors would seem to be unlikely in most accidents or falls. The contribution of physical changes to accidents is seen in the fact that persons liable to falls were judged to be less fit medically (41 per cent) than individuals not liable to falls (18 per cent) (*Droller, 1955*). There is a suggestion that persons who maintain physical exercise or engage in gymnastics will have better control over their movements than untrained persons. To what extent sustained physical exercise can maintain fine motor control and prevent weakness and deterioration of skills is uncertain. For those persons who are undergoing pathological changes, a more appropriately designed physical environment is highly desirable to minimize risks. Attention is being given to the proper engineering of the environment for the older person, but more needs to be done along the lines of "human engineering" of equipment used by young adults (*Fitts, 1951*).

Recognizing that age changes in psychomotor speed and sensory acuity contribute importantly to accidents in older persons, attitudes and experience are also important influences. For example, older persons frequently have accidents on sidewalks and streets because they do not conform to safe pedestrian rules. Also, many of the pedestrians in the older population who are killed are nondrivers. The lack of personal experience with driving may lead a pedestrian to underestimate the dangers of walking habits, such as walking between cars and crossing between intersections. Never having driven a car, it is difficult for the older pedestrian to appreciate the problems of seeing someone along the road at night or of stopping suddenly for a pedestrian in the flow of traffic. More than half of the pedestrian deaths involve unsafe behavior. Not being able to assess the risks, the older person tends to expose himself unduly to traffic accidents, and because of his physiological limitations, he is less able to avoid or minimize a crisis if it arises.

Automobile Drivers and Transportation Problems

Automobile driving is a good example of a psychomotor skill that could with profit be studied in more detail in relation to age, both as to learning by young adults and as to the conditions under which effective and safe driving are maintained throughout the adult years. Two important issues are involved: the interest of the individual in being able to drive and the interest of the public, which wishes to protect itself from the mistakes of drivers of any age. To this might be added the relations of age to effectiveness of performance by commercial transportation workers; e.g., airline pilots, truck drivers, and bus drivers, in which there is a triangle of interests: the public, the individual employee, and the employer. Many older pilots, private automobile drivers, bus drivers, and truck drivers perform excellently in terms of safe miles covered or other criteria. However, with advancing years there is a trend toward higher *probability* of involvement in accidents. If the probability of accidents is largely a function of the individual's skill or capacity for safe driving, then there is a need for an individual assessment program. Such programs, however, are costly, and it is by no means certain that some of the more critical elements could be determined exactly. For example, some individuals may undergo dramatic and progressive decrements in component physiological and psychological functions within a period of a few months. Such changes might easily be missed, even if there were semi-annual examinations for psychomotor skills.

The number of older automobile drivers—i.e., sixty-five years and over—is increasing in relation to the increase of older persons in society. In 1940, about 3 per cent of the total drivers were over sixty-five, whereas in 1959, about 7 per cent were over sixty-five. In 1940, there were 1,400,000 drivers aged sixty-five and over, whereas in 1959, there were 5,700,000 (*Marsh, 1960*). The accidents per 100,000 miles driven by age of drivers indicates that the accident rate diminishes for both men and women up to about the age of fifty, after which it tends to rise in both sexes, although perhaps it rises slightly earlier for women. The driver above the age of seventy is more likely to have a highway accident than is the driver in the more widely discussed critical age range of sixteen to twenty. Within the usual adult employed age range—i.e., up to sixty or sixty-five years—accidents are really not closely related to age, but thereafter they become increasingly probable.

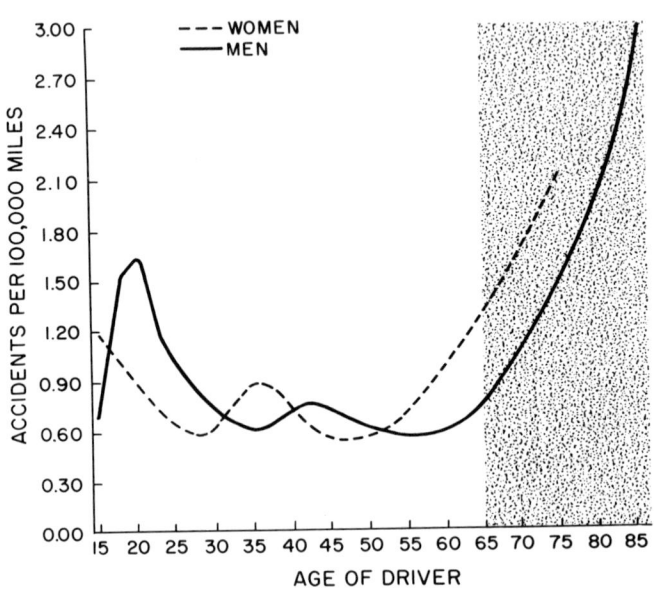

FIGURE 6-1. Accidents per 100,000 miles driven, by age of driver. *Source:* B. W. Marsh. Aging and driving. *Traffic Engineering* (November, 1960), pp. 3-21.

Many factors combine to make individual drivers over sixty-five more likely to have accidents; diminished visual acuity, less resistance to glare, hearing loss, and impairments of physical movements. Also, the increased reaction time known to occur with age is involved, as drivers must respond quickly to unpredictable events. Any of these factors alone would only slightly increase the probability of having an accident, but their combination can result in an appreciable risk. The additive effect on the probability of having an accident from independent contributory causes is considerable. As more information is available concerning the nature of accidents, it should be possible to make progress in sorting out precipitating factors, including those of judgment and motivation. To cite just one example, it has been said that young drivers are impulsive and older drivers conservative. Halting, uncertain patterns of driving should result in a different pattern of accidents than should aggressive driving. To some extent, this is confirmed by existing survey data. Drivers under thirty are about twice as likely as drivers over sixty-five to have speed as a contributing factor in accidents, whereas drivers over sixty-five are about twice as likely to have right-of-way conflicts (*Marsh*,

TABLE 6-1. CAUSES OF AGRICULTURAL ACCIDENTS

CAUSE	Number of Cases	Percentage of Each Kind of Accident by Age Group					
		15-20	21-30	31-40	41-50	51-60	61-80
Significant increases with age:							
Falls from heights or machines	252	7.6	8.4	10.5	14.5	19.2	16.4
Falls through slipping or tripping on ground	201	3.8	6.3	9.4	13.4	11.0	16.4
Hit by falling or moving object	339	14.0	15.7	13.9	17.6	21.4	21.3
Significant decreases with age:							
Caught in machine	202	13.4	11.8	11.5	9.1	7.9	6.6
Injury inflicted by own tool	184	13.4	11.8	10.7	5.8	6.6	9.3
Continued activity	127	4.5	9.2	7.9	6.2	2.8	4.4
Starting an engine	98	12.7	7.9	4.1	4.5	1.3	1.1
No significant change with age:							
Moving heavy objects	103	3.2	4.8	6.8	4.2	7.5	1.6
Knocked against, or trod on, object	90	6.4	3.6	5.3	4.9	3.4	3.8
Action of animals*	79	1.3	3.9	4.3	4.2	5.3	2.7
Trapped, other than in machine	48	1.3	3.1	1.9	2.7	1.6	3.8
Miscellaneous	127	9.5	6.0	7.7	4.7	6.0	6.0
Cause not specified	141	8.9	7.5	6.0	8.2	6.0	6.6
Total	1991	100	100	100	100	100	100

* Some cases in which animals were involved were classified under "Hit by falling or moving object." This group constitutes the remainder.

Source: H. F. King, An age-analysis of some agricultural accidents. *Occupational Psychol.* (1955), **29**, 245-253.

1960). Improper manipulation of a car during turning is also a factor in the accidents of older drivers. This involves misjudging speed, as well as turning into or from a wrong lane. The disproportionate number of automobile accidents in the over sixty-five group represents a combination of driving habits, sensory-motor control, and attitudes. The deterioration of performance that can be observed in an individual because of physical changes is disturbing, since the individual may never have had an accident during his entire driving career. He may not be aware that his capacities have changed and will insist upon, if not overassert, his independence of action by still driving. Driver evaluation and reeducation of those over sixty-five is a particularly sensitive but important social and psychological problem requiring attention.

Data on agricultural accidents reveal that some kinds of accidents increase with age, whereas others decline (*King, 1955*). Older persons are generally more susceptible to falls, and perhaps the additional element of speed (or its lack) in avoiding sudden moving objects is involved. Accidents due to the person's own tools decrease with age. There is a trend in the data showing that accidents preventable by judgment based upon experience decrease in older workers, whereas accidents preventable by rapid evasive response to sudden events increase.

Occupational Skills

The data on automobile accidents and age do not follow the data from industry. Table 6-2 shows that the number of disabling injuries per 500 workers is among the lowest for workers sixty-five and over. Very possibly the employed group over sixty-five is indeed an unusually well-selected sample of the population with respect to health, skill, and personal characteristics compared with all drivers over sixty-five.

TABLE 6-2. INJURY EXPERIENCE BY AGE OF WORKER

Age Group	Injury Frequency			Injury Severity (Disabling)	
	Disabling		Nondisabling Per Million Man Hours	Average Days' Disability	Average Days' Healing
	Per Million Man Hours	Per 500 Workers			
15-24	6.6	5.9	1328	20.2	29.5
25-34	9.1	8.8	1475	9.2	29.0
35-44	11.9	9.2	1145	12.7	31.3
45-54	8.7	8.8	855	17.7	37.0
55-64	9.9	9.0	604	18.0	40.8
65 and over	8.3	7.2	408	12.9	49.0

Source: R. A. McFarland and B. O'Doherty, Work and occupational skills. In J. E. Birren (ed.), *Handbook of Aging and the Individual* (Chicago: University of Chicago Press, 1959), p. 469.

If the older worker is injured, he is likely to take longer to recover, suggesting that, although he is less likely to have an accident, once an injury occurs, the consequences are more severe. Other evidence on sickness among the employed indicates that with advancing age there are fewer, but longer, absences.

After the mid-thirties, men tend to be stable in their jobs. Being more skilled and more interested in holding their present jobs, they can avoid impulsive acts likely to lead to accidents, and they can better manage their own activities to conserve themselves physically.

Airplane Pilots. The relation of age to flying an airplane is most interesting. Flying is a highly developed skill of a highly select group of men. Not many data are available on age and accidents, but inferences can be made. What little evidence is available suggests that pilots between the age of forty and the retirement age of sixty show no tendency for increased accidents; if anything, a slight decrease is seen. Since age and experience are correlated, there is a somewhat higher rate of accidents in Air Force pilots under thirty compared with those over thirty. Because of the relationship between experience and age, it is not surprising that accidents decline in middle age. However, for any experience level (hours of flying), there is a decline in accidents with age.

Another way to study the relation of age to pilot performance is to analyze the attitudes and opinions of pilots. Since it has been known for some time that not all aspects of performance change in the same direction or in the same way with age, it is useful to ask experienced men how they think age is related to different kinds of performances. A study of Air Force pilots used the "critical incident technique," which focused the attention of the respondent on critical incidents that might reveal situations showing improvements or decrements in skilled performance with age. The value of this approach lies in the respondent's focusing his attention on a specific instance rather than on generalizations or on the folklore of the profession.

A total of over 500 air crewmen were interviewed using the critical incident method. The results gave information on five kinds of changes: retention of physical abilities, learning and practicing skills, flight performance, relations with co-workers, and job morale and adjustment. Typical of many findings on aging, the results show interaction of influences. Air crewmen who are aging adversely show: (1) physical and physiological deterioration, (2) changes in motivation and ability to absorb new skills and improve their present level of skill, as well as, (3) lowered level of performance of critical aspects of the job. They also reveal: (4) a tendency toward lower morale and less satisfactory adjustment to their jobs (*Miles and Shriver, 1953*). While changes toward more effective behavior in these areas are also reported, these are, in general, reported on younger persons and can be considered to be sensitive indicators of resistance to deleterious effects of aging. "Age" takes on a somewhat unusual meaning in a group that has a mean age of about thirty years. Air Force pilots may be viewed as a highly sensitive in-group in which changes in specific skills are overreacted to by the individual and by his peers. A pilot who suffers vertigo or blackout in laboratory tests given to determine his resistance to the effects of acceleration would feel that his ego had been dealt a blow.

It is important to question the relevance of body change to total skilled performance in middle-aged persons. May not an individual with a hearing aid and glasses often have better flight performance because of greater relevant experience? To a group known to be of superb physical and mental condition, the minutiae of test performance can well be overly provocative. It is suggested that psychological and medical test results be kept in perspective as one part of the total context of aging in pilots or other skilled persons.

Changes in physical abilities and capacities necessary for effective performance as reported in the study of air crewmen appeared to be particularly age-related in visual and auditory perception. More surprising and perhaps of greater significance is the finding that low motivation to improve job performance was related to age. Thus lack of interest in learning new methods and willingness to accept criticism was found to be descriptive of "older men"; i.e., mean age 35. Younger men were more interested in enlarging their experience with different kinds of planes and procedures. The subtlety of age-related aspects of job performance can be enhanced by studies using the critical incident method, since it uses the observations of men and women most skilled in the performance and therefore most likely to be highly sensitive to age or other influences.

Issues arise that make the study of occupational skills complex and prevent simple statements about the results. For example, an industry itself may age relative to the economy and employ "out of date" types of skills. If an industry builds a new factory to manufacture a new product or to produce a more highly developed form of the same product, it tends to employ new workers. It has been observed that the oldest workers in an industry are often employed at the oldest machines on the oldest processes under the least modern type of working conditions. Thus the kinds of occupational skills found in older workers may not be representative of the whole range of contemporary industrial skills or reflect the individual's capacity. There tends to be resistance to moving workers to new types of occupations—both on the part of the industry, which would rather have longer service from younger workers in a new type of position, and on the part of the workers themselves, who would rather continue in the practice of already acquired and familiar skills.

Older workers who remain employed are obviously selected from a population initially employed. To some extent, the less skilled, uninterested, and less healthy leave employment earlier. There is thus a survivor bias in the continuingly employed group. Accordingly, the skills displayed by the older person still employed hardly represent the average skill of the population that started or could have started in a particular type of employment many years earlier. The foregoing indicates that there are many influences underlying the selection of the kind of worker who remains employed as he grows older. The general evidence about occupational skills and age would seem to indicate that over the conventionally employed age range—i.e., up to sixty or sixty-five—the age-associated differences in psychomotor skills are small. If total job behavior is considered, the older worker is sometimes found to be better in comparison with the young worker, particularly if such characteristics as accuracy, absenteeism, and motivation are considered.

An analysis of the percentage of workers who survive in their occupations until age sixty-five was carried out for British industries (*LeGros Clark and Dunne, 1956*). From their analysis they estimated that, for reasons of physical capacities, about 30 to 40 per cent of all male workers could not continue in their normal jobs after age sixty-five. Furthermore, they estimated that about 20 per cent of men over sixty-five will have to be found other jobs if they are to continue in the labor force. Jobs show considerable variability in survival rates; i.e., the proportion of older men who survive or continue to work at their customary jobs varies with the type of job. Physical endurance as well as fine motor skills are important factors, with self-paced fine skills (watch making) showing better survival of older workers than do jobs with high physical activity (coal miners).

Athletic Skills

The records of champion amateur and professional athletes provide excellent data for consideration of changes in human psychomotor skills. Professional athletes wish to remain at championship level for as long as possible, since the level of their performance directly influences their income. Continued motivation and interest in top level athletic performance may be taken for granted. An examination of the ages at which championships tend to be won and the range over which they are maintained reveals a pattern that reflects the analysis of the major components of the skill; i.e., strength, precision or accuracy, endurance, critical nature of the timing, complexity of the stimulus and response variations. Certain data, for example, indicate that golf champions tend to be relatively older than boxing champions (*Lehman, 1953*). The boxer

TABLE 6-3. AGES AT WHICH INDIVIDUALS HAVE EXHIBITED PEAK PROFICIENCY AT "PHYSICAL" SKILLS

TYPE OF SKILL	Number of Cases	Median Age	Mean Age	Years of Maximum Proficiency
U.S.A. outdoor tennis champions	89	26.35	27.12	22-26
Runs batted in: annual champions of the two major baseball leagues	49	27.10	27.97	25-29
U.S.A. indoor tennis champions	64	28.00	27.45	25-29
World champion heavyweight pugilists	77	29.19	29.51	26-30
Base stealers: annual champions of the two major baseball leagues	31	29.21	28.85	26-30
Indianapolis Speedway racers and national auto-racing champions	82	29.56	30.18	27-30
Best hitters: annual champions of the two major baseball leagues	53	29.70	29.56	27-31
Best pitchers: annual champions of the two major baseball leagues	51	30.10	30.03	28-32
Open golf champions of England and of the U.S.A.	127	30.72	31.29	28-32
National individual rifle-shooting champions	84	31.33	31.45	32-34
State corn-husking champions of the U.S.A.	103	31.50	30.66	28-31
World, national, and state pistol-shooting champions	47	31.90	30.63	31-34
National amateur bowling champions	58	32.33	32.78	30-34
National amateur duck-pin bowling champions	91	32.35	32.19	30-34
Professional golf champions of England and of the U.S.A.	53	32.44	32.14	29-33
World record-breakers at billiards	42	35.00	35.67	30-34
World champion billiardists	74	35.75	34.38	31-35

Source: H. C. Lehman, *Age and Achievement* (Princeton: Princeton University Press, 1953), p. 256.

must respond suddenly to rapidly changing cues, whereas the golfer initiates the response after he is set and thus maximizes the opportunity to benefit from experience.

Experimental Studies of Skill

Many skills are such highly complicated processes that the experimental psychologist often finds it difficult, even when an age difference in total performance is observed, to localize precisely what the main factor is that accounts for the age difference. There are no simple generalizations that identify the limiting factors in psychomotor skills. A skill may change because of perceptual speed, short-term memory, fineness of timing, coordination of muscular movements, and dexterity or the capacity to monitor closely an ongoing activity. Excellent descriptions of analytical experiments on age changes in human skill have been reported (*Welford, 1958*).

Detailed studies of age changes in human skill indicate that the conditions which can be modified to overcome limiting factors characteristically involve: raising the level of sensory input, giving the subject a long time to anticipate or preview the stimulus conditions; allowing for self-pacing of the response; and giving immediate knowledge of results, so that the appropriate modifications of behavior can be made within the attention span of the individual. The two areas where most evidence has been gathered have been in perception and in the slowing of psychomotor performance, both of which were discussed in the previous two chapters. These two facets of performance can interact. For example, if an individual must continually modify his actions in response to signals reporting the outcomes of his actions, he may have to divert his attention from his own manipulations to the signals reporting the outcomes. In this case, sensory and motor slowness may become confounded, and if continuous activity in relation to external signals is required, pressure is put on the individual. Older persons tend to react unfavorably to situations requiring continuous activity under time pressure; e.g., driving an automobile in traffic or industrial production line work. In industry, older workers tend to drift out of jobs that require continuous activity under pacing (*Belbin, 1953*). Workers may be unconsciously seeking the kind of job best suited for their age-related capacities. Psychological experiments have been done on age changes in the interference effect of mirror vision on a skill. The basic question being asked is whether the use of a mirror in disrupting (reversing) normal relations between vision and hand movements is more disturbing to old than to young adults. In one study, the subjects were required to keep a stylus on a moving spot, similar to a spot on a phonograph disc (*Ruch, 1934*). The subjects were given the same tracking task under normal vision and using a mirror in which the normal vision and movement relations were reversed. Older subjects were relatively better in the direct vision condition, suggesting that mirror reversal was more disrupting to their performance than to that of the young subjects.

TABLE 6-4. SCORES MADE ON A PURSUIT-ROTOR* TASK
SEEN IN DIRECT AND MIRROR VISION

VISION	Age Group			60-82 Group as Percentage of 34-59
	12-17	34-59	60-82	
Direct	285.7	280.5	239.2	82
Mirror	77.2	74.0	40.6	55

* The pursuit rotor turned only while the subject's stylus was in contact with the button. Its speed when it turned was about 32 rpm. The scores are the average numbers of times per subject the rotor was made to turn during a total of 25 half-minute trials. There were 40 subjects in each group.

Source: F. L. Ruch, The differentiative effects of age upon human learning, *J. Genetic Psychol.* (1934), **11**, 261-286.

Subsequent studies have substantiated the fact that mirror reversal tends to be more disrupting of the older person's performance. The interpretation of the results in terms of basic processes is not simple. Perhaps the more distant the responses in space and time are from the sources of sense data, the more difficulty the older person will have relative to the young. Why this should be is not clear. Contributing to this may be life-long adaptations to conventional sensory-motor relationships. The extent to which the relations of sense information and limb position can become fixed over time are seen in the phantom limb illusion in amputees. Thus if a recent amputee is asked to describe the sensation when moving the remaining portion of a limb near a wall or table, he may report sensations as if the whole limb were still there (*Jalavisto, 1950*). Young amputees (seventeen to twenty-four years) showed a more rapid rate of adaptation to the phantom limb illusion than did the older group (twenty-five to forty-five years). The persistence of a phantom may be less a matter of current sensory motor capacities than of the relative strength of long-standing adaptations. This would seem reasonable, since men in the age range twenty-five to forty-five years are not "old" by most current standards for measurements of sensory motor capacities.

While part of the changes in psychomotor skills occur in specific components, such as rigidity of joints, muscular strength, or sensory acuity, there is a tendency for many kinds of psychomotor skills to show intercorrelations with advancing age. The interdependency of skills with age probably reflects a physiological change in the nervous system that limits the speed of neural events, but adaptation may also play a role. Not only does the individual adapt to his external environment and its demands, he also adapts to his own body. It has been pointed out that the body forms part of the environment to which the aging individual must adapt (*Kleemeier, 1959*). The nervous system in adapting to the limitations of a changing organism and the demands of the external environment can be viewed as continuously attempting to optimize behavior, although the limits within which behavior is controlled become more and more circumscribed.

Summary

A psychomotor skill is defined as an acquired pattern of finely coordinated voluntary movements. Skills should not be looked upon merely as muscle movements, but rather as complex chains of events in the nervous system, with resulting muscle movement. Skills improve with practice, so that levels of quality of performance may be distinguished, and also personal styles become apparent that characterize an individual's performance in many familiar behaviors, such as walking, writing, or playing a musical instrument or engaging in a sport. The control of voluntary movements involves continuous excitation and inhibition of nerve cells, so that muscle movements are a distribution of activity over time. Movements never involve one muscle. Modification of movement in the light of sensory information is a continuous process. Thus any delay in securing information about muscle position will disturb the relation of the movement to the "purpose" of the individual.

Over the employed years, individuals develop work methods or approaches, and by so doing simplify their tasks. The inexperienced worker is more apt to be working near the limits of his physiological capacities. Compensations are developed by the individual so that limitations on performance are circumvented or minimized. There is thus no one-to-one or simple relation between complex occupational or athletic skills and specific physical or physiological capacities. Older workers tend to drift from jobs requiring continuous activity under paced conditions. This confirms the evidence from experimental studies that slowness of perceptual and motor processes is a rather basic correlate of aging of the nervous system. With age during the usual employed years, there is generally a reduction in accidents resulting from failure of judgment and an increase in accidents in which rapid evasive movements or falls are involved.

Much of the evidence from industrial studies indicates that little change in worker performance is found up to age sixty or sixty-five. How definitive are these facts is uncertain, since older workers have a survivor bias and are a highly select subpopulation from a total initial population. Except for individuals with cumulative injuries or problems of health, worker performance up to age sixty should be little influenced by physiological changes in aging. Exceptions are instances where time pressures are great. Since the individual performs in some context, his capacities and his adaptation to his working conditions are significant for his total effectiveness. Few studies have attempted to measure long-term consequences of practice and experience on psychomotor skills. From laboratory studies and data from athletes, it is known that from about age forty there is commonly found a reduction in such capacities as strength, sensory acuity, and an increase in reaction time. The individual's limits are not often taxed in occupational performance and tend to be well counterbalanced by experience and better work methods. Capacities change so gradually that adaptation is almost an unconscious process. When dramatic changes in skills occur, they are likely to be the result of injury or disease, with accompanying neurological damage. It is perhaps only after age seventy that skills have a more distinctive quality of being "old," primarily because of the slowness of action and the tendency to work according to an internal tempo rather than to an external pace. Some researchers believe that individual differences in skills increase in persons over age seventy, so that group averages, or norms, are less useful than they are for younger persons. Individual differences in rates of aging, specialization of experience and skills over the life span, consequences of diseases and injuries, including sensory defects, make the increased range of individual differences a likely and important fact, though not many studies have been done on the skills of persons over the age of sixty-five.

References

Belbin, R. M. Difficulties of older people in industry. *Occupational Psychol.,* 1953, **27,** 117-190.

Droller, H. Falls among elderly people living at home. *Geriatrics,* 1955, **10,** 239-244.

Fitts, P. M. Engineering psychology and equipment design. In S. S. Stevens (ed.), *Handbook of Experimental Psychology,* pp. 1287-1340. New York: John Wiley & Sons, Inc., 1951

Jalavisto, Eeva. Adaptation in the phantom limb phenomenon as influenced by the age of the amputees. *J. Geront.,* 1950, **5,** 339-342.

King, H. F. An age-analysis of some agricultural accidents. *Occupational Psychol.,* 1955, **29,** 245-253.

*Kleemeier, R. W. Behavior and the organization of the bodily and the external environment. In J. E. Birren (ed.), *Handbook of Aging and the Individual*, pp. 400-451. Chicago: University of Chicago Press, 1959.
LeGros Clark, F. and Agnes C. Dunne. *Ageing in Industry*. New York: Philosophical Library, Inc., 1956.
Lehman, H. C. *Age and Achievement*. Princeton: Princeton University Press, 1953.
McFarland, R. A. *Human Factors in Air Transportation*. New York: McGraw-Hill, Inc., 1953.
——— and B. M. O'Doherty. Work and occupational skills. In Birren (ed.), 1959, *op. cit.*, pp. 452-500.
Marsh, B. W. Aging and driving. *Traffic Engineering*, Nov. 1960, 3-21.
Miles, W. R., and Beatrice M. Shriver. Aging in airforce pilots. *J. Geront.*, 1953, **8**, 185-190.
Norman, L. G. *Road Traffic Accidents*. Geneva: World Health Organization, 1962, No. 12.
Paillard, J. The patterning of skilled movements. In J. Field, H. W. Magoun, and V. E. Hall (eds.), *Handbook of Physiology*, pp. 1679-1708. Washington, D.C.: American Physiological Society, 1960.
Ruch, F. L. The differentiative effects of age upon human learning, *J. Genetic Psychol.*, 1934, **11**, 261-286.
Simonson, E. Physiological fitness and work capacity of older men. *Geriatrics*, 1947, **2**, 110-119.
Welford, A. T. *Aging and Human Skill*. London: Oxford University Press, 1958.
———. Psychomotor performance. In Birren (ed.), 1959, *op. cit.*, pp. 562-613.

* Suggested additional reading.

7. Learning

There is great interest in whether the capacity to learn during the adult years constricts or, barring ill health, continues to expand. While proverbs and anecdotes might satisfy the casually interested person, the educator and psychologist must turn to technical information to form opinions about the changes in adult capacities to learn. Such knowledge is useful in creating learning situations to maximize the individual's potential for learning, whether it be for academic, occupational training, or avocational reasons. It is of interest to note that when Thorndike published his book on adult learning in 1928 he compared two age groups—"twenty to twenty-four" and "thirty-five and over," the latter group having an average age of forty-two years. A contemporary study of aging would hardly regard a group with an average age of forty-two as "old," and, indeed, the dialogue concerning aging and capacity to learn has shifted to the comparison of adults over sixty-five with those in their twenties. Contemporary society expects older individuals to display greater capacity for learning than it did in the past, and individuals expect more of themselves. In recent years, a dramatic example of the expectancy of adult capacity for learning was shown by the decision of the Government to allow commercial airline pilots to shift from flying piston-motor airplanes to jet planes up to the age of fifty-five. The idea of an individual's learning to fly such a dramatically new type of plane in his early fifties would have come as quite a shock to students of learning in the days of Thorndike. With the gradual rise in years of educational attainment, more adults reach their older years with a positive attitude toward abstract learning, as well as toward learning of new occupational skills.

Definitions

In order to discuss the relation of adult age to learning, certain definitions and distinctions are useful. Learning may be defined as "a relatively lasting modification of behavior as a result of experience." Three aspects of learning may be distinguished. The "experience" must be *registered, retained,* and *recalled.* It is only by testing or examining for the effects of the experience sometime later that it may be judged whether learning has taken place. "Intuition" suggests that learning is a matter of sheer plasticity of behavior. Without evidence, however, of the nature of the neurophysiology of this ultimate plasticity of behavior, we must for the time being be satisfied with descriptions of learning that cannot be reduced to a physical-chemical basis. There is little reason to doubt, however, that it will be possible in the future to point to a physical-chemical modification corresponding to the registration and retention of an experienced event. Many important principles of learning may be established prior to having a knowledge of the basic process, for the primary mechanism of learning is surely not concerned with whether Greek or English is registered and retained—although this is of considerable interest to the individual acquiring the experience.

One discussion of theories of learning in relation to aging quoted James's discussion of plasticity as "possession of a structure weak enough to yield to an influence but strong enough not to yield all at once" (*Kay, 1959*). In relation to aging, the *balance* between plasticity and permanence particularly needs emphasizing, for if the nervous system were excessively plastic in response to experience, much of what is regarded as important would be excessively temporary in its influence. In the definition of learning as a relatively permanent modification of behavior, the term "relative" includes the advantages of further modifications of behavior, yet retains the advantages of stability. At the same time that the teacher of formal subject matters, such as mathematics and foreign languages, may regret the shifting impermanence of a day's classroom results, the psychotherapist may be bewailing the permanence of certain undesirable characteristics. In relation to aging, it may be equally difficult for "toast to be buttered on both sides" by having a permanent quality for those aspects of experience regarded as advantageous and a highly plastic quality for those considered disadvantageous.

Certainly for organisms with specialized nervous systems, and quite possibly for those without, some behavior is learned and organized by experience and some is genetically determined. Proceeding up the phylogenetic tree, the ratio of behavior organized through experience or learning increases in relation to behavior that is organized on a genetic or instinctive basis. In addition, man, as he advances in age, shows an increasing experiential determination of the behavioral output. Since the older adult has already acquired elementary social and academic skills, such as language and arithmetic computation, there is more interest in specific aspects of learning—or rather in the adult capacities to modify certain areas of behavior—than in the over-all plasticity, as with the child who has "the whole row to hoe."

Modifying Conditions

Many conditions affect over-all learning performance that are not regarded as primary to the learning process itself. One of these conditions is motivation. Motivation might be defined as "the intensity or frequency of the individual's exposing himself to the learning experience." In studies of animal learning, it is common practice to deprive the animals of food for a short length of time so that they will learn to make appropriate discriminations to get food as a reward. Food deprivation is therefore regarded as a way of motivating the animals. With older animals, however, the same amount of food deprivation will produce less motivation than with young animals. It is necessary to manipulate conditions of motivation independent of age and the learning material in order to decide the order of importance of the variables. Endocrine changes of aging very likely change other levels of drive or motivation that affect the exposure of the animal to learning situations. Another example of change is speed of performance, which may limit the amount of exposure that the older organism has to the learning situation. A slow human or animal, by stretching out the elements of a learning task, may seriously interfere with the acquisition of new material, since temporal contiguity is an important aspect of learning. From this point of view, the slow organism does not get the same amount of practice per unit time.

While changes in physiological drive states, speed, and perceptual acuity may limit the older individual's learning performance, other factors may facilitate it. Novelty of a learning situation would seem to operate in favor of the older person's learning. Although it is often thought that a learning situation is more threatening to an adult than the same situation is to a young person, it is also true that the learning situation is in itself sufficiently novel to intrigue the adult, and therefore make more intense the learning situation. Just as the child who is hard of hearing or who has a visual limitation is moved to the front of the classroom to make his exposure to the learning situation comparable to that of the other children, so the circumstances in which the older adult learns can be maximized by controlling contributory factors. However, there remains much to be done in studies of the relative contributions of secondary factors in adult learning.

Conditioning

A prototype of the learning experience is conditioning. One type of conditioning that has been studied in relation to aging is that of the conditioned eye blink. In one study, the blink reflex was conditioned to a small illuminated patch that was exposed in front of the subject for one second (*Braun and Geiselhart, 1959*). After a half second, a puff of air was directed at the cornea of the eye, causing the subject to blink. Each subject was given eighty such conditioning trials followed by twenty extinction trials, during which the conditioned response of the eye blink to the exposure to the light could be expected to be extinguished or modified. The experimenters compared the conditioning and extinction of the eye blink reflex in male subjects eight to ten years, eighteen to twenty-five years, and sixty-two to eighty-four years. The result, as seen in Figure 7-1, showed a difference between the young and old subjects in the frequency of conditioned responses. The older subjects proved to be relatively unconditionable. The authors interpreted the data as showing that in many years of living the eye blink itself had become more adapted to environmental conditions and thus less susceptible to conditioning.

Conditioned hand withdrawal has also been studied in relation to age (*Marinesco and Kreindler, 1934*). In this study, the unconditioned stimulus was an electric current that passed through the hand from a plate on which the hand was placed. The conditioned stimulus was the ringing of a bell or the lighting of a colored lamp. The aged subjects took about twice as long as the young to develop the conditioned hand retraction. It is interesting to note that differentiation among unconditioned stimuli also took longer in the older subjects, and two very aged men failed to make the discrimination between a red and a yellow light.

These and other results of conditioning and learning studies may have some bearing upon the concept of set (*Botwinick, 1959*). It is more difficult to arouse in the older person the same set or expectancy for a stimulus and to maintain this state over long intervals. Another study of conditioning and extinction of the galvanic skin response used electric shock as the unconditioned stimulus and a tone as the conditioned stimulus (*Botwinick and Kornetsky, 1960*). The thirty-nine older subjects

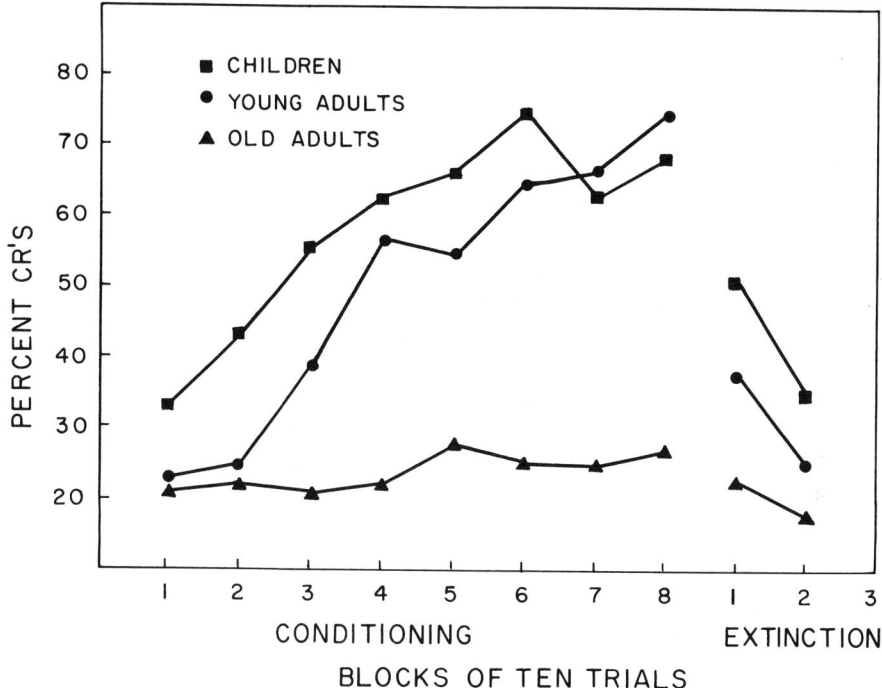

FIGURE 7-1. Relative frequencies of conditioned eye-blink responses on successive blocks of trials for three age groups during conditioning and extinction procedures.

Source: H. W. Braun and R. Geiselhart. Age differences in the acquisition and extinction of the conditioned eyelid response. *J. Exper. Psychol.* (1959), 57, 386-388.

extinguished their response to the tone without pairing with shock more readily than the nine young control subjects. They also conditioned less readily. The authors concluded that the older subjects were less reactive.

The basis for a lowered reactivity on the part of older subjects is not established. It may be an adaptive phenomenon with age, or it may be a result of an endogenously reduced neural activity. Regardless of their ultimate basis, the findings have implications for human learning, particularly learning of speeded perceptual tasks. The stimulus presentation must be carefully controlled, so that the older subject is exposed to the stimulus with maximum intensity. In a more general way, the attention of older subjects may have to be "shaped up" more explicitly in order to equalize the task. Learning should be analyzed while holding more nearly constant conditions of stimulus input for the age groups.

The aged subjects of these and related studies were considerably older than those studied by Thorndike (*e.g., Gakkel and Zinina, 1953*). In Braun and Geiselhart's study, the subjects had a mean age of seventy years, and when Marinesco and Kreindler referred to the fact that they could not establish a certain type of trace condition reflexes in older subjects, they were discussing eight subjects between the ages of seventy-five and ninety years. Certainly in the latter age range, it is quite reasonable to be suspicious of the presence of deteriorative disease states as influencing conditioning, in addition to an intrinsic change with age in the plasticity of the nervous system itself. It is also important to be sensitive to paralearning variables, those variables that surround the learning situation but that in themselves are not intrinsic learning phenomena. It is probable that more detailed future studies will help determine in very aged subjects whether all or only a few subjects show some decrement in conditioning. If only a few, then there will be presumptive evidence that the cause is not uniformly distributed in the population; e.g., a disease found in aged persons.

Animal Studies

Animal learning studies in relation to age should be thought of as models for experimental analysis rather than as having direct relevance to the phenomena of human learning. Certain studies indicate that the age deficit in learning in rats may not be distributed uniformly among the population (*Verzár-McDougall, 1957*). The experimenter had rats of different ages learn a multiple T-maze to obtain a food reward. The learning criterion was not more than three total errors in three consecutive runs. As a group, the older animals showed inferior learning of the maze. However, the experimenter did point out that half of the rats in the age range of twelve to twenty-seven months learned the maze just as well as the young adult rats of eight to nine months, indicating that the deficit condition affecting the rats is not continuously distributed in the population. A follow-up study indicated that those rats which showed inferior retention probably had an excessive loss in nerve cell mass in the frontal lobes of the brain (*Gömöri, 1959*).

Earlier studies, using a multiple discrimination box, did not find age differences in learning in the rats between the ages of thirty-one days and 770 days (*Stone, 1929*). At each of five choice points in the discrimination box the rat had to choose an exit through one of two windows. The correct window was that which was illuminated on a given trial.

One study of learning in the rat used a swimming tank with a two-choice maze (*Birren, 1962*). Little evidence was obtained in this study of a deficit in the older rat's ability to learn the two-choice T-maze. The study added the further information (shown in Figure 7-2) that when animals are matched for initial ability to learn, reversal of the two-choice situation does not produce any greater interference for the older animal. One aspect of this study that did show a deficit in the performance of the older rat was that the older rat swam back and forth along the side wall of the tank and by so doing avoided a choice point. This was interpreted as indicating a long-standing habit on the part of the older rat to cling to a wall as a type of tropism. Perhaps this is another example of a secondary interference with the learning process; the undue intru-

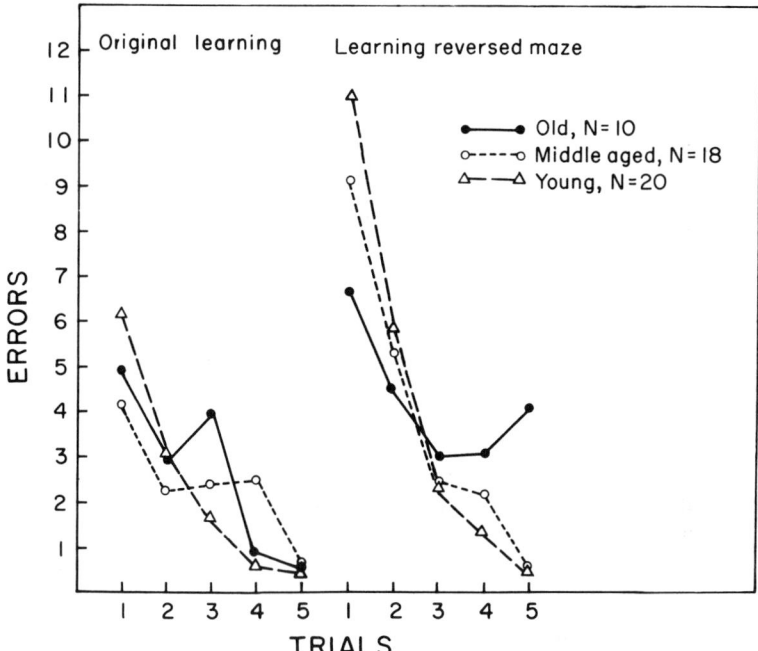

FIGURE 7-2. Mean errors per trial in learning a two-choice water maze by rats. Age groups were equated for original learning in order to study age differences in interference when the maze choices were reversed.

Source: J. E. Birren, Age differences in learning a two-choice water maze by rats. *J. Geront.* (1962), **17**, 211.

sion into the learning situation of a long-standing habit pattern of the older organism. The rat with advancing age may come to depend more and more upon tactile and kinesthetic orientation, somewhat like the adult human who appears to be increasingly dependent upon vision.

What may appear to be a deficit in learning may in fact be a necessity to depend excessively upon information via one sensory modality.

Certain studies also lend themselves to the interpretation that, while rat learning performance and age may be related under some conditions, the age difference may be attributed to something other than intrinsic learning change, in this instance to a difference in perception in the rats (*Kay and Sime, 1962*). Certainly the conclusion must be drawn from the many studies of aging and learning in rats that, at the very least, there is not regularly seen a learning deficit. When deficits of learning do occur, they are more likely than not due to some para-learning variable, such as perception, motivation, or senile debilitation not typical of all animals (*Margolin and Bunch, 1940*).

Speed in Learning

Almost as difficult as separating motivation and learning is the task of ascertaining the influence of speed on the learning performance. With greater speed, younger subjects attempt more trials per unit time; it may then be expected that they will also show greater learning per unit time. Data on the relation of learning and practice clearly must be adjusted or controlled for the unit of practice. Speed of performance may also affect the amount of learning per attempt by separating the rewards or knowledge of results from the behavior so as to give a lessened reinforcement effect. It should not be concluded from these remarks about the necessity to examine the speed of performance in relation to learning that these two processes cannot be intrinsically involved. The ability of the organism to perform quickly under certain conditions may be associated with the plasticity of behavior itself, independent of the increased exposure of the organism to learning per unit of time. This leads to the suggestion that not only learning per unit of practice must be investigated, but also the distribution of practice over time. There is, however, a lack of information on the optimum conditions for the distribution of practice in different age groups. The massing of practice, the timing of reinforcements, and, in complex tasks, the provision for knowledge of results may differentially affect adults of different ages.

Interference Effects

One of the most interesting topics in relation to age and learning performance is the possibility that with increasing age there is a greater likelihood of interference from past habits with present learning. It is perhaps not implausible to believe that the acquisition of habits through many years of experience does tend to intrude into new learning situations. With greater experience, there is an increasing probability of negative as well as positive transfer in future learning situations. One of the earliest experiments designed to test the effects of age on reorganization of long established behavior patterns used a rotary pursuit task in which the subject followed with a stylus a spot on a rotating phonograph-like disc (*Ruch, 1934*). One part of the study used direct vision, whereas another used mirror vision, which required a considerable reorganization of visual motor habits. Assuming a greater consolidation of visual-motor habits in older persons, a reversal situation should produce greater decrements in the performance of older persons. Under the conditions of the mirror reversal, older subjects gave a relatively poorer performance than they did in the direct-view situations. It should again be noted that in these circumstances there were only trivial differences in the performance of subjects age twelve to seventeen compared with ages thirty-four to fifty-nine; the older subjects were sixty to eighty-two. It must be stated again that "age" in this sense is outside the range normally considered by adult educators, and, in fact, deficits in learning, if, indeed, that is what they are, are seen only after the age of conventional employment is ended. In the mirror-reversal situation, it need not be the long-standing habits themselves that intrude, but rather, if kinesthetic imagery is weaker in older persons, they must necessarily place greater reliance upon vision, which is, to a disproportionate extent, interfered with in the reversal situation. Thus it need not be so much an undue intrusion of habit patterns as a reflection of a necessary dependence upon certain elements of information in the task or task context.

In a study designed to produce marked interference effects, the effects of age on learning and recall of paired associates was examined (*Gladis and Braun, 1958*). In this study, each subject learned an eight-item, paired associate word list. After the initial learning, the subjects had to learn paired associates having varying degrees of similarity in meaning to the original lists. Each subject relearned the original list of paired associates two minutes after he learned one of the interpolated lists of words of varying relationships to the original materials. In all instances, the lists were learned to the criterion of a perfect trial each. The data of this study are presented in Table 7-1. Jerome pointed out that the analysis of these data indicated that there is a superiority in absolute amount of transfer for the older subjects when the raw scores are considered. However, a reliable superiority in favor of youth is shown when the scores are transformed to reciprocals and adjusted for vocabulary and rate of original learning. Since vocabulary normally increases with age, the proper method of equating young and old subjects in verbal learning experiments is difficult (*Korchin and Basowitz, 1957*). In terms of verbal comprehension, older people would on the average be expected to know more words than would young adults. What this study in fact shows is that the amount of transfer or interference effect depends upon the kinds of controls used in the learning situation—i.e., the rate of original learning—and the matching of subjects. However, such interference effects are ideally obtained

TABLE 7-1. AVERAGE LEARNING RATE AND RECALL SCORES
FOR PAIRED ASSOCIATES IN SEVERAL AGE GROUPS

TYPES OF SCORE	Age Groups		
	20 to 29	40 to 49	60 to 72
Mean raw scores:			
Original learning	14.8	19.7	23.3
Interpolated learning	10.9	15.2	17.7
Gains	3.9	4.5	5.6
Recall	4.3	4.0	3.3
Transformed scores:			
Original learning	79.98	59.65	53.30
Interpolated learning	116.88	80.88	72.30
Gains	36.90	21.23	19.00
Adjusted scores:			
Original learning	85.78	59.18	48.10
Interpolated learning	112.23	83.48	73.81
Gains	26.45	24.30	25.71
Recall	3.90	4.14	3.52

Source: M. Gladis and H. W. Braun, Age differences in transfer and retroaction as a function of intertask response similarity. *J. Exper. Psychol.* (1958), **55**, 25-30.

only under laboratory conditions. What people usually have in mind when they speak of interference effects in learning, however, are lifelong habits which antedate any experimental condition that may be imposed.

Set or Expectancy

One of the relevant conditions in learning is the focusing of attention on that which is to be learned; another is the intensity with which the individual expects a particular stimulus. One study has shown that there is a difference with age in the expectancy for sound signals in simple reaction time experiments (*Botwinick, 1959*). Older persons perform fastest by lifting a finger when the sound signal to which a reaction is to be made occurs at a regular interval after a warning signal. With a regular preparatory interval, they are at their relative best in speed of response, which suggests that the conditions of stimulus presentation may be designed to maximize expectancy and thereby the intensity of the registered event. The use of regular warning signals and preset intervals of associated stimuli may minimize tendencies to distraction or irrelevant associations during the course of learning. The development of set and its maintenance appear to be a physiological phenomenon, although there is a possibility that the individual learns how to anticipate stimuli. In its broadest aspect, set, or expectancy, to learn may be a matter of long-standing habit; i.e., the better educated subject has learned how to learn and has a set that encourages associations to novel stimuli.

Basically, learning to learn may be a matter of learning what to attend to in order to develop a strategy for seeking out the crucial elements in a learning task. The individual learns to concentrate on these elements, rather than on irrelevant features of the learning context. It may well be that years since school does affect both expectancy to learn and the ability to seek out crucial elements in a learning situation. Here again, however, emphasis is being given to a para-learning variable, a variable not intrinsic to the process of acquisition *per se,* but one that governs the intensity of registration of important task elements.

Studies of Occupational Learning

Because of new methods of production and automated control over industrial methods, workers are often required to retrain or to acquire totally new skills if their previous jobs have been eliminated. Retraining of adult workers has become a major activity in industries subject to rapid technological change. As the rates of learning of workers of different ages are studied and attempts are made to provide optimum learning conditions, valuable information will be obtained about the adaptability of individuals over the whole span of their work life. A survey was made of industrial training of workers of different ages (*U.S. Department of Labor, 1963*). Data were obtained from four companies in which training was required because of technological changes. There were about 2220 workers in different occupations: oil refinery production workers; airline maintenance mechanics; aircraft factory engineers, technicians, and craftsmen; and telephone company operators.

It would seem that there is a somewhat different cognitive load placed on the worker in an automated plant; he has to return to a classroom-like learning situation for extensive retraining. The petroleum company studied changed dramatically from a step-at-a-time process to a "straight-through" method of production. In the new system, the whole plant worked as one unit or not at all; no part could stop for twelve hours without the whole plant's stopping. This required the operators to depend upon a highly instrumented control system and to have knowledge about processes in all parts of the plant. The workers's skill changed from mastery of a limited operation in time and place to one of strategy and an anticipatory function. Speed, strength, and dexterity became less important than long-term integration of abstract information and planning of strategy.

In preparing for the plant changeover, the petroleum company gave a series of courses of instruction to eighty-two operating workers and eighteen instrument workers. For the operators, two sets of courses were given; each was given eight hours a day, five days a week. One course went for a total of 120 hours and another for 160 hours. A third set of courses was given four to eight hours a week over a two-week period.

For the instrument workers, one set of courses was arranged by company staff and the other by a local university staff. The content ranged from elementary physics through electronics and construction to maintenance of specific instruments.

TABLE 7-2. PRODUCTION WORKERS AT OIL REFINERY: LEVEL OF PERFORMANCE OF YOUNGER AND OLDER TRAINEES ON TRAINING COURSES

NAME AND DURATION OF COURSE	Younger Trainees			Older Trainees*		
	Number of Trainees	Per cent		Number of Trainees	Per cent	
		Above Average Grade	Below Average Grade		Above Average Grade	Below Average Grade
1. Zone A (3 weeks)	12	58	42	10	40	60
2. Zone B-D (3 weeks)	10	50	50	11	45	55
3. Zone C (3 weeks)	10	60	40	11	36	64
4. Zone D (3 weeks)	5	80	20	5	20	80
5. Zone A (4 weeks)	15	47	53	15	53	47
6. Zone B (4 weeks)	12	58	42	13	46	54
7. Zone C (4 weeks)	15	53	47	13	31	69
8. Zone D (4 weeks)	4	50	50	3	33	67
9. Zone A (2 years)	10	50	50	10	40	60
10. Zone B (2 years)	7	75	25	8	50	50
11. Zone C (2 years)	8	63	37	8	50	50
12. Zone D (2 years)	5	60	40	6	33	67

* Because of the small number of trainees in each course, it was necessary to use a different age criterion for each course. In Courses 1 and 2, older trainees included those 47 years and over; Courses 3, 5 and 12, 43 years and over; Course 4, 51 years and over; Course 6, 52 years and over; Course 7, 49 years and over; Course 8, 48 years and over; Courses 9 and 11, 39 years and over; Course 10, 42 years and over.

Source: U.S. Department of Labor, Industrial Retraining Programs for Technological Change (Washington, D.C.: Government Printing Office, Bureau of Labor Statistics, Bull. No. 1368, 1963), p.10.

Table 7-2 gives the results of the production worker training in relation to worker age. Each trainee is compared in grade with the median group performance, and comparisons are made between the proportion of younger and older workers above and below the median. Using this method of analysis, the age differences are not impressive, and they are minimized if workers with the same level of education are compared, as in Table 7-3. The older instrument workers were, if anything, somewhat better than the young (under forty) in the training courses, as shown in Table 7-4.

The data on retraining of long distance telephone operators provides an interesting contrast to the petroleum industry. The new task of the

TABLE 7-3. PRODUCTION WORKERS AT OIL REFINERY:
LEVEL OF PERFORMANCE OF OLDER AND YOUNGER TRAINEES
WHEN DIFFERENCES IN EDUCATION ARE TAKEN INTO ACCOUNT

Name and Duration of Course	Younger Trainees			Older Trainees*		
	Number of Trainees	Per cent		Number of Trainees	Per cent	
		Above Average Grade	Below Average Grade		Above Average Grade	Below Average Grade
1. Zone A (3 weeks)	12	50	50	9	45	55
2. Zone B-D (3 weeks)	10	40	60	9	67	33
3. Zone C (3 weeks)	10	50	50	10	50	50
4. Zone D (3 weeks)	3	33	67	4	50	50
5. Zone A (4 weeks)	12	58	42	13	46	54
6. Zone B (4 weeks)	12	67	33	10	40	60
7. Zone C (4 weeks)	11	82	18	13	31	69
8. Zone D (4 weeks)	5	40	60	2	100	0
9. Zone A (2 years)	12	58	42	6	33	67
10. Zone B (2 years)	6	50	50	4	50	50
11. Zone C (2 years)	8	50	50	8	63	37
12. Zone D (2 years)	4	25	75	4	75	25

* See footnote to Table 7-2.

Source: U.S. Department of Labor, Industrial Retraining Programs for Technological Change (Washington, D.C.: Government Printing Office, Bureau of Labor Statistics, Bull. No. 1368, 1963), p. 11.

TABLE 7-4. INSTRUMENT MECHANICS AT OIL REFINERY:
PER CENT OF OLDER AND YOUNGER TRAINEES
WHO RECEIVED GRADES ABOVE AND BELOW AVERAGE TEST SCORES

Name of Course	Younger Trainees			Older Trainees*		
	Number of Trainees	Per cent		Number of Trainees	Per cent	
		Above Average Grade	Below Average Grade		Above Average Grade	Below Average Grade
1. Company course: Arithmetic	7	29	71	6	67	33
2. Company course: Fractions and decimals	8	47	53	7	71	29
3. Vendor course: Control valves	8	50	50	7	43	57
4. Vendor course: Control and valves	8	50	50	6	67	33
5. Vendor course: Level indicators	8	50	50	6	50	50
6. University course: Generators and AC circuits	7	43	57	6	50	50

* Older trainees include those 40 years of age and over.

Source: U.S. Department of Labor, Industrial Retraining Programs for Technological Change (Washington, D.C.: Government Printing Office, Bureau of Labor Statistics, Bull., No. 1368, 1963), p. 12.

operators involved the substitution of an IBM card for a paper form. The changes were more a shift in a well-established psychomotor skill than a fundamental change, as with the petroleum workers' task. Rather than writing numbers on slips of paper, the operator was required to read down and mark small spaces in vertical columns that corresponded to numbers. To process the card accurately in the computer at the next stage, the marking had to have been done accurately; marking errors result in billing errors. The operator also had to mark rapidly. To establish the new pattern, each operator was given a two-day period of retraining, involving both marking of cards and reading of cards. The trainees were called on standard telephone apparatus, as in an actual working situation, and the trainee was required to record and place the call in the new manner. The second phase involved the use of the marked IBM cards in placing calls. Trainees were required to place calls that had been recorded on a deck of thirty cards; both speed and accuracy were emphasized. Performance was described by five measures: total number of tickets marked, total number of errors, total number of items omitted, ratio of omissions to tickets marked, and the difference between the total tickets marked and the sum of errors and omissions. Table 7-5

TABLE 7-5. TELEPHONE OPERATOR TRAINEES: LEVEL OF PERFORMANCE ON VARIOUS TESTS, BY AGE GROUP

TEST AND PERFORMANCE LEVEL	Age Group (Per Cent)			
	18-24	25-34	35-44	45 and over
Number of trainees	176	202	70	55
Number of tickets marked:				
Above average*	54.0	51.5	41.4	25.5
Below average	46.0	48.5	58.6	74.5
Total number of errors:				
Above average	43.7	49.5	58.6	52.7
Below average	56.3	50.5	41.4	47.3
Total number of omissions:				
Above average	62.5	59.4	58.6	40.0
Below average	37.5	40.6	41.4	60.0
Ratio of omissions to tickets marked:				
Above average	55.7	52.0	47.1	29.1
Below average	44.3	48.0	52.9	70.9
Marking efficiency index:				
Above average	59.7	53.0	42.9	27.3
Below average	40.3	47.0	57.1	72.7

*Above average always indicates superior performances (e.g., more tickets, fewer errors).

Source: U.S. Department of Labor, Industrial Retraining Programs for Technological Change (Washington, D.C.: Government Printing Office, Bureau of Labor Statistics, Bull. No. 1368, 1963), p. 28.

TABLE 7-6. TELEPHONE OPERATOR TRAINEES:
LEVEL OF PERFORMANCE OF TRAINEES
WITH 8-11 YEARS OF EDUCATION, ON VARIOUS TESTS, BY AGE GROUP

	Age Group (Per Cent)			
TEST AND PERFORMANCE LEVEL	18-24	25-34	35-44	45 and over
Number of trainees	33	31	21	31
Number of tickets marked:				
Above average*	57.6	51.6	33.3	19.3
Below average	42.4	48.4	66.7	80.7
Total number of errors:				
Above average	45.4	64.5	61.9	38.7
Below average	54.6	35.5	38.1	61.3
Total number of omissions:				
Above average	63.6	77.4	61.9	45.2
Below average	36.4	22.6	38.1	54.8
Ratio of omissions to tickets marked:				
Above average	51.5	61.3	38.1	25.8
Below average	48.5	38.7	61.9	74.2
Marking efficiency index:				
Above average	60.6	67.7	47.6	22.6
Below average	39.4	32.3	52.4	77.4

*Above average always indicates superior performances (e.g., more tickets, fewer errors).

Source: U.S. Department of Labor, Industrial Retraining Programs for Technological Change (Washington, D.C.: Government Printing Office, Bureau of Labor Statistics, Bull. No. 1368, 1963), p. 29.

shows that the proportion of trainees with above average scores declined with increasing age on four of the five measures: errors tended not to be different with age.

When differences in educational level are adjusted, the age differences in performance are reduced (Tables 7-6 and 7-7). When the results of interpretation of tickets are examined with respect to speed and errors, trainees over forty-five did not do as well as the younger group. The authors observed:

> It is noteworthy, however, that the performance record of older trainees, based on error using the old method of interpreting tickets, was about the same as the record for younger trainees. This suggests that, with further experiences using the new method, older trainees would probably achieve about the same level of performance as younger trainees (*U.S. Department of Labor, 1963, p. 27*).

This type of performance involving psychomotor coordination where speed is important has long been regarded as being especially difficult for older persons. One might express surprise that the age groups were not found to have even greater differences.

TABLE 7-7. TELEPHONE OPERATOR TRAINEES:
LEVEL OF TICKET-MARKING PERFORMANCE OF TRAINEES
WITH 12 YEARS OR MORE OF EDUCATION, BY AGE GROUP

TEST AND PERFORMANCE LEVEL	Age Group (Per Cent)			
	18-24	25-34	35-44	45 and over
Number of trainees	142	158	44	18
Number of tickets marked:				
Above average*	53.5	52.5	45.4	38.9
Below average	46.5	47.5	54.6	61.1
Total number of errors:				
Above average	43.7	48.7	63.6	77.8
Below average	56.3	51.3	36.4	22.2
Total number of omissions:				
Above average	62.7	56.3	54.6	27.8
Below average	37.3	43.7	45.4	72.2
Ratio of omissions to tickets marked:				
Above average	57.0	50.0	52.3	38.9
Below average	43.0	50.0	47.7	61.1
Marking efficiency index:				
Above average	59.9	50.0	40.9	38.9
Below average	40.1	50.0	59.1	61.1

*Above average always indicates superior performances (e.g., more tickets, fewer errors).

Source: U.S. Department of Labor, Industrial Retraining Programs for Technological Change (Washington, D.C.: Government Printing Office, Bureau of Labor Statistics, Bull. No. 1368, 1963), p. 30.

Although the authors of the report point out that this was a pilot study, the results do suggest that the chronological age of an adult is secondary to other identifiable individual characteristics that bear upon learning and occupational retraining.

The introduction of automated equipment into office procedures has also had implications for adult learning. The Department of Labor issued a report of a survey on this subject which indicates that persons selected for the newer programming and planning jobs tended to be men between the ages of twenty-five and thirty-four with some college education (*Bull. 1276; May, 1960*). While four out of five employees assigned to the new positions were upgraded, few women or older workers were chosen. Although the job status of older workers was not much affected, there was a tendency not to promote them to the newly created positions. Educational qualification was among the factors given for the lack of older worker promotion to the newer electronic positions. Presumably, the lack of sufficient education of older workers would preclude their mastery of the newer, more abstract skills.

TABLE 7.8. TELEPHONE OPERATOR TRAINEES:
LEVEL OF PERFORMANCE ON TESTS INTERPRETING TICKETS,
BY AGE GROUP

	Age Group (Per Cent)			
TEST AND PERFORMANCE LEVEL	18-24	25-34	35-44	45 and over
Number of trainees	92	165	55	57
Speed using old method:				
Above average*	52.2	52.7	50.9	33.3
Below average	47.8	47.3	49.1	66.7
Errors using old method:				
Above average	63.0	68.5	69.1	64.9
Below average	37.0	31.5	30.9	35.1
Speed using new method:				
Above average	60.9	54.6	38.2	28.1
Below average	39.1	45.4	61.8	71.9
Errors using new method:				
Above average	56.5	60.6	60.0	39.3
Below average	43.5	39.4	40.0	60.7
Speed difference:				
Above average	55.4	54.6	49.1	31.8
Below average	44.6	45.4	50.9	68.2

* Above average always indicates superior performances (e.g., more tickets, fewer errors).

Source: U.S. Department of Labor, Industrial Retraining Programs for Technological Change (Washington, D.C.: Government Printing Office, Bureau of Labor Statistics, Bull. No. 1368, 1963), p. 31.

These examples of industrial studies of adult learning indicate the context within which contemporary adult learning may take place. The pattern of industrial learning seems to be moving toward that found in educational institutions. The distinction between "real life" learning and school learning would seem to be breaking down. However, just as there are qualifications that must be introduced before laboratory studies of learning are generalized to daily life context, so results of industrial studies must be qualified before they are generalized to the population at large. Industries select personnel upon entry, and over time there is both voluntary and forced selection of those workers remaining on the job. Furthermore, years of job experience make interference or negative transfer effects to new job requirements more probable. Laboratory experiments characteristically control for the level of initial experience, so that age differences in rates of learning can be studied. Thus the laboratory deliberately studies a learning task that has never before been learned in order to minimize unequal positive or negative transfer.

In industry, duration of experience varies with chronological age in a manner that is difficult to control, preventing specification of the factors involved in individual differences in learning and in response to the learning context.

Incidental Learning

Incidental learning is another aspect of acquiring information that should be explored in relation to aging. One study of incidental learning under laboratory conditions showed that older subjects displayed relatively good incidental learning compared with their intentional learning (*Wimer, 1960*). The task was to associate six different words ("middle," "agile," "gloomy," "sturdy," "cautious," and "wicked") with the color in which they were printed (green, red, yellow, turquoise, orange, and violet). In one experimental condition, subjects were told that they were going to be asked later about the colors; in the other condition, subjects were merely told that the procedure was a study of the effects of color upon reading speed. Under the latter condition, the subject was unfocused, rather than set to learn. Wimer had fifteen subjects over sixty-five and seventeen subjects under thirty learn the word-color relationship. There was a significant age difference in learning under the intentional conditions, but not under the incidental conditions. Why older subjects showed comparable incidental learning but not intentional learning is not readily explained. This study, while by no means conclusive, suggests that the role of set and attention, so well developed by Botwinick and Brinley in speed of performance of simple tasks, should be examined in relation to the broader learning context of older persons.

Practically, it is most difficult to attempt to measure the amount of incidental learning that goes on during daily life, although it seems plausible that a large part of the information acquired over a lifetime is acquired incidental to other activities that were at the time more central to the individual's purposes. For example, in comparing the incidental learning of individuals going into a modern department store for a particular item, age and motivations would be very influential. Much intelligence would be gathered about new products and available choices of articles remote to the immediate purpose. Emphasis tends to be given to information that is intentionally learned and little to other information that may also be registered and retained. Perhaps future research will be able to deal with the relations of age to the incidental learning of daily life and the accompanying strengths and variety of motives. The findings would make it more nearly possible to say what the total uptake of information is over a lifetime and how the rate of uptake varies with age, and would lead to better descriptions of the facilitating conditions of learning.

Summary

The evidence that has been accumulating on both animal and human learning suggests that changes with age in the primary ability to learn are small under most circumstances. When differences do appear, they seem to be more readily attributed to processes of perception, set, attention, motivation, and the physiological state of the organism (including that of disease states) than to a change in the primary capacity to learn. Since Thorndike's studies in 1928, there has been a general tendency to advance the age at which subjects in learning research are regarded as aged. At the present time, there is little evidence to suggest that there is an intrinsic age difference in learning capacity over the employed years; i.e., up to age sixty. This is not to say that learning of certain psychomotor skills may not show limitations in older persons because of problems of performance, of speed limitations, or of life-long habits that elude laboratory study. Clearly, further studies are needed to indicate the optimum conditions for adult learning over the life span. These include studies on the massing or distribution of practice, the focusing of attention and set, and the encouragement of learning strategies by the older subject. The latter may fall into disuse as a consequence of long years since schooling.

Because of the rapid changes in industry, particularly those brought about by automation, occupations change rapidly. Some jobs are eliminated and new ones created. Generally, the new jobs emphasize control over production rather than primary productive skills, hence automation brings with it an emphasis on abstract learning rather than on psychomotor skills. Training and retraining is becoming a commonplace characteristic of adult employment. It is expected that increasing information about adult learning and the conditions that best facilitate it will be provided by industrial studies of learning. Attitudes will change still more as training becomes an accepted feature of a work life in which individuals spend more time in training and less time in direct production. Years of schooling is a more important variable than is age in relation to learning over the work life.

References

Birren, J. E. Age differences in learning a two-choice water maze by rats. *J. Geront.*, 1962, **17**, 207-213.
*Botwinick, J. Drives, expectancies, and emotions. In J. E. Birren (ed.), *Handbook of Aging and the Individual*, pp. 739-768. Chicago: University of Chicago Press, 1959.

---

* Suggested additional reading.

────── and C. Kornetsky. Age differences in the acquisition and extinction of the GSR. *J. Geront.*, 1960, **15**, 83-84.

Braun, H. W. and R. Geiselhart. Age differences in the acquisition and extinction of the conditioned eyelid response. *J. Exp. Psychol.*, 1959, **57**, 386-388.

Gakkel, L. B. and N. V. Zinina. (Changes of higher nerve function in people over 60 years of age.) *Fiziologicheskii Zhurnal SSSR im. I. M. Sechenova*, 1953, **39**, 533-539.

Gladis, M. and H. W. Braun. Age differences in transfer and retroaction as a function of intertask response similarity. *J. Exp. Psychol.*, 1958, **55**, 25-30.

Gömöri, Z. Histologische Veränderungen in der Grosshirnrinde von Ratten mit Verlust des Erinnerungsvermögens im Alter. *Gerontologia*, 1959, **3**, 288-304.

*Jerome, E. A. Age and learning-experimental studies. In Birren (ed.), 1959, *op. cit.*, pp. 655-699.

*Kay, H. Theories of learning and aging. In *ibid.*, pp. 614-654.

────── and M. E. Sime. Discrimination learning with old and young rats. *J. Geront.*, 1962, **17**, 75-80.

Korchin, S. J. and H. Basowitz. Age differences in verbal learning. *J. Abnorm. Soc. Psychol.*, 1957, **54**, 64-69.

Margolin, S. E. and M. E. Bunch. The relationship between age and the strength of hunger motivation. *Comp. Psychol. Monogr.*, 1940, **16**, No. 4.

Marinesco, G. and A. Kreindler. Des réflexes conditionnels, troisième partie: application des réflexes conditionnels à certains problèmes cliniques. *J. Psychol.*, 1934, **31**, 722-791.

Ruch, F. L. The differentiative effect of age upon learning. *J. Genetic Psychol.*, 1934, **11**, 261-286.

Stone, C. P. The age factor in animal learning. *Genetic Psychol. Monogr.*, 1929, No. 5, pp. 1-130; No. 6, pp. 125-202.

Thorndike, E. L., E. O. Bregman, J. W. Tilton, and E. Woodward. *Adult Learning*. New York: The Macmillan Company, 1928.

U.S. Department of Labor. *Adjustments to the Introduction of Office Automation*. Washington, D.C.: Government Printing Office, Bureau of Labor Statistics, 1960, Bull. No. 1276.

──────. *Industrial Retraining Programs for Technological Change*. Washington, D.C.: Government Printing Office, Bureau of Labor Statistics, 1963, Bull. No. 1368.

Verzár-McDougall, E. J. Studies in learning and memory in ageing rats. *Gerontologia*, 1957, **1**, 65-85.

Wimer, R. E. Age differences in incidental and intentional learning. *J. Geront.*, 1960, **15**, 79-82.

8. Thinking and Intelligence

The ability to solve abstract problems and to verbalize and communicate these solutions to others seems to characterize man's superiority over other species. There are many important implications, both scientific and personal, in the evolution of the higher cognitive processes over the life span. Research in this area involves the study of principles by which the higher thought processes are acquired and organized so that they may be more easily transferred or used in a broad variety of problem situations. This touches upon the question of the degree of transfer of training from higher education to problem-solving situations in daily life and in specialized technical and professional activities. While there is justifiable reason to believe that training in the scientific method does transfer to other activities, it is also known that such training does not unfailingly lead to contributions to human activities. The trend in society toward an increased emphasis on higher education is placing a premium on the higher thought processes and logical problem solving in comparison with psychomotor skills, which were more important in past generations. Not many years ago, all major precision tasks were performed manually. Now man has built machines that do dexterous tasks more efficiently than he can. Thus man is free to exercise his more special, abstract talents.

Elements of Problem Solving

Perhaps the first element of the problem-solving process is the perception of the essential nature of the problem. Unless the individual has a clear grasp of the problem facing him, he can hardly be expected to recognize a solution when it is presented or attained. Trial-and-error solutions imply that while the individual may not know exactly how to solve the problem, he may try to do so in semi-random fashion, but that once he stumbles upon a solution, he will be able to recognize it as such.

In addition to having a problem-solving set, or orientation, the individual must be sufficiently motivated to continue trying to solve the problem. While certain kinds of perceptual tasks may be solved by quick insight, perhaps involving a sudden perceptual reorganization of the stimulus, most problems are solved by several cycles of attention to the nature of the problem, selection of elements from experience related to the problem, and evaluation of the potential solutions. This process can be regarded as the formulation and testing of various hypotheses.

Having once defined a particular problem, to solve it the individual must select relevant items from his own experience. Thus the amount of relevant information, or stored experience, and the fluidity of selection of items from experience according to some purpose or set govern the quality of the final problem-solving activity. As indices of the higher thought processes, tests of intelligence to a great extent measure achievement or stored information. The (often implicit) assumption is that if the individual has already gained familiarity with, or mastery of, certain elements or facts, he can probably be effective in future situations in applying concepts he has already mastered or in forming new ones like them. Tests of intelligence are therefore more practical tools or guides to the assessment of individuals' capacities than they are methods of analyzing the nature of higher thought processes.

The kinds of problems and tests used in assessment of adult mental abilities have often been criticized on grounds that they are unfamiliar, often trivial, do not elicit the adult's interest for serious effort, or inherently penalize the older adult by stressing some extraneous element or requiring contemporaneous knowledge of a very specialized sort. The use of time limits in measuring the performance of older persons has frequently been questioned. Granted that many of these criticisms are appropriate, some are open-ended comments that cannot be evaluated Those who have not worked with older individuals tend to assume that the material of tests and problems cause them to be defensive. Quite the contrary point of view is usually held by those who have spent a great deal of time working with older adults. Rather than being more defensive, the very old may be more candid than young adults and feel less on trial about their performance. Furthermore, the very element of unfamiliarity of the tests and problems may elicit a greater curiosity about the materials and a greater desire to manipulate them. Most older adults are probably less concerned than the young with the relative success or failure of their test performance and are thus not particularly high in avoidance motivation. But although the curiosity of older persons may be readily elicited in many kinds of problem-solving or intelligence test situations, it does not follow that their attitudes are necessarily particularly relevant or helpful or that the ensuing problem-solving behavior is efficient. For example, as a consequence of adapting to the conditions of daily life, an individual may have a very narrow range of situations in which he adopts a problem-solving approach. Most daily interactions of adults occur without the need for behaving under novel instructions. In experimental situations, it would be relatively more difficult to impart to such an individual a novel instruction or set that would persist through a series of solution attempts. Another way of saying this is that the existence of curiosity does not in itself imply that the individual will attend to the instructions and develop alternative problem-solving strategies.

The subject's quickness or promptness of response in problem-solving situations is in itself susceptible to many alternative explanations, such as the need or desire of the individual to consider the stimulus elements for a long time before responding. Some alteration of behavior may be expected in particular individuals after middle age as a result of disuse of skills, organic involution or disease, and the consequence of mental sets momentarily aroused by trivial or idiosyncratic elements in the situation.

Some Studies of Thinking

A group of 480 subjects aged twelve to eighty years was studied (*Friend and Zubek, 1958*). The investigators used the Watson and Glaser Critical

TABLE 8-1. SUBJECTS OBTAINING SCORES EQUAL TO OR GREATER THAN THE PEAK MEAN*

Age Group	Number of Subjects	Mean Raw Score	Number over Peak Mean	Percentage over Peak Mean
40's	82	65.09	23	28.0
50's	67	62.19	14	20.9
60's	57	58.05	9	15.8
Over 70	35	53.31	3	8.6

*Peak mean was 70.34, obtained by the 20-39 age group.

Source: Celia M. Friend and J. P. Zubek, The effects of age on critical thinking ability. *J. Geront.* (1958), **13**, 410.

Thinking Appraisal, which purports to evaluate the ability to draw inferences, recognize assumptions, draw deductions from brief syllogisms, weigh evidence, and evaluate arguments. The results indicated a marked difference in the performance of the older and younger subject.

The investigators pointed out that although the elderly subjects as a group scored poorly on the tests of critical thinking, many of them showed performance at a level as high as, or higher than, young adult subjects. After making a detailed analysis of the results, they came to the conclusion that there were two reasons for the poorer scores of the older subjects. The first was a lower "objectivity" in answering certain types of questions; the other was a greater "inflexibility." The latter was defined as a tendency to choose the absolute category of true or false rather than to consider other alternative answers. It would seem that attitudes and emotional factors were influencing performance on the critical thinking test. Figure 8-1, showing the age changes in ability to weigh evidence and interpret data, does not include a time factor. Since the test itself was untimed, the older person could take as long as he wanted.

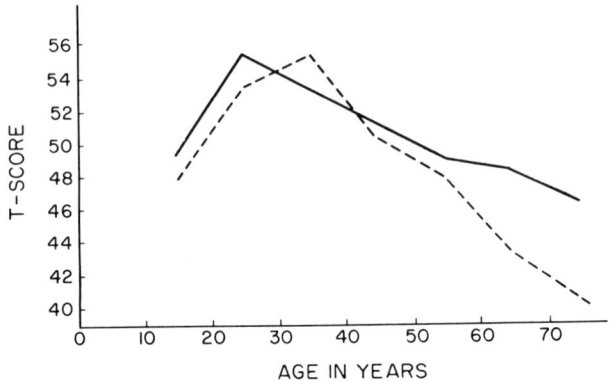

FIGURE 8-1. Ability to weigh evidence and interpret data (continuous line) and changes in deductive thinking (broken line) in relation to age. Based upon results obtained from 484 subjects ranging in age from twelve to eighty years using the Watson-Glaser Critical Thinking Appraisal Test.

Source: Celia M. Friend and J. P. Zubek. The effects of age on critical thinking ability. J. Geront. (1958), 13, 410.

Another way of approaching the problem of constructive and creative mental activity is through the use of proverbs. One study gave proverbs for interpretation to three different adult age groups (*Bromley, 1956*).

Perhaps more important than the results, which showed a tendency for the oldest subjects to give a somewhat lower proportion of good interpretations of proverbs, is the theoretical statement by Bromley. He proposed that the changes with age in normal intellectual performance could be due to: "(a) a loss of performance potentialities, which govern mainly the quantity of output, and (b) a loss of performance evaluation, which governs mainly the quality of output." There was an implication in the study that the older person does not have the same amount of information about his performance as has the younger person; i.e., does not have the same knowledge of results. This could be the result of a change in attitude toward a standard of performance or it could mean that the older subject, having less clearly in mind what he is trying to achieve, cannot compare his performance with a standard.

Inflexibility of Approach and Low Objectivity

Without an orientation to problem-solving, individuals may tend to evade the analysis of the logical components of problems and to proceed on the basis of what they think is involved. One exploratory study used a set of statements on topics of general interest (*Welford, 1958*). There were two sets of statements, one consisting of mutually compatible items and the other containing statements that were inconsistent with at least one other of the total group. Subjects of a wide age range were asked to give answers to specific questions, which required both identification of the members of the subset as compatible statements and, from this subset, the derivation of a valid conclusion. A disproportionately large number of older subjects gave answers inconsistent with the request for logical analyses and derivation. Rather they made comments about the statements and premises and expressed opinions that were quite independent of those embodied in the test statements. They did not adhere to the logical restraints of the task, but felt free to reject or correct the premises if they believed them to be in error. The subjects' conclusions thus seemed to be based upon attitude rather than analysis. The comment might be added that past experience can result in a larger number of associations. Therefore, the task of selecting relevant items is greater for the old than for the young subject. Furthermore, the older subject may find that his personal associations tend to compete with a logical grasp of the nature of the problem or task.

In another study on problem solving, subjects of a broad age range were given four resistance boxes in which the terminals were interconnected internally in various patterns (*Welford, 1958*). The subject was given an ohmmeter and a wiring diagram of the net of connections and asked to discover how each of the six terminal posts of the four black boxes was associated with the internal resistances. In comparison with the young, the older subjects identified as many, or slightly more, terminals per problem, but they required 85 per cent more time and made 37 per cent more readings in their identification. It would appear that the older subjects had more difficulty in assigning meanings to the readings that they did make. Since these readings were "immediate experience," they could not be elicited from the repertory of past experience, but either they were too readily dropped from immediate memory or the subjects had a weakness in their set, or orientation, for the problem.

Logical problem solving in two adult age groups was studied using an even more elaborate procedure (*Jerome, 1962*). In this study, subjects pressed buttons that illuminated lights in a sequence, the task being to integrate in an orderly arrangement the sequentially elicited light-key pairings. Problems were given at four levels of difficulty in an ascending order of complexity. If a subject failed to solve a problem, he was given an alternate form of the problem at the same level of difficulty. The performance of the old and young subjects differed markedly. In all the indices of performance, except the rate of inquiry, the young were superior to the older subjects by a factor of at least two. An important aspect of this study was that the localization of the differences in the process of logical problem solving was to some extent possible. The older subjects appeared to show an inability, or unwillingness, to apply a strategy that was repeatedly demonstrated to all subjects and that every young subject employed *skillfully;* an apparent lack of appreciation of the value of early identification of the specific goal condition of a problem; a disorderly search behavior; a high degree of redundancy of inquiry; and a disinclination to keep notes. Jerome concluded from these results that "the patterns of heuristic control so laboriously acquired during youth through formal education and emulation of skillful acquaintances, decay significantly with disuse and with age" (*Jerome, 1962, p. 822*). What are known as *work methods* in psychomotor skills and as *problem-solving orientation* in higher cognitive processes may indeed change with age. Perhaps in the years after leaving school, adults allow their problem-solving skills to fall into disuse, except in specialized areas of their daily life. An attitude that encourages the avoidance of concept formation for problems will be associated with the failure to generate hypotheses for testing.

While the data are most scant, what evidence there is suggests that the higher thought processes of many older persons tend toward simple associations rather than toward analysis. What is lacking is a strong problem-solving orientation that involves the formulation of hypotheses based upon relevant items from experience and then the systematic testing of these hypotheses.

The Nature of Intelligence Tests

It is a truism in psychology that predicting what a man will do in the present situation is most efficiently based upon an estimate of his performance in similar past situations. As commented upon earlier, the content of most intelligence tests is really a sample of achievement (*See Conrad, 1930*). Intelligence tests do not directly measure the more labile qualities displayed by individuals who are able to integrate simultaneously available, but previously disparate, facts into some new synthesis. This might be described as "inventive concept formation" or "inventive conceptualization." The moment of conceptual integration is very fleeting, and people who have spent time solving problems know that they may come again and again to the moment of integration only to fail. Concept formation partly involves primary capacities and partly a willingness to endure the "mental strain" involved in persistently facing the problem. There is a need to keep in one's immediate memory the necessary elements to be combined, while at the same time keeping clearly in the foreground the purpose of the mental manipulations. Some part of the inductive leap or inventive concept formulation is facilitated by an increased familiarity or redundancy of the elements to be combined. For this reason, several cycles of task reconsideration often facilitate the solution.

The acquisition of words in our vocabularies reflects an ability to form concepts. It is thus not unreasonable that one of the best measures of intelligence or predictors of intelligent behavior in scholastic situations is a vocabulary test. A vocabulary test at its simplest level—e.g., a definition or synonym test—measures the number of stored words known or yields an index that is proportionate to the number of words known.

Test Results

One study found that scores in perceptual and dexterity tests declined from the teens to the seventies, whereas other test scores—e.g., comprehension and verbal fluency—held up well until the mid-forties (*Bilash and Zubek, 1960*). Of interest are the correlations of these tests with education.

The correlations in Table 8-2 of tests with education are somewhat lower than those obtained when the negative correlation between age and education in the population is not controlled for, and may be compared with those obtained using the Wechsler Adult Intelligence Scale seen in Table 8-3. The relation between age and test performance may be studied removing the effects of education, and the relation of education and test performance may be studied removing the effects of age.

Table 8-2. Correlations of Mental Tests with Education: Age Has Been Partialled Out

Test	r
Memory	.20
Perception	.25
Dexterity	.29
Numerical	.37
Reasoning	.37
Comprehension	.37
Space	.40
Fluency	.42

Source: I. Bilash and J. P. Zubek, The effects of age on factorially "pure" mental abilities, *J. Geront.* (1960), **15**, 178.

These points are illustrated in an analysis of the subtests of the WAIS in relation to age and education (*Birren and Morrison, 1961*).

A subset of the standardization data of the WAIS was drawn; results were based upon 933 subjects, native-born white, aged twenty-five to sixty-four years. All tests showed a significant correlation with years of education. In this age range, the correlation of test scores with years of education was greater than with chronological age. This may be seen graphically in Figure 8-2, which gives the mean curves by level of education. The results parallel those previously cited for the industrial studies, wherein education level was significantly related to learning.

These findings do not imply that educational level was the cause of

Table 8-3. WAIS Correlation Matrix: 11 Subtests and Age and Education Based on 933 Native-Born White Males and Females, Age Range 25-64*

	1	2	3	4	5	6	7	8	9	10	11	12
1. Information												
2. Comprehension	67											
3. Arithmetic	62	54										
4. Similarities	66	60	51									
5. Digit span	47	39	51	41								
6. Vocabulary	81	72	58	68	45							
7. Digit symbol	47	40	41	49	45	49						
8. Picture completion	60	54	46	56	42	57	50					
9. Block design	49	45	48	50	39	46	50	61				
10. Picture arrangement	51	49	43	50	42	52	52	59	54			
11. Object assembly	41	38	37	41	31	40	46	51	59	46		
12. Age	−07	−08	−08	−19	−19	−02	−46	−28	−32	−37	−28	
13. Education	66	52	49	55	43	62	57	48	44	49	40	−29

*Decimal points omitted.

Source: J. E. Birren and D. F. Morrison, Analysis of the WAIS subtests in relation to age and education, *J. Geront.* (1961), **16**, 363-369.

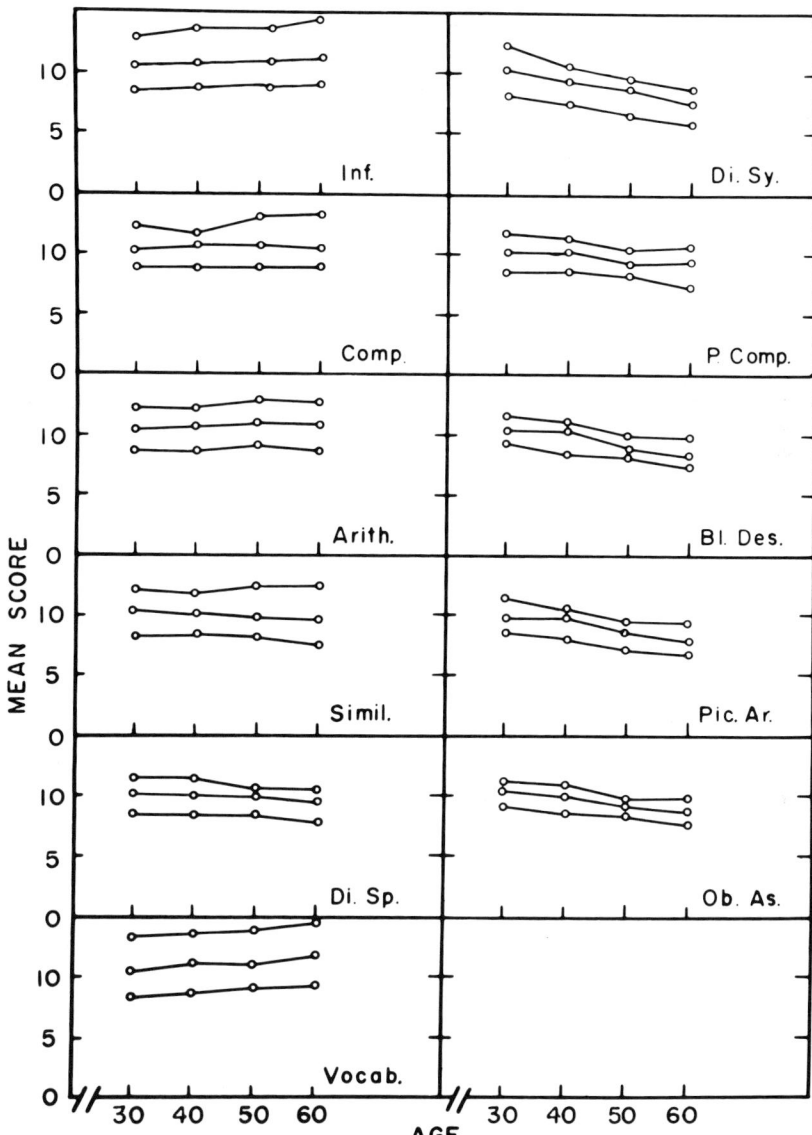

FIGURE 8-2. Mean scores on the Wechsler Adult Intelligence Scale in relation to age and education. For each subtest the upper curves are for individuals having an educational level of thirteen years and above; middle curves for eight to twelve years; and lower curves for less than eight years. Age intervals: 25-34, 35-44, 45-54, 55-64.

Source: J. E. Birren and D. F. Morrison. Analysis of the WAIS subtests in relation to age and education. *J. Geront.* (1961), **16**, 366.

high test scores, since initial mental ability influences the years of schooling. They also do not imply that there is no change with age in component mental abilities. In terms of relative variance, it may be said that more variance is associated with level of education than with age. Age has a significantly positive relationship for a number of subtests—e.g., information and vocabulary—and a significantly negative relationship for others—e.g., Digit Symbol and Picture Arrangement. Again, this is not unlike the industrial learning studies in which the long distance telephone operators showed some decrement with age in a relatively high speed perceptual motor task, while in the others, which could be approached verbally and with no time limit, workers showed little decrement with age.

Obviously the pattern of mental abilities changes with age. This leads to the issue of differential weighting of intelligence test results; e.g., should greater weight be given to the increments in scores or to the few tests showing decrements? This raises the question of which items have greatest validity as indicators of adult mental capacity. With children,

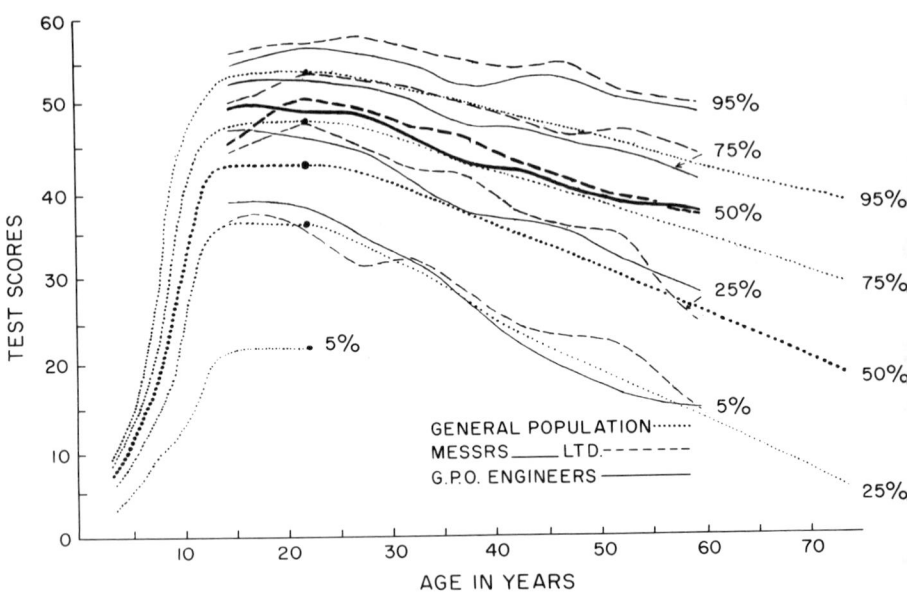

FIGURE 8-3A. Performance of a non-verbal intelligence test, progressive matrices, in relation to age and occupational status.

Source: G. A. Foulds and J. C. Raven. Normal changes in the mental abilities of adults as age advances. *J. Ment. Sc.* (1948), **94**, 133-142.

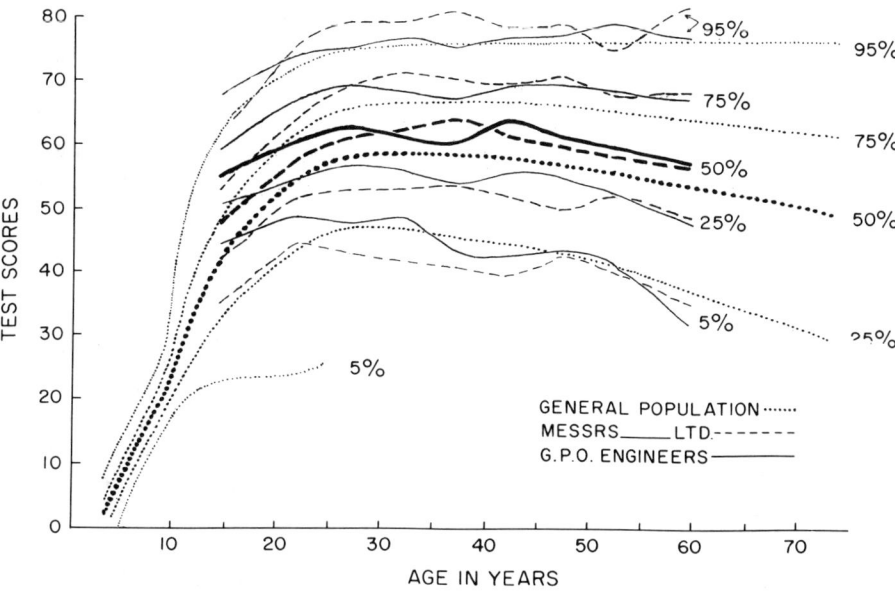

FIGURE 8-3B. Performance on the Mill Hill Vocabulary test in relation to age and occupational status.
Source: Ibid.

this has been settled somewhat by generally adopting the criterion of school success. Therefore, for children or young adults, a valid intelligence test item is one that bears a relationship with performance in mastering school subject matters. Lacking a similar obvious criterion, it is not simple to make decisions either about the appropriate content of adult intelligence tests or how to weight types of items differentially. The content of adult intelligence tests has been rightfully criticized as an unthoughtful borrowing from children's tests. Yet until there is agreement upon what factor or group of factors can provide a criterion of adult intelligence, there is little but intuition to guide efforts in selecting the content of adult tests.

The issue may be drawn even more specifically with verbal tests, the results of which show a rise with age in a synonym test and a decline with age in a word selection test (*Riegel, 1959*). Whether there is interference in the selection of a word when more are known with advancing age is not settled, but the issue is one of differential verbal performance. Is a synonym or a word selection test a more valid measure of adult mental capacity? Obviously, differential validity must be approached cautiously until the criterion problem is advanced.

In contrast with many verbal intelligence tests, nonverbal tests generally show decrements in average scores after mid-life. The Raven Progressive Matrices Test, shown in Figure 8-3, is one such widely used test. That this test has something to do with abstract problem solving is shown by the mean differences in scores obtained by different occupational levels in the same utility company (*Foulds and Raven, 1948*).

Criteria of Adult Intelligence

In deciding what is the best measure of adult intelligence, or what is the best measure of intelligence in aged adults, the question of criteria arises. What is meant by "intelligence" in adults is less certain than what is meant by intelligence in children. By "intelligence" is usually meant that capacity or combination of psychological capacities which equips the individual to master school-like subject matter if given proper tuition and motivation. Intelligence is that variable which governs the upper limit of mastery or the rate of mastery of the school curriculum. It is less certain whether there is a similar homogeneity of purpose in relation to older adults where more varied criteria may be involved, such as the possibility of the individual's profiting from an occupational retraining program or the test's being used for diagnostic purposes in relation to health assessment. An important aspect of effective behavior in the adult years is social behavior, or the skill with which relationships with other people are managed, usually with the effective use of words. If "social intelligence" is to be emphasized as a criterion of adult intelligence, then the measures of verbal comprehension might be weighted more heavily than measures of perceptual function. By contrast, emphasis might be given to intellectual achievement as a criterion of intelligence in relation to age. Extensive studies on age of notable achievements in science and the creative arts indicate that the single work of a man's career generally regarded as most outstanding tends to come at a relatively early age (*Lehman, 1953*). Do these curves better reflect intellectual capacity than intelligence test results? There are, of course, arguments against a literal interpretation of the biographical data of outstanding scientists and artists. For example, it has been pointed out that the drive toward achievement may be stronger in younger men. Also, once having achieved a few early successes in a chosen career, there may be less reward in each subsequent accomplishment.

It must always be kept in mind that any discussion of age and outstanding achievement, or age and intellectual productivity, concerns average trends; there are considerable individual differences. Furthermore, there are long-lived scientists who maintain intellectual productivity well into their eighties. Physical influences on intellectual productivity must also be noted. Lehman emphasized the fact that physical changes contribute to changes in intellectual productivity with age. In addition to possible changes in the nervous system itself due to ill health, the annoyance and distraction of physical disabilities and the inability to maintain sustained activity are undoubtedly influences in the age trends.

Mental-Physical Correlations in Aging

It has been pointed out that an essentially biological interpretation of the changes over the life span is based on the assumption that favorable traits tend to be intercorrelated (*Jones, 1959*). Correlated genetic influences should express themselves through favorable maturation and aging. This suggests that there should be correlations between physiological and psychological phenomena in older adults. In part, this is verified by studies of senescent identical twins (*Jarvik, et al., 1960*). As with young children, the psychological characteristics of aging twins tend to be more closely related than do those of fraternal twins or siblings.

Another indication that there is a relation between cognitive processes and physical well-being in older adults comes from a study done at the National Institute of Mental Health (*Birren, et al., 1963*). This was an intensive two-week study of forty-seven men over the age of sixty-five. These men were relatively healthy volunteers, yet when they were divided into two groups, those regarded as in optimum health (twenty-seven men) and those having subclinical or asymptomatic disease (twenty men), there were significant differences in the two groups' verbal intelligence scores. The results were interpreted as suggesting that when physiological changes in the body appear, especially those related to cerebral circulation, they began to pace cognitive regression. Unlike the verbal tests, however, the digit substitution tests and measurements of speed of reaction time showed similar results for the two groups, both being significantly different in these measurements from young adults. This provides a clue that there may be age-related increments and decrements in mental abilities as well as disease-paced decrements.

One study gave a group of twenty-five psychological and physiological tests to 102 males and females aged twenty to seventy years. A single large or general factor was found, involving nineteen of the twenty-five measures and accounting for almost all of the variance associated with age. The researcher concluded that "at the level of this analysis, aging occurs along a single dimension, measured best by blood pressure, lens accommodation, and sound threshold and less well by ability and speed tests" (*Clark, 1960, p. 186*). These results are important, for they lend

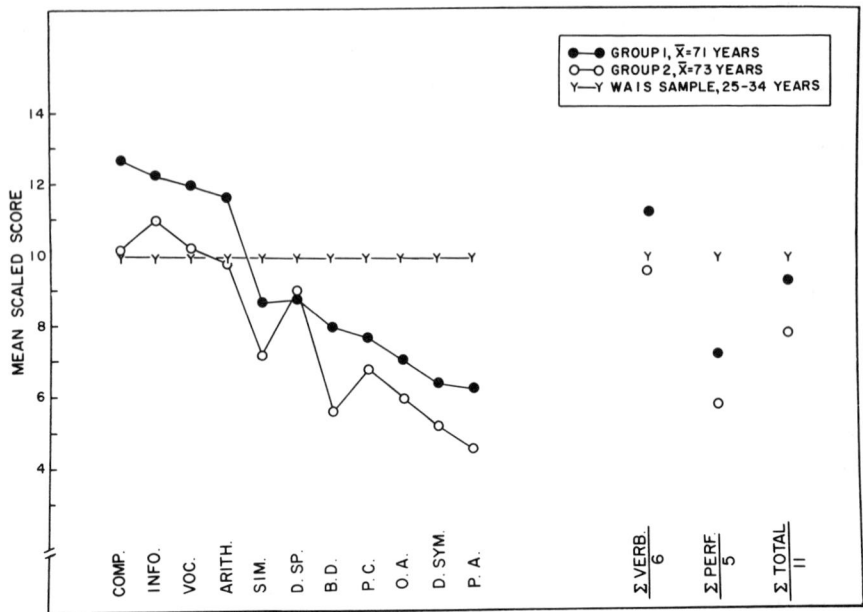

FIGURE 8-4. Comparison of the subtest scores of the Wechsler Adult Intelligence Scale for three groups of subjects: young standardization group, healthy elderly men (group 1), and elderly men with mild asymptomatic disease (group 2). The expected mean value for young adults is ten on each subtest.

Source: J. E. Birren, R. N. Bulter, S. W. Greenhouse, L. Sokoloff, and Marian R. Yarrow. *Human Aging* (Washington, D.C.: Government Printing Office, Public Health Publication No. 986, 1963), p. 151.

substance to the view that there is a typical pattern of psychological changes associated with advancing age which has a normal psychophysiological, rather than pathogenetic, basis.

A further differentiation of this concept has been reported *(Birren and Spieth, 1962)*. While the investigators found, as did Clark, a correlation of age with both psychomotor speed and blood pressure, their age-speed correlation was higher than the age-blood pressure correlation. They concluded that the trend toward higher blood pressure with advancing age could not be regarded as the "cause" of slowing of psychomotor performance but that possibly it is a reflection of a common change with advancing age in the regulation of the central nervous system of vegetative and behavioral functions. Patients with hypertension and those with coronary artery disease appear to show more marked psychomotor slowing than would be expected from age alone. The evidence again points to a separation of the effects of disease from a pattern of measurements representative of normal psychophysiological aging.

Twins over the age of sixty-nine have been reported upon in an important series of papers (*Falek, et al., 1960*). One of the basic findings is that the correlations between mental abilities of one-egg twins persists into the later years. Very significant for both the psychological and biological viewpoints was the fact that intrapair differences in length of life remained smaller for one-egg than for two-egg twins (of the same sex). It would appear that both longevity and mental abilities in later life are controlled or paced to some extent by hereditary factors.

In view of the fact that information measures generally increase with age and that perceptual and speed measures decrease, there is interest in knowing which are more closely related to length of life. A ten-year

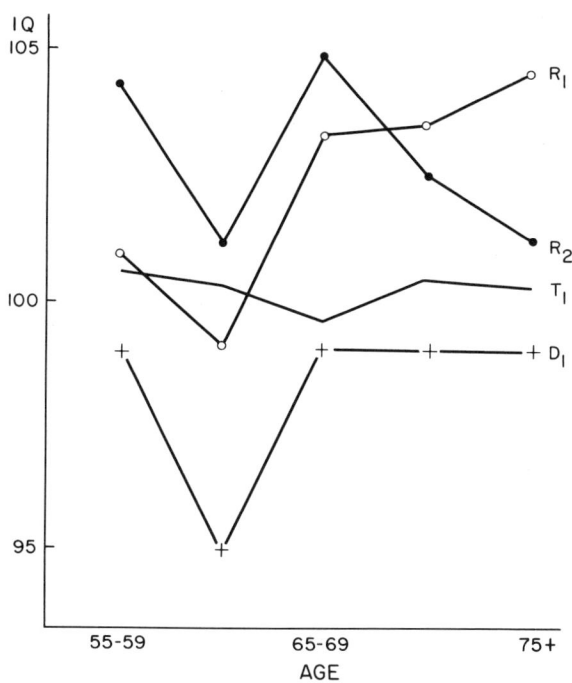

FIGURE 8-5. Retesting of a contemporary adult German population with the Wechsler Adult Intelligence Test. Curves are given by age for several groups: T_1 is the total original population (N = 380); R_1 is the portion of the total group available for retesting (N = 202); R_2 is the retested group (N = 202); D_1 is the group deceased since original testing (N = 62).

Source: Unpublished data by permission of K. F. Riegel.

186 *Thinking and Intelligence*

longitudinal study was carried out on 268 senescent twins; forty-eight were tested on three occasions, and a positive relationship was found between high test scores and survival. It is of great interest that "comparison of mean scores of first, second, and third testings revealed statistically significant losses only on the two-speeded performance tests (Tapping and Digit Symbols). The decline trend on the other tests was less pronounced, although there was an interval of seven years between the second and third testing" (*Jarvik, et al., 1960, p. 293*). The decline in tapping test speed over the three testings and the lower initial score of nonsurvivors clearly place the changes in psychomotor speed in the middle of an important matrix of relationships. The generality of the speed changes indicates that the speed changes may not be regarded as noncognitive, but rather that they imply changes in control over the

TABLE 8-4. STUDY OF HUMAN AGING:
RETEST WAIS TOTAL SCALED SCORE

Group	Subject	Age	Follow-up in Months	1956 Total Scaled Score	1961 Total Scaled Score	Difference		
I	6	72	57	72	56	− 16		
	12	70	56	97	92	− 5	\multicolumn{2}{c}{*Difference*}
	1	80	60	82	82	0	\multicolumn{2}{c}{*Total Subjects*}
	47	65	46	147	149	+ 2	$\overline{X} =$	−9.59
	15	75	58	98	99	+ 1	$\sigma =$	7.78
	20	73	57	106	92	− 14	$\sigma_m =$	1.47
	14	68	59	82	80	− 2	$t =$	6.52
	5	69	61	126	114	− 12		
	16	71	61	101	79	− 22	\multicolumn{2}{c}{*Group I*}
	9	67	64	87	79	− 8	$\overline{X} =$	−8.32
	36	69	54	82	69	− 13	$\sigma =$	7.63
	19	70	62	103	84	− 19	$\sigma_d =$	1.80
	51	71	53	105	90	− 15	$t =$	4.62
	58	71	52	112	97	− 15		
	59	74	52	126	115	− 11	\multicolumn{2}{c}{*Group II*}
	54	73	54	137	138	+ 1	$\overline{X} =$	−12.0
	55	65	54	153	147	− 6	$\sigma =$	7.48
	53	81	54	115	120	+ 5	$\sigma_d =$	2.49
	56	69	58	113	104	− 9	$t =$	4.81
II	28	74	49	79	72	− 7		
	35	74	47	89	76	− 13		
	10	92	57	45	37	− 8		
	18	66	55	104	93	− 11		
	39	69	47	91	88	− 3		
	32	77	50	70	38	− 32		
	27	66	55	128	112	− 16		
	23	74	57	94	84	− 10		
	42	68	51	104	92	− 12		
	8	71	64	83	75	− 8		

Source: J. E. Birren, unpublished manuscript.

the way stored information is used (*Birren, Riegel, and Morrison, 1962*).

A comprehensive study of cognitive and personality changes with age in a sample of the German population also found significant differences in test scores for survivors and nonsurvivors; i.e., dividing initial measurements according to subsequent length of life gave significant differences in scores (*Riegel, 1963*). Figure 8-5 shows Riegel's results.

Somewhat similar findings were obtained in a follow-up of the Mental Health study. Several of the cognitive sets of measurements show initial discrimination between the subsequent survivors and nonsurvivors. Low information scores were found, for example, in the nonsurvivor group.

There is thus substantial evidence indicating that how well an adult performs on cognitive and sensorimotor tests is related to the probability of survival.

Longitudinal studies of mental abilities have given more precise information about changes in individuals, though they have not resolved the problem of the criterion of adult intelligence (*Owens, 1953; Bayley, 1955; Kleemeier, 1961; Jarvik, 1962*). One criterion suggested by the longitudinal studies is that of the prediction of survival. The use of such a criterion assumes that mental ability to some extent should parallel the remaining duration of life and that as individuals approach the end of their lives, mental test scores should decline. There is actually some evidence for this in the studies of Kleemeier and Jarvik. What is bothersome in this concept is the fact that the cause of death may influence the course of terminal decline, with some individuals showing dramatic interruption of a full-facultied existence and others undergoing a protracted involution.

The longitudinal studies of mental abilities generally show significant decline for individuals after seventy years of age. From this it may be suspected that if mental decline is sometimes seen in middle-aged adults, it is probably the result of diseases influencing the central nervous system rather than a part of a normal senescent program of aging. Cerebral arteriosclerosis, hypertension, and even coronary artery disease may have psychological concomitants (*Spieth, 1962*). Their effects and relationships should properly be distinguished from those age-related behavioral characteristics that all members of the population eventually show.

Age, Brain Damage, and Mental Abilities

A commonly expressed opinion about the deficits in mental ability that appear in mental test performances of some older individuals is that the deficit arises from brain damage. In one study of thirty psychiatric patients, mortality and verbal learning were shown to be related

(*Sanderson and Inglis, 1961*). In selected patient populations, the investigators found a significant relationship between scores on verbal learning tests and mortality within two years. The obtained relationship between mental capacity and survival was greater between the psychological measurements and survival than between survival and original diagnosis.

In one investigation, performance on a complex psychomotor task was studied, among other reasons, "to obtain additional evidence pertinent to the possibility that the normal aging process exerts an influence on performances in this kind of task situation similar to that of clinically established brain damage (*Reed and Reitan, 1962, p. 193*). In this study, fifty brain-damaged subjects were compared with fifty control subjects matched for age, education, sex, and race. The subjects were given three trials on the Sequin-Goddard form-board, and the data were analyzed with respect to levels of performance and improvement in relation to both age and brain damage. Both proved to have a significant and marked influence on the absolute levels of performance, but little on measurements of improvement over successive trials. Insofar as the task involves learning, the variables of age and brain damage did not affect ability to improve performance with practice.

In a study of the electroencephalogram in relation to mental functioning in older subjects leading normal lives, little evidence was found of a relationship between the EEG and intelligence test performance. However, in subjects with medical and psychiatric disorders, low intelligence test scores were found to be associated with EEG's that deviated from young adult norms. The investigators concluded: "The results suggest that age, *per se*, is not a crucial factor influencing the magnitude of EEG-intelligence test correlations. Rather it would appear that health status is the critical determinant of the degree of relationship" (*Obrist, et al., 1962, p. 203*). It should also be noted that correlations for individuals with arteriosclerosis were consistently higher than for those without. These findings lead us to view the older subject more individualistically and to expect that he will show mental test performance influenced by the absence or presence of forms of brain pathology more common in late life. Present evidence suggests that the effects of cerebral pathology are superimposed on, or interact with, a pattern of change prototypic of normal aging.

Sex Differences

One of the persistent characteristics of mortality data is the fact that women outlive men. If there are indeed correlations between psychological and physiological characteristics, there should be a more favorable life course in psychological abilities of women than of men, consistent with their greater survivorship. Unfortunately, not much evidence is available on American populations regarding sex differences in mental abilities with age. A rather comprehensive study in Japan reported that in a sample of twelve subtests, women scored consistently lower than men at all ages (*Kurihara, 1934*). The data even include a sex difference in favor of men on verbal tests, whereas available evidence from America suggests that females equal or slightly outperform men on verbal tests. The psychological correlates of the greater survivorship of women clearly remain to be studied in detail.

Rigidity and Problem Orientation

Research has shown that with advancing age, individuals appear to be less disposed to adapt or modify their behavior in accordance with changes in the conditions of the stimuli. For example, it has been discovered that individuals over the age of fifty-five tend to agree more frequently with clichés than do younger subjects age seventeen to nineteen (*Riegel and Riegel, 1960*). This has been interpreted as indicating an increase in dogmatism. A study in England also found evidence for increased rigidity with age in 200 subjects aged twenty to eighty-one. The investigator defined rigidity as "lack of change of behavior, where a change is necessary for success at the task, and where the subject knows that a change is likely to be demanded" (*Chown, 1961, p. 353*). By intercorrelating all items of the rigidity scale with each other and with chronological age, and with independent measures of verbal ability and nonverbal intelligence, Chown obtained a correlation matrix that was factor-analyzed. She identified three factors: normal obsessionality, liking for habit (related most closely to increasing age), and agreement with clichés (this was related to nonverbal intelligence). It is important to note that agreement with clichés was related to a nonverbal measure of intelligence, suggesting that rigidity in behavior may be in considerable part the result of a cognitive factor rather than one of affect or attitude. In order of magnitude of variance, the effects of general intelligence were largest, then came age, and then "spontaneous flexibility." Age and general intelligence were closely correlated, and between them they accounted for 30 per cent of the total variance. The factors of rigidity, conceived of as being independent of intelligence, seem discrete and of much smaller magnitude. Certainly there is no evidence for invoking a concept of general behavioral rigidity in explaining test performance of older persons. Rather it is more reasonable to regard the constraints of behavior as primarily cognitive in nature and as being due only secondarily to rigidity of a minor, specialized sort. It is noted in the data that with age, the effects of speed became more diffuse, again suggesting that with advancing age, the speed factor becomes a more pervasive factor.

Similar questions are raised by research based upon 500 subjects in the age range twenty to seventy years (*Schaie, 1958*). The basic question here concerns the basis of the apparent linear increase in personality rigidity with increase in age. While several studies have also shown that with increasing age there is a trend toward lack of flexibility in intellectual or motor performance, a change characterized as one of increased rigidity, the explanation for the changes is not readily apparent (*Mangan, 1958*). A common interpretation of rigidity of behavior in younger persons is that it is due to a personality constraint stemming from insecurity or anxiety. Excessive cautiousness based on insecurity or anxiety is assumed to lead to protracted time to review an environmental situation and a proneness to cling to a previous response pattern. The anxious person is thought to take a long time rather than incur the uncertainties of responding. However, it has been found that there may be a tendency to perseverate when the stimulus is weak or unclear. When the stimulus is uncertain, the individual tends to base his response to it on the previous response. In Chapter 5, a study was discussed that illustrates this relationship (*Landahl and Birren, 1959*). It was found, however, that while older subjects tend to show a kind of perseveration in judging weights, once their performance is adjusted for the level of weight discrimination, the perseveration effect disappears; i.e., what is involved is fundamentally an ability to discriminate weights rather than an attitudinal disposition to perseverate. Put another way, if the older subjects could discriminate as well as the younger ones, they would not show the tendency toward perseveration. Thus the tendency toward inflexibility or cautiousness in certain tasks may not be due so much to an anxious, uncertain disposition as to the need for more information; i.e., there is a need for older persons to have more information than younger ones in order to yield an equivalent level of behavior.

It has been found that the individual's confidence about his judgments decreases with age (*Wallach and Kogan, 1961*). Furthermore, older subjects require a higher probability of success before they would approve of a high-risk, high-reward course of action. As in the studies of rigidity, it is not immediately obvious what factors are operating. The terms "increased rigidity" or "increased caution" are a way of describing behavior; they do not directly lead to inferences about the mechanisms involved.

A comprehensive study of the relation of age to performance of twenty-one speed tests (versions of word, number, and perceptual-spatial tests) has been made (*Brinley, 1963*). Rigidity was operationally defined as the additional time required to do a mixed (alternation) task compared with time to do a nonshift task. In each of the nonshift tasks, the subject successively performed one type of operation; there were three different operations in each of the categories. The shift task alternated all three operations. In the sense that older subjects (fifty-nine to eighty-two years) took more time than the young (eighteen to thirty-six) on the shift tasks, the older subjects exhibited greater rigidity. However, both from the results of a factor analysis and from an analysis of average trends, the performance of the older subjects on the alternation tasks was predictable from their performance of nonshift tasks. Thus it was not necessary to invoke a new variable (rigidity) to explain slower performance under shift conditions. As in other studies, a general speed factor, associated with accuracy, was found in the older group but not in the young (e.g., *Birren, Riegel, and Morrison, 1962*). Speed was positively correlated with accuracy in the older group. The findings led Brinley to conclude that the speed of performance of older subjects is a measure of the extent to which these subjects maintain effective control over cognitive sets. While older subjects appear to be slow in task performance when different tasks are mixed, apparently it may not be inferred that the characteristic is other than cognitive; e.g., that it is attitudinal or affective in basis.

Because of the tendency to link behavioral traits of cautiousness and rigidity in young subjects to attitudinal or personality factors, it is easy to assume that the same factors may be operating in the cautious behavior of older persons. The delay of decision sometimes seen in older people, the time taken to review a stimulus, and the apparent conservatism in behavior may not be caused by an increase in the level of certainty required. Rather the difficulty may lie in not being able to attain the same level of certitude as previously, or as compared with a younger person. Limitations in perception and intelligence, age differences in set or expectations, as well as changes in drive, motivation, and caution all interact in providing the psychological basis for the apparent increased behavioral rigidity with advancing age.

Abstract-Concrete Orientation

Two contrasting terms used in describing individuals' intellectual behavior are *concreteness* and *abstractness*. An abstract orientation leads one to form a broad concept embracing all elements in a situation, whereas a concrete approach leads one to attend to each stimulus as an individual item. Older persons tend to make few alternative sortings of the Wiegel figures which may be alternatively sorted according to size, shape, or color (*Thaler, 1956*). If an individual forms one possible concept, say that of size, he may be inordinately inclined to cling to this view of the stimuli to the exclusion of any alternative. Such an impoverishment of performance might come about if an individual were extremely anxious, so that once having found a suitable way of classifying stimuli, he would be most eager to avoid any possible alternative. Similarly, however, a reduced cognitive capacity for concept formation might limit the individual's shifting from one form of classification to another. That is, the capacity to form continually expanding superordinating concepts within which to group stimuli may require high level perception and a clear and intense problem solving orientation, in addition to the mastery of certain problem solving strategies. The latter would include the willingness and even the disposition to seek deliberately an alternative point of view toward the same stimulus complex.

There is some evidence that older persons showed relatively greater skill at word associations between concrete nouns than between abstract nouns (*Riegel, 1959*). Such a tendency toward concreteness of association might be regarded as a consequence of daily speech patterns of individuals. The favored use of concrete nouns may be a reflection of the general level of daily speech exchanges but, nevertheless, exclusive use of concrete nouns would represent a form of impoverishment in that few superordinating and hence simplifying concepts would be employed or formed.

Behavioral Load

A useful concept in describing the context of the behavior of individuals is that of behavioral, or cognitive, load. If an individual is required to make discriminations beyond his capacities he feels a certain inner tension and senses a desire to escape from the situation and possibly to avoid it in the future. However, there are social rewards for enduring the cognitive strain of complex situations. Individuals are constantly surrounded by a stream of complex information that they are expected to assimilate and form concepts leading to some behavioral output. This behavioral output also has constraints placed upon it. Some of these constraints arise from the individual's personal standards; some are molded by outside influences, such as those provided in school examinations; and some are defined by the expectations of friends and relatives.

Some individuals show behavior indicative of tenseness, which suggests that they are faced with a heavy load even though the objective circumstances are such that the situation ought to be treated lightly or with little difficulty. For example, in school the retarded child may react with aggression or crisis behavior when faced with the rather simple task of learning to read—which for most children is a task of moderate or low cognitive load. In this way, the emotional behavior arises from the inability to perform under the load conditions; i.e., to integrate the information presented and yield a behavioral output satisfactory to the standards imposed. A behavioral, or cognitive, load on an individual is thus a combination of the difficulty and complexity of the information presented to him in relation to constraints on the behavioral output, and to the behavioral capacities of the individual. Those individuals who appear to have a low capacity because of undue sensitivity to the situation are regarded as manifesting a form of psychopathology; e.g., a neurosis. Those who show a low capacity for a behavioral load because of cognitive limitations are characterized as being dull or backward; e.g., the mentally retarded. Since there are rewards for sustaining high-load conditions in school, in employment, and under certain family circumstances, individuals come to inhibit the tendency to escape or avoid. However, if the load does become relatively heavy or nearly intolerable, individuals engage in load-shedding, using various social devices.

Load-shedding is a way of avoiding high-strain conditions, whether due to perceptual limitations or to a situation that is of special symbolic significance to the individual. For some persons, the resolution of a complex input of many unfamiliar items of information may itself become an experience to be sought. Scientists and mathematical problem solvers tend to court such high-load situations. Their motivation to seek out the conditions that normally lead to high cognitive load and strain results from the reward implicit in obtaining the solution and in the relaxation that occurs after the previously highly aroused pattern of thought and effort.

It has been noted that with advancing age, the total behavioral output of individuals tends to diminish. Some part of this diminished behavioral output may be the result of load-shedding. The reduced behavioral output can also represent a shift in the load that the environment places on individuals. A comfortable way of life is one in which the individual can adjust the input of information that must be processed and responded to. For example, watching a movie or a television program is, depending upon the motivation of the individual, more or less involving; there are few constraints placed upon his behavioral output. By contrast, however, a complex traffic situation involves many simultaneous and changing perceptual elements, and the demands on the individual's behavior require that it be effective at a precise moment in time. The complexity of the information and the length of time over which the stimulus elements have to be assimilated contribute to cognitive load. The motivations and values of an individual determine his readiness to avoid high-load situations and engage in load-shedding or to seek and work through high-load conditions.

Summary

Many species show superiority to man in their sensory acuity and their speed, strength, and endurance of movements. Man appears to be distinguished by his ability to form abstract concepts of his environment, to use these concepts in the solutions of problems, and to communicate the solutions to others. Problem solving involves many component abilities, each with its own limit, which may change with age. The changes with age in component abilities are both incremental and decremental, and some show no change over the adult years. Generally, the amount of information possessed by an individual rises over the life span. The extent to which a problem has familiar elements determines whether it will be solved more efficiently by the old or young adult. If a problem emphasizes perceptual capacity or memory-held instructions, the young adult will probably perform more effectively. It seems plausible that the adult enlarges his repertory of ready-made solutions over a lifetime and becomes more effective by virtue of them. The mode of address to a problem thus tends with age to be one of searching within the existing repertory of responses rather than of looking to the generation of novel approaches. Therefore, age brings with it not only differential changes in component mental abilities, but it involves the adaptions of the individual to problem-solving situations. Because of adaptation, the problem-solving orientation probably declines as a function of years since school. While the disposition to solve problems in terms of known methods is efficient, it can, in extreme instances, lead to an avoidance of looking at a current problem on its own terms.

"Rigidity" is a descriptive term referring to a tendency to hold to a particular point of view and resist change when the situation suggests that change is called for. Most rigidity in problem solving seems not to lie in attitudes *per se,* but in changes in abilities. Rigid behavior can result from disease and brain damage occurring with age, although this is not a factor in every individual. Thus a population of individuals over the age of sixty is a mixture of those who have limitations of mental abilities because of somatic disease affecting the brain and those who are relatively healthy. In the healthy, up to about age sixty-five, years of education show a greater relationship to mental abilities than does chronological age. Furthermore, healthy individuals over the age of seventy will tend to perform better than young adults on certain mental tests, such as vocabulary, comprehension of verbal statements, and arithmetic operations; they will perform poorer than young adults on tests involving spatial perception and rapid decoding of information. Because of these differential changes with age, no simple answer can be given to the question of whether problem-solving and intellectual capacity rises or falls over the adult years.

Longitudinal studies of mental abilities indicate that some individuals decline rapidly in abilities over a short period of time, reflecting changes in health. If many such persons are included in a sample, the averages show gradual decline, when in fact the results are a mixture of two populations—those who are stable in their abilities and those who decline abruptly and seriously. In statistical terms, this means that changes in ability in later life are not randomly distributed, but that with age there is an increasingly skewed distribution of abilities. Several studies show that the likelihood of survival is related to mental test performance. The probability of survival is less in the persons showing drops in test performance. This seems reasonable, since performance on psychological tests is a result of complex activity in the nervous system. Such activity may be particularly sensitive to disturbances in blood flow to the brain, arteriosclerosis, and loss of cells in senile brain disease. A new field of research is being defined, that of behavioral measurements, which identifies persons who have latent or active somatic disease and which shows the relations of mental abilities to brain damage in later life.

Tests of mental ability have been criticized as being inappropriate for use with older adults because much of their content was developed for children and young adults. Intelligence tests for children are mostly used in school-like situations for the prediction of school success. With older adults, no such simple criterion can be agreed upon. Adult intelligence is difficult to define in general. It has meaning in a particular context, such as occupational training, vocational guidance, or medical diagnosis and therapy. Measurements of behavior will increasingly have to indicate the extent to which particular areas of the nervous system and the body are involved in a disease process. By contrast, a criterion of social effectiveness changes the emphasis of test content to reflect those abilities used in effective interpersonal relationships.

As progress is made in research on the analysis of logical problem-solving behavior of persons over a wide age range, it will be possible to specify the individual differences in the sequence between some problem input and the resulting solution, or behavioral output. These sequences will no doubt be found to differ with age between the healthy person of high initial ability and with good education and supporting environment and the individual with poor health, low initial ability, poor education, and an unsupporting environment. At present there are only intimations about the nature of these efforts.

References

Bayley, Nancy and Melita H. Oden. The maintenance of intellectual ability in gifted adults. *J. Geront.*, 1955, **10**, 91-107.

Bilash, I. and J. P. Zubek. The effects of age on factorially "pure" mental abilities. *J. Geront.*, 1960, **15**, 175-182.

Birren, J. E., J. Botwinick, A. D. Weiss, and D. F. Morrison. An analysis of mental and perceptual tests given to healthy elderly men. In J. E. Birren, R. N. Butler, S. W. Greenhouse, L. Sokoloff, and Marian R. Yarrow (eds.),

Human Aging. Washington, D.C.: Government Printing Office, 1963, Public Health Publication No. 986, pp. 143-156.

——— and D. F. Morrison. Analysis of the WAIS subtests in relation to age and education. *J. Geront.*, 1961, **16**, 363-369.

———, K. F. Riegel, and D. F. Morrison. Age differences in response speed as a function of controlled variations of stimulus conditions: evidence of a general speed factor. *Gerontologia*, 1962, **6**, 1-18.

——— and W. Spieth. Age, response speed, and cardiovascular functions. *J. Geront.*, 1962, **17**, 390-391.

Brinley, J. F. *Rigidity and the Control of Cognitive Sets in Relaton to Age Differences in Speed and Accuracy of Performance.* Ph.D. dissertation, Department of Psychology, Catholic University, Washington, D.C., 1963.

Bromley, D. B. Some experimental tests of the effect of age on creative intellectual output. *J. Geront.*, 1956, **11**, 74-82.

Chown, Sheila M. Age and the rigidities. *J. Geront.*, 1961, **16**, 353-362.

Clark, J. W. The aging dimension: a factorial analysis of individual differences with age on psychological and physiological measurements. *J. Geront.*, 1960, **15**, 183-187.

Conrad, H. S. General-information, intelligence, and the decline of intelligence. *J. Appl. Psychol.*, 1930, **14**, 592-599.

Falek, A., F. J. Kallmann, I. Lorge, and Lissy F. Jarvik. Longevity and intellectual variation in a senescent twin population. *J. Geront.*, 1960, **15**, 305-309.

Foulds, G. A. and J. C. Raven. Normal changes in the mental abilities of adults as age advances. *J. Ment. Sc.*, 1948, **94**, 133-142.

Friend, Celia M. and J. P. Zubek. The effects of age on critical thinking ability. *J. Geront.*, 1958, **13**, 407-413.

Jarvik, Lissy F., F. J. Kallmann, and A. Falek. Intellectual changes in aged twins. *J. Geront.*, 1960, **15**, 289-294.

Jerome, E. A. Decay of heuristic processes in the aged. In C. Tibbitts and Wilma Donahue (eds.), *Aging Around the World,* pp. 808-823. New York: Columbia University Press, 1962.

*Jones, H. E. Intelligence and problem-solving. In J. E. Birren (ed.), *Handbook of Aging and the Individual,* pp. 700-738. Chicago: University of Chicago Press, 1959.

Kleemeier, R. W., W. A. Justiss, A. Jones, and T. A. Rich. Intellectual changes in the senium. Unpublished manuscript, 1961.

Kurihara, H. (General intelligence test and its norm. I: Standardization of intelligence tests for children, adolescents and adults. II: Mental development of the Japanese.) *Rep. Inst. Sc. Labour, Japan,* 1934, **25**, 1-22.

Lehman, H. C. *Age and Achievement.* Princeton: Princeton University Press, 1953.

Mangan, G. L. Method-of-approach factors in the testing of middle-aged subjects. *J. Geront.*, 1958, **13**, 55-59.

Obrist, W. D., E. W. Busse, C. Eisdorfer, and R. W. Kleemeier. Relation of the electroencephalogram to intellectual function in senescence. *J. Geront.*, 1962, **17**, 197-206.

---

* Suggested additional reading.

Owens, W. A., Jr. Age and mental abilities: a longitudinal study. *Genetic Psychol. Monogr.*, 1953, **48**, 3-54.

Reed, H. B. C., Jr., and R. M. Reitan. The significance of age in the performance of a complex psychomotor task by brain-damaged and non-brain-damaged subjects. *J. Geront.*, 1962, **17**, 193-196.

Riegel, K. F. A study of verbal achievements of older persons. *J. Geront.*, 1959, **14**, 453-456.

────── and Ruth Riegel. A study on changes of attitudes and interests during later years of life. *Vita Humana*, 1960, **3**, 176-206.

Sanderson, R. E. and J. Inglis. Learning and mortality in elderly psychiatric patients. *J. Geront.*, 1961, **16**, 375-376.

Schaie, K. W. Rigidity-flexibility and intelligence: a cross-sectional study of the adult life span from 20 to 70 years. *Psychol. Monogr.*, 1958, **72**, 26 pages.

Spieth, W. Abnormally slow perceptual motor task performance in individuals with stable, mild to moderate heart disease. *Aerospace Med.*, 1962, **33**, 370 (Abstract).

Thaler, Margaret. Relationships among Wechsler, Weigl, Rorschach, EEG findings, and abstract-concrete behavior in a group of normal aged subjects. *J. Geront.*, 1956, **11**, 404-409.

Wallach, M. A. and N. Kogan. Aspects of judgment and decision making: interrelationships and changes with age. *Behavioral Sci.*, 1961, **6**, 23-36.

Welford, A. T. *Ageing and Human Skill.* London: Oxford University Press, 1958.

Wimer, R. E. Age differences in incidental and intentional learning. *J. Geront.*, 1960, **15**, 79-82.

9. Employment, Productivity, and Achievement

Like most issues in the psychology of aging, employment, productivity, and life achievement cannot be considered without regard to social and biological influences. The contemporary adult can expect to live much longer than he would have in previous generations. He thus spends more time in the labor force or in productive activities; however, he also spends more time out of the labor force. In 1900, he spent, on the average, thirty-two years in the labor force and sixteen years outside. By 1950, he spent forty-two years in the labor force and twenty-four outside. While the work life has increased by one third, the period of retirement has increased by one half. There are indications that in the coming years, the work life will not expand as much as will the period of retirement. This means that there is a greater economic burden on the worker, in that he has to accumulate more resources during his work life. This is especially true for the unskilled worker, who tends to drop out of the labor force early. As a result of longer retirement, an economic problem has been created for the United States, which has a relatively high proportion of older people compared with many other countries.

Although most persons over the age of sixty-five need employment to maintain their standard of living, and indeed more than half are physically capable of working, there is not much chance that the trend toward decreasing employment of older persons will be reversed. In 1900, 63 per cent of males sixty-five and over were in the labor force; by 1962 only 29 per cent were. If persons over the age of sixty-five were encouragd to remain in, or return to, the labor force, great pressure would be exerted on the young who are about to start their work life. Their delayed entrance would tend to create other kinds of social problems. While retirement is a good period for those with means, most older persons need the income from work to maintain their standard of living. Behind many negative attitudes toward retirement is a basic economic motive. Half of the married couples sixty-five and over have incomes of less than $2530 per year, and half of the older persons living alone have incomes less than $1055.

Leisure time can be productive in that the expressive arts are productive, yet retirement tends to be enforced leisure, since many, if not most, persons would rather still be working for income. The philosophy of work that is thought to dominate our society has at its root in middle age and later life not only habit, but also the preservation of a standard of living that is threatened by reduced income. Very likely, most middle-aged adults, when their grown children have left home, would not want to work continually to raise their standard of living. It is probable that they would rather shift to a higher proportion of leisure, including full retirement, providing income was not greatly reduced. Exceptions might be the self-employed or those salaried persons for whom work is the central social force in their pattern of living *(Friedmann and Havighurst, 1954)*. It is worth noting that most Federal Civil Servants do not wait until the compulsory retirement age. Possibly this reflects the willingness to shift to retirement if there is a pension that appears to provide the worker with sufficient income for his needs and wants.

Complicating the picture of employment of those over sixty-five is the role of education, since older persons tend to have less education. In general, the number of unemployed among those completing high school is double that of those completing college, and the same ratio holds between those completing elementary school and those completing high school. Probably only those of average or more education who leave the work force with a pension can be regarded as retired; the others are "out of work."

Productivity

Surveys made to determine the relative productivity of workers of different ages usually find that output remains rather stable through the mid-fifties, with a slight falling off thereafter (*U.S. Department of Labor, 1956, Clark, 1959*). Results vary somewhat with the type of job. Women office workers, for example, show little change in output over the employed span.

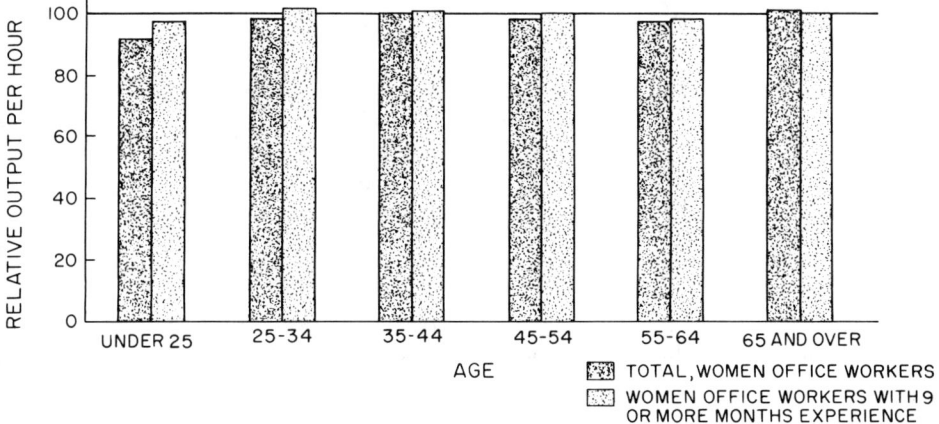

FIGURE 9-1. Relative output per man-hour of women office workers, by age group and experience on the job.
Source: USDL, Bureau of Labor Statistics, 1962.

In contrast to office workers, men and women in footwear and furniture plants show a tendency to decline in output over age fifty-five. However, even in these data, variations among individuals are large, with many older workers being superior to the average young worker.

The complications surrounding the data on productivity of workers with age limit their value in indicating the probable changes, if any, in work capacity. For one thing, there is an early turnover in employees as young workers try different jobs and as industries encourage those whom it wishes to hold for longer employment. Since the turnover rates vary with age, the population of employed men and women in successive age groups cannot be accurately described. Also, most working conditions are such that output is well within the limits of the individual's performance. A moderate fixed level of production is characteristic of most industries.

A number of factors other than capacity to work operate to make the older worker less likely to be re-employed. Older workers have seniority

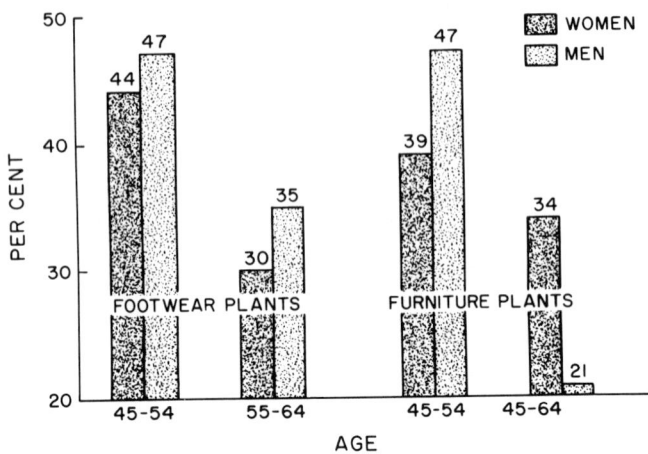

FIGURE 9-2. Percentage of workers aged forty-five and over with output per man-hour greater than the average for age group thirty-five to forty-four.

Source: Ibid.

and secure higher wages than the young. Also, older workers tend to be less interested in training for new types of jobs, and industries are less willing to train older workers because of the number of years needed to receive a return on the investment. Sometimes union agreements give the older worker security in his job, but once unemployed, the worker may find it difficult to get another job. Collectively, the influences operate to lead to a continuing increase in long-term unemployment as a function of age (Cottrell, 1960).

Not only does the worker age, but his job also tends to be age-graded and may also be a "dated" kind of job. Because of having specialized skills, older workers prefer to remain in their usual jobs. The industry that employs him may "age," with its products being sold to a particular age segment of society. Consumer habits tend to persist in the population, and specific items may be still used by older persons although rarely purchased by young consumers. In a period of rapid expansion, the older worker is at a disadvantage, for as industries create new divisions, they tend to employ younger persons to fill the new jobs, though not necessarily with intentional prejudice against the older worker. Consider, for example, the manufacture of pipe organs, in which older workers may have constructed only the more complicated wooden pipes. With the introduction of the electronic organ, younger workers tend to be employed to make them.

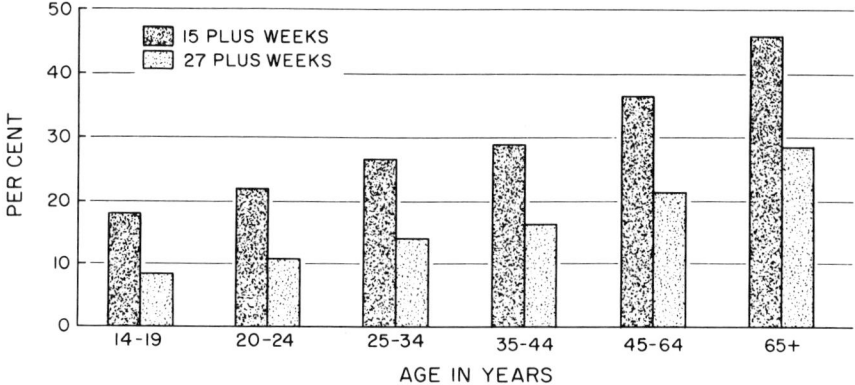

FIGURE 9-3. The rate of long term unemployment in relation to age. *Source: Ibid.*

As new industries develop, a generation is apt to elapse before significant numbers of men reach an age considered suitable for retirement. The airline industry, for example, which began as an industry around the early 1930's, employed young men as pilots. A twenty-five-year-old man employed as a pilot in 1930 would not reach the conventional age of retirement until 1970. Until recently, therefore, very little concern was expressed about age and retirement of airline pilots by either the pilots or the industry. An opposite pattern to the airline industry is seen with farmers; the decreasing number of farmers results in a much greater proportion of older farm owners, supervisors, and managers. The population shift from the farm to the city is a young man's, rather than an old man's, move.

Young members of the labor force change their place of residence and type of job for larger incomes. Young men tend to change jobs for the better, older men for the worse. The older worker, with less interest in changing jobs, will actually be less likely to initiate a move toward a more advantageous position. When under pressure to change, his respect will more likely suffer because of a downgrading in occupational group and income.

In certain data, employed men in selected industries between the ages of thirty and thirty-four showed stable employment of 42 per cent and upward mobility of employment of 33 per cent, with a downward mobility of 3 per cent; the balance of 22 per cent was fluctuating employment (*Gordon, 1960*). In contrast, workers in the age range of sixty to sixty-four showed 78 per cent stable employment, 10 per cent upward mobility, 6 per cent downward mobility, and 6 per cent fluctuating.

Employment rates indicate that single, widowed, divorced, or separated men have relatively low participation in the labor force. Tending to be outside the labor force, they are more likely to be socially isolated and to have lower incomes. Single persons of both sexes appear to have a greater opportunity for the accumulation of consequences of independent and correlated unfortunate environmental influences and comprise a group of high social cost.

Age, Sex, and Employment

A striking change in employment pattern has been shown by women in recent years. The proportion of women in the labor force drops after the middle twenties, presumably because of responsibility for young children at home. It then rises to a second peak after the age of forty-five. When the married woman re-enters the labor market at age forty-five, her attitudes are quite different from those of her single peers and of married men. Her employment, while of considerable value to her, probably does not have the overriding importance that it has to the man who is the major wage earner for a family. She thus appears as a stable, mature worker without drive to achieve higher job grades. These psychological qualities of the middle-aged married woman are being recognized by industry and government. The married woman seeking employment after age forty-five is perhaps in a more favored position than is the man whose skills are probably more specialized and whose employment is often the major feature of his life pattern.

Women tend to stop working somewhat earlier than men. In the age range over sixty-five, between 30 and 40 per cent of the single women are in the labor force, compared with between 5 and 10 per cent of the married women. For the same age range, about a third of all men are in the labor force. The percentage of working women in both the middle and young age groups has tended to increase since 1900 and to remain relatively constant in the sixty-five and over group, fluctuating between about 6 and 9 per cent.

Availability of Social Security benefits may keep older men out of the job market after they have become frustrated by failing to secure employment; i.e., the tendency to provide small pension benefits, coupled with the pressure of new industrial methods, probably results in the trend to decreasing participation in the labor force by men past age sixty-five. The ratio of workers to nonworkers over sixty-five will probably continue to diminish. The same forces that have contributed to the decline of employment of older men have, if anything, increased in recent years and have been augmented by the consequences of automation.

Particularly for a man, the period following retirement represents a time of considerable readjustment. However, once they have adjusted to the retired state, it is apparent that relatively few workers are interested in returning to full-time or even to part-time employment. Sampling of attitudes toward work in the period just before or after retirement will yield different results than will a sample of attitudes and feelings about retirement taken two years later.

One of the distinguishing characteristics of American culture has been its emphasis on upward striving and economic gain through individual effort. The younger worker has traditionally felt that through his own efforts he could rise significantly in economic class and upgraded occupation. This pioneering emphasis on gain through individual effort and striving has been important, and, coupled with good natural resources, has produced a most highly technically developed society. Implicit, almost to the point of an ethical principle, is the conviction that there is an inherent moral value in paid employment. It is not surprising, therefore, that the older worker may feel a considerable loss of meaning in his life when he is separated from his employment, even if he has an adequate pension. An emphasis that is desirable for the young worker and for society as a whole is not to the advantage of the older man, since it is difficult for him to accept time-filling activities other than paid employment as being important and meaningful. As the number of retired older workers becomes greater and as retirement income levels become more adequate, there will undoubtedly be a shift toward the acceptance of nonpaid activity as being meaningful and productive.

The Uses of Time. A definition of "work" has always been a puzzling matter, since individuals often expend more energy in leisure-time activities than in their occupations or "work." In the past centuries, work generally implied sustained high-level muscular activity because of obligation or for financial gain. Work, then, was directly productive, in contrast to leisure activity, which was unproductive because it was individually determined rather than deemed necessary by society. Since modern machinery and labor-saving devices have relieved man of most physical work, the distinction between work and nonwork activities is less clear. For example, is the man who engages in oil painting during his leisure—i.e., nonpaid—time not working? Furthermore, does this time become productive only if someone buys the painting? If so, productive activity would thus be something that an individual does for which another is willing to pay. However, one is reminded that the activities of college students are very intense and yet the students are not reimbursed. Studying is desired by society and results in higher economic gain for the individual after graduation. The frequent use of scholarships implies that many students are in truth employed by society to study. It is becoming more important to have men and women over the employed age ranges spend a large proportion of their reimbursed time in continued study. These considerations lead to the point of view that in a modern society terms like "work" and "leisure" are less useful than they once were in describing the uses of time.

Man, because of the rather fixed upper limit of his life span, has finite capacities for achievement. For example, he can be expected to read only a limited number of books during his lifetime. In the present context, the basic questions are: How do people of different ages use their time over the life span and how is achievement measured? Leisure-time activities in the aged have been examined in great detail (*Kleemeier, et al., 1961*). It appears that in a complex society, the concept of "productive activities" will have to be considerably broadened. Many activities that have been regarded as beneficial only to individuals doing them and so thought of as leisure-time activities will in the future be brought into the scope of productive activities benefiting society as a whole.

In a period of shifting meanings of work, the measurement of achievement over the life span is problematic. Some activities, like research, would generally be accepted as being productive, and perhaps for these, achievements in relation to age should be discussed.

Scientific Productivity and Achievement

Francis Galton was a well-to-do Englishman who became interested in the psychology of development and aging during the 1870's. His research was carried on as a leisure-time activity in the sense that he paid for it out of his own fortune and did not expect economic gain from it. His collection of psychological and anthropological data led him into statistical interests and to the development of the first index of correlation, or association, between two variables. When he died, he left his money to establish the first professorship of statistics in Great Britain. A modern society could not function without statistics, and thousands of people are employed and paid for their time in statistical jobs. What began as one man's leisure-time activity has become a highly salaried profession in contemporary society. Thus it is obvious that the terms "work" and "leisure" are not sufficiently descriptive. In retrospect, Galton was engaged in a form of productive activity. Furthermore, since his day, research itself has come to be a salaried activity widely accepted as productive. In the past century, however, research was a matter of personal interest and was conducted as a hobby. The modern researcher does very little "work" in the sense of the expenditure of energy, and yet the results of his activity increase the productivity of society.

The evolution of the activities of modern man appears to be accomplished by a language lag, in which words and folkways are associated with the period when man indeed supplied much of the energy in society. Now man contributes less than 1 per cent of the energy required in America. If it was by the sweat of his brow that man previously made his way in the world, modern man has a sweaty brow because of the thought that must go into expanding his competence and productivity. Productivity may be defined as the process of providing larger amounts and choices of goods available to consumers, an enlarged variety of personal services, an enlarged body of knowledge and information, and, finally, an enlarged amount of free-time or individually programed activities. It is worthwhile to repeat that while research and scholarship began as leisure-time activities and efforts on the part of individuals to enlarge their own knowledge and development, research is now a highly salaried activity. If education, training, and self-development generally result in an expanded productivity of society, perhaps all education beyond elementary school will come to be placed on a salaried basis.

Since research and scientific activities have so recently become salaried, researchers in previous generations may have entered them under a different complex of personal motivations than do present-day scientists, who are highly encouraged by current society. Keeping in mind the changing motivations of society and their influence on scientists, the curves showing the changes in scientific accomplishments and contributions as a function of age are instructive. An exhaustive survey has been made of the quality and quantity of creative output of scholars and researchers in relation to age (*Lehman, 1953*). By scanning biographies, publications of scientific and scholarly societies, and other library sources, Lehman described quantitatively the relationship between chronological age and outstanding achievements. Figure 9-4 shows the relationship between chronological age and the occurrence of chemical discoveries. Several observations may be made about such curves. The age at which most outstanding contributions are made occurs early in the professional life of individuals. For chemists, the most distinguished discoveries tend to be made around age thirty. However, as stated earlier, outstanding contributions are made throughout the life span, and for any one individual, the greatest discovery could well be made after the age of sixty or sixty-five. Thus there is both a general trend and also a wide range of individual differences. Since not all individuals live the same length of time, some obviously have their careers interrupted. Figure 9-5 shows a line that would reflect contributions by chemists if they had all lived to age eighty. In these curves, the five-year interval in which the most contributions were made was accepted as 100 per cent. The contributions made in other five-year intervals are then expressed as a percentage of the five-year interval of maximum contribution. Thus chemists at age sixty made about one fifth of the contributions that chemists made at age thirty to thirty-five.

In medicine, discoveries are made somewhat later and extend over a much wider portion of the life span. Figure 9-6 shows the relationship between medical discoveries and chronological age.

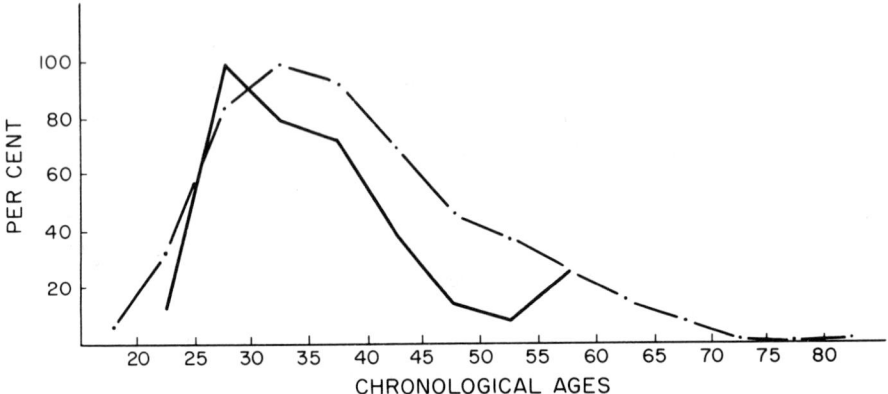

FIGURE 9-4. Age and production in chemistry. Solid line: 52 of the greatest discoveries by 46 chemists now deceased. Broken line: 993 contributions of lesser average merit by 966 chemists now deceased.

Source: H. C. Lehman. *Age and Achievement* (Princeton: Princeton University Press, 1953).

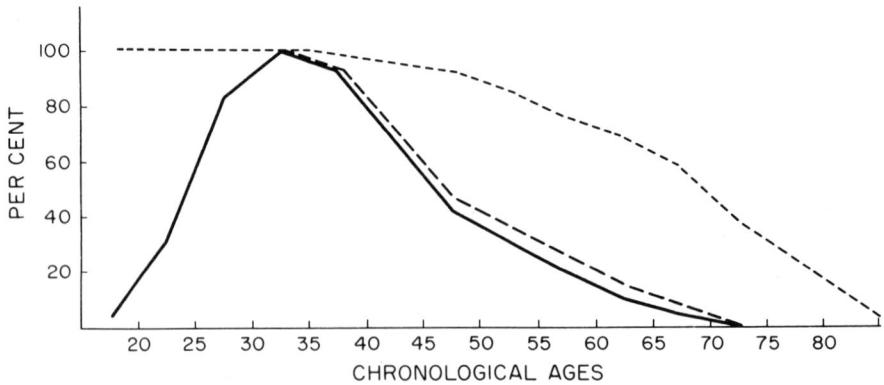

FIGURE 9-5. Age and contributions by chemists. Solid line: 993 significant contributions by 244 chemists. Broken line: hypothetical output if each chemist had lived to 80. Dotted line: percentage of the original number of chemists still alive at successive age intervals.

Source: Ibid.

Since the practice of medicine entails social responsibility, individuals must be qualified before they can practice and be in a position to make significant discoveries. Chemists, being able to start on their careers

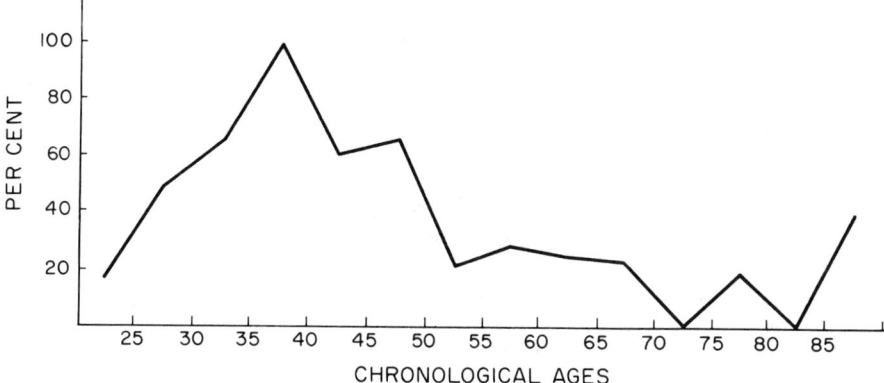

FIGURE 9-6. Medical discoveries and inventions in relation to age. Data for 139 individuals who made 188 medical discoveries and inventions.
Source: Ibid.

earlier, are able to make contributions earlier. There is also an influence of the degree of integration or articulation of the information available in a field. Some vocations require a mastery of a great array of incidental information and experience that is not necessarily integrated into a tight conceptual system. Thus a specialty within mathematics can be mastered relatively early by an individual of high capacity. Philosophy, on the other hand, consists of many more disparate elements of experience; hence one finds that philosophers make their contributions somewhat later in life. Figure 9-7 shows the relationships between quality and quantity of output in philosophy.

In comparison with the sciences, it might be expected that the skills necessary to begin creative productions in music and other arts are achieved earlier in life. The musician may begin his training very young, so that his contribution may be noted early. It is necessary, however, to distinguish between skilled performances of exceptional quality and creative musical composition, such as symphonies or operas. Musicians tend to be somewhat younger when they write instrumental music and vocal solos than when they write symphonies, chamber music, and operas. While the best-respected and -loved works of music tend to be produced in the earlier parts of careers, musical productivity continues over much

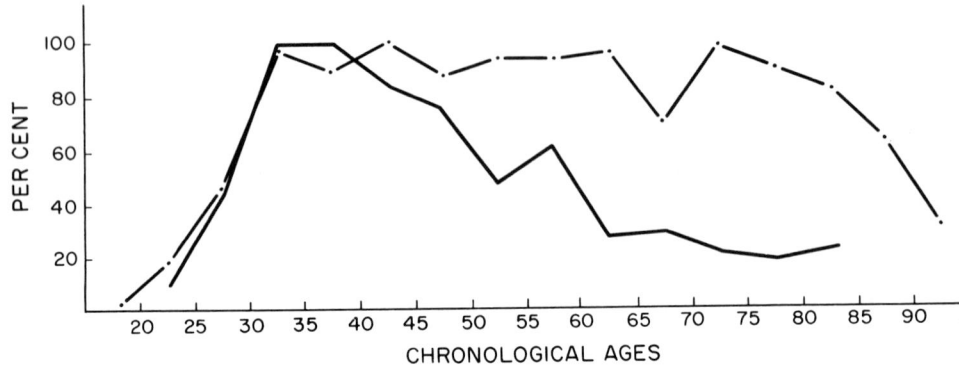

FIGURE 9-7. Philosophical output, quality and quantity, in relation to age. Solid line: the one best treatise (as determined by consensus) by each of 182 deceased philosophers. Broken line: the ages at which these same 182 men first published 1,593 other books, an average of 8.75 books per man.

Source: Ibid.

of the life span. Figure 9-8 shows the production of orchestral works in relation to age, both with respect to contemporary writing and to very superior orchestral works of the past. It is interesting that musical composition may have a late middle-age peak; i.e., for many composers, the most prolific period occurs in the fifties. This does not mean, however, that the peak of their efforts, in terms of quality or recognition, does not occur much earlier in life. While creative productivity is a highly personal matter, it is also obvious that there are general trends to artistic careers, for there is a greater likelihood that recognized production of high quality will come between the ages of thirty and forty than at other periods in the life span. A somewhat similar trend is seen in the graphic arts. Figure 9-9 shows the most recognized painting by individual artists in relation to age. In art, as in music, men may remain prolific throughout their life span, although there is a greater probability that their most widely recognized works will be produced during their thirties.

A somewhat similar trend is seen for literature. Yet literature, even more than painting, continues at a high level of output for much of the life span. For most types of writing, around age thirty is the time when an author's best works will be written. It occurs a few years earlier for poets and a few years later, in the thirties, for writers of religious prose. The composite curves of Figure 9-10 illustrate the age trends for miscellaneous literary works.

Employment, Productivity, and Achievement 211

Of considerable significance is that of all the highly developed intellectual skills, the production of literary works continues to show greatest productivity late in life. Compared with other fields, a surpris-

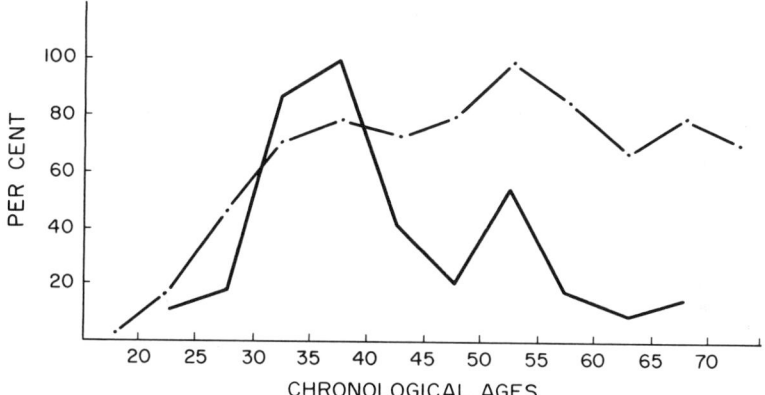

FIGURE 9-8. Orchestral works in relation to age. Solid line: 53 very superior orchestral works which have survived the test of time. Broken line: 510 contemporary orchestral works written by Americans between 1912 and 1932.
Source: Ibid.

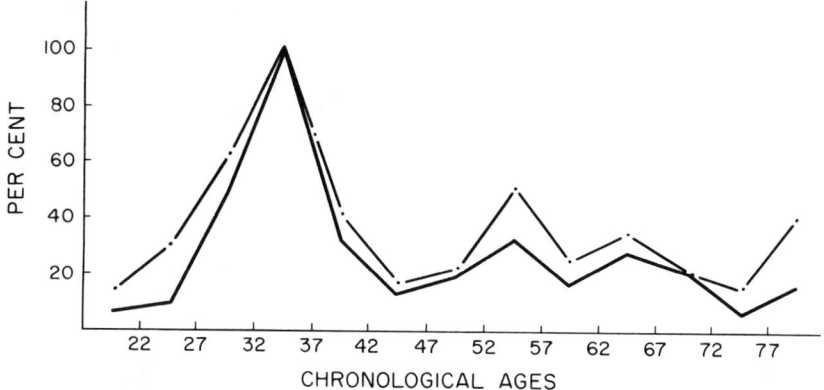

FIGURE 9-9. Age and the one best painting by 61 artists each of whom lived to be 70 or more. Solid line: each painting counted only once. Broken line: each painting counted as many times as it appeared in a composite list.
Source: Ibid.

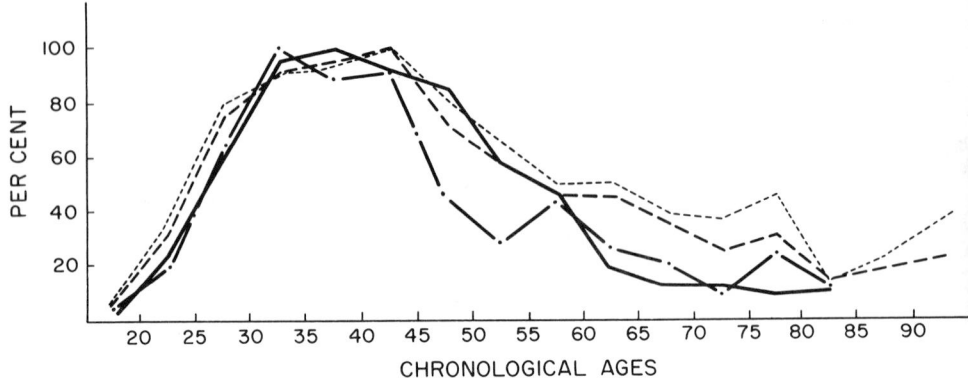

FIGURE 9-10. Age and the production of miscellaneous literary works. Solid line: 843 works by 330 American authors. Broken line: 461 works by 152 German authors. Dash line: 376 works by 149 French authors. Dotted line: 2,250 works by 543 British authors.

Source: Ibid.

ingly high level of literary productivity is maintained after the age of sixty-five—and even after age eighty. Poetry, for example, may decline only by about 50 per cent in productivity between the age of peak, around thirty, and late life. Together with motivation, this undoubtedly reflects the data previously discussed concerning mental ability. Granted good health and opportunity, vocabulary continues to expand throughout the life span. Thus the literary worker continually has more experience and skill available for his productions. If one were going to select a career for late life, a literary career would seem to be an ideal choice.

Since women did not enter the sciences in appreciable numbers until relatively recently, it is difficult to assemble data on the relations of age and scientific and other kinds of intellectual productivity for women. Lehman has noted that he found it difficult to assemble separate age data for women. For example, many biographical sources fail to list the ages of women; i.e., their birth dates and, as a result, the age at which various contributions were made. It will thus be some time before the creative years of women can be compared with those of men.

Athletic Achievements. As in the arts and sciences, the age at which distinguished achievement is made in athletics varies with the type of sport. Surprisingly, physical endurance is not as much a limiting factor as are speed and timing. Endurance runners are frequently in their late forties, or even older, whereas championship boxers are usually much younger. Boxing apparently requires a combination of accurate and rapid perceptions, ability to change expectancies or set rapidly, and strong, rapid, and coordinated movements. Unlike boxing, in which the boxer must respond suddenly to unexpected moves on the part of his opponent, the golfer may get himself set for a shot with considerable preparation. Thus sports in which the performance allows for the maximization of experience, rather than depending heavily on sudden activity, change more slowly over the adult years. Tennis, baseball, and boxing tend to be early peak performance sports, whereas golf, billiards, and bowling tend to be later developing sports. The difference between the ages of peak proficiency between the two extremes is about ten years, ranging roughly between ages twenty-five and thirty-five. The comparison between productivity in

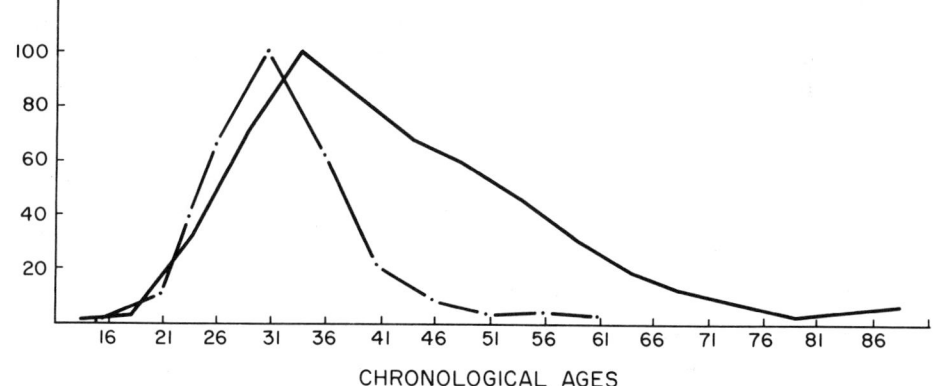

FIGURE 9-11. Age and scientific output compared with age and proficiency in vigorous skills. Solid line: superior contributions in various scientific fields. Broken line: championships in 17 classes of vigorous sports.

Source: Ibid.

science and sports is most interesting. The one feature that stands out above all else is the fact that the age at peak performance is nearly the same for sports and for scientific output. Figure 9-11 shows this comparison. By age forty-five, peak proficiency in sports declines to a level that is not reached until about seventy in scientific achievement. Perhaps the curves for peak productivity would be more nearly the same if there were no time lag in the recognition of a scientist's output. A scientist must not only prepare and complete his work, he must also write it for publication. Thus the time that his work is recognized may be two to three years after the creative activity which originally went into the accomplishment.

Age and Income. One estimation of the productivity of individuals is in terms of their average income. Average income trails the ages previously described for peak output in terms of creativity or skills. The average man's income is likely to reach a peak around age forty, although the peak of total family income is somewhat later, perhaps as late as age fifty-five. Using only the data on income of unrelated individuals, peak income is reached around age thirty, which, in a general way, is the most likely age of peak productivity for many activities. Income can trail by quite a few years the accomplishments of individuals. One result of this disparity between age at peak income and age at peak productivity, as well as age at greatest family responsibilities, is that it puts the greatest strain on the young family unit. The male, at about age thirty, is very likely to be at his peak period of productivity and at a relatively peak period of family responsibilities and financial needs. His income will, however, not reach its peak for ten years or more. This phase difference in reward for effort must play an important function in the motivations of middle-aged employed persons, since psychologically the effects of a reward are related to the time interval between the activity and the reward. It is of interest that, unlike income for men, women's income shows little or no evening out in middle age. Occupationally, of course, the male tends to be more specialized and therefore, if displaced from his job, he has less likelihood of re-employment, whereas the middle-aged woman at the low- to middle-income level tends to be a more general employee.

Individuals in the older group who are in positions of control and power in society must guard against making decisions that unnecessarily delay the period when young men and women can enter into full career responsibilities. Of course there is no doubt that the ever-increasing amount of knowledge and skills required results in individuals' being delayed in achieving peak income and responsibility. Regulating the attainment of "journeyman status" in order to insure public protection is necessary; however, adding time-consuming educational or experience requirements that do not enhance proficiency is a waste of talent. Attention should be given to moving downward the age of full responsibility, perhaps to somewhere between the ages of twenty-five and thirty in the professions. Attention should also be given to the continuing role differentiation of the older men and women. Unless there is an opportunity for continuing growth from worker to supervisor to manager to adviser and counsellor, the older adults will be reluctant to relinquish responsibilities to youth. Psychologically, therefore, attention must be given to the development of employed roles throughout adult life.

Values, Employment, and Leisure. In America, religion generally emphasizes work as a desirable spiritual value. In a discussion of the impact on values of the changing patterns of employment and free time, it has

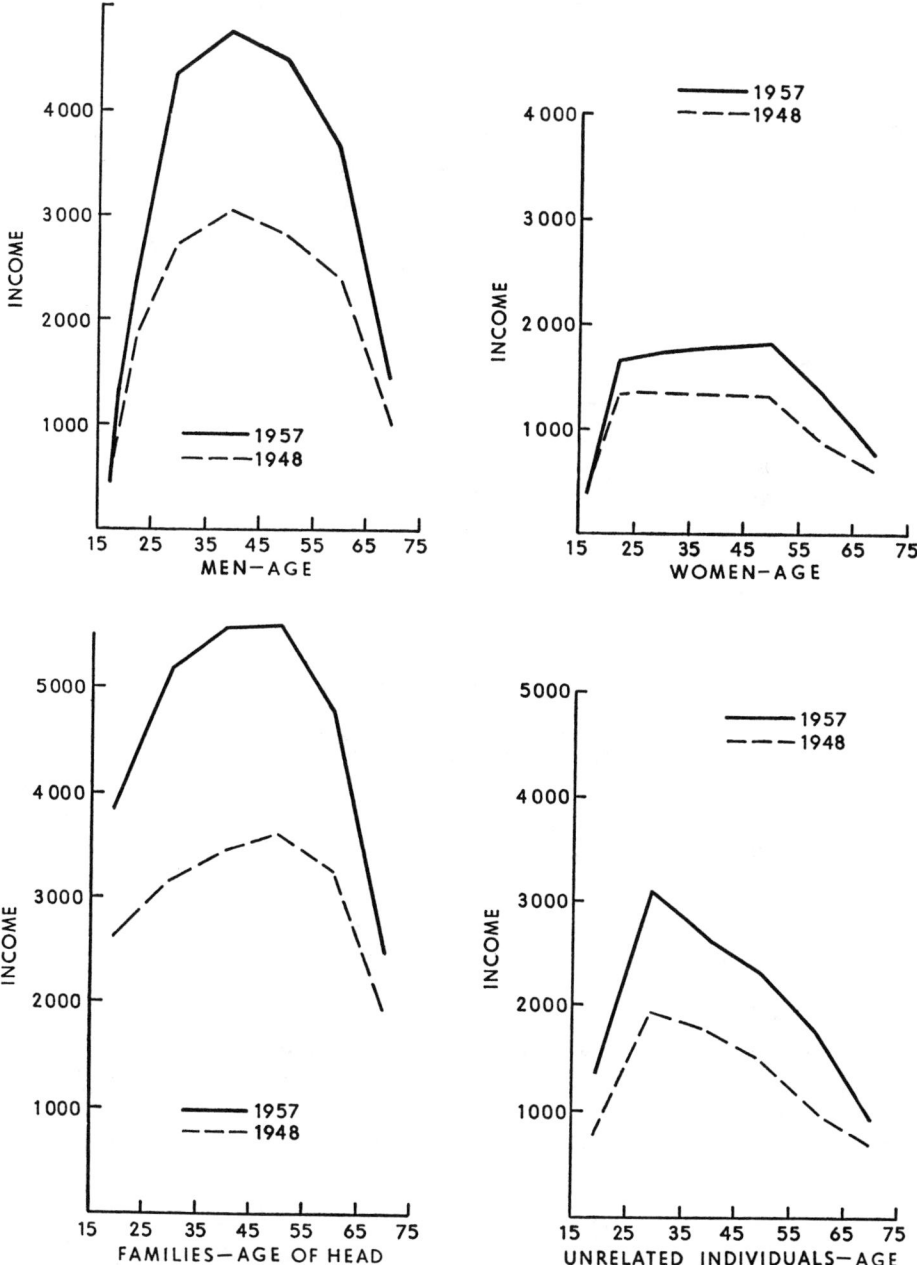

FIGURE 9-12. Median income by age: for men and women with income, families, and unrelated individuals, United States, 1948 and 1957.

Source: Margaret S. Gordon. Aging and income security. In C. Tibbitts (ed.), *Handbook of Aging and the Individual* (Chicago: University of Chicago Press, 1960), p. 212.

been pointed out that "the average middle-class home in America has in it enough vacuum cleaners, waffle irons, air cleaners, dishwashers, clothes scrubbers, and other gadgets to equal the energy of ninety male servants" (*Kaplan, 1960, p. 295*). Some part of the free time from household tasks goes into television viewing. Generally, our cultural values do not regard television viewing as being as good a use of time as "work" or as other forms of recreation, because it is "too passive." An average of sixteen hours of television viewing per week is possible because of lightened household chores and of a shortened work week for wage earners. Figure 9-13 shows the hours free each day after necessary requirements are met.

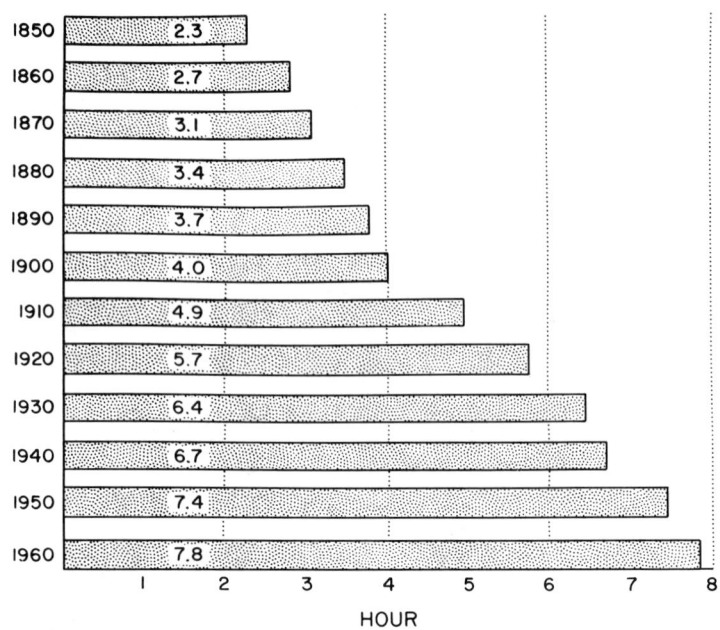

FIGURE 9-13. Hours free after work, eating, and necessities, 1850-1960. Projected on a six-day work week. Includes seven hours sleep, one hour eating, two hours miscellaneous.

Source: M. Kaplan. *Leisure in America* (New York: John Wiley & Sons, Inc., 1960).

It can be seen from this figure that the number of free hours has nearly doubled since 1900. Such a large addition of free time brings with it some uncertainty about social roles and where the time should be invested. Previous centuries might have placed great emphasis on prayer and contemplation during a considerable portion of this additional time. More recently, however, the emphasis has been on individual development through study and creative and expressive activities. It is through an individual's choices of leisure-time activities that he most clearly expresses his personality and what he wishes to "stand for" in his own eyes and in the eyes of society. With a strong achievement drive, the individual probably conceives of leisure time as something to be "used." An individual with a more passive or responding outlook toward life will "pass" time by exposing himself to stimulation, but not without necessarily feeling a necessity to force a pattern upon it. In current society, it is possible to settle quite early the implicit or explicit contractual relations of adult life; i.e., the number of hours to be given to work, to family responsibilities, to the church, and to the community. Those remaining hours of uncommitted time may be devoted to activities determined by internal needs and values.

The aged, as well as the young, are involved in an important change in society, a change that is of interest not only to the social and biological scientists, but also to the clergy, philosophers, and political leaders, who are especially concerned with questions of social and personal values. Perhaps in the future, adults will not feel worthless if they are not full-time employees. Younger persons will probably acquire values that look upon leisure activities as being as potentially productive as "on-line" production.

Along with the decline in the number of agricultural and unskilled industrial workers in recent years, there has been an increase in the number of white collar and professional persons. As machines continue to take over more of the labor of society, it may be expected that many more individuals will be rendering personal services of a semi-professional and professional nature. There will be, therefore, a great increase per capita in the number of educators, psychologists, social scientists, and many other types of specialists who will be knowledgeable about the structuring of time and activities in a complex society.

Continuing Productivity in the Aged. Consideration of such distinguished elderly persons who remain highly effective very late in life as Winston Churchill, Oliver Wendell Holmes, Jr., Charles de Gaulle, Konrad Adenauer, Somerset Maugham, and others leads to the question of whether such lives should be thought of as ideal, but rarely achieved, models, or as the common expectation. Survival to age eighty is, of course, itself a sort of accomplishment. In America, approximately 10 per cent of the population is over the age of sixty-five. While it is true that the population is still expanding and that the absolute number of elderly individuals will increase, a relatively "old" country may have 12 per cent of its people over the age of sixty-five. Perhaps 17 to 20 per cent of the population born today may be expected to reach the age of eighty. From results of a study of healthy elderly men at the National Institute of Mental Health, it may be inferred that many, or most, people who undergo degradation of behavior with advancing age do so because of disease and social deprivation rather than because such behavior is a pattern of normal senescence (*Birren* et al., *1963*). Given good physical health and an environment that contains physical and psychological supports for the individual and opportunities for psychological involvement, the now relatively rare example would become the average.

An analogy has been drawn between the older and the younger individual in terms of the great significance of the immediate physical and social environments. Healthy men who had undergone environmental losses tended to show poor performances on cognitive and psychomotor tests (*Birren* et al., *1963*). Thus the current life circumstances of the older individual are regarded as being of considerable significance in governing the individual's affective state and his "social productivity" in the sense of adequate interpersonal relationships. What seems to happen is that a downward spiral, initiated by reduced capacity because of disease, renders the individual less capable of coping with environmental losses, leading to depressive trends and then to a further reduction in the capacity of the individual to maintain adequate interpersonal relations. Thus at each stage in a degradative spiral, enviromental losses, disease, and physiological status, as well as the integrity of the nervous system, play roles as dependent and independent factors. This does not mean, however, that the spiral may not be arrested or slowed with intervention.

Individuals always tend to emphasize the consequences of their unique life experiences and the habitual attitudes in their reactive patterns. A finding that seems to be emerging from studies of the aged, however, is a greater dependence of the individual's functioning upon his current life circumstances than was previously realized. While the nervous system apparently does undergo a pattern of senescent changes found in very aged persons, the integrity of the nervous system may respond to chronic environmental influences. There are differences in the environments of older persons that affect their tendency to promote and maintain effective involvement and behavior, which in turn increases their resistance to deteriorative attitudes and behaviors typified as "senile." While there may be constellations of positive factors occurring by chance alone (good health, favorable environment, good habits), habitual patterns of adaptation are also relevant; i.e., the effective use of insight and the adoption of an information-seeking and active role rather than a passive, submissive one would appear to be more likely to lead to compensations for social losses that commonly occur with advancing age. What the results of research seem to show is that effective behavior in the aged is much more a consequence of interactions between social, sociological, and physiological factors than was previously realized.

A side effect of increased machine control over production is a reduction in the physical activity of contemporary adults. The optimum level of physical activity probably varies for individuals, but there are indications from research that good health is sustained by some amount of exercise. At present it cannot be said with confidence what the optimum level or form of the physical or cognitive load should be to maintain adults at or near their peak of mental and physical well-being.

Summary

As the average life span of modern man has increased, the amount of time outside of the labor force has increased more than the amount of time in it. The length of time before entering employment has lengthened, but more dramatic has been the doubling of the length of retirement. This creates a special problem for the individual, for he must provide sufficient income during the work life to provide for the lengthening phase of retirement. With low incomes after retirement, the standard of living drops; thus the need for income to meet needs and maintain previous activities is a primary concern for most older persons. It is not likely that there will be a reversal of the trend toward decreasing employment of older persons, since their employment would in many instances necessitate competition for jobs with young adults.

In periods of high technological change, older persons and those with low education tend to be dropped from employment. Industrial trends are such that education and continuing training through the employed life are becoming characteristic. The distinction between working and training is less distinct than it once was. Previously, the worker trained before entering the labor market; now, as industrial processes are modified, there is continuing on-the-job training. Older workers tend to have skills most out-of-date with industry in general (obsolescence of skills). The unemployment is thus more technological in its basis than lack of worker capacity. Redundancy or antiquation of skills should not be interpreted as lack of physical and mental capacities, which over the usual work life do not change markedly except in persons suffering from disease.

Although society has not solved the economic problems of maintaining an adequate standard of living for retired persons, it is clear that the period of retirement is increasing. Because of the work orientation of society, the transition to free-time activities is not easy for individuals. Along with the expansion of leisure-time activities there goes a need for a reorientation in attitudes toward the uses of time; the meaningful use of time in retirement can be a major problem of personal values.

The effects on career patterns of the high value placed by contemporary society on scientific research is not known. Past generations of scientists and scholars tended to show peak productivity during their thirties. Major contributions to mathematics, chemistry, and physics tend to come earlier in life than those in medicine and philosophy. While sustained productivity occurs in most learned fields over the life span, the most notable works appear to be produced by individuals in their thirties. Not much is known about scientific and artistic achievement in women, since few women entered these fields until recently and women often do not indicate their ages in their biographies.

Athletic achievements tend to peak only slightly earlier than achievements in the arts and sciences, but they decline more rapidly. Thus top-level achievement in sports declines by age forty-five to a level not reached until age seventy in the sciences. There seems some basis for accepting the general view that physical capacities develop and decline earliest, while psychological capacities develop later and permit high-level achievements over most of the usual employed life span. Social skills mature latest and, in individuals in good health and in a favorable environment, are maintained at a high level throughout the life span.

Total family income is at peak in the mid-fifties, suggesting that income trails somewhat the age of maximum productivity and also the age of maximum need. What effects the current emphasis on education and research will have on productive careers and life achievement is not apparent. Working for income, recognition, achievement, and the more subtle motive of understanding are probably differently affected by age and social climate. A change in the social climate is giving increasing emphasis to maximum self-development, particularly through education, in contrast to the older ethic of work, which held that it was more moral to work hard than to study hard. Because of conflicts with earlier formed attitudes, older adults necessarily show some lag in responding to evolving attitudes toward education, work, and the uses of free time.

References

Birren, J. E., R. N. Butler, S. W. Greenhouse, L. Sokoloff, and Marian R. Yarrow (eds.), *Human Aging*. Washington, D.C.: Government Printing Office, 1963, Public Health Publication No. 986.

Clark, S. D. The employability of the older worker. Ottawa, Canada: Economics and Research Branch, Department of Labor, 1959.

*Cottrell, F. The technological and societal basis of aging. In C. Tibbitts (ed.), *Handbook of Social Gerontology*, pp. 92-119. Chicago: University of Chicago Press, 1960.

Friedmann, E. A. and R. J. Havighurst. *The Meaning of Work and Retirement*. Chicago: University of Chicago Press, 1954.

---

* Suggested additional reading.

Gordon, Margaret S. Aging and income security. In Tibbitts (ed.), *op. cit.*, pp. 208-260.

Kaplan, M. *Leisure in America.* New York: John Wiley & Sons, Inc., 1960.

*Kleemeier, R. W. (ed.) *Aging and Leisure.* London: Oxford University Press, 1961.

*Lehman, H. C. *Age and Achievement.* Princeton: Princeton University Press, 1953.

U.S. Department of Labor. *Job Performance and Age: A Study of Measurement.* Washington, D.C.: Government Printing Office, Bureau of Labor Statistics, 1956, Bull. No. 1203.

10. Personality and Aging

Probably no topic in the psychology of adult life and aging can arouse as much interest as that of personality. The word "personality" carries connotations of the most personal and unique qualities of the individual. Perhaps because it has such powerful connotations, it is difficult to describe what the term means or to define it rigorously. It is probably impossible to state any definition of personality that all serious students of the subject would accept (*Hall and Lindzey, 1958*). A working definition of personality with reference to aging is that it is "the characteristic way in which an individual responds to the events of adult life." The kinds of choices he makes and his characteristic behavior in making choices and in relating to other people would be included in this definition. It also implies that if we know an individual's present style of responding, we can predict what he is likely to do in some future situation. There are two broad categories of responses that the individual makes, an inner, or covert, response and an outer, or overt, response. Inner responses consist of the ways in which we see ourselves, other people, and events; our thoughts and associations about them; and the meanings we read into them. We also respond in terms of moods. Our perceptions and motivations may lead to actions controlled in a way typical of us. Our overt, actions involve other people; e.g., whether we characteristically move toward or away from others. Among other traits, whether we are friendly and interested in other persons or are suspicious and withdrawing, whether we are disposed to action or passivity, characterize our styles of responding and acting and are elements of our personality.

The objects and processes that individuals desire and seek and those that are disliked and avoided are thought to fall into patterns. If it would be possible to have a comprehensive sample of what an individual does with his time—the type, frequency, and duration of his activities—it would be possible to compare him with others, grouping him with those most similar and contrasting him with those most dissimilar. This would lead to attempts to describe the underlying reasons for, or the origins of, the differences and similarities.

Personality Types. The essential element in personality theories is that there are certain nuclear themes in the organization of the individual's responses, which, if discerned, lend themselves to future predictions of responses. If one knows what type of personality an individual has, presumably one can understand him better. That is, once a personality style or type is discerned in the individual, generalizations can be made about his probable behavior in a broad range of situations. In order to be useful, a personality type should not be descriptive of all people, but only of some limited subset of the population.

Personality is thus regarded as the intervening variable between the events of adult life and the behavior of the individual. If there are relatively enduring individual patterns of behavior characteristics, these should lead to predictions about the way the individuals will adapt or adjust to the major events of adult life. One important reservation must be made, and that is: The existence of mutually exclusive adult personality types is relative to the kinds of measurements used.

How many adult personality types there are—and even the question of whether or not there are types—depends upon the concepts and measurements employed. It is true, of course, that most investigators of personality using a particular type of observation—e.g., handwriting, ink blots, spontaneous speech, expressive body movements, or physiological arousal—expect that their measurements are related to major themes or principles of organization of a much broader scope of behavior. The validity of each such measurement as a predictor or explanatory key to what are thought to be significant areas of behavior has to be established.

One review cautions that we are not fully justified in speaking of "personality types" of aging adults (*Riegel, 1959*). With reservation, however, the term "personality type" can be used here to mean large segments of behavioral characteristics that seem to distinguish individuals and that lead to useful discourse and predictions. One way of studying the subject of personality and aging is to analyze the way in which individuals characteristically react to critical events in adult life as financial crises, the home leaving and marriage of children, occupational changes, death of close associates, and so on.

Theoretical Issues. Personality may in part be described in terms of the characteristic motives of an individual. That is to say, personality is a term that stands for the controls over the characteristic directions of an individual's behavior. The traditional view of motivational states was that the organism had needs, which if not fulfilled, produced tension states. Thus, as hunger or thirst increased, the internal tension state rose and the individual was directed in his behavior to a goal that yielded tension reduction. Anxiety was also considered a tension state to be avoided or reduced. The modes of behavior that the individual displayed in anxiety reduction to a large extent consisted of his personality.

Recent research has indicated that there are both excitatory and inhibitory systems of control over lower brain centers involved in the initiation of patterns of behavior. Animals with minute electrodes implanted in selected areas of the brain will press a lever to secure a small electric shock. They will do this for long periods, implying that drive reduction *per se* is not the goal of many behaviors. Electrodes planted in other brain centers will produce avoidance motivation, whereby the animals will actively seek to avoid the electric shock. Thus at a very basic level of the nervous system, it is necessary to consider that behavior has a dual form of control; inhibition and facilitation, approach and avoidance.

Play is an obvious example of the fact that the organism under many conditions is stimulation seeking as well as stimulation avoiding. Kittens, puppies, and children engage in a large amount of spontaneous activity, or activity that is stimulation seeking. They initiate action when comfortably fed and in good health. In fact, if a child or young animal does not engage in much spontaneous activity, he is regarded as being ill. To some extent, this is also true for adults; i.e., the healthy adult whose somatic and visceral drives are relatively well met should also be expected to show stimulation-seeking behavior. The child has an omnivorous appetite for stimulation and is constantly creating games so that he can act and react. Less commonly thought of in these terms are adult games. Cards and other games that adults create follow implicit principles which reflect human stimulation-seeking activities. Games have several properties: a moderate element of suspense governing gains or losses; a semi-ritualized setting with familiar aspects; activities carried out in a setting of social approval, at least by the in-group; and some element of skill or mastery, which makes a difference in overcoming the

226   *Personality and Aging*

level of suspense. Were humans not actively stimulation seeking, after achieving moderate satiation of visceral drives, they would hardly engage in many hours of repetitive play in such games as golf, basketball, and baseball. The small amount of novelty embedded in a larger setting of familiarity is apparently very appealing or stimulating to the human. As adults grow older, their games usually involve less energy expenditure, but they still engage in stimulation-seeking activities involving ritualized uncertainties.

A study of spontaneous activity in rats using wheel turning provides data on the relations of age and experience to activity (*Jones*, et al., *1953*). Figure 10-1 shows that while young animals show more spon-

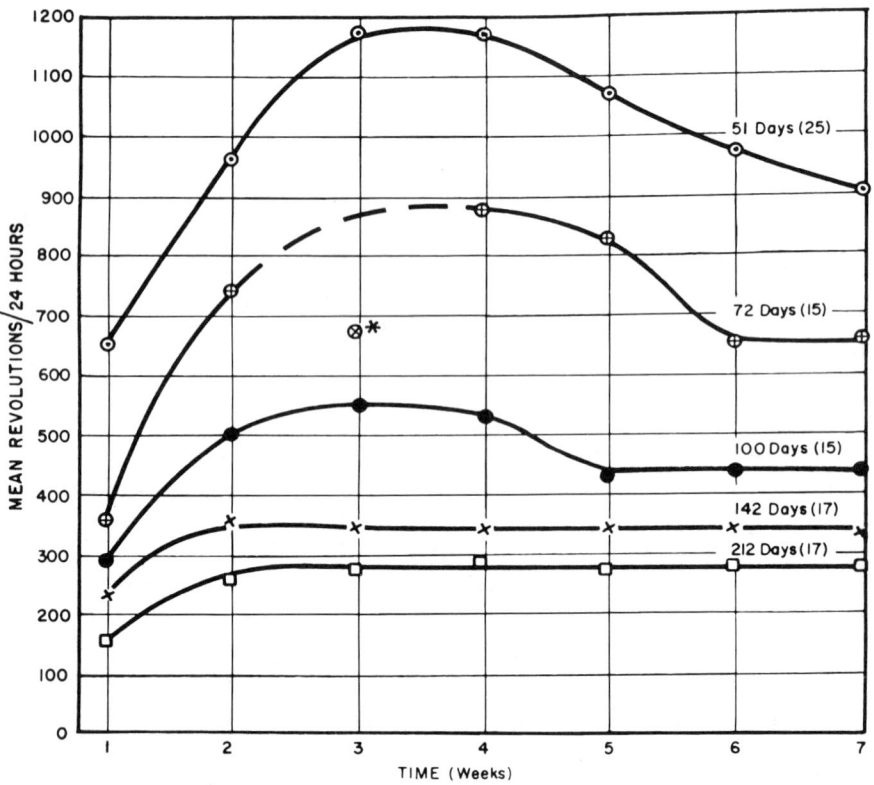

FIGURE 10-1. Activity of the rat as a function of age and time in wheel cage. Activity is measured in mean revolutions of the wheel per day.

Source: D. C. Jones, D. J. Kimeldorf, D. O. Rubadeau, and T. J. Castanera. Relationship between volitional activity and age in the male rat, *Amer. J. Physiol.* (1953), **172**, 109-114.

taneous wheel turning than do the older rats, they also tend to decrease their activity more with additional experience. It would appear that both age and adaptation to a particular environment are influences on the levels of activity.

A common assumption made by students of adult life is that as the individual ages, his previous goals decline in reward value. This may be due to a general reduction in the central motivated states, such that the threshold of an excitatory state for instituting a behavior pattern is rarely reached. If the notion of a generalized drive reduction in aging is valid, it would be expected that more elements in adult life would approach a level of affective neutrality; i.e., neither approached nor avoided. There is, of course, evidence that the older adult engages in fewer activities, particularly those involving high physical activity. In addition to a generalized reduction in drive level with advancing age, it is also commonly assumed that there is a change in the relative balance of avoidance versus approach motivation. If in late life the individual finds himself sustaining more losses and negative events than positive happenings, he may tend toward a nonactive pattern of behavior in which he attempts to conserve what he considers his psychological and physical resources.

Disease in late life can be associated with a generalized reduction in activity level. Along with the reductions frequently induced by disease, there are changes in the pattern of the environment that may constrict the individual's life space and result in a low level of stimulation. Patterns of motives that lead to the avoidance of stimulation and affiliation with other persons are often not easily reversible. When one considers how difficult it is to break a habit, such as smoking, one can appreciate that long-standing motivational patterns may not be highly plastic.

Hunger and Thirst. Because of the tendency for adult men and women with adequate incomes to overeat, it would be worthwhile to have information about the level of deprivation that would lead to the sensation of hunger and thirst in adults. No such evidence has yet been collected. There is some indication from animal research that hunger contractions are more frequent and persistent in younger than in older dogs. There have been other studies on food-deprived rats of different ages (*Margolin and Bunch, 1940*). In these studies, the number of times that the rats would cross an electrified grid to secure food was used as a measure of food deprivation as a motivator of behavior. Figure 10-2 shows that food deprivation had a much greater effect on young animals. If, for example, a food reward were going to be used to motivate animals to learn, it is obvious that the food reward would be less motivating for the old than for the young animal. Any differences in learning that might result would therefore be a consequence of the difference in the

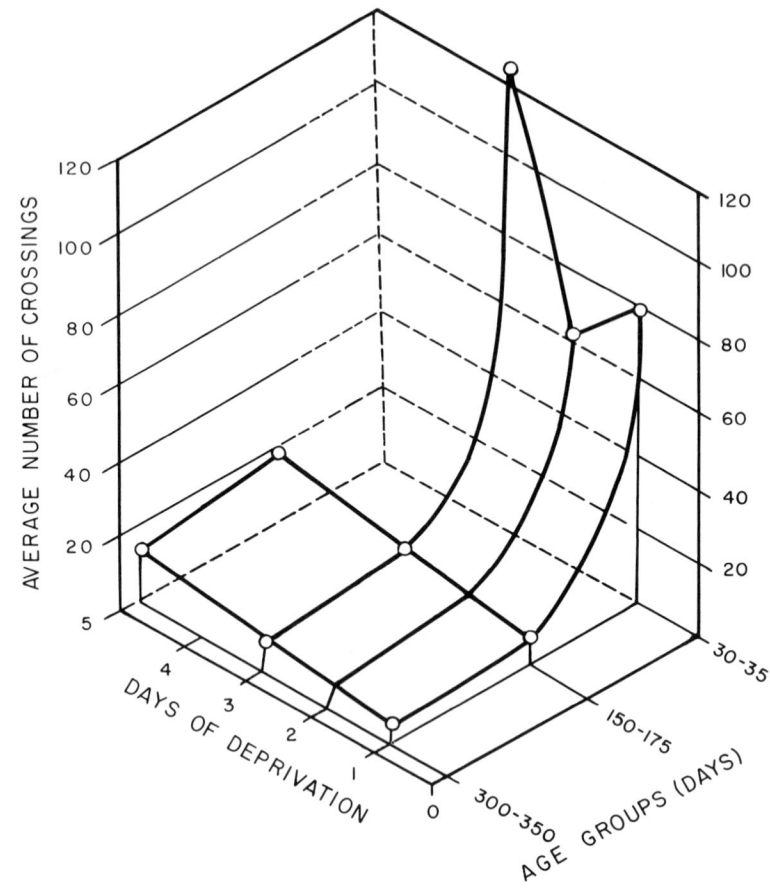

FIGURE 10-2. Average number of crossings per rat on a thirty-minute test in the Columbia Obstruction Apparatus by three age groups of rats after varying durations of food deprivation.

Source: S. E. Margolin and M. E. Bunch. The relationship between age and the strength of hunger motivation, *Comp. Psychol. Monogr.* (1940), **16**, No. 4.

incentive value of the food reward rather than of an intrinsic age difference in capacity to learn. Some unpublished research indicates that older animals might be motivated by a larger food reward than that needed to motivate young animals (*Botwinick,* et al.). Specifically, older rats were more motivated to learn a T-maze when given a larger food pellet reward. Whether this is due to some perception of the reward object or some effect on hunger satiation is not known at this time.

Sexual Behavior. Evidence on sexual behavior is more systematic than that on thirst and hunger drives, since information can be gotten by interview (*e.g., Kinsey,* et al., *1948*). Using as the criterion of sexual behavior the sensation of orgasm, the survey of Kinsey reported that in the male the frequency of orgasms declined from the late teens almost linearly throughout the life span. Figure 10-3 shows the frequency of orgasms per week for human males of different ages. The effects of novelty associated with new sex partners is such as to increase the fre-

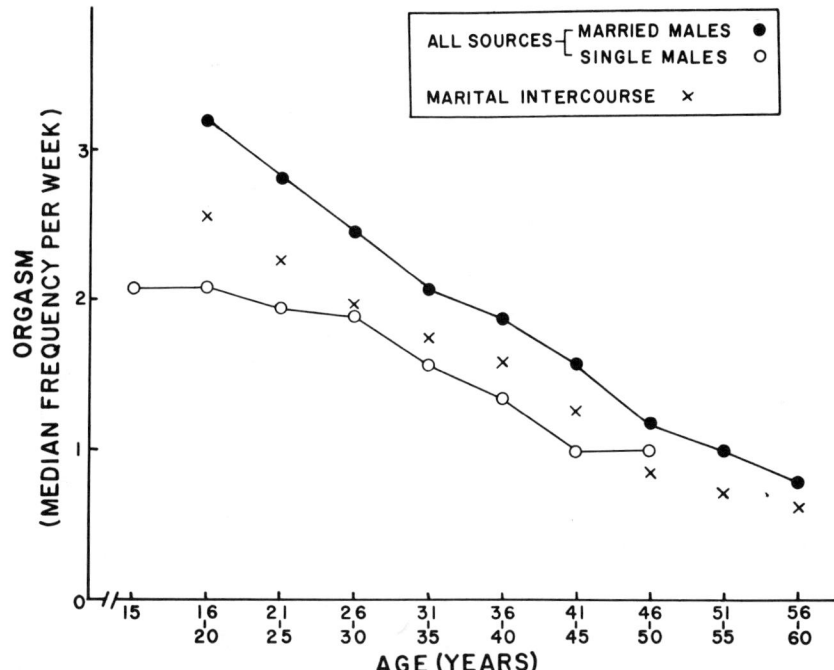

FIGURE 10-3. Age and the median frequency of orgasms per week for men. Orgasms from all (six) sources include marital intercourse.

Source: A. C. Kinsey, W. B. Pomeroy, and C. E. Martin. *Sexual Behavior in the Human Male* (Philadelphia: W. B. Saunders Company, 1948).

quencies in older males. However, previous rates of orgasm frequency are relatively soon re-established, implying that while novelty may have a stimulating effect on the sex drive, it probably must be considered in the context of a general drive reduction over the adult life span. There is evidence indicating that some men in their nineties continue to have marital intercourse. One of the great limitations of the effects of both social and biological influences on sex drive is the relative unavailability of an appropriate mate in the older age group. This is particularly important in the case of the female, since only about one-third of the females over sixty-five live with a husband. Also, the known decline in marital intercourse of the female may be more a function of the potency of the husband than her own sexual drive or capacity. Because of the greater dependence of the woman upon the availability of an appropriate mate in late life, it may be, as Kinsey suggests, that frequency of masturbation may be a more appropriate measure of female sexuality. Although the rate of masturbation is lower in females than in males, the decline in reported masturbation frequency with advancing age is less in females than in males (*Kinsey, et al., 1953*). This may be an indication that sexuality changes very slowly and only to a small extent in the female.

In the expression of sexual behavior, there appear to be at least three major components: the hormone level of the individual, the threshold of the centers in the brain controlling the elicitation of sexual behavior (in the monkey, a specific center for penile erection has been identified), and the factor of central control over the pattern of sexual behavior that has been acquired as a result of experience and learning. In aging, an important problem for research is to study the relative effects of age changes in the hormonal factors compared with the central nervous system control of sexual behavior. Animals raised in isolation and those raised in groups tend to show differences in frequency of ejaculation. Curiously, the rat and the guinea pig react differently to isolation. Previously isolated guinea pigs have difficulty in mating, whereas previously isolated rats tend to show a higher frequency of ejaculation when exposed to females. It is not unreasonable to suspect that in the human, the differences in hormone levels, thresholds of brain centers controlling sexual behavior, and previous learning will result in considerable individual differences in sexual behavior of older adults under identical environmental conditions.

Differentiation of the Adult Personality. Given some individual differences in the biological bases for temperament and behavior, the format of personality is established by the individual's social environment. The directions of parental behavior in such things as suppressing or encouraging autonomy of behavior, affective expression or neutrality, and hostility or love lead to selectivity and specialization of behavior. Early maternal influences tend to be especially significant for the development of the individual; the consequences of paternal influences are likely seen more clearly as the individual grows into the responsibilities of adult life. The personality is further differentiated in adults as they are presented with problems and developmental tasks typical of an age level. Thus the readiness with which certain behavior is evoked comes as a consequence of successes and failures in occupations, in sexual relations, and in acquiring new social roles in an evolving society. Because we have an awareness of our personal continuity in time, we may be relatively unaware that the "I" is continually evolving. Because new tasks and experiences do not equally involve past experience, and because drives, appetites, and other somatic changes are not uniform, the continuity of personality from childhood onward is not equal for all traits. What appears to happen is that some personality traits show rather close continuity or stability from childhood onward and others evolve and differentiate over the adult life span.

One study reviewed the available research on stability of personality over the life span, with the finding that some traits, like relative masculinity or masculine interests and attitudes, tend to persist (*Neugarten, 1963*). By contrast, evidence indicated that certain children who were hostile and dependent in childhood were friendly and outgoing as adults. One has the impression that perhaps something less than half of the variations in adult personality characteristics are predictable from the individual's childhood personality. This neither denies the early origins of the adult personality nor regards personality as a book closed early in life. While there is measurable continuity in personalities from early childhood onward, continual evolution of the personality over the life span would seem to characterize the healthy, adaptive adult. Rigidly regarding each new situation and dogmatically fitting it into the tight mold of what has already been experienced, while typical of some individuals, is by no means universally characteristic of older adults.

Hypochondriasis, depression, and other maladaptive patterns of meeting crisis situations occur in older adults. The relative role of the premorbid personality, somatic change, and contemporary social environment in these late-life mental crises will be discussed in the next chapter.

Personality Development in Young Adults

Some indication of the stability of adult personality characteristics was obtained in a sixteen- to eighteen-year follow-up of 300 couples engaged to be married (*Kelly, 1955*). The 600 individuals were initially given, among other measurements, a battery of psychological tests, a thirty-six variable personality rating scale, and a biographical information questionnaire. Of the 300 engagements, 278 couples married and twenty-two broke off their engagements; all but five of these latter forty-four individuals married someone else. Of the 278 who married as planned, twelve marriages were ended by death and thirty-nine by divorce. Of the original 600 individuals, retest data were obtained on 215 of the males and 231 of the females. After 16 to 18 years of married life, there was no apparent increase or decrease in the correlation of personality variables between mates. At original testing, there was a low positive relationship between the scores of engaged couples, indicating some amount of initial similarity, but, as stated, no increase was seen over the years of marriage. Of the personality variables, personal values and vocational interests seemed most stable (48 and 45 per cent consistency); self-ratings of personality showed about 31 per cent consistency; and least stable were attitudes (8 per cent consistency). Thus between the mid-twenties to the mid-forties, men and women show considerable change in personality characteristics. The changes are not so great that the individual loses his feeling of continuity or stability of person, yet it is clear that change is at least as characteristic as is stability in relation to the adult personality. Presumably, the changes represent the adaptations of the normal healthy adult to the interactions between himself and his environment. It is important to note that over the same age range (twenty-five to forty-five) where many of the personality variables are showing change, mental abilities, as discussed in Chapter 8, are relatively stable. From this it may be gathered that the personality adaptations over much of adult life, along with other influences, are a function of the mental capacities of the individual's interacting with the environment.

Intelligence and Personality Change. A study of personality changes with age in relation to intellectual functions has been carried out (*Edwards and Wine, 1963*). The investigators used biographical data, a personality inventory, and the Raven Progressive Matrices in a study of a group of hospitalized men twenty-two to seventy-six years of age. When the forty-one personality variables studied were correlated with age, fourteen were found to be significantly related. However, when the groups were equated for intelligence, most of the correlations with age disappeared. The authors interpreted the results as indicating that the personality changes were not related to the process of aging, but to intellectual change. Since the study was done with hospitalized patients in a medical and surgical hospital, the implications of the results, while important, are tentative.

As a nonverbal measure of intelligence, the Raven Progressive Matrices have been found to correlate with psychomotor speed in adults (*Chown, 1961: Birren, et al., 1963*). Thus behind the changes in nonverbal intelligence may indeed lie a basic process of aging. In the Chown study of 200 subjects over the age range twenty to eighty-two years, it was found that scores on sixteen tests of rigidity were more closely related to intelligence than to chronological age. However, Chown pointed out that it was impossible to separate the factors of age and intelligence. In accord with the discussions in Chapter 5, Chown also found that while speed tests in young subjects formed their own cluster, in the older subjects they were highly related to nonverbal intelligence. Birren, *et al.*, have also reported a significant correlation between nonverbal intelligence, as measured by the Raven Progressive Matrices test, and reaction time.

Here is one of the most basic issues in the psychology of aging—that psychomotor speed in its changes with age is correlated with measures of nonverbal intelligence, and that these in turn are related to personality variables. One senses not only that the variable of speed is expressing a change in a basic property of the nervous system of the older organism, but also that the changes involve the personality and the individual's social functioning. Speed tends not to be related to other mental measures that emphasize stored information. The structure of experience as it is stored is not the same as the more labile component of intellectual abilities expressed in speed of mental functioning. What very likely happens is that the changes in the nervous system, expressed as a slowing psychomotor speed, occur earlier than changes in social functioning. This point is stated here in anticipation of information to be presented later on the tendency of older adults to decline in activities and to disengage themselves from previous social relationships. Changes in psychomotor speed with age may be closely related to what some students of personality describe as an age change in "ego energy."

The Berkeley Studies of Personality

One of the common events of late life is retirement from gainful employment. Since an individual's occupation has so many meanings, including that of income, that it is not unusual that the years just before and after retirement tend to be somewhat unsettled (*Streib, 1956*). One may ask, as did the Berkeley investigators, whether there are not personality differences in adapting to retirement (*Reichard,* et al., *1962*). Using psychoanalytical concepts of personality structure, these investigators examined changes in self-concept, adjustment, and the effect of retirement upon individuals' psychological life. Aging and retirement were regarded as independent variables, with psychological adjustment being a characteristic dependent upon the previous personality of the individual. Since retirement is such a definite and broad change in social role, it poses a problem for the individual of maintaining a stable image of himself. For example, an aggressive, hard-working, businessman who has taken special pleasure in his occupational achievement might well undergo a considerable psychological upheaval in retirement since he would be removed from the activities that gave him his feeling of self-worth.

With these kinds of issues in mind, the Berkeley investigators studied eighty-seven men over the age range of fifty-five to eighty-four years, forty-two of whom were retired and forty-five not yet retired. These men were interviewed from seven to twelve hours each, with a nine-hour average.

Results showed that some of the older men appeared to be more satisfied with their earlier lives than were the younger men. For them, it was as though growing older had led to acceptance of the past and to a kind of renunciation of unattained, perhaps somewhat irrational, goals of earlier life. The older persons interviewed presented a more benign picture of their early family lives than did the younger men. The investigator said that "the preretirement period . . . is characterized by a sense of insecurity and instability. It seems that after retirement the individual has less need to be defensive in his relations with others" (*Reichard et al., 1962, p. 491*).

Older persons are perhaps more willing than the young to discuss what would seem to the interviewer to be sensitive topics (perhaps because there is less at stake). The Berkeley investigators said that defensive efforts to ward off anxiety evoked in the interview were more common in the younger than in the older respondents. Also, projection of hostility was seen less in older respondents. Their data suggest that, in general, men who adjusted successfully to retirement were psychologically better equipped to stand up under stress; find satisfaction in their activities; accept changed circumstances of their lives; and, importantly, seek, rather than avoid, social contact. In general, the more intelligent men were better educated, tended to be healthier, and participated in more organizations. There is thus a constellation of positive contributing factors to successful adaptation to aging, as was reported earlier for studies of gifted children and adults (*Terman and Oden, 1959*).

The Berkeley investigators tried to isolate the personality factors in their matrix of relationships by separate studies of 115 personality ratings of forty persons rated high in relation to personality adjustment to aging, and of thirty persons rated as low. Their statistical analysis led to the identification of five clusters of persons having similar personality profiles. Among the five clusters, there appeared to be three groups of people who were well adjusted to aging. One group of fourteen was defined as the *mature* group. They were described as having a *constructive approach* to life and were neither excessively impulsive nor defensive in their relations. Another successful type, the *rocking chair type* had six persons. These were the individuals who tended to lean heavily on others. The third type, seven individuals, was the *armored type,* who had well-developed defenses or were concerned with maintaining high defenses against anxiety. In the poorly adjusted category there were two groups. Sixteen men were described as *angry;* they were hostile and characteristically blamed others for shortcomings. There was another smaller group of four poorly adjusted individuals who were described as *self-haters*. These personality types may not have universal validity. For example, the "mature type" may be but the result of a collection of positive factors having no, or limited, essential interrelationship other than that they independently contributed to a pattern of successful adaptation.

The University of Chicago Studies of Personality and Adjustment

A number of very important contributions to our knowledge of the changes in adult life have been made by researchers at the University of Chicago (*Cavan, et al., 1949; Friedmann and Havighurst, 1954; Havighurst and Albrecht, 1953; Neugarten, 1963; Cumming and Henry, 1961; and others*). These studies have been characterized by large samples of community residents of a rather wide range of social characteristics. The Kansas City Study of Adult Life involved the study of two samples of men and women, age fifty and seventy, who were studied over a period of six years. Excluded were the chronically ill and physically impaired. Previous information on groups had indicated a slowing in activities and social roles with age, and the follow-up of the Kansas City group clearly supports this; i.e., if individuals are followed longitudinally over the later adult years, in general they show a reduction in activities. Some part of this may be not unlike the studies of spontaneous behavior in animals with age; ie., the older organism will tend to emit fewer spontaneous behaviors than will the young. An obvious example of this is the decline in play behavior with age. What complicates the picture for humans is the fact that older persons are responding to changes outside themselves which lead to reduced activities; thus widowhood and retirement tend to restrict the number of possible behavior alternatives and also to reduce the stimulation value of the environment. In the context of personality changes with aging, an important question is whether the aging individual is less involved with his environment. Collectively, the University of Chicago studies indicate that, other things being equal, those persons who have highest satisfaction with their lives are those with close interpersonal interactions (*Tobin and Neugarten, 1961*). The disposition to move toward interaction or personal relations with others can be regarded as a personality characteristic. This leads to a distinction between psychological and social engagement with age (*Phillips, 1961*).

The structure of daily life and the social roles that an individual has evolved over his adult life contain many stimuli to which he reacts. He may, as he grows older, be less involved psychologically with these objects and stimuli. Thus an individual could remain socially engaged with his environment and yet over time, become psychologically disengaged. Presumably, habit systems could keep the role activities intact despite a lowering in psychological (affective) involvement. This implies a degree of affective investment and has been called "ego investment" (*Havighurst, Neugarten, and Tobin, 1963*). The follow-up of the Kansas City study showed that both psychological and social disengagement occur with advancing age. In the investigators' view, life satisfaction and level of activity are functions of the personality. The independent element in changing personality with age is the changing level of "energy," such as might be reflected in the extent to which an individual is willing to make an effort to replace a lost role. This leads to a complex issue, for the amount of psychological engagement and ego energy not only responds to psychological losses but also initiates reductions in activities. In the study of the healthy older men at the National Institute of Mental Health, it was found that psychological and social losses appeared to be related to physiological functioning (*Birren, et al., 1963, p. 303*). What may be required in explanation is a concept that allows for a greater probability of a relatively irreversible physiological functioning in response to psychological events, a depletion that is accelerated by social and psychological losses in advancing age and is protected by a matrix of social roles and interpersonal relations.

One study clearly indicates a relationship with age among cognitive and affective components in personality changes with age (*Rosen and Neugarten, 1960*). In this study, 144 individuals varying in age, sex, and social class gave responses to five cards from the Thematic Apperception Test. The scores developed by each subject were analyzed for introduced characters, introduced conflict, activity-energy expressed, and affect intensity. With age, lower scores were obtained on all four measures. The findings were interpreted as implying a decline in ego energy and its distribution. On the other hand, the older subjects seemed less inclined to deal with complicated aspects of the stimuli, and less capacity for dealing with complexity may also be implied. Similarly, the tendency on the part of older persons to perceive affect and to describe more passive modes of behavior may reflect differences in mood due to somatic changes, as well as shifts in major conflicts with age. There is a trilogy of relationships between: somatic changes with age and resulting lowered disposition to activity, changes in cognitive capacity, and changes in environmental stimulation of the aging person. The role of the habit systems of the individual in mediating these changes is not easily described. In some instances, the personality should be regarded as the dependent variable in aging, and in others, the independent factor (*Britton, 1963*).

The extent to which environmental changes may have consequences for the individual is seen in death rates for widows and married persons of the same age (*Kraus and Lilienfeld, 1959*). Death rates are much higher for widowed persons than for married persons of the same age. The death rates for young widows from cardiovascular diseases is especially interesting and important, for it suggests that the consequences of bereavement and widowhood are such as to impress, over time, a disease pattern on the individual that would otherwise be most uncommon in an age and sex group. The effects of the environment are also apparent in a study on death rates of elderly patients moved to new institutions (*Aldrich and Mendkoff, 1963*). Movement to a new environment appears to accelerate death rates in such a group. Again there is the question of the stimulus value of the environmental changes, which in this instance were intense and protracted, and their relation to the individual's capacity to deal with the implications and to his capacity for appropriate somatic adaptation. In aging, there is evidence for both physiological consequences of psychological events and psychological consequences of physiological events, and very likely a continuing reciprocity of these influences is typical of the adapting individual. Generally, high social participation and being an active member of a matrix of personal interrelationships seem to be conducive to successful aging and may also have implications for physiological functioning. Partly, the social matrix in which the individual finds himself supports him in his adaptations to aging. However, he has also been influential in determining the particular kind of social matrix in which he finds himself as an older person.

Criteria of Successful Aging

The meaning of "successful aging" is elusive and is particularly susceptible to one's own social value or judgments of what is important in life. As used, "successful aging" has two principal implications. One is the life satisfaction that the individual himself experiences; e.g., is he reasonably content with his life and does he have positive self-regarding attitudes. However, an individual may have rather high self-regarding attitudes and display some contentment with his life and yet not be regarded by his peers as being successful in growing older. The other criterion of successful aging appraises the adequacy of the individual's fulfilling his social roles or interpersonal obligations. Successful aging has thus an inner, or psychological, criterion and an outer, or social, one. Generally, some congruity between these criteria is expected; however, it cannot be assumed that there is a one-to-one relationship between a psychological and a social criterion of successful aging.

One of the current views about the personality changes of aging is that older individuals often tend to dissociate themselves from some part of their social interactions; i.e., the individual is a willing accomplice in this process of disengagement (*Cumming and Henry, 1961*). Changes in health, feelings of energy, and mental debility may all limit the individual's capacity to maintain extensive and intensive interpersonal relationships. Viewed from this standpoint, disengagement is a process of cognitive and affective load-shedding, or an adaptive constriction of psychological involvement and activities in order to conserve energy and move toward a more optimum equilibrium of demands and rewards. Just as it was necessary to examine carefully the theory personality types stated in the Berkeley studies, it is necessary to examine the ideas of disengagement theory for their inclusiveness; i.e., how many individuals show disengagement with age and how many would benefit from increased activity. It is conceivable that the movement toward or away from social activities and the basal level of social interaction of an individual are related to certain health and mental capacities. Socially deprived or isolated older persons will show, and have shown, an improvement in self-regarding attitudes and life satisfaction when moved to a higher level of social interaction and increased diversification in social roles. Similarly, other persons, having many diversified and intensely involved social roles, may show a better form of adjustment if they disengage themselves from certain of these activities. Successful aging, then, may be viewed as how close the individual has come to the optimum equilibrium of satisfactions, demands, and capacities.

What has emerged from recent research in the social psychology of aging is the fact that whether disengagement or activity is an important variable depends upon the position of the individual along several dimensions. One of these dimensions consists of the amount of psychological or affective involvement with other persons; another consists of the variety of social roles engaged in; others consist of the mental abilities in solving problems and physical stamina for initiating and enduring sustained activity. By analogy, a limited exposure to an infectious disease may develop antibodies, resulting in protection, whereas too great an exposure may lead to an active infection. Activity in an appropriate amount, as well as a diversity of social roles, may protect the older person against some of the major limitations of aging, just as excessive social pressure for interaction and activity may lead to an unproductive and involuting form of adaptation.

Personality Processes. One convenient way of describing personality is in terms of three components: biological drives, behavior controls, and personal standards. These can be regarded as corresponding to the id, ego, and superego of psychoanalytic psychology, although Freud did not discuss their relationships to aging. All three appear to change with age: our food and sexual wants diminish, our concept of reality changes, and our ideals and standards, though relatively stable, keep evolving over the life span (*Zinberg and Kaufman, 1963*). Marked change in any one of them can result in personality difficulties.

One of the problems of personality theory and aging is the difficulty of describing the interaction with biological processes, drives, appetites, and impulses. That part of the personality which directs relations with the environment is commonly called the "ego." It refers to the administration of the needs and impulses of the body in relation to the environment. The ego also seems to vary in the energy available to it to initiate actions. What is implied is that in aging there are interactions between the personality and the environment and body for which there are no readily found analogies in childhood. An important mechanism by which young persons can maintain a personal equilibrium is through having a sense of futurity, a sense that the future will bring a reward or balance more in accord with his needs and ideals. This confidence in future gratification or attainment is not as appropriate to an older person, measuring his life as he does in terms of some estimated remainder. Reaction to a change or loss depends upon the previous role the object played in the individual's life and the individual's present investment in it.

Gradual decline in sexual potency with age is reacted to in relation to the previous importance that sexual prowess had to the individual. Some individuals, perhaps fearing loss of function, overcompensate with athletic feats, sexual relations, social relations, and undue attention to physical attractiveness. How the self has been viewed and how integrated the "executive functioning" of the ego is influence the individual's reactions to the change in his body with age and to the changes in his environment. Over the life span, there is a continuous redistribution of energy and interests, and at some phase in late life, the individual moves from involvement with the outer world to a more internalized state.

As the needs of the young adult become satisfied, the motivational pattern of the individual changes (*Kuhlen and Johnson, 1952*). Some psychologists have suggested that there is a normal progression of motivational changes from a personal achievement and gratification orientation to more concern with gratification of the needs of others. The very young may seek thrills, whereas the elderly may avoid threats to their well-being. Some part of the tendency to avoid threats may come from a greater awareness of the consequences of poor judgment. An older man may not risk expressing a strong adverse opinion in his job because loss of a job is a more severe problem for an older man.

While some of the motivational changes of age can be described as psychologically conservative—avoidance of risk, frustration, reduction of challenges to the mind or body, conservation of time and emotional energy—another aspect of motivation has to do with the satiety or boredom with a long-standing pattern of living that had significance for earlier needs. A pattern of life with little apparent change may cause deep frustration and prompt middle-age flings.

At all stages of life, a more satisfactory balance of impulse, control, and ideals may be expected if the individual has the energy to realign the personal focus in his life. However, initiative and energy are less commonly found in the aged, possibly because the cost of energy relative to a short future appears too great. A woman who has always taken great satisfaction in her physical attractiveness to men may be disconcerted at the sight of middle-age wrinkles and require readjustment of her attitudes, including reinvestment or attachment of her feelings of self-worth to some other personal characteristic, activity, or relationship. Men have analogous problems of physique and physical prowess. The reinvestment of psychological attachments is one of the more demanding aspects of aging and the personality, particularly so if the early life attachments were unrealistic and did not lend themselves to a transition to a more differentiated adult life.

Interests

From the previous discussion of personality and the tendency to lower psychological involvement with age, one would expect some shift in interests as well *(Riegel and Riegel, 1960)*. Some shift is likely to occur because of changes such as those in appearance and physical capacities. Others represent differentiation of earlier interests; e.g., an older sports spectator might have been a younger participant. Generally, with age there is less interest in strenuous physical activity and active participation in sports, and in later life in spectator sports as well. There is also a tendency for individuals to become more interested in relatively solitary activities rather than in those involving large groups. It has been pointed out that there are social class differences in leisure-time interests. Taken in perspective, the values of leisure-time activity seem to be more related to social class and personal adjustment than to age and sex *(Havighurst,*

TABLE 10-1. PROPORTION OF ADULTS WHO READ BOOKS AND PREFER SERIOUS RADIO PROGRAMS, BY EDUCATION LEVEL AND AGE

	Proportion of People Who State that They Read a Book During Past Month			Proportion of People Who Want More Serious Programs on Radio		
	Educational Level			Educational Level		
Age	College	High School	Grade School	College	High School	Grade School
21-29	57	31	1	31	14	12
30-49	52	27	10	33	16	16
50 and over	45	28	10	29	18	18

Source: R. Meyersohn, An examination of commercial entertainment. In R. W. Kleemeier (ed.), *Aging and Leisure* (New York: Oxford University Press, 1961), p. 263. Adapted from P. F. Lazarsfeld and P. Kendall, *Radio Listening in America: The People Look at Radio—Again* (Englewood Cliffs, N.J.: Prentice-Hall, Inc., 1948), Appendix Tables 9, 18.

1961). An interesting trend is that of the older person's increased interest in "cultural" reading and decreased interest in being amused. This trend is illustrated in Table 10-1. These figures may be compared with the 56 per cent of young adults age twenty-one to twenty-nine who indicate that they like to listen to popular and dance music and with the 29 per cent of those over fifty who so indicate. An even greater age decrement is seen in movie attendance; 50 per cent of the individuals age twenty to twenty-nine went to a movie at least once a week in 1957, whereas only 8 per cent of those over fifty went that often. Lest this seem to imply that the older individual simply vegetates, Table 10-2 shows the time

TABLE 10-2. AVERAGE MINUTES PER DAY PER PERSON IN UNITED STATES SPENT VIEWING TELEVISION, BY AGE AND DAY OF WEEK

AGE	Average Monday to Friday	Saturday	Sunday	Average Daily
Under 6	72	89	54	72
6-11	111	157	102	117
12-17	114	115	134	117
18-34	100	109	113	103
35-49	102	106	121	105
50 and over	106	112	113	108
U.S. Total	102	113	110	105

Source: R. Meyersohn, An examination of commercial entertainment. In R. W. Kleemeier (ed.), *Aging and Leisure* (New York: Oxford University Press, 1961), p. 266.

Data from Television Bureau of Advertising, Inc., 1957, p. 3. Results are based on personal interviews conducted with all household members, in a representative U.S. cross section of 3000 households, drawn on the basis of a modified probability sample. Information on the number of minutes spent was obtained by a research technique called by its authors "association-recall," which encouraged the respondent to reconstruct his personal activities during the preceding day, and then to associate media exposure with these personal activities.

spent in watching television. These figures indicate that the average amount of time spent in television viewing remains approximately constant throughout the adult life span. With regard to program preferences, older individuals tend to like quiz, variety, and talent shows, and are less interested in the serious drama and mystery programs. In agreement with the trends in adult reading selections, older people tend to like non-fictional, rather than fantasy, entertainment.

Meyersohn feels that adult and later-life themes are underrepresented in fiction, movies, and television; i.e., most of the topics are organized around the young. Thus it may well be that older adults find it difficult to identify with the major themes of fictional and fantasy material.

There is a tendency, however, to expect older people to begin to identify with the major cultural trends and therefore to read biography in preference to fiction and to be somewhat more identified with the continuity in life rather than with the fantasy departures from real life. By no means do all interests decline over the adult age range. Figure 10-4 shows that some interests—e.g., bird watching, gardening, and visiting museums—rise over the adult years, while interest in other sorts of activities tends to decline. If one identifies interest in strenuous and dangerous activities as being masculine, then males tend to become more feminine

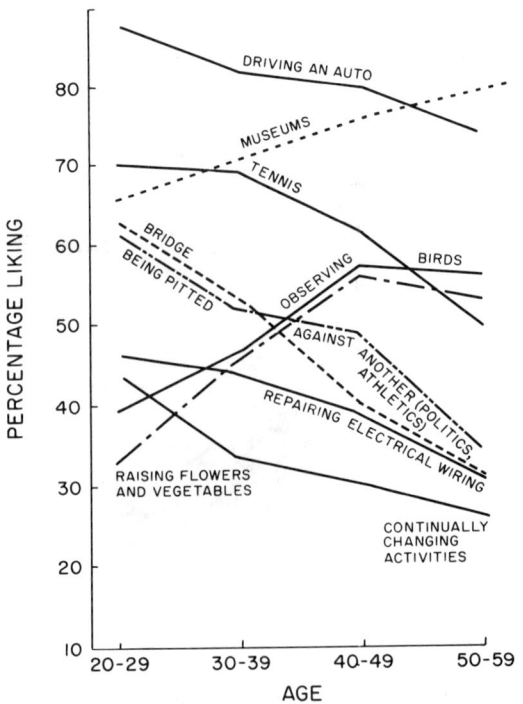

FIGURE 10-4. Changes with age in various interests as measured by the Strong Test (E. K. Strong, *Change of Interest with Age* [Stanford, Calif.: Stanford University Press, 1931]).

Source: S. L. Pressey and R. G. Kuhlen. *Psychological Development Through the Life Span* (New York: Harper & Row, Publishers, 1957).

in their interests over the life span. After age twenty-five, men tend to become less interested in hobbies that produce excitement and involve danger and rapid adjustment, and to become involved in more stable activities, like gardening and activities associated with their occupation. While there undoubtedly is an age trend toward decreasing interest in strenuous activity, there is also clear evidence that man maintains an intellectual curiosity about the natural world throughout the life span.

It is interesting to note that although younger individuals tend to be highly active and quick in their reactions, their subjective impression of the passage of time indicates that they regard time as a slower moving entity than do older people. Older people, possibly because of their changing perspective about the amount of time left in their lives, or perhaps because of changes in their internal biology, regard time as highly fleeting. Concomitant with this change in the subjective impressions of time, older people tend to be more conserving in their uses of time.

Attitudes

With the changes in personality and interests that come with age, it is reasonable to expect that social attitudes also change. The dominant concerns of many older persons, with health, income, and immediate circumstances of living, have consequences for their social attitudes. If a majority of older people express an unfavorable attitude toward retirement, it need not imply a preference for the activity of work compared with leisure, but may merely reflect their concern over income. Thus many of the more important issues concern why people hold the attitudes they do rather than the content of the attitudes.

Individuals have a tremendous variety of opinions about other people, objects, and processes. These opinions come from family influences, groups in society, and individual experiences and personalities. Furthermore, attitudes are commonly held about objects and groups with which the individual has had little or no personal experience. Thus some people may express opinions about Eskimos or Indians merely on the basis of preformed ideas along the dimension of "foreignness." The following topics suggest the vastness of the variety of attitudes: attitudes toward the opposite sex, ethnic groups, children, parents, religion, politics, artistic creations (paintings, sculpture, architecture, music), naturally occurring objects (woods, birds, stars), consumer habits and attitudes (food, clothing, housing, home furnishings).

An important type of attitude involves different age groups. To the school child, it makes a great deal of difference in his attitudes whether another child is the same age or a year or two younger or older. At the school playground, the child would be most reluctant to play with another from a grade "beneath" him, although in his home neighborhood, with a shortage of playmates, he might condescend to play with the slightly younger child. Throughout the life span, individuals have such age-related attitudes. The developing child tends to regard the slightly older person as being in a more desirable phase and the younger person as being somewhat inferior. Two kinds of attitudes are involved: the attitude of the individual toward his own age group and the attitudes of the members of his age group toward different age groups. Seventy-year-olds might be asked how they like being seventy, and thirty-year-olds asked how they would like to be seventy. The seventy-year-old might express a liking for his age. However, differentiation in his attitude might be found by asking him to compare being seventy with what he recalls of being thirty.

From the foregoing, it may be apparent that an attitude may be defined as "an individual's characteristic way of regarding an object, person, or process." It involves evaluation—whether he likes or dislikes, approves or disapproves, seeks or avoids a particular person, object, or process. In addition to the like-dislike aspect of an attitude is the intensity of feeling. Voters who cast their ballots for a candidate for public office express approving attitudes, yet they may vary considerably in the degree to which they approve of their candidate, ranging from near neutrality to intense feeling.

The affect, or strength of feeling, involved in an attitude determines the likelihood of an individual's taking action concerning the object of the attitude. The answer to the question whether an individual likes the Democratic or Republican party carries with it the implication that he might vote for one or the other on election day. In addition to the qualities of affect and action implied in attitudes, there is an informational, or cognitive, element. Attitudes that have been evolved after one has sought information and reasoned through the issues may be contrasted with those adopted without information primarily on the basis of affect or defensiveness. Defensive attitudes exist less because of the inherent qualities of the object than because of the individual's strong need to hold a given position. Thus the middle-aged man who, with strong emotions, rejects the necessity for Social Security for persons over sixty-five may be doing so less from his knowledge of economics and financial structure than from his own conflicts. Similarly, a middle-aged woman, feeling threatened by potential diminishing physical attractiveness, may make disparaging comments about older people. Attitudes toward and of the aged are determined by the availability of information, prior defensiveness and affective involvement, and the individual's own value system.

Differentiation of attitudes would be revealed, for example, in answers to questions about what people might like to see if they visited the Smithsonian Institution in Washington. Very likely, more women would express interest in the gowns of former presidents' wives and more men in objects from military activities. On the other hand, another question might be asked about the individual's desire to make a trip to Washington in order to visit the Smithsonian. To the latter question, it might be expected that a greater number of younger persons would answer "yes." The threat of travelling is not the same to old and young adults, just as moving a household or changing jobs does not pose the same threat to both groups. Attitudes expressing underconcern with risks is as inappropriate as overconcern. There may be overly constricting or overly liberal attitudes toward behavior risks in later life, just as there often are in early parent-child relationships. Hostile control in which discipline is not for the good of the child but is an outlet for the parent's tensions and hostility is obviously not conducive to optimum development. There are similar parent-child attitudes in later life. Hostile rejection of aging parents can be expressed by highly controlling attitudes. In this context, the importance of attitudes lies in whether they promote the interaction of aged persons with others or build barriers between relationships.

Sex Differences in Attitudes

Differences in attitudes have been found between age groups and between the sexes within an age group. Young women tend to view older persons' appearance in more negative terms than do either young or older men. While our society emphasizes youthful appearance in general, particular emphasis is placed on the appearance of women. Thus concern with age-linked changes in appearance is a sex-related factor. Evidence about more general attitudes of the sexes in relation to age has also been obtained. In this study, a specially designed picture was shown to older and younger men and women. The picture showed a young man and an older woman, and an older man and an older woman. The subject was asked to tell a complete story about the picture, one that had a beginning, a middle, and an end. Then "the interviewer, moving clockwise around the picture, beginning with the picture of the young man, asked the respondent to assign an age and to give a general description of each of the four figures. Again moving clockwise, the respondent was asked finally to describe what he thought each figure in the picture was feeling about the others" (*Neugarten and Gutmann, 1958, p. 5*). A striking result of this study was that the older man and woman reversed roles regarding family authority. Younger men and women saw the older man as the authoritative one, whereas older men and women cast the older woman in the dominant role. It is necessary to decide whether the individuals are reflecting a stereotype that they have acquired in society, or whether their impression is realistically based. Whatever the interpretation, it should be emphasized that, generally, older men are regarded as being more submissive and less authoritative than older women. Quite conceivably this reflects a fundamental change in the roles of the sexes during the later years. Young men are task oriented, impelled toward action and achievement, and they become increasingly power conscious and authoritative because of their position in society and in the family. Later, physiological changes in the male and his loss of authority upon retirement may, indeed, place him in a more dependent role than that of the woman.

In one study of changes in attitudes and values with age, subjects were required to indicate their ratings of a list of concepts, checking on a seven-point scale along the dimensions: fair-unfair, strong-weak, active-passive, safe-dangerous (*Kogan and Wallach, 1961*). Older men tended to have more favorable reactions to the concepts of "foreign" and "imagination." Older women were more favorable than young women in their evaluation of "death" and less favorable in their evaluation of "love" and "myself." Of considerable interest, in view of the changes in our society, is that older subjects of both sexes viewed both the Negro and retirement as being more favorable than did young subjects. It might be speculated that older persons, being in a rather dependent position in society, would tend to be more sympathetic toward others who are also deprived. Although the study was remarkably comprehensive, other age and sex differences in attitude remain to be explored; e.g., attitudes touching upon work and leisure, family and interpersonal relations, developmental stages of the life span, physical and psychological attributes, and attitudes toward the future. Perhaps future studies of attitudes should investigate not only general areas of inquiries, but also specific relationships, such as those among family members; e.g., wife-husband, father-son, brother-sister, natural child-stepchild, and so forth. Should older people be found to possess generally stronger nurtural feelings toward underprivileged persons, then constructive, affiliative outlets for their interests could well be encouraged in appropriate ways.

Beliefs about the Aged

When an attitude is simply acquired from the social environment and is based on slight information, it may be said to be a "stereotype" (*Tuckman and Lorge, 1953*). Young people frequently have stereotyped views of the aged, and aging persons themselves often accept such stereotypes. Stereotypic opinions can arise about the aged from the 1 or 2 per cent of all aged persons who may be institutionalized for mental illness. From this small group, the erroneous generalization may be made that most persons over the age of seventy have "senile" qualities about them. A study of aged and young persons' attitudes toward older people was done using a sentence completion test. Completion of such sentences as "most old people's friendships are . . ." and "when I am with an old person I . . ." reflect the attitude of the subject. Certain data indicate that the attitudes of older and younger subjects regarding old people are less far apart than attitudes about religious or ethnic group differences; i.e., older and younger people tend to be affectively or attitudinally closer together than are members of different racial or religious groups (*Kogan and Shelton, 1962*). One difference in response between the two age groups was to the question: "One of the greatest fears of many old people is. . . ." The younger subjects mentioned death, or dying, as the greatest fear, while the older individuals stressed lack of money and financial insecurity. This corroborates the currently developing point of view that the attitudes of older persons reflect more a concern with conditions of living than a fear of death. Many of the expressed attitudes indicate that, as a group, younger persons are regarded as being capable of giving the assistance that they feel the older people need. Elderly people seem to be quite concerned with whether or not they are rejected or accepted by younger persons.

While the study revealed greater similarities than differences in the beliefs of the younger and older subjects about older people, it nonetheless revealed obviously important differences. The authors suggest that the relationship between the two groups resembles a majority-minority group conflict, in which the older persons are considered as having less desirable characteristics, such as the need for financial and affective assistance, as well as various other negative traits. However, unlike minority groups (as described in the usual stereotype), the older group does not strive for dominance in power. It is judged as having few attributes which might suggest that it considers power desirable, and it seems in fact to be quite dependent. Thus regarding older people as a typical minority group in the population is not a particularly discriminating viewpoint, even though there are a number of areas in which they do have qualities that might lead to such a classification. Persons who tend to reject most groups that they regard as being different from their own tend also to reject the aged as a group. Conversely, individuals who have nurtural personality dispositions regard older people favorably (*Kogan and Wallach, 1961*).

The attitudes of an aged person toward "old people" may be differentiated from his attitudes toward himself in growing old. A study was done of self-judgments of the aged (*Mason, 1954*). In general, the self-regarding attitudes of the older subjects implied negative feelings of self-worth, although an independently living group of older persons regarded itself somewhat less negatively than did an institutionalized group. Within the aged sample itself, there was no correlation between attitudes and chronological age. This suggests, as do other studies, that the personal circumstances of the individual over the age of sixty tend to be more important in determing his attitudes and his level of functioning than does his chronological age.

Summary

"Personality" is a difficult term to define, since there is such a wide variety of theories and measurements. In general, "personality" refers to the distinctive behavior patterns of individuals. Presumably, with a large enough sample of the behavior of an individual, it would be possible to predict behavior in future situations and to be able to group the individual with those most similar and to contrast him with those most dissimilar. The differences and similarities in behavior characteristics give rise to the notion of "types" of personality. How many types there are—and whether there *are* types—depends upon the kind and breadth of observations and measurements used in classification.

With advancing age, in the adult organism there are reductions in drive level, including a reduction in spontaneous physical activity and sexual behavior. Studies of many kinds of activities have shown a tendency toward declining social activities and interpersonal relationships. This has given rise to concepts of psychological and social disengagement, since both psychological and social involvement with the environment decline in later life. To some extent, social role decline is initiated by the environment's placing the individual in a less engaged position; e.g., retirement. In addition, there is also a quality of affective detachment from the environment in which older persons have less ego involvement in their roles and activities. Students of personality and aging have described this as in part a consequence of reduced "ego energy."

Generally, personality traits are more variable over the adult years than are mental abilities. But the former are themselves not uniform for some traits—like those of personal values and vocational interests—are relatively stable, whereas self-regarding attitudes change markedly. Studies of personality traits in relation to age and intelligence indicate that age is less important than intelligence in the personality adaptations over adult life. An important qualification must be made, however, in that nonverbal intelligence becomes highly correlated with psychomotor speed in older adults. In three aspects of the individual—psychomotor speed, nonverbal intelligence, and personality adaptations—there may lie a factor of central nervous system change. What the student of personality observes at one level and calls "ego energy" may at another level be measured as reaction time and be called a "change in psychomotor speed."

The evidence indicates that the adult is a constantly adapting organism. The possibility exists that there is physiological registration of the effects of psychological events of later life, as well as physiological changes leading to behavioral consequences. This does not imply either a complete persistence or a complete fluidity of behavior. There are relative fixations of habit systems and physiological adaptations that make the older adult a more differentiated organism than the child. Changes with age in the environment and within the individual continually provoke further differentiations of behavior. Because of the increased differentiation, there would appear to be less probability of novel adaptations as a function of age. However, there is always some environment that is optimum for the age and state of a particular organism. Changes in interests and activities of adults reflect the changing position of the older adult in his environment as well as his motivations and long-established patterns of behavior.

The habit systems that are built up in the individual over time impose controls over the behavior elicited in response to somatic changes in internal drives and external stimulation. One stable element in the choices of behavior is personal values, although these too may be modified or superceded if the cognitive load placed on the individual becomes excessive, or if the values are in dramatic conflict with the changes and drift in the content of the individual's life. The adaptive person continually modifies his behavior over time, thus aging "successfully." The internal habit systems that promote adaptation are not fully known, and successful adaptation may be brought about by quite different and almost opposite types of personality organization.

References

Aldrich, C. K. and Ethel Mendkoff. Relocation of the aged and disabled: a mortality study. *J. Amer. Geriatric Soc.,* 1963, **11**, 185-194.

Birren, J. E., R. N. Butler, S. W. Greenhouse, L. Sokoloff, and Marian R. Yarrow (eds.), *Human Aging.* Washington, D.C.: Government Printing Office, 1963, Public Health Publication No. 986.

Britton, J. H. Dimensions of adjustment of older adults. *J. Geront.,* 1963, **18**, 60-65.

Cavan, Ruth S., E. W. Burgess, R. J. Havighurst, and H. Goldhamer. *Personal Adjustment in Old Age.* Chicago: Science Research Associates, Inc., 1949.

Chown, Sheila M. Age and the rigidities. *J. Geront.,* 1961, **16**, 353-362.

*Cumming, Elaine and W. E. Henry. *Growing Old.* New York: Basic Books, Inc., 1961.

Edwards, A. E. and D. B. Wine. Personality changes with age; their dependency on concomitant intellectual decline. *J. Geront.,* 1963, **18**, 182-184.

Friedmann, E. and R. J. Havighurst. *The Meaning of Work and Retirement.* Chicago: University of Chicago Press, 1954.

Hall, C. S. and G. Lindzey. *Theories of Personality.* New York: John Wiley & Sons, Inc., 1958.

Havighurst, R. J. The nature and values of meaningful free-time activity. In R. W. Kleemeier (ed.), *Aging and Leisure,* pp. 309-344. London: Oxford University Press, 1961.

---

*Suggested additional reading.

———. The social competence of middle-aged people. *Genetic Psychol. Monogr.,* 1957, **56,** 297-375.

——— and Ruth Albrecht. *Older People.* New York: David McKay Company, Inc., 1953.

———, Bernice L. Neugarten, and S. S. Tobin. *Disengagement and Patterns of Aging.* International Social Science Seminar of Social Gerontology, August 1963.

Jones, D. C., D. J. Kimeldorf, D. O. Rubadeau, and T. J. Castanera. Relationship between volitional activity and age in the male rat. *Amer. J. Physiol.,* 1953, **172,** 109-114.

Kelly, E. L. Consistency of the adult personality. *Amer. Psychol.,* 1955, **10,** 659-681.

Kinsey, A. C., W. B. Pomeroy, and C. E. Martin. *Sexual Behavior in the Human Male.* Philadelphia: W. B. Saunders Company, 1948.

———, ———, ———, and P. H. Gebhard. *Sexual Behavior in the Human Female.* Philadelphia: W. B. Saunders Company, 1953.

Kogan, N. and Florence C. Shelton. Beliefs about "old people": a comparative study of older and younger samples. *J. Genetic Psychol.,* 1962, **100,** 93-111.

———, ———. Images of "old people" and "people in general" in an older sample. *J. Genetic Psychol.,* 1962, **100,** 3-21.

——— and M. A. Wallach. Age changes in values and attitudes. *J. Geront.,* 1961, **16,** 272-280.

Kraus, A. A. and A. M. Lilienfeld. Some epidemiologic aspects of the high mortality rate in the young widowed group. *J. Chronic Dis.,* 1959, **10,** 207-217.

*Kuhlen, R. G. Aging and life-adjustment. In J. E. Birren (ed.), *Handbook of Aging and the Individual,* pp. 852-897. Chicago: University of Chicago Press, 1959.

——— and G. H. Johnson. Changes in goals with increasing adult age. *J. Consult. Psychol.,* 1952, **16,** 1-4.

Margolin, S. E. and M. E. Bunch. The relationship between age and the strength of hunger motivation. *Comp. Psychol. Monogr.,* 1940, **16,** No. 4.

Mason, Evelyn P. Some correlates of self-judgments of the aged. *J. Geront.,* 1954, **9,** 324-337.

Meyersohn, R. A critical examination of commercial entertainment. In R. W. Kleemeier (ed.), *Aging and Leisure,* pp. 243-272. London: Oxford University Press, 1961.

*Neugarten, Bernice L. Personality changes during the adult years. In R. G. Kuhlen (ed.), *Psychological Backgrounds of Adult Education,* pp. 43-76. Chicago: Center for the Study of Liberal Education for Adults, 1963.

——— and D. L. Gutmann. Age-sex roles and personality in middle age: a thematic apperception study. *Psychol. Monogr.* 1958, **72,** No. 470.

———, R. J. Havighurst, and S. S. Tobin. The measurement of life satisfaction. *J. Geront.,* 1961, **16,** 134-143.

Phillips, B. S. Role changes, subjective age, and adjustment: a correlational analysis. *J. Geront.,* 1961, **16,** 347-352.

*Reichard, Suzanne, Florine Livson, and P. G. Petersen. *Aging and Personality.* New York: John Wiley & Sons, Inc., 1962.

*Riegel, K. F. Personality theory and aging. In Birren (ed.), *op. cit.,* pp. 797-851.

——— and Ruth M. Riegel. A study on changes of attitudes and interests during later years of life. *Vita Humana,* 1960, 3, 177-206.

Rosen, Jacqueline L. and Bernice L. Neugarten. Ego functions in the middle and later years: a thematic apperception study of normal adults. *J. Geront.,* 1960, **15,** 62-67.

Streib, G. F. Morale of the retired. *Social Problems,* 1956, **12,** 270-276.

Terman, L. M. and Melita H. Oden. *The Gifted Group at Mid-Life.* Stanford, Calif.: Stanford University Press, 1959.

Tobin, S. S. and Bernice L. Neugarten. Life satisfaction and social interaction in the aging. *J. Geront.,* 1961, **16,** 344-346.

Tuckman, J. and I. Lorge. Attitudes toward old people. *J. Soc. Psychol.,* 1953, **37,** 249-260.

Wallach, M. A. and N. Kogan. Aspects of judgment and decision making: interrelationships and changes with age. *Behavioral Sc.,* 1961, **6,** 23-36.

Zinberg, N. E. and I. Kaufman (eds.), *Normal Psychology of the Aging Process.* New York: International Universities Press, Inc., 1963.

11. Aging, Maladjustment, and Psychopathology

A literal definition of "psychopathology" is "the study of mental diseases"—the anatomical and functional origins of disturbances of thought, affect, and overt behavior. Its importance to the student of the psychology of aging is that there is a relationship between the age of an adult and the likelihood of his having certain types of maladjustments and mental disorders. Mental illnesses of advancing age show considerable interaction with the life-long experiences of the individual, his current environment, and his changing anatomy and physiology. There is a broad range of implications of the mental disorders and maladjustments of later life that are important for the health professions as well as for the biological and social sciences. There are many questions to be answered about origins and precipitating factors, as well as more practical ones, such as a legal definition of personal competence and responsibility for behavior. The presence of an older person with a mental disorder creates side effects within families and communities; questions about management as well as responsibility for the maintenance of an aged person with serious maladjustments or a mental disorder are by no means easily answered (*Goldfarb, 1959; Roth and Kay, 1960*).

It is useful to try to distinguish between the age-related and non-age-related contributing factors in mental disorders. Even with a relatively stable personality pattern, the social changes of later life may precipitate mental crises (*Busse,* et al., *1960; Kral, 1962*). Involved in mental disorders associated with aging are the pre-existing personality and temperament, the habit systems of the individual, the nature of the affective investments of the individual, and the extent to which the central nervous system and body organs are free of functional limitations. An individual late in life, for example a widow, may be called upon to make major decisions about issues that she has not considered for years, if ever. The increased cognitive load and the associated tension can lead to crisis behavior. The mechanism may be more clearly seen in children in whom irritable and aggressive behavior may appear when they are faced with an overload on their capacity for problem-solving.

If losses occur too rapidly and the cognitive load of adaptation becomes too great, the individual may not be able to develop appropriate compensations or otherwise be able to accept the decrements; his previous ways of handling situations—e.g., working through, avoiding, denying, dependent load-shedding on other persons, and fantasy—may no longer be adequate. It is not surprising, therefore, to find discussions in the psychiatric literature of individuals who are precipitated into severe mental illness by a laterlife personal crisis. The precipitating factor is viewed as occurring to a person who, because of the physiological and psychological changes of advancing age, is less able to cope with the emotional impact of a given situation. He also may be in a considerably less supportive social environment, thereby not getting the assistance from others that would help him to perceive the essential nature of a situation. A large proportion of persons who suffer from affective disorders of later life appear to recover, indicating that a significant part of serious mental illness in late life is reversible.

Age and Maladjustment. Before considering those forms of psychopathology that are apt to be seen by the professional staff in clinics and mental hospitals, it will be well to consider maladjustments that result in age-related crime, suicide, or attempted suicide. These acts reflect a breakdown in customary controls over behavior. Whether there is a sudden loosening of controls or an increase in motivation leading to the impulse to act, the result is that the strength of the behavior controls is insufficient. Some indications of age changes in the relative strength of behavior controls and drives and motivation may be seen from the data on age and crime. For example, rape tends to be a relatively young man's crime, with 34 per cent of the arrests for rape being in the under twenty-year group and 58 per cent in the twenty- to thirty-nine-year group. Only 8 per cent of the men arrested for forcible rape are over the age of forty, whereas other sex offenses, including exhibitionism and statutory rape, are more common in the older group. Statutory rape laws are designed to protect young girls who may be willing cohabitants but are judged not mature enough to be responsible for their participation. Figure 11-1 shows the arrest for sex offenses by age.

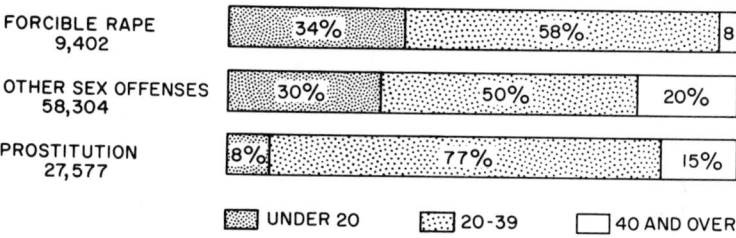

FIGURE 11-1. Age and the percentage of arrests for sex offenses, 1962.
Source: U.S. Department of Justice. *Crime in the United States,* Uniform Crime Reports, 1962 (Washington, D.C.: Federal Bureau of Investigation, 1963).

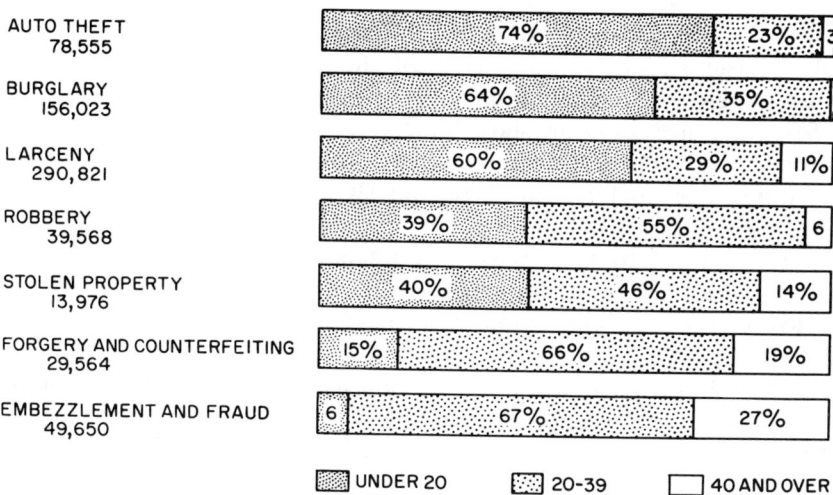

FIGURE 11-2. Age and the percentage of arrests for types of stealing, 1962.
Source: *Ibid.*

Impulsive crime would seem to be more characteristic of youth than of old age, as shown by the arrests for types of stealing. For example, over 74 per cent of the automobile thefts are committed by individuals under the age of twenty. By contrast, only 15 per cent of the forgery and counterfeiting crimes are committed by individuals under twenty and only 6 per cent of those involving embezzlement and fraud. Thus a direct attempt to achieve a goal is characteristic of the young offender. He steals the immediate object he wants, whereas the older adult tends to deal in stolen property obtained by others or in embezzlement and forgery. Figure 11-2 indicates that experience and the opportunity for certain crimes goes up with age. Dealing in stolen properties, forgery, counterfeiting, and embezzling require considerable skill in criminal activity. Therefore they are not usually attempted by the young. The crimes of assault also show an age distribution suggesting that the young person is given to impulsive action. He is most apt to be arrested for carrying and possessing dangerous weapons, 30 per cent of such arrests being in the under-twenty-year group. By contrast, only 15 per cent of the individuals committing murder and manslaughter by negligence are under the age of twenty.

One pattern of crime in older adults is seen in their involvement in illegal business operations (embezzlement, forgery, counterfeiting, prostitution, narcotic law violations, and gambling). Another criminal pattern seen with advancing age is that of drunkenness and vagrancy. Only 3 per cent of the arrests for drunkenness were from the under-twenty-year group, whereas 56 per cent were in the age group forty and over. The generalization may be made that adult crime has aspects of long-established patterns, whereas the crime of the young tends to be more impulsive, characterized by burglary, rape, or stealing automobiles.

Sex differences in crime show some evidence that the male is the more adventurous and perhaps more impulsive criminal. In thefts, men outnumber women: 36 to 1 for burglary, and 30 to 1 for automobile thefts. In embezzlement, men outnumber women only 6 to 1, and in forgeries and counterfeiting, 5 to 1. In possessing weapons of a dangerous sort, male offenders outnumber female offenders 18 to 1. However, murder is committed only four times as often by men as by women. To some extent, the rates for female crimes are lower because, although she often plays an implicit role in crime, the woman is not as subject to arrest; i.e., a wife, girl friend, or mistress of a man gaining his living by crime may also profit from it, but she is less likely to be apprehended and arrested. Crime interacts with family stability and the availability of employment. Nevertheless, there is an age difference in this interaction. In men aged twenty-five to thirty-five, there is a tendency for arrests for property offenses to

Aging, Maladjustment, and Psychopathology

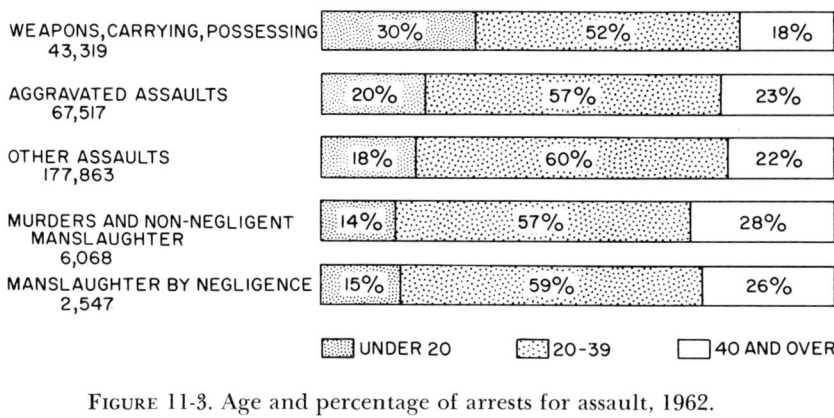

FIGURE 11-3. Age and percentage of arrests for assault, 1962.
Source: Ibid.

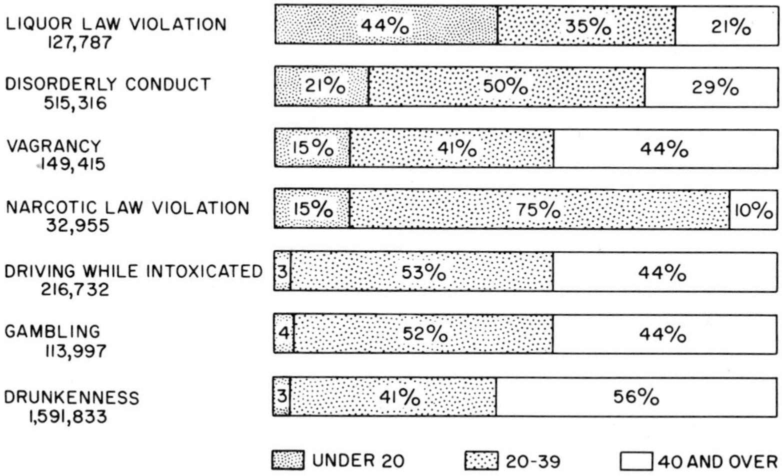

FIGURE 11-4. Age and the percentage of arrests for vice and conduct violations, 1962.
Source: Ibid.

be highly related to current unemployment; however, a somewhat negative relationship is obtained for individuals under age 17. One suggestion is, of course, that as fathers are unemployed, they spend more time with their families. Thus unemployment can lead to a more tightly organized family and greater parental control over children. In periods of unemployment, children under seventeen commit fewer crimes, but unemployed men are more disposed to crime, due to both economic pressure or insecurity and free time. Somewhat puzzling is the tendency for crime to drop in older males during periods of unemployment. Perhaps both older males and younger children are more tightly organized in family patterns during periods of unemployment. One possibility is that since alcohol tends to be used increasingly with age, the unemployed older male seeks solace in alcohol. In contrast, the unemployed younger adult may take some direct action against society by stealing or committing a misdemeanor or some other crime. It may well be that the individual over the age of thirty-five tends to abandon impulsive crime, and if he has a tendency to alcohol, he adopts the use of alcohol as an important element in his way of living. Until there are more detailed statistics on the age trends in crime as a function of unemployment, it is difficult to go further into its psychological or sociological factors.

Suicide and Sex Differences. One of the more puzzling issues is the greater vulnerability of men to depression and suicide in late life (*O'Neal, et al., 1956; Sainsbury, 1955; USDHEW, 1956*). Suicide in males shows a consistent increase over the adult life span. Females show a lesser rise and then a later-life decline. The curves in Figure 11-5 show these remarkable age and sex differences. Generally, the suicide victim (or suicide attempt) appears to have greater than average representation of unfavorable items in his personal history; e.g., more history of family members being institutionalized for mental illness, broken homes in childhood, and prior indication of depression. While these factors may predispose to suicide, they hardly reveal what might be the basis of the sex difference or the age-related variable leading to the increased tendency.

Physical infirmity, chronic illness, or the diagnosis of an incurable disease often leads to depression and a suicide attempt by an older person (*Dovenmuehle and Verwoerdt, 1962*). Rarely does a child attempt suicide when faced with a crippling illness. This suggests that in childhood, stress is not reacted to with a self-directed, hostile act. The reaction on the part of the person seemingly involves the more self-directed feeling that "I am worthless," whereas the young person says, "You have abandoned me, take the blame for my death." The older person seems to have difficulty in evolving new values or a new image of himself that can tolerate an infirmity. Older men in particular find it difficult to accept illness, and when they react by committing suicide, they do so in direct and often violent ways.

Another feature of the age and suicide data which implies that some of the suppositions based upon studies of childhood depression should be re-examined is that of the white-nonwhite differences in suicide. The

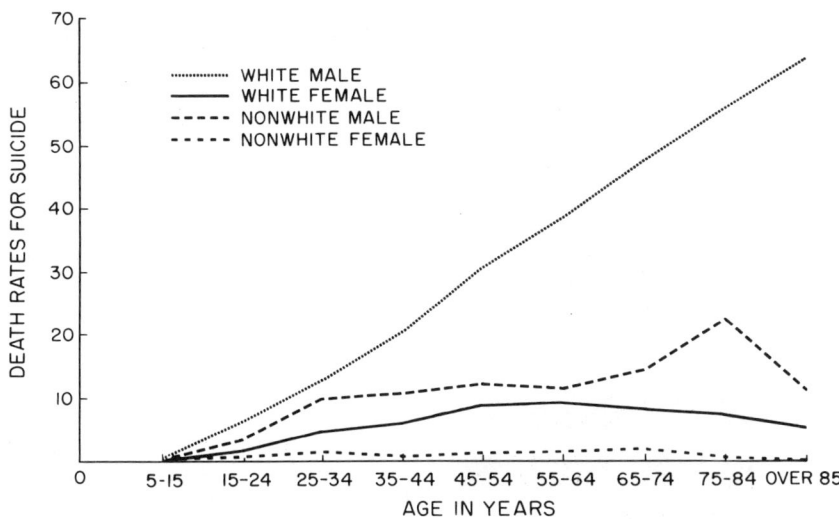

FIGURE 11-5. Suicide death rates by age, sex and race.
Source: USDHEW. *Special Reports* (Washington, D.C.: Bureau of Vital Statistics, 1956).

nonwhite suicide rate is much lower than the white, despite the fact that the nonwhite would generally be expected to grow up under less privileged economic circumstances and to show more social maladjustment during development. A tentative explanation is that the culture surrounding the nonwhite encourages an outwardly aggressive pattern of reaction rather than a self-directed one. These considerations relate to differences in predisposing personality characteristics and not to the dynamics of aging *per se*.

Most older persons are at some time or other involved in a depressive reaction to physical illness. In addition to the frequency of bereavement and other losses, there is a strong likelihood that the depressive reaction is less well prevented and tolerated in an older person and leads to suicide. The total complex of issues may thus involve a body that is less able to withstand the effects of depression and that is also more frequently exposed to precipitating influences. Blindness to an older person who always had excellent vision and was proud of it is quite a different problem from blindness in a child.

Mode of Suicide. Suicides of older persons, particularly men, are usually such as to leave little doubt that they were intentional. Violent acts, such as shooting, jumping out of windows, and drowning, leave little room for the feeling that the older persons expected or wanted to be interrupted in the act. Women are somewhat more passive in their suicide attempts—e.g., they tend to use poison—and for this reason register more unsuccessful attempts than do men. The statistics on deviant behavior, such as crimes and suicide, are perhaps data on caricatures of normal processes, yet the problems are important in themselves and offer clues to shifting motivations with age that may, to lesser degrees, be found within normal personality ranges.

Classes of Mental Illness. The major causes of institutionalization in mental hospitals are shown in Figure 11-6. The late-life diseases of

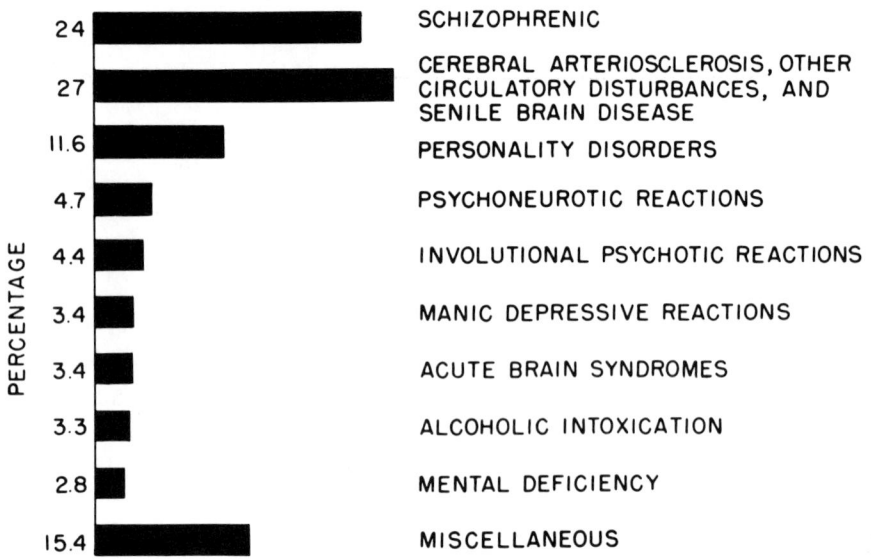

FIGURE 11-6. Diagnostic distribution of first hospital admissions.
Source: *What Are the Facts about Mental Illness?* (National Committee Against Mental Illness, Inc., 1957).

cerebral arteriosclerosis and senile brain disease comprise the most important category of first hospital admissions, followed by schizophrenia. Schizophrenic patients tend to remain in the hospital longer, averaging over ten years, whereas the senile patients, of whom over 70 per cent die in the hospital, have an average stay of about two and one-half years (*Confrey and Goldstein, 1960*). Because the hospital stay of schizophrenic patients is four times longer than that of senile patients, the schizophrenic population in mental hospitals is much greater, perhaps approaching one half of all mental patients, whereas the senile group is probably between 10 and 15 per cent. It should be remembered that relatively few persons of any age group will ever be institutionalized; at any given time, about 1 per cent of all persons age forty-five and over may be mental hospital paitents. Between 1 and 2 per cent of the older population may be expected to be institutionalized for senile mental disease. It should not be assumed that this is an accurate indicator of the true incidence of severe mental disorder in later life, inasmuch as widowed, divorced, and single persons occupy more hospital beds than do the married. Thus social isolation is an important factor in coping with a mentally ill person. The willingness and capability of the social environment to cope with mental illness influences the rate of institutionalization as well as who becomes institutionalized. The tractable but deteriorating senile patient is more apt to be maintained in the community if he is part of a large family than if he is relatively isolated. Furthermore, the types of alternative facilities will determine the kind of hospitalization that the individual will receive; e.g., if it will be a nursing home or a chronic disease hospital. If there are few other facilities available for the geriatric patient, there will be more mental hospital beds occupied by older persons.

It can be assumed that as research on the nervous system and behavior advances, more older individuals will be found to have diagnosable conditions. This does not imply that hospitalization will increase. It has been commented upon that although hospitalization rates of middle-aged persons in western European countries tend to resemble those in America, the hospitalization rates for older patients is much higher in America. This suggests that institutionalization in late life may be more a function of the general social setting than of specific symptoms displayed by any one individual. It is worth mentioning that the uselessness felt by the older, isolated person may be a reflection of urban society's not offering an appreciable number of alternative social roles to give the individual a feeling of significance. Thus social, environmental factors not only enter into the development and precipitation of mental illness, but also determine the "threshold" of institutionalization.

From the foregoing it should not be concluded that the environment is especially hostile to older persons with mental illness. Actually, deviant behavior tends more to be tolerated in older persons than in young adults. Presumably, the "queer" old person is tolerated in public because it is assumed that, while queer, his behavior is benign. In most communities, the permissiveness of the social environment toward deviant behavior tends to increase in relation to age. How much queer behavior will be tolerated from an individual will depend not only upon his age, but also upon the social class of the community, its size, and other background factors.

Several psychiatrists have pointed out that mental illness in older persons can be a side effect of somatic illness; i.e., an infection in an older person may be accompanied by mental aberration (*Roth, 1955; Busse, 1959*). The mental symptoms may not disappear immediately upon recovery of physical health. It might be expected that in relatively undeveloped countries, the associated higher rates of infectious diseases and undernutrition would lead to higher incidence of mental disorder in later life. However, the highly developed social organizations in such societies result in more social and psychological support for individuals than is found in technologically developed countries. An aged rural person living with a large family will probably never come to the attention of the health authorities, even if he has a severe mental illness. In contrast, the relatively isolated, urban, lower class male, without female relatives to ease his burdens, will almost certainly need public assistance and will come to be represented in health statistics.

Elsewhere we have considered the relation of suicides to age. It is perhaps appropriate here to point out an interaction between depressive psychosis and tendency to suicide. The social stresses of growing older in an urban community are much more likely to lead to suicide by an individual who has a disposition to a depressive psychosis than by others. Also, stress on the individual is particularly likely to lead to suicide in a society undergoing a disintegration of previous traditions. There are seasonal variations both in suicide rates and in mental hospital admissions. This emphasizes the fact that the appearance of mental illness in an elderly person is a complex function of a number of factors, including declining physical health, psychological and social isolation (particularly in the disintegrating cultural pattern), and a predisposition (perhaps genetic) to mental illness.

Brain Syndromes. There are some patterns of change in older people which are so specific that they are regarded as distinct clinical entities. One age-related disease of apparent genetic basis is Alzheimer's disease, which has its onset in the middle fifties. It is an unusual disease in that it appears more commonly in women than in men. In Alzheimer's disease there is gross brain atrophy, with widespread degeneration of nerve cells. Pick's disease, which appears in middle age and progresses rapidly to death probably also has genetic basis. As in Alzheimer's disease, there is gross brain deterioration. There are behavioral characteristics that distinguish Alzheimer's and Pick's disease, including the fact that Alzheimer patients appear to have more emotional distress and to be more overactive, whereas in Pick's disease emotional reactions are more blunted (*Busse, 1959; Jervis, 1956*).

Circulatory Disorders

Since the brain is very sensitive to lack of oxygen and cannot survive if deprived of it for more than a very few minutes, any interference with circulation of the blood is extremely serious. One of the relatively common changes in the blood vessel with age is the narrowing of the central lumen, or passage, of the vessel as a consequence of atherosclerosis or arteriosclerosis. These terms refer to deposits in the blood vessel causing a smaller inside diameter and a relative reduction of blood flow to the area supplied.

Cerebral arteriosclerosis with accompanying diminished blood flow leads to a condition known as "cerebral ischemia," or lack of sufficient blood. The state of oxygen deficiency is known by the term "hypoxia"; no oxygen is termed "anoxia." Since interference with blood flow due to arteriosclerosis can develop over a long period, symptoms are slow to appear and there is the opportunity for compensations to develop. When an acute interruption of blood supply occurs, there are disturbances of function within the local regions of the brain that will appear, for example, in motor behavior, speech, hearing, or other functions, depending upon the precise localization of the interruption. The dying cells may be hyperirritable, and the local disturbance that they may initiate may lead to epileptic-like seizures, as observed in connection with cerebral arteriosclerosis. An individual with frequent complaints of headaches, dizziness, and emotional outbursts may often have fainting attacks and convulsions. Since the vascular system is involved, there also may be evidence of elevated blood pressure. Because of the frequency of arteriosclerotic conditions and the relative difficulty in diagnosing them in the brain, there is perhaps a tendency to overdiagnose cerebral arteriosclerosis. There seems little doubt, however, that in individuals in whom there is a disturbance of circulation in late life, arteriosclerosis is the dominant pace-maker of the behavior changes. A study was made of 505 patients who, upon entering a mental hospital, were initially diagnosed as either being senile or as having arteriosclerotic psychosis (*Simon and Neal, 1963*). All of these patients died in the hospital and were studied neuropathologically. About one third of them showed senile brain disease. In about one fourth of the cases, cerebral arteriosclerosis was the main finding, with about one fifth of the total cases displaying a mixed picture of senile and arteriosclerotic changes. Of the total 505 cases, 61 per cent displayed significant senile brain diseases and 44 per cent significant arteriosclerotic brain disease. Thus according to these findings, the most frequent diagnostic error was that of diagnosing more cerebral arteriosclerosis than in fact existed.

It is evident from the studies done on healthy older men at the National Institute of Mental Health that reduction in cerebral blood flow and metabolic rate are not necessary concomitants of growing older. In general, men above the age of sixty-five who were judged to be healthy, or free from significant somatic disease, had blood flows and cerebral metabolic rates approximately equivalent to those of young men. In related studies, it was apparent that with individuals in whom there was a reduction in cerebral metabolic rate, the reduction in blood flow appeared to be the antecedent cause. It seems plausible that a change in the blood vessels from a sclerotic process was reducing the blood flow. Thus the interpretation that an interference with blood flow leads to brain deterioration and alterations of behavior is appropriate for a significant proportion of older persons. However, a somewhat larger proportion of individuals who need hospitalization for mental illness are not covered by this explanation. These are the individuals who are appropriately diagnosed as having senile brain disease.

Senile Brain Disease. There have been studies reported by neuropathologists and neuropsychiatrists on the relationships between the changes found in the brains of hospitalized individuals when compared with their previous clinical picture and behavioral symptoms. Earlier studies reported that brains of distinguished elderly men who were competent shortly before death showed changes that, when present in large amounts, are characteristic of senile brain disease; e.g., senile plaques. Indeed, some studies attempted to show that, on the basis of the condition of the brains, it would not be possible to distinguish elderly patients who had been hospitalized for mental illness and those dying from other causes. These studies—although qualified because of more recent findings—did establish that considerable changes may occur in the brains of older persons without producing clear-cut behavioral symptoms or the appearance of mental illness. These results suggest the need for finer observation of the pathological, as well as the behavioral changes. It seems most necessary to assume an interrelation of brain and behavior, for without it one is in the unrealistic position of believing that the integrity of the brain has no influence on the adequacy of behavior. Obviously, all the changes in the behavior of an older person cannot be explained as being caused solely by changes within cells and in the circulation of the brain.

A study was made of the brains obtained in 300 consecutive postmortem examinations of patients in a mental hospital (*Corsellis, 1962*). The case histories of the individuals were analyzed separately from the postmortem examination, and the two sets of data were then compared. Patients were divided by diagnostic groups according to whether the disorder was associated with vascular, cerebral-senile, or mixed vascular and senile changes. The functional psychoses included affective disorders, schizophrenia, paranoia, and psychoneurotic and psychopathic disorders.

The brains were categorized as to their macroscopic changes, including cerebral atrophy and changes in blood vessels, and as to their microscopic anatomy. In the total sample, 40 per cent were judged to have had cardiovascular disease as a cause of death. Even though the patients died from the common causes, the diagnostic groups did show different characteristic patterns of brain changes. Moderate or severe cerebral atrophy was found in 71 per cent of the brains of the senile group and in 39 per cent of the vascular group.

At the microscopic level of observation, it was found that the senile plaques in the cortex occurred in 36 per cent of those judged to have had an organic basis for their psychosis and in only 9 per cent of the functional cases. Patients diagnosed as having senile dementia showed both microscopic and macroscopic changes in their brains that differentiated them as a group from the patients diagnosed as having cerebral vascular disease. The mixed diagnosis group, indeed, showed a mixed proportion of brain changes. One of the more important implications of the study is that patients diagnosed as having a functional disorder —i.e., affective, schizophrenic, or paranoid—can be expected with advancing age to show vascular or senile changes in the brain in proportion to what might be expected from the population as a whole. Thus being schizophrenic neither raises nor lowers the probability of developing a senile brain disorder. The fact that senile brain disease occurs concomitantly with the functional psychoses in the same proportion as in the general population clearly underscores the fact that there are distinct etiologies to these diseases. The largely separate, though concomitantly occurring, vascular and senile changes are shown by the differing proportions of the findings. In patients judged to have had a vascular basis for their psychoses at postmortem examination, 76 per cent were found to have had moderate to severe vascular changes. The senile psychotic group, by contrast, had 37 per cent similarly judged. At the microscopic level, 27 per cent of the vascular group were found to have had senile plaque formation, in contrast to 80 per cent in the senile group. These figures can also be compared with the affective disorders, in which 28 per cent showed moderate or severe vascular change and none showed moderate or severe senile plaque formation.

It has become apparent that in order to discover relationships between the organic and functional disorders, with their probable antecedents and resultant behavior, more discriminating studies need to be made at the cognitive and personality, as well as at the neuropathological level. Some studies are in fact now being made. As part of one such study, an analysis was made of a group of 534 patients admitted after the age of sixty to the psychiatric receiving wards in San Francisco (*Simon and Neal, 1963*). The role of organic brain deterioration in cognitive functioning is seen in the fact that patients judged to have senile disorders had a mean weighted score of 16.1 on four of the Wechsler Adult Intelligence subtests, in comparison with a mean weighted score of 32.2 for problem drinkers. In the National Institute of Mental Health study, normal elderly men scored equal or higher values than did young adults on these same tests. Thus there is no reason to doubt that organic brain disease of later life does lead to involution of cognitive functioning. Further quantitative studies should permit an even more definitive separation of disease types, as well as a more accurate assessment of therapy. Even though there is a high correlation between the individual's cognitive level of functioning and the integrity of his brain, it does not follow that there exists a one-to-one relationship between these two variables and the affective status of the individual or his ability to maintain himself in the community. The latter, of course, is largely dependent on personal living arrangements and the support found in the environment. Since an isolated individual is much more likely to be institutionalized at any given stage of disease, a proper assessment of the many factors contributing to mental disorders of later life depends upon an accurate description of the physical and social environment of the individual, his present affective and cognitive functioning, and his physiological and psychiatric status.

Studies of Psychopathology in the Population. In the study of hospital admission of older persons in the city of San Francisco, it was found that some of the factors contributing to the hospitalization of older people are apparent in the fact that about one half of the city's population over the age of sixty-five lives alone *(Simon and Neal, 1963)*. Of this group, 55 per cent had no income other than Social Security, pension, or public welfare. Thus these individuals were largely dependent upon public out-patient clinics for medical attention. It is of interest to note that San Francisco had about twice the rate of hospitalization of older persons than other urban areas. The authors thought that this reflected the fact that in San Francisco there are very few alternatives of domiciliary and nursing care facilities available for low-income groups.

A sample of 534 individuals who had never entered a psychiatric ward before the age of sixty was also studied. It was found that they were relatively socially isolated, for only 27 per cent of the men and 18 per cent of the women were married; this is significantly lower than in the general population. Diagnosis tends to be multiple in the older person, and alcoholism and somatic illness often seem to be involved in the psychiatric problem presented. Only 13 per cent of the sample were diagnosed as having a depressive disorder. This is a lower proportion than is found in England and perhaps suggests some differences between England and the United States in diagnostic criteria and in the social factors involved in hospital admission for affective disorders. It is of interest to note at this point that in the San Francisco area the successful suicide is usually a man. In a one-year period, 71 per cent of the successful suicides were men. Of the attempted suicides, 53 per cent were men and 47 per cent women. An analysis of suicide based on studies of those who have attempted suicide will probably give a biased representation of the total group, since individuals who use active methods are more likely to succeed.

The study of Simon and Neal emphasizes the role of physical disability in hospitalization for mental illness in late life. In their study group, 80 per cent of the patients "required extensive care or supervision for physical reasons alone."

Sensory changes in late life may amplify the consequences of mental illness; i.e., a higher proportion of elderly paranoids or schizophrenics are found to have auditory or visual defects. These sensory impairments further isolate the individual from persons in the environment who may be available to help him. Since schizophrenic patients usually remain hospitalized for a long time, they may suffer sensory impairments as well as other brain changes during their hospital stay. The question arises whether aging, paranoia, and schizophrenia may interact. Similarly, there is a question concerning the late-life fate of patients earlier diagnosed as obsessive compulsive neurotics. It has been reported that compulsive obsessive neurotics become more tolerable in their compulsion with advancing age (*Müller, 1963*). It is interesting that in late life, compulsive traits may actually have some utility, in that they trigger the individual to action in structuring an ambiguous environment; e.g., retirement (*Perlin and Butler, 1963*).

Actively hallucinating schizophrenics may calm down in old age. As a result of his study of 101 aged schizophrenics, Müller found that thirty-two of them had some organic brain syndrome. The presumed senile processes had no affect on the form or content of the schizophrenic psychosis in one half of the patients. In the remaining one half, however, he found a marked change, although not a simple one, since it was either in the disappearance of delusions or in the expansion and consolidation of the delusional state. The reduction of affectivity played a useful role in symptom reduction in some patients, whereas presumably the cognitive deterioration adversely affected the psychotic manifestations in others. It is apparent that aging and schizophrenia are not at opposite poles of a continuum. No simple summarizing statement can be made about the changes in schizophrenic patients in whom senile brain disease may appear in later life with appreciable frequency.

Elements of Geriatric Psychiatry. Most of the mental disorders of later life have no specific therapeutic measures. In particular, the organic psychoses are not at all well understood. It is to be anticipated that control over cerebral arteriosclerotic psychoses will advance rapidly once the process of arteriosclerosis is known. However, the somewhat larger group of senile mental disorders will still remain. Insight into their basic processes will require detailed studies of the metabolism and biochemistry of the aging brain. Studies of neurophysiological and psychological functioning in the affective disorders give great promise of effective treatment, because both psychopharmacological agents and electroshock therapy prove beneficial. In addition to geriatric psychiatry's concern with the treatment of mental disorders in the individual, there is a small but growing field of the social psychiatry of aging. Social changes, such as the disruption of social customs by war, tend to have a severe effect on the aged. Changing conditions of employment are particularly stressful for older persons. These broad factors contributing to the occurrence of mental illness in later life need study from the point of view of public mental health.

The question may be raised about the legitimacy of the term "geriatric psychiatry"; i.e., whether there is a geriatric, as distinct from child, psychiatry. One point of view holds that the developmental principles of personality are applicable to a person of any age. A more balanced point of view suggests that while many of the same mechanisms may be involved in mental disorders of later life as in childhood, the antecedents have different proportions and the problems themselves appear in quite different environmental and organic contexts. Thus the child is generally an expanding organism moving toward a goal of increased capacities, whereas the older adult has begun to limit his activities, if only because of the normal process of adaptation. Adapting to the demands of his environment over a great number of years restricts the individual's potential for responding to crisis situations. In addition, there is a great probability that organic disease is present in the older person. Recognition of this, however, frequently leads to the assumption that all behavior disorders in older persons have organic causes. This error is equivalent to the opposite error, often made by professionals most familiar with young children; i.e., the error of assuming that organic factors contribute little compared with the events in the individual's life history. Between the excesses of an overly functional approach to behavior disorders of later life and the overly organic emphasis, there is a balanced point of view that attempts to discern proportions of contributing factors both in individuals and in the population.

Families often need to seek medical and psychiatric assistance for an aging member who displays behavior described as having "senile" qualities. These include overly simplified and dogmatic points of view toward the environment and self, reduced capacity for abstract reasoning, and limited recent memory, with a resulting tendency toward confusion. In a study of qualities that predispose toward the psychiatrist's making a diagnosis of "senile," it was indicated that ". . . cognitive disfunction, alterations in behavior, and disturbances in affective expression . . ." cause others to view the individual as being or becoming senile (*Perlin* and Butler, 1963, p. 167). Frequently masquerading as "aging" is depression in response to environmental loss. The apathy associated with depression in an older person is often perceived as senility rather than as a reversible emotional state.

Late-life mental disorders can arise from the individual's having had a long-standing pattern of psychopathology that proves inadequate to meet the special circumstances of later life. New psychopathology can emerge, however, without organic antecedents. The question then becomes: What is the likelihood of personality, environment, or organic disorders producing constellations of typical behavior in the later life? The National Institute of Mental Health studies of healthy elderly men clearly indicate that cerebral blood flow and the cerebral metabolic rate are not necessarily reduced in men in their seventies and eighties, although severe reductions in blood flow and cerebral metabolic rate are seen in individuals diagnosed as having chronic brain syndrome (*Dastur*, et al., *1963*). Such individuals also show severe impoverishment on psychological tests and frequently are beyond the range that permits testing. Early failures to find a precise relationship between organic changes in the brain and prior alterations in personality and behavior led to the impression that there was a considerable disparity between neuropathology, or brain lesions, and alterations of behavior. Recent studies have modified this overinterpretation. When considering only those patients who enter mental hospitals late in life, of whom there are large numbers, questions arise as to the extent to which their brains differ from those of individuals still maintaining a satisfactory life in the community and the extent to which the brains of patients with different diagnoses resemble, or differ from each other.

Many problems of mental disorders and maladjustment have not been discussed in this chapter, some because they are regarded as being too specialized, others because no general principle is involved or because there is so little information about them. Much of the professional writing is based upon statistics of individuals who seek attention for their problems by virtue of their own or others' initiative. Clinics and professional persons see a highly select sample of the population. Consider the period of menopause in women, which has been regarded in the folklore as "difficult." Studies at the University of Chicago indicate that most women adjust well during this period, suggesting that the small proportion of women who require medical attention are not typical. Because of the recognition that institutional samples may be highly unusual, research in psychiatry and related fields is now being directed to portions of the population that would not ordinarily be seen in institutions or by professional persons.

There are many issues to be explored more fully in relation to aging, such as what happens in late life to the early compulsive neurotic, to the homosexual and erotomaniac when their drives are lessened with age.

The results of the superimposition of aging and senile brain changes upon early life psychosis may reveal something about the basic processes of both. The aged subnormal is yet another member of a group that will "age" in perhaps a special manner (*Kaplan, 1956*). There is much that tends to screen the scientist from the basic facts, yet improvements in research methods can now lead to better distinctions beween the transient emotional states and moods of aging and the persistent symptoms of underlying pathology and those symptoms which appear in such regular form that they are found to comprise a syndrome. As the normal psychology is better defined and understood and more detailed attention is given to older deviant individuals, it seems likely that new syndromes will be identified in the older population. Knowledge in this area is far from static, and it is to be expected that finer discriminations will continually be made among the mental problems associated with advancing age.

Summary

Many forms of deviant behavior and mental illness change in their frequency with age. The relative frequencies of forms of socially deviant behavior suggest that with age there are shifts in the motivation to act as well as in the controls over behavior. Rape tends to be a young man's crime; arrests for exhibitionism, by contrast, are greater with age. In terms of arrests, younger men steal automobiles and older men deal in stolen property or engage in embezzlement and forgery. Men seriously outnumber women in thefts (36 to 1 for burglary), although arrests for murder is only four times more common in men than in women. Property offenses tend to be related to unemployment, but it affects younger and older men differently; crime rises with unemployment in the group aged twenty-five to thirty-five but declines in those over thirty-five.

Suicide shows a consistent and large rise with age in men, and is higher for whites than for nonwhites. A sex difference is also seen, with women showing a slight rise in the middle years and then a decline after sixty, in the same age range in which the male suicide rate is increasing. Illness and physical infirmity seem to play a precipitating role in the suicides of men. The large age, sex, and white-nonwhite differences in suicide indicate that the social environment, as well as personal values, is of major importance. The violent modes of suicide chosen by older men leave little doubt of their serious intent, in contrast to more ambivalent suicide attempts of younger persons.

Although patients with mental diseases of later life comprise the largest group of first admissions to mental hospitals, they do not constitute the largest group in the hospital since their death rates are high. Schizophrenic patients tend to remain in hospitals longer (average ten years) than senile patients (average two and one half years), most of whom die in the hospital. Relative to the total population, few persons over sixty-five ever become mental hospital patients; only about 1 to 2 per cent. This figure, however, does not fully represent the frequency of mental disorder in the older population. Populations differ in their capacity to contain the older deviant person, although in general, the community is more permissive toward the deviant behavior of older than of younger persons. The widowed, single, and divorced occupy many more beds in institutions than do married persons. Thus social isolation is a factor in the likelihood of institutionalization.

Circulatory impairment and senile brain deterioration occur both separately and together in older patients. Studies indicate that advancing age is not necessarily related to a reduction in blood flow to the brain. Recent studies show that the type of brain deterioration is related to the kind of symptoms shown by a patient, but that mixtures of organic and functional factors are frequently found. Diagnosis tends to be multiple in the older person, with interaction taking place between somatic and mental illness and the social environment throughout the course of the illness. Physical factors are being increasingly recognized as having functional consequences in older persons, not only in depressive affect, which may lead to suicide, but also as factors in precipitating mental disorder.

Geriatric psychiatry is giving more emphasis to mixed causality, or etiology, in mental illness in older persons, and finding that fewer persons have symptoms regarded as categorically either functional or organic in background. It is expected that further disease patterns in the older population will be defined as research methods now available are applied to representative samples of the populations as well as to clinically-selected groups. As more knowledge of the normal psychology of aging is acquired, the treatment of the older patient will become more specific and more rationally based.

References

*Busse, E. W. Psychopathology. In J. E. Birren (ed.), *Handbook of Aging and the Individual,* pp. 364-399. Chicago: University of Chicago Press, 1959.

———, R. H. Dovenmuehle, and R. G. Brown. Psychoneurotic reactions of the aged. *Geriatrics,* 1960, **15,** 97-105.

*Cameron, N. Neuroses of later maturity. In O. J. Kaplan (ed.), *Mental Disorders of Later Life,* pp. 201-243. Stanford, Calif.: Stanford University Press, 1956.

*Cavan, Ruth S. *Criminology.* New York: Thomas Y. Crowell Company, 1962.

Confrey, E. A., and M. S. Goldstein. The health status of aging people. In C.

---

* Suggested additional reading.

Tibbitts (ed.), *Handbook of Social Gerontology,* pp. 165-207. Chicago: University of Chicago Press, 1959.

*Corsellis, J. A. N. *Mental Illness and the Ageing Brain.* London: Oxford University Press, 1962.

Dastur, D. K., M. H. Lane, D. B. Hansen, S. S. Kety, R. N. Butler, S. Perlin, and L. Sokoloff. Effects of aging on cerebral circulation and metabolism in man. In J. E. Birren, R. N. Butler, S. W. Greenhouse, L. Sokoloff, and Marian R. Yarrow (eds.), *Human Aging,* pp. 59-76. Washington, D.C.: Government Printing Office, 1963, Public Health Publication No. 986.

Dovenmuehle, R. H. and A. Verwoerdt. Physical illness and depressive symptomatology. I: Incidence of depressive symptoms in hospitalized cardiac patients. *J. Amer. Geriatrics Soc.,* 1962, **10,** 932-947.

Glaser, D. and K. Rice. Crime, age, and employment. In M. E. Wolfgang, L. Savitz, N. Johnston (eds.), *The Sociology of Crime and Delinquency,* pp. 163-169. New York: John Wiley & Sons, Inc., 1962.

Goldfarb, A. I. Depression, brain damage, and chronic illness of the aged; psychiatric diagnosis and treatment. *J. Chronic Dis.,* 1959, **9,** 220-233.

Himler, L. E. and Virginia Morrisey. Factors influencing prognosis in psychiatric illness of the aged. *J. Amer. Geriatrics Soc.,* 1955, **3,** 811-816.

Jervis, G. A. The presenile dementias. In Kaplan (ed.), *op. cit.,* pp. 262-288.

Kaplan, O. J. The aged subnormal. In *ibid.,* pp. 383-397.

Kral, V. A. Stress and mental disorders of the senium. *Canadian Med. Serv. J.,* 1962, **18,** 363-370.

*McGill University Conference on Depression and Allied States. *Canadian Psychiat. Assoc. J.,* 1959, **4,** Special Suppl.

Müller, C. The influence of age on schizophrenia. In R. H. Williams, C. Tibbitts, and Wilma Donahue (eds.), *Processes of Aging,* **1,** 504-511. New York: Atherton Press, 1963.

O'Neal, Patricia, E. Robins, and E. H. Schmidt. A psychiatric study of attempted suicide in persons over sixty years of age. *Arch. Neurol. Psychiat.,* 1956, **75,** 275-284.

Perlin, S., and R. N. Butler. Psychiatric aspects of adaptation to the aging experience. In Birren, *et al.* (eds.), *op. cit.,* pp. 159-213.

*Post, F. *The Significance of Affective Symptoms in Old Age.* London: Oxford University Press, 1962.

Roth, M. The natural history of mental disorder in old age. *J. Ment. Sc.,* 1955, **101,** 281-301.

——— and D. W. K. Kay. Enquiries into mental disorder in old age. *Postgrad. Med. J.,* 1960, **36,** 270-275.

*Rothschild, D. Senile psychoses and psychoses with cerebral arteriosclerosis. In Kaplan *op. cit.,* pp. 289-331.

Sainsbury, P. *Suicide in London,* Mandsley Monogr. No. 1. London: Chapman & Hall, Ltd., 1955.

Simon, A., and M. W. Neal. Patterns of geriatric mental illness. In Williams, *et al.* (eds.), *op. cit.,* pp. 449-471.

Stenbäck, A. On involutional and middle age depressions. *Nordiska Psykiaterkongressen,* **13,** p. 19.

U.S. Department of Health, Education and Welfare. *Suicide.* Washington, D.C.: Government Printing Office, Vol. 43, No. 30, 1956.

12. Life Review, Reconciliation, and Termination

The lives of individuals may be reviewed looking backward from the end toward their beginning. However, unlike with historical reconstruction of biographical information, an individual lives his life in a forward direction from its beginning. The reader of the diaries of a deceased person can know what the outcome will be; the person writing did not. Thus the historical reader who knows something about the end is in a position to judge the significance of passing events. It is only after the individual has arrived at a resting stage of development that he can look back and review the path by which he came. This chapter will examine some aspects of the last phase of life, in which the imminence of death may provoke an individual to review his life. It will require a shift in tone and content from the preceding chapters, since the last phase of life has not usually been treated in a scientific context. Thus one function of this chapter, in addition to providing facts, is to help supply concepts and language to aid in bringing this period of the life span into an objective context, so that relationships between variables may be posed and explored empirically.

As individuals move from middle age to late life, they

face new issues in ways consistent with the way in which they have lived their life to date. An interesting example of this is the book *Senescence*, written by G. S. Hall upon his retirement as Professor of Psychology and President of Clark University. Hall was known for his work in adolescence, so the developmental theme of his book on later life was a natural one. What is of interest is Hall's implicit conviction that thought and logic would put his concerns in order. His book on senescence, while developed in scholarly form, contains his personal attempt to reconcile his views on old age and death. One senses in his scholarship an attempt to exorcise his concerns and fears with a demonstration of crystal-clear reasoning. Others less well educated might have the same anxieties about the future, about being alone, or about disabling illness, yet not be able to verbalize them.

Those who deny that death might be imminent have no need to review. Perhaps one might "type" persons in their approach to the end of life as follows: welcomers, accepters, postponers, disdainers, and fearers (*cf. Schneidman, 1963*). Some will be concerned about getting in order what they are leaving, some with where they are going, and some will not think about anything. It is perhaps too easy to take the writings of educated persons as expressing models for reactions. Although it is emphasized in the following pages that nearness to the end of life is provocative of life review, it is highly uncertain whether many persons are inclined to the major attempt at a theoretical integration of their lives that Hall undertook. Reminiscing in the aged has implications of a life review without the overtones of evaluation of the educated, somewhat compulsive person. Fantasy and confabulation may also serve to reconcile the past, present, and expected future.

Death is a *social, psychological,* and *biological* phenomenon. For the individual, the imminence of death has psychological consequences not explained by a sequence of chemical changes. An awareness in late life of the likelihood of death can set in motion a more complete review of life's events than might characterize previous periods, when an individual may have been halted in his forward motion and led to review his actions and values. The task is to integrate one's life as it has been lived in relation to how it might have been lived. The individual thus is integrating and reconciling what he sees in this retrospective account with his earlier life values, as well as the values he has come to accept over his adult life. The empirical basis of the concept "life review" lies in the experiences of psychiatrists and religious leaders, as well as in those with broad family experience who have seen the aged "set their house in order." One psychiatrist has said, "The universal occurrence of an inner experience or mental process of reviewing one's life in older people is postulated" (*Butler, 1963, p. 65*). Not everyone is privileged to experience the process of life review and reconciling his omission and commissions of behavior with his personal system of values. Illness may be so abrupt or so cloud the intellect that a process of life review is seriously interfered with or prevented. Hall has commented upon the occurrence of a period of "Indian Summer clarity," implying that psychic life has a period of extreme lucidity before death. To the mental clarity should be added a phase of emotional stabilization when the individual is freed from the struggles of his life.

Life review is not a passive process; it is a constructive effort to achieve an active, purposeful form of reminiscense. The reminiscences of older persons are not only to recall facts, but also to weave them into an acceptable perspective. Perhaps the individual is provoked into a life review by somatic changes or by information from the environment telling him that he is highly vulnerable and may not have much longer to live. The realization of one's vulnerability or approaching death can be accompanied by the progressive return to consciousness of details of events and unsolved conflicts from the past.

Futurity

Futurity is often an escape from present conflict, as well as a sign of the developing individual. Hope that the future will bring gratifications not found in the present is a common and normal mechanism of maintaining our psychological equilibrium. An unrealistic hope for the future uses fantasy as an easy way of escaping present action to solve conflicts in life. With the likelihood of death in the near future, futurity may no longer be a useful or acceptable mechanism to the individual. He thus reorganizes his attitudes toward the events of his life and attempts to square the content of his life with his early values and expectations. The point is repeated that life review is not a garrulous story telling or passive, reminiscing review but a response to a need for a reorganization of attitudes toward the content of one's life. By reconciling his past life with his wishes and values, the individual is preparing for the uncertainties of death, which appear to be more acceptable if he evolves an acceptable image of himself and of the influences he will leave behind.

The forms of the life review may vary from a mild, nostalgic recall to severe depression with anxiety, guilt, and suicidal tendencies (*Butler, 1963*). Life review should not, however, be viewed as a psychopathological phenomenon but as a common, normal experience.

Certain elements of the life review are seen in other, earlier experiences. For the woman, it might have come at the time the last child left home. A man may have had somewhat the same reaction to reviewing his life when faced with retirement or with an earlier sudden realization that his career was no longer expanding. In addition to the grief, death of a spouse is another precipitator of a life review. Such events, and more particularly the review associated with one's own imminent death, may be helped by the special qualities of a sympathetic listener. While for some individuals, a goodly portion of this may involve content best reviewed with a religious adviser, much of it lies outside direct religious concerns. Resolution of such early issues as one's behavior in relation to a brother or sister or to one's mother or father may not involve religious concepts. In the life review, there is much concern with the image that the individual believes he is leaving or wishes to leave behind. This leads to deathbed gifts, forgiveness, reconciliation of lifelong hates and loves, and the transmitting of one's interpretation of the meaning of life. Not only does the essential meaning of life appear to need clarification, but also the stewardship of one's life has to be reconciled. The personality of the individual during his life is obviously relevant to how he handles this situation. Also, whether the individual feels he has much time or only a few days to get his psychological house in order influences his approach. His techniques of early-life conflict reduction are also employed in terminal conflict resolution and in the quality of integration. For example, does he tend to involve other people, or does he try to think things through by himself? Successful terminal conflict reduction also has important implications for the surviving friends and relatives of the individual. There is thus a need for a sophisticated terminal counsellor to help the dying, his relatives, and friends, lest past conflicts get increasingly distorted and perpetuated for another generation.

Content of the Review. The tendency to think more often about the past and to talk about it to others can be easily misinterpreted, for several motivations of the speaker and listener are likely to be involved. Because the reminiscences may be annoying to others, they are often depreciated as either a sign of degradation of the aged person or as aggressive behavior in order to "capture the ears" of others without the obligations of an interpersonal relationship. But in the conversations of the aged there are other elements as well, and because these may be disquieting, it is easier for family members to disparage and to avoid such conversations.

More than must a young person, the older individual must see and reconcile his past place in the world of people, places, and things. He is under pressure to integrate his views of his past, faced as he is with an inevitable but uncertain future. In an aggressive vein, the older person may exhort the young to follow in his footsteps, in order to insure his own immortality in the material world that he expects to be leaving soon. This may involve the wish to have the young succeed, and the old undoubtedly believe their values and folkways define the proper life for the young. Thus urging the young may be a matter of deep conviction, and not merely an attempt to recruit in a last minute maneuver. Less constructive, and perhaps less admirable, are attempts by the old to insure the young's preserving their memory by gifts of money and promises of what they will receive in willed property.

Relationships of many years' standing are such complex matters of checks and balances that the interest on the part of the aged person to reconcile or relieve tensions may be upsetting or even painful. Children of mature years will find this difficult, and it is not unlikely that the aged themselves will try to spare their children some of the implications of parental thoughts.

The extent to which the sorting, integrating, and jettisoning of the details of one's life go on at various times is indicated by remarks made by G. S. Hall upon his retirement:

> As preliminary to even this, it slowly came to me that I must, first of all, take careful stock of myself and now seek to attain more the self-knowledge that Socrates taught the world was the highest, hardest, and last of all forms of knowledge (p. 14). As my horizon changed and I became more at home with myself, and personal problems grew nearer and clear, I realized that I must make a new plan of life, in which both tasks and also a program of renunciation played a very prominent initial part. This began with a literal house cleaning (p. 17). I had for years collected pamphlets and bound volumes on many topics in the vague hope of some future use, but which I now realize will never be warmed up again (p. 18).

He also weeded out his old lecture notes.

> How crude and impossible now were these earlier reminders of my professional activity! What a prodigious amount of work, time, and even manual labor they involved! What hardihood of inference and conclusion! What immaturity and even foolhardiness of judgment on some of the greatest problems of life! If I wanted to dignify or even glorify my old age at the expense of my youth, here are abundant data for so doing. But I do not, and so I found peculiar pleasure in consigning, with my own hands, armfuls of such manuscript to the flames (p. 19).

Such a physical weeding out of papers is probably a preliminary step to the later sorting over of memories of personal events. Some psychological elements may be evoked when the letters of youth to youth and of youth to parents and those between lovers are handled and read and the question arises about what to do with them. One suspects that the thoughts of most people in such a situation are that those to follow will have little interest in the letters and it is better to destroy them in a respectful way than leave them for some later, less feeling disposal.

At the time of physical house cleaning, often at retirement, a man may become more aware than he was before that not everyone is reluctant to see him leave his job. Later still, one wonders whether one's death might not indeed be welcomed by some. This realization may be tinged with the desire to repair certain relationships. As he comes nearer the end of his life, the aged person needs more and more psychological support from fewer and fewer available individuals. His ability to secure this rapport and support involves not only his skills, but also the capacity of his listener to discern what he is doing and saying, both manifestly and latently. Since a very old person may have lost all close peers, the listener may well be considerably younger than he. Hopefully, such a young person will have his own relationships with parents and other older persons sufficiently in order so that lingering resentments or unsolved childhood relations will not intrude into the rational conduct of the present. Not all that is stored in memory need be recalled and impressed with determination into an ear captured by filial or professional duty. A discerning interest and supporting rapport for the excesses of verbalization and emotion should insure that the desired point will emerge. Few modern individuals will believe that they can tidy up their lives so readily as did King John of England, of Magna Carta note, who before he died in 1216 requested that he be buried between two saints already buried in Worcester Cathedral, because he said that on Judgment Day he might slip into Heaven unnoticed between the two saintly figures of St. Oswald and St. Wulstan.

In his review and reconciliation, the older person looks to his parents who went before and to children, relations, and friends following after. He might still wonder if his parents treated him fairly, and if he in turn treated his old parents well. If he turned away from his own parents in late life, he realizes that now is the moment for the consequences to emerge, perhaps to become aware that he is receiving attention as a matter of duty rather than because he is loved.

Sudden emergence of long-standing memories of a seemingly bizarre sort need not be indicative of psychopathology, but simply of the fact that the individual has a new intent or strong purpose. Many memories may sweep through the individual and flood him with more information and affect than he can integrate. Faced with imminent death, the controls and inhibitions of many years are broken down and the individual may speak afresh of events of long ago with new candor. Thus although life review is considered to be a universal and normative process, it may have varied and include strong psychopathological manifestations and violent outcomes; e.g., suicide.

Attention must be drawn to both the adaptive and maladaptive aspects of the life review. It is believed that the process often involves personality reintegration following re-evaluation of life's experiences. It was earlier pointed out that the older individual, provoked by the fear of an uncertain future, may actually devote more time than previously to squaring relations with those to be left behind. In this sense, the individual wants to "write" a corrected autobiography to be left in the hands of those of special concern. To some extent, the major figures in the person's life may change positions; i.e., while the mother may have assumed considerable significance in the feelings of security and love throughout the life span, the father may stand for the values and goals to which the individual aspired. Thus there may be a new balance created in the psychological identification of the individual with the mother and the father. An actively upward mobile individual may have crossed several social class boundaries during his life span and transiently adopted the social values of the class in which he was a member. What form of effective reconciliation might be found in the terminal life review of such individuals is a matter of conjecture.

Impending death also brings with it problems of transmission of property. Contemporary American society and families place less value upon keeping the family estate intact than did past societies. Nevertheless, transmission of possessions links the ancestors with the succeeding generation, and inheritance is associated with emotional issues that go far beyond the material value of the possessions. It is not surprising therefore that the life review and reconciliation may lead to reconsiderations of earlier made wills. In the novel *Memento Mori,* Muriel Spark describes characters who show the overconcern that some older people may have with wills. Some individuals with psychopathological deviousness attempt to control those around them by promises of inheritance.

In families in which there is a strong emphasis on farm lands, for example, the transmission of lands to the children has strong overtones in which the dying person may feel he is the present steward for his ancestors. He must resolve the potential conflicts over inheritance in terms both of his personal feelings toward his children and of his attitudes toward the values of his ancestors. There are also conflicts over inheritance by the implied differences in affection and recognition given to the children, and family ties are often weakened or broken as a result of the way in which property is transmitted. Reconciling matters involves a rather complex matrix of influences; how well a man resolves them influences the generation to follow. Rituals and manner of transmission of family control and property also bear a relation to familial conflicts.

Published candid life reviews of the successful and unsuccessful, the notable and the obscure, should add much to our knowledge of the psychological development of the individual over the life span. This would not only lead to knowledge useful in terminal counselling, but would also serve as a contribution to developmental psychology.

Terminal Decline

It is important to distinguish the terminal stage of life from normal aging. Terminal decline may extend from a few days or weeks to over a year. The terminal stage of life commonly has such distinctive characteristics, both psychological and biological, that it may not be easily explained by the previous pattern of the individual's life.

The individual himself may or may not be aware of diffuse changes in mood, in mental functioning, or in the way his body responds. Terminal decline may be paced by a disease initially remote from the nervous system, such as a cancer of the stomach. Thereafter, over a few months, a rapid sequence of changes might be observed in overt behavior or in measured psychological characteristics of the individual. It is as though at some point the physiology of the individual had started on a new phase that the organism is unable to stop.

Depending upon the nature of the terminal illness, there are individual differences in the conscious awareness of changes in the body and in the relative sensitivity to such changes. There apparently are individuals who remain supremely parental to the end of their lives and attempt to protect those around them from their self-knowledge, just as there are more hysterical persons who amplify the circumstances in which they find themselves and preoccupy those about them with their concern. It is necessary, of course, to distinguish psychological capacities from attitudes and physiological states. In 1904, William Osler commented upon the fact that in 500 deaths of which he had records, the great majority of individuals displayed little distress.

Terminal Cognitive Change. Research seems to indicate that sudden declines in mental tests or psychomotor skills should be viewed with the suspicion of probable serious changes associated with terminal decline (*e.g., Kleemeier, 1961; Jarvik, 1963*). It is the abruptness of the changes that occur in mental abilities which distinguishes the terminal state from the normal adult period. The terminal decline commonly appears, then, as a marked break or departure from a previously relatively stable series of measurements. Figure 12-1 indicates the relation of psychological changes to probability of survival in older adults.

From the work of Jarvik comes the clue that the more stable adult characteristics, such as verbal abilities, may indeed be more indicative of survival than those functions that are known to be susceptible to age decline, such as psychomotor speed and the Digit Symbol test of the Weschler Adult Intelligence Scale. A distinction should be made between the normal age declines and those declines precipitated by terminal illness. In the terminal stages of life, the perception of one's body may change, and it is thus not unreasonable that human figure drawings may to some extent be predictive of imminence of death in older persons.

Grief and the Task of Dying

The dying individual faces four major tasks: the management of his reactions to the symptoms of his terminal state and altered physiology, reactions to the impending separation from loved ones and friends, reac-

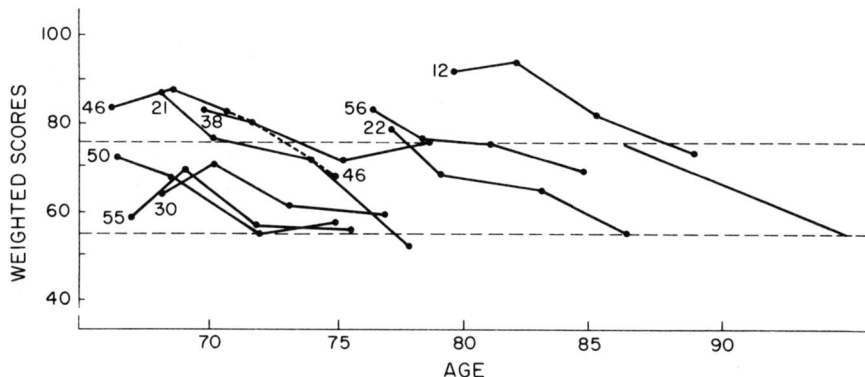

FIGURE 12-1A. Successive total weighted Wechsler-Bellevue scores, by age, of nine aged men living on January 1, 1961. Upper horizontal line represents the mean first test score of all 13 subjects who were given a total of four tests; lower line represents mean of last test. The diagonal connecting the two horizontal lines represents the average rate of decline over the mean interval between the first and the last of the four tests (8.9 years). Individual curves are indicated by subject number.

Source: R. W. Kleemeier, W. A. Justiss, A. W. Jones, and T. A. Rich. *Intellectual Changes in the Senium*, unpublished manuscript, 1961.

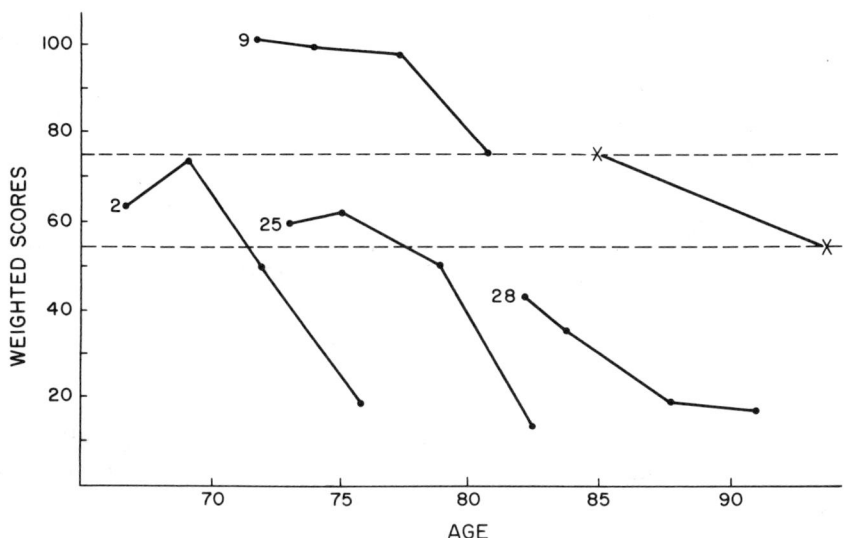

FIGURE 12-1B. Successive total weighted Wechsler-Bellevue scores, by age, of four aged men who died shortly after the fourth test (January 1, 1961).

Source: Ibid.

tions to the prospect of a transition to an unknown state, and adjusting his perception of how he lived his life in relation to how he wanted to live it.

Perhaps the above is not unlike saying that the individual dies in the following order: socially, psychologically, and biologically. Terminal illness separates the individual from his previous social roles, and social death may occur relatively early in protracted illness. Psychological death would seem to occur at a somewhat later stage, when the individual is no longer aware of other persons or accessible to affective relationships. Biological death occurs latest, but it is no less simple. The death of cells is distributed over time, since they are differently susceptible to oxygen want and toxicity as a result of the failure of respiration and circulation.

A persistent pattern of depressed affect in reaction to the loss of a love object or the loss of some element of systematic significance in one's life may be called depression. Whereas anxiety is a diffuse physiological arousal in reaction to threat or anticipated loss, depression is a reaction to a loss or perceived loss. Animals, particularly dogs, will show a retarded form of behavior, including loss of appetite, if they lose their master or mate. The reaction of grief includes an altered somatic state initiated by a sudden loss of pervasive significance, which, once initiated, seems difficult to allay. Grief has been described as waves of sensations lasting from twenty minutes to an hour; e.g., tightness in throat, sighing, lack of strength, and mental pain (*Lindemann, 1944*). Among other symptoms described, were dilated pupils, a sign of sympathetic nervous system stimulation.

Grief is defined as "an acute state of despair and disconsolate anguish because of the immediate loss of a person or object." However, unlike the grief in losing a spouse, child, or friend, the feelings of a dying individual may be organized around the fact that he is leaving others.

Depression has elements similar to grief (dejection and hopelessness), but it also has an overtone of being unduly protracted or having a depth of mōōd disproportionate to what has been lost. Being told of an incurable illness may bring on depression, and perhaps suicidal thoughts as well. For this reason, there are varying opinions as to the advisability of a physician's informing a patient of the reality of an incurable illness. The hopelessness invoked in being informed that one has an incurable illness might seem to be better faced if the patient were a "strong" person and believed in immortality. Belief in immortality can in fact be a denial of the fact of death, and many supposedly "strong" individuals do not meet the facts of incurable illness well, but become depressed and suicidal. Grief of a dying individual would appear to be a function of "(1) the extent and quality of his interpersonal relationships; (2) the use he makes of denial; and (3) the extent of his regression and the retraction of his ego boundaries secondary to his illness" (*Aldrich, 1963, p. 331*).

One has the impression from clinical literature and from folklore that open mourning has a constructive influence. The widow who grieves openly is believed to recover faster from the abysmal sense of loss and removal from normal interpersonal relationships. Whether an intense and open mourning rather than stoicism is prophylactic of the consequences of loss or restitutive of the personality needs systematic study.

Some change in reaction to loss seems to take place in development and aging. In childhood, emphasis is given to the real loss of, or separation from, parents, particularly from the mother, whose nurtural and protective role are especially significant. In the child, the reaction might be called a "sense of abandonment," with rejection of the parent by the child occurring when the separation is ended, as after a required hospitalization of the child. In adulthood and old age, that which is lost may have been struggled for; e.g., a child, or a social cause, or a scientific experiment. Thus the little child tends to blame the parent for going away, whereas the adult may blame himself for not being sufficiently potent or omniscient to prevent the loss of that which he loves. Presumably, adolescents and young adults in their reactions to loss would be mixed in blaming the outer world and themselves.

When the loss can be clearly identified, grief and a possible subsequent depression are reactive; reactive depressions commonly occur after the death of a close friend or relative, loss of property or money, job, health, reputation, and many other highly personal objects and processes. A common element would seem to be that in order to have the potential for evoking a reactive depression, the object must have central or systematic significance to the individual; i.e. many responses are organized or patterned around the lost element. The systematic meaning of the lost element tends to keep the depressive state intact and ongoing. One aspect of the depressive state is the continuity in mood extending over days, in contrast to the transient unhappiness experienced with loss of an important, but psychologically limited, object. Highly differentiated adults can be much involved with abstract ideas, religious beliefs, art forms, and social groups. Destruction or loss of these can result in grief or depression accompanied by the feeling that life no longer has meaning and feelings of personal worthlessness.

If the losses seem to be merely releasers or precipitators of a depression for which the individual was poised or ready, the depression is called "endogenous" to give greater relative recognition to the contribution of the host's psychological vulnerability, including his somatic disposition. While there appear to be some older individuals who seem to be searching for events around which to crystallize "a-beginning-to-form" depressive mood, it cannot be denied that old age is indeed a period of frequent losses of a major sort. Mixed reactive and endogenous depressions tend to be more common in older persons because of the high frequency of losses and the somatic changes of aging.

The study of the National Institute of Mental Health of healthy older men indicated that social psychological losses were related to evidence of depression and also to cerebral-physiological functions (*Yarrow,* et al., *1963*). This would imply that there are adverse somatic reactions to essentially psychological losses of later life. Since the deaths of friends and relatives come frequently in late life, there is a problem for the aged individual in avoiding becoming a grief-ridden, depressively preoccupied person. There may be a partial dampening of reaction, in that the lowered drive states are accompanied by psychological disengagement or reduced affective involvement. Also, the affect may retrench from its previous attachments. The psychoanalysts have described this as the withdrawal of libido from external objects. In aging and dying, there is presumably some anticipatory affective withdrawal or renunciation of relationships. The withdrawal of the affective ties from external objects makes the aged person perhaps more narcissistic, but it is adaptive in that he is less vulnerable to the changes outside his control.

With the experience of many bereavements, individuals may tend to avoid the somatic stress and pain of an intense period of grief. Students of grief and mourning in young persons are prone to believe that the period of grief may be postponed, but not avoided. If older persons seem better able to manage bereavements in late life, it may well be that they have withdrawn some investment. This view implies that older persons, when faced with frequent losses, withdraw their affective investment in persons and objects in order to avoid the consequences of likely loss. What is missing in the pattern of explanation is the possibility that an individual may be able to reach a generalized state of abstract involvement in which he is convinced that "this is the nature of life and one should go on." In the process of "going on," his behavior is a reflection of a set of principles in which he has invested.

Many psychiatrists have given us insightful pictures of the reactions of grief, including reactions of older adults. What must be kept in mind is that the individuals most likely to be included in clinical investigations of grief and mourning are those who are not able to manage well the psychic and somatic concomitants of bereavement by themselves. Studies of community residents might better reveal the mechanisms by which the aged generally manage their losses.

Studies of depressions suggest that they are of lower frequency in the elderly who continue to work (*Busse, 1961*). Perhaps this gives some support to the notion that the individual should "keep on going" in order to prevent a spiral of debilitating moods and somatic reactions. The bereaved often finds himself surrounded by continuing reminders; the empty chair and the unused cup provoke waves of emptiness and lack of purpose. This lack of deep meaning is less likely to be experienced when working, and working itself may also provide new affective investment. Furthermore, physical activity may be useful in managing the somatic aspects of grief and depression and the interpersonal relations of work situations may help restructure behavior.

In addition to the kinds of individuals ordinarily included in clinical investigations of grief and depression, those who require or seek help, there is a disproportionate professional orientation toward explaining the old in terms of the young. Most commonly, the young are left, people move away from them; but the aged individual may himself be dying, hence moving away. Grief of the dying aged individual seems hardly explained as a compound of abandonment and hostility toward those who have left him. He may have feelings about his own inadequacy in having to leave because of ill health, thus abandoning his loved ones to an uncertain future. Thus self-reproachment can arise in the dying aged until such time as the individual can establish a principle whereby he can accept death without remorse for leaving his responsibilities and his unfinished life's business. It is suggested that because of their different roles in life, grief may be different in the aged man and woman. While early-life grief may involve more elements of the nurturant role of the mother, later-life grief may be more entwined with principles by which the group functions and which are more reflected in the father.

Political refugees, particularly men, have been known to be susceptible to depression and suicide. However, the pattern of feeling might not be unlike that associated with the death of a spouse; the all-encompassing loss leading to a feeling of hopelessness and impotence to manipulate the situation. What is probably involved, more often in the male, is an identification with action and ideas, hence if the individual is in a position where he can no longer act for the ideas, he feels worthless. This repeats the idea that men and women derive their sense of personal worth from different qualities—the man from his capacity for action, the woman from her capacity for being supportive.

Generally it would be predicted that the more adequate the interpersonal relations of the individual, the more likely he is to have an appropriate social input to help manage the reaction to loss. This is not to suggest that the social isolate may not be able to cope successfully with loss, but merely that the probability is against it. Being isolated means fewer available effective outlets to compensate for the loss and less social restructuring of behavior to help overcome the uncertainty. However, it has been pointed out that successful aging may be achieved by at least two modes of living: an outward-directed style with much interaction with other persons and a more passive home-centered style (*Havighurst, 1961*). Havighurst's criterion of successful aging is one of life satisfaction. Being reasonably happy and satisfied with one's life would appear to be a defense against excessive and persistent depressive reactions to real or perceived losses in late life. Several patterns or personalities would seem to provide such protection, some by heavy use of denial and little involvement with others. Such persons would seem to have their Achilles heel, particularly when they themselves suffer change, such as occurs in illness.

The Normal Psychology of the End of Life. The previous discussion may cloak the end of life in an aura of psychopathology. What was being emphasized were the kinds of issues that the older person faces. The manner of handling these issues may fit a normal pattern, or it may make use of a pattern so organized in its extreme that it forms a part of psychopathology. While extreme forms of late-life reactions occur, they need not obscure a normal adaptive pattern, what might be called the normal psychology of the end of life.

Age itself plays a role in which persons who die in their sixties are in a sense dying prematurely and may be expected to show more deviancy than persons in their eighties and nineties. Adaptation occurs over time, and time pressure may produce aberrations. Thus a person aged ninety has lived twenty-five more years than one of sixty-five, and the adaptations during these twenty-five years enter into his reactions and attitudes toward events. In this sense, studies of centenarians and the very aged offer some basis for extending the normal developmental psychology of late life. Those who survive beyond eighty seem to enjoy relatively good health; some physicians have even suggested that the highly disease-prone have already died, leaving a more sturdy group physiologically and psychologically. One thing is very obvious—centenarians are not like ill younger persons. While infirmity is common in the aged, creeping illness is not typical. If somatic and environmental changes occur slowly enough, and if the individual has been successful in his adaptations in early life, he can compensate physiologically and psychologically. While it is not to be expected that a centenarian will be like an adult half his age, it should also not be expected that his nervous system and behavior will resemble those of younger persons in the terminal stages of a fatal disease.

The last stage of life, terminal decline, may not be highly related to the previous life pattern and functioning of the individual because rapid physiological changes in the nervous system may occur. Since there may be a limited relevance of the terminal morphological changes and the pre-morbid behavior, reconstruction of the psychological and physiological characteristics of the individual in relation to brain morphology must be approached with caution. Such caution is in relation to the interpretation of findings and not to the need for further study.

There is a tendency to approach the subject matter of aging—and particularly the termination of life—with a heavy mood, without the lightness and deftness of thought that might be given early development. This is a mistake, for in the end as in the beginning, thinking, enthusiasm, and vitality will carry the day, in research and in daily life.

Summary

This chapter discussed the last stages of life in terms of individual reactions. The end of life can be provocative, with surprising recall of early life events. Sometime before the terminal stages of life, an individual can become involved with a review of his life. Individuals react differently to the stimulus provided by the indications that life may be ending: some may deny it, some react passively, and some welcome it without reflection. Many people become involved in varying degrees in re-examining their lives in the face of an uncertain future. The life review is an active, or purposeful, examination of the events of one's life accompanying an impression of impending death. The intent of the life review is to reconcile one's values with the behavior of one's life and to leave behind an acceptable image.

What has just been described is an important event in the life of an individual. At present, there is not much in the way of systematic research on reminiscing and the life review, so it is not possible to contrast individuals and experiences in a quantitative manner. This facet of the psychology of aging will no doubt become increasingly recognized. As more information becomes available, professional services will become more constructive for the aged.

Meeting and coping with bereavement and frequent loss is one of the particular tasks of old age. Individuals learn to manage their grief by many devices, some by diverting their thoughts or avoiding provocative situations, others by developing abstractions of life principles.

The experience of loss is, of course, life-long, and one of the elements of maturity is the management of the reactions to loss and the restitution of acceptable behavior.

The dying person has four tasks: management of his reactions to the symptoms of his terminal state and altered physiology, reacting to the impending separation from loved ones and friends, reacting to a transition to an unknown state, and adjusting his perception of his life.

Because of the frequency of deviant reactions in later life and the dramatic circumstances surrounding the end of life, the late years tend to be clouded in an aura of pathology, somatic and psychic. Terminal decline should be separated conceptually from the normal adaptations to living in the later years. Centenarians are not debilitated; they often have reasonably good health and mental lucidity. The normal psychology of later life is beginning to be understood, leading to expectations for successful adaptations for most persons. As further research is done on the relations of psychological, physiological, and social changes in later life, the characteristics that promote optimum adaptations should become better known.

References

Aldrich, C. K. The dying patient's grief. *J. Amer. Med. Assoc.*, 1963, **184**, 329-331.

Birren, J. E., R. N. Butler, S. W. Greenhouse, L. Sokoloff, and Marian R. Yarrow. Interdisciplinary relationships: interrelations of physiological, psychological, and psychiatric findings in healthy elderly men. In Birren, Butler, Greenhouse, Sokoloff, and Yarrow (eds.), *Human Aging*, pp. 283-305. Washington, D.C.: Government Printing Office, 1963, Public Health Publication No. 986.

Busse, E. W. Psychoneurotic reactions and defense mechanisms in the aged. In P. H. Hoch and J. Zubin (eds.), *Psychopathology of Aging*, pp. 274-284. New York: Grune & Stratton, Inc., 1961.

*Butler, R. N. The life review: an interpretation of reminiscence in the aged. *Psychiat.*, 1963, **26**, 65-76.

*Feifel, H. (ed.). *The Meaning of Death*. New York: McGraw-Hill, Inc., 1959.

Hall, G. S. *Senescence*. New York: Appleton-Century-Crofts, Inc., 1922.

*Havighurst, R. J. The nature and values of meaningful free-time activity. In R. W. Kleemeier (ed.), *Aging and Leisure*, pp. 309-344. London: Oxford University Press, 1961.

Jarvik, Lissy F. and A. Falek. Intellectual stability and survival in the aged. *J. Geront.*, 1963, **18**, 173-176.

Kleemeier, R. W., W. A. Justiss, A. Jones, and T. A. Rich. Intellectual changes in the senium. Unpublished manuscript, 1961.

Lindemann, E. Symptomatology and management of acute grief. *Amer. J. Psychiat.*, 1944, **101**, 141-148.

Mueller-Deham, A. Diagnosis, prophylaxis and treatment in old age. In E. V. Cowdry (ed.), *Problems of Ageing*, pp. 855-889. Baltimore: The Williams & Wilkins Company, 1942.

Schuster, D. B. A psychological study of a 106-year-old-man. *Amer. J. Psychiat.*, 1952, **109**, 112-119.

Shneidman, E. S. Orientations toward death: a vital aspect of the study of lives. In R. W. White (ed.), *The Study of Lives*, pp. 201-227. Englewood Cliffs, N.J.: Prentice-Hall, Inc., 1963.

Spark, Muriel. *Memento Mori*. New York: The Macmillan Company, 1959.

*Zinberg, N. W. and I. Kaufman. Cultural and personality factors associated with age. In Zinberg and Kaufman (eds.), *Normal Psychology of the Aging Process*, pp. 17-71. New York: International Universities Press, Inc., 1963.

---

*Suggested additional reading.

Name Index

A

Adenauer, Konrad, 217
Albrecht, Ruth, 48, 235, 250
Aldrich, C. K., 237, 249, 282-283, 288
Alexander, Edith A., 109
Allara, E., 100, 108
Altman, P. L., 20
Anderson, Edythe M. S., 109
Anderson, J. E., 22

B

Basowitz, H., 105, 106, 108, 109, 159, 170
Bayley, Nancy, 187, 195
Beasley, W. C., 84, 108
Belbin, R. M., 145, 148
Belloc, Nedra B., 94, 108
Belt, E., 10, 22
Beresford, J. C., 19
Berg, B. N., 79
Bick, M. W., 91, 94, 108
Bilash, I., 109, 177, 178, 195
Birren, J. E., 9, 22, 55, 78, 89, 91, 92, 94, 104, 105, 108, 109, 116, 117, 118, 119, 120, 121, 122, 123, 124, 126, 130, 131, 156, 157, 169, 178, 179, 183, 184, 186, 187, 190, 191, 195, 218, 220, 232, 236, 249, 288
Bondareff, W., 53, 55, 56, 78
Boring, E. G., 106

Botwinick, J., 89, 105, 106, 109, 121, 122, 123, 125, 126, 130, 131, 154, 160, 169, 195, 228
Bourlière, F., 99, 100, 109
Braun, H. W., 109, 154, 155, 156, 159, 160, 170
Bregman, E. O., 170
Brinley, J. F., 109, 123, 125, 126, 131, 190, 191, 196
Britt, L. P., 117, 131
Britton, J. H., 236, 249
Brody, E. B., 117, 131
Brody, H., 55, 78
Bromley, D. B., 174, 175, 196
Brown, R. G., 271
Brozek, J., 94, 109
Bunch, M. E., 158, 170, 227, 228, 250
Burgess, E. W., 48, 249
Burstein, Sona R., 9, 22
Busse, E. W., 196, 254, 262, 271, 284, 288
Butler, R. N., 130, 184, 220, 249, 267, 269, 272, 274, 275, 288

C

Cameron, N., 271
Casperson, R. C., 89, 109
Castanera, T. J., 226, 250
Cavan, Ruth S., 48, 235, 249, 271
Cendron, H., 109
Chapanis, A., 88, 109

289

Name Index

Chown, Sheila M., 189, 196, 232, 233, 249
Churchill, Winston, 217
Clark, J. W., 183, 196
Clark, S. D., 201, 220
Comalli, P. E., Jr., 110
Comfort, A., 72, 78
Confrey, E. A., 260, 271-272
Conrad, H. S., 177, 196
Cooper, R. M., 100, 109
Corsellis, J. A. N., 264, 272
Cosh, J. A., 103, 109
Cottrell, F., 202, 220
Coules, J., 109
Crook, M. N., 105, 109
Cumming, Elaine, 6, 22, 48, 235, 237, 249

D

Dastur, D. K., 269, 272
Davies, D. F., 79
da Vinci, Leonardo, 9
de Gaulle, Charles, 217
Dittmer, Dorothy S., 20
Dovenmuehle, R. H., 258, 271, 272
Droller, H., 136, 148
Dunne, Agnes C., 143, 149

E

Eastman, A. A., 93, 109
Edwards, A. E., 232, 249
Eisdorfer, C., 196
Emmers, R., 119, 132
Erickson, E. H., 7, 22

F

Falek, A., 185, 196, 288
Fanshel, D., 27, 48
Farrimond, T., 98, 109
Feifel, H., 288
Feldstein, M., 109
Fieandt, K. von, 119, 131
Fitts, P. M., 136, 148
Foulds, G. A., 180, 182, 196
Fox, Charlotte, 91, 108
Frenkel, Else, 6, 22
Friedmann, E. A., 16, 22, 200, 220, 235, 249
Friend, Celia M., 173, 174, 196

G

Gakkel, L. B., 156, 170
Galton, F., 114, 206
Gebhard, P. H., 250
Gee, M. V., 54, 79
Geiselhart, R., 154, 155, 156, 170
Gladis, M., 159, 160, 170

Glaser, D., 272
Glick, P. C., 19
Goldfarb, A. I., 253, 272
Goldfarb, W., 120, 131
Goldhamer, H., 48, 249
Goldstein, M. S., 27, 28, 36, 48, 66, 78, 260, 271-272
Gömöri, Z., 156, 170
Gordon, Margaret S., 48, 203, 215, 221
Greenhouse, S. W., 130, 184, 220, 249, 288
Guedry, F. E., Jr., 99, 109
Guth, S. K., 93, 94, 109
Gutmann, D. L., 245, 250

H

Hall, C. S., 223, 249
Hall, G. S., 274, 275, 277, 288
Handler, P., 51, 78
Hanley, T. D., 124, 131
Hansen, D. B., 272
Hanson, J. A., 109
Harrison, J., 3, 23
Havighurst, R. J., 16, 22, 31, 48, 200, 220, 235, 236, 240-241, 249, 250, 251, 285, 288
Heer, D. M., 19
Henry, W. E., 6, 22, 48, 235, 237, 249
Herrington, L. P., 28, 48
Himler, L. E., 272
Himwich, H. E., 68, 78
Himwich, Williamina A., 68, 78
Hollingshead, A. B., 30, 31, 33, 48
Holmes, Oliver Wendell, Jr., 217
Howell, T. H., 103, 104, 109
Huhtala, A., 131

I

Imus, H. A., 55, 78
Inglis, J., 188, 197

J

Jalavisto, Eeva, 146, 148
James, W., 152
Jarvik, Lissy F., 15, 59, 64, 78, 183, 186, 187, 196, 280, 288
Jeffries, N. T., Jr., 109
Jerome, E. A., 170, 176, 196
Jervis, G. A., 262, 272
Johnson, F., 65, 78
Johnson, G. H., 239, 250
Jones, A., 196, 281, 288
Jones, D. C., 226, 250
Jones, H. B., 60, 61, 78
Jones, H. E., 183, 196
Justiss, W. A., 84, 109, 196, 281, 288

Name Index

K

Kagan, J., 3, 22
Kallmann, F. J., 15, 59, 64, 78, 196
Kaplan, M., 216, 221
Kaplan, O. J., 270, 272
Karis, C., 109-110
Kaufman, I., 238, 251, 288
Kay, D. W. K., 253, 272
Kay, H., 119, 130, 131, 152, 158, 170
Kelly, E. L., 231, 250
Kety, S. S., 272
Keys, A., 94, 109
Kimeldorf, D. J., 226, 250
King, H. F., 139, 140, 148
King, John, 278
Kinsey, A. C., 229, 230, 250
Kleemeier, R. W., 84, 109, 147, 149, 187, 196, 206, 221, 280, 281, 288
Knowlton, G. C., 117, 131
Koga, Y., 114, 115, 116, 131
Kogan, N., 190, 197, 246, 247, 250, 251
König, E., 86, 97, 98, 109
Korchin, S. J., 105, 106, 108, 109, 159, 170
Kornetsky, C., 154, 170
Kornsweig, A. L., 94, 109
Koskenoja, M., 99, 109
Kral, V. A., 254, 272
Kraus, A. A., 236, 250
Kreindler, A., 128, 131, 154, 156, 170
Kuhlen, R. G., 34, 48, 239, 242, 250
Kullberg, P., 131
Kummick, Lillian S., 96, 109
Kurihara, H., 189, 196
Kutner, B., 26, 27, 48

L

Landahl, H. D., 72, 78, 104, 109, 190
Lane, M. H., 272
Langner, T. S., 27, 48, 49
Lansing, A. I., 57, 65, 74, 78
Laslett, P., 3, 23
Lawrence, P. S., 67, 78
LeGros Clark, F., 143, 149
Lehman, H. C., 143, 144, 149, 182, 183, 196, 207-213, 221
Lesse, H., 117, 131-132
Lilienfeld, A. M., 236, 250
Lindemann, E., 282, 288
Lindzey, G., 223, 249
Livson, Florine, 250
Lorge, I., 196, 246, 251

Mc

McConnell, J. W., 39, 48
McFarland, R. A., 96, 109-110, 140, 149
McGill University Conference, 272

McNelis, J. F., 93, 109

M

Magladery, J. W., 120, 131
Mangan, G. L., 190, 196
Margolin, S. E., 158, 170, 227, 228, 250
Marinesco, G., 128, 131, 154, 156, 170
Mark, D. D., 54, 79
Marsh, B. W., 137, 138, 139, 149
Martin, C. E., 229, 250
Mason, Evelyn P., 247, 250
Mathers, Ruth A., 23
Maugham, Somerset, 217
Maurizio, Anna, 62, 78
Maves, P. B., 45, 48
Medawar, P. B., 57, 78
Mendkoff, Ethel, 237, 249
Meyersohn, R., 240, 241, 250
Michael, S. T., 49
Mildvan, A. S., 54, 79
Miles, W. R., 141, 149
Misiak, H., 94, 110
Morant, G. M., 114, 115, 116, 131
Moriyama, I. M., 28, 48
Morrisey, Virginia, 272
Morrison, D. F., 120, 130, 178, 179, 187, 191, 195, 196
Moss, H. A., 3, 22
Mueller-Deham, A., 288
Müller, C., 267, 272
Myers, J. K., 30, 48
Mysak, E. D., 124, 131

N

National Center for Health Statistics, 36, 37
National Committee Against Mental Illness, 260
Neal, M. W., 263, 265, 266, 267, 272
Neugarten, Bernice L., 31, 48, 231, 235, 236, 245, 250, 251
Nienstedt, C. W., Jr., 88, 110
Norman, L. G., 149
Norris, A. H., 117, 131

O

Obrist, W. D., 188, 196
Oden, Melita H., 31, 49, 195, 234
O'Doherty, B. M., 140, 149
O'Neal, Patricia, 258, 272
Opler, M. K., 49
Orma, E. J., 99, 109
Osler, W., 280
Owens, W. A., Jr., 187, 197

P

Paillard, J., 134, 149
Pavlov, I., 61
Pell, S., 97, 110
Perlin, S., 267, 268-269, 272
Petersen, P. G., 250
Phillips, B. S., 235, 250
Pomeroy, W. B., 229, 250
Post, F., 272
Pressey, S. L., 242

Q

Quetelet, A., 9, 23

R

Rabbitt, P. M. A., 87, 110, 113, 131
Rapaport, A., 109
Raven, J. C., 180, 182, 196
Redlich, F. C., 30, 31, 33, 48
Reed, H. B. C., Jr., 188, 197
Reichard, Suzanne, 233, 234, 250
Reichenbach, Maria, 11, 23
Reitan, R. M., 188, 197
Rennie, T. A. C., 49
Rice, K., 272
Rich, T. A., 196, 281, 288
Riegel, K. F., 120, 123, 130, 181, 185, 187, 189, 191, 192, 196, 197, 224, 240, 250-251
Riegel, Ruth, 189, 197, 240, 251
Robbin, J. S., 109, 123, 126, 131
Roberts, B. H., 30, 48
Robillard, E., 101, 110
Robins, E., 272
Rockstein, M., 62, 65, 78
Rosée, Graf de la, 97
Rosen, Jacqueline L., 236, 251
Ross, S., 88, 110
Roth, M., 253, 262, 272
Rothschild, D., 272
Rousel, F., 95, 110
Rubadeau, D. O., 226, 250
Ruch, F. L., 145, 146, 149, 159, 170

S

Saari, K., 131
Sainsbury, P., 258, 272
Sanderson, R. E., 188, 197
Schaie, K. W., 190, 197
Scheinfeld, A., 79
Schmidt, E. H., 272
Schneider, J., 109
Schneidman, E. S., 274, 288
Schorr, A. L., 46, 48
Schuster, D. B., 288
Semenovskaia, E. N., 95

Sheldon, J. H., 99, 110
Shelton, Florence C., 247, 250
Sherman, E. D., 101, 110
Shock, N. W., 52, 66, 79, 92, 109, 131
Shriver, Beatrice M., 141, 149
Sime, M. E., 158, 170
Simmons, L. W., 48
Simms, H. S., 67, 79
Simon, A., 263, 265, 266, 267, 272
Simonson, E., 149
Singleton, W. T., 118, 131
Sinnott, E. W., 63, 79
Smith, J. Maynard, 75, 76, 79
Sokoloff, L., 130, 184, 220, 249, 272, 288
Spark, Muriel, 279, 288
Spieth, W., 124, 126, 131, 184, 187, 196, 197
Srole, L., 29, 49
Stenbäck, A., 272
Stevens, S. S., 86, 110
Stone, C. P., 156, 170
Strehler, B. L., 52, 53, 54, 79
Streib, G. F., 35, 49, 233, 251
Strong, E. K., 242
Strong, L. C., 65, 78
Szilard L., 64, 79

T

Tanner, J. M., 17
Terman, L. M., 30, 31, 49, 234
Thaler, Margaret, 191, 197
Tharp, R. G., 7, 23
Thompson, W. E., 35, 49
Thorndike, E. L., 151, 170
Tibbitts, C., 49
Tilton, J. W., 170
Tobin, S. S., 235, 236, 250, 251
Togo, Alice M., 27, 48
Townsend, P., 49
Tuckman, J., 246, 251

U

U.S. Department of Health, Education, and Welfare, 49, 69, 70, 71, 82, 84, 110, 258, 259, 272
U.S. Department of Justice, 255-258
U.S. Department of Labor, 161-167, 170, 201, 221
U.S. President's Council on Aging, 21, 40-43, 49

V

Verkhutina, A. I., 95
Verwoerdt, A., 258, 272
Verzár, F., 52, 79
Verzár-McDougall, E. J., 156, 170
von Mering, O., 3, 18, 23, 49

W

Wagman, I. H., 117, 131, 132
Wall, P. D., 117, 118, 131
Wallach, M. A., 190, 197, 246, 247, 250, 251
Wapner, S., 88, 110
Warren, B., 109-110
Wayner, M. J., Jr., 119, 132
Weekers, R., 95, 110
Weiss, A. D., 90, 110, 195
Welford, A. T., 132, 135, 145, 149, 175, 197
Weniger, F. L., 3, 18, 23, 49
Werner, H., 110
Williams, R. H., 34, 49
Wimer, R. E., 168, 170, 197
Windle, W. F., 55, 78
Wine, D. B., 232, 249
Woodward, E., 170

Y

Yarrow, Marian R., 130, 184, 220, 249, 284, 288
Yiengst, M., 94, 108

Z

Zinberg, N. W., 238, 251, 288
Zinina, N. V., 156, 170
Zobel, H., 101, 102, 110
Zubek, J. P., 109, 173, 174, 177, 178, 195, 196

Subject Index

A

Absolute threshold, 84
Abstract behavior, 191
Accident theories of aging, 10
Accidents:
   age of driver (fig.), 130
   agricultural, 139
   annual rates (fig.), 70
   injuries (fig.), 71
   rate per 1000, 38
   speed, 128
Accommodation, 89
   and age (fig.), 90
Accumulation of experience, 11
Achievement, problem of, 5
Activities, reduction in, 227
Adaptation to aging, 234
Adaptive organism, description, 13
Adjustment to social role, 33
Adolescents and social mobility, 29
Adult learning, 151
Adult life:
   problems, 3
   tempo, 6
Affective disorders, 266
Affective investment, 236
Age as an index, 9
Age at:
   adulthood, 17
   marriage, 18

Age grading of behavior, 13
Age, husband and wife, 19
Aging:
   accident theory, 10
   adaptation to, 234
   behavioral theory, 11
   biological definition, 51
   biological theory, 72-73
   cells, 52
   and chronological age, 9
   and clock analogy, 68
   contrasting views, 9
   counterpart theories, 10, 72-73
   and development, 74
   and disorganization, 72
   DNA, 52
   emergent features, 19
   evolutionary viewpoint, 61
   genetic theories, 10
   kinds, 10
   and pigment, 53
   and post-mitotic cell, 53
   and radiation injury, 52
   rate, 16
   RNA, 52
   and social class, 25
   successful, criteria, 237-238
   "wear-and-tear" theories, 10
Agricultural accidents (table), 139
Air crewmen, 141
Air Force pilots, 142

Subject Index

Airline pilots, 141
    retirement, 203
    shift, 152
Alternation index, 126
Alternation tasks, 190-191
Ambiguous illustration (fig.), 106
Amputees, 146
Angry type, 234
Animal learning, 156
Animals, differences in life span, 57-59
Appearance, changes, 16
Armored type, 234
Arrests for stealing, 255
Artists, productivity, 210-211
Assault, arrests for (fig.), 257
Association time, 123-124
Athletic achievements, 212-213
Athletic performance, 144
Athletic skills, 143
Attitudes:
    about the aged, 246-247
    changes, 243-244
Attractiveness in women, 240
Audition, high tone perception, 96-97
Auditory reaction time, 114
Automation, effects, 19, 20, 166
Automobile drivers, 137

B

Bee, differences in life span, 62
Behavior:
    abstract, 191
    concreteness, 191
    cyclical, 12
    degradation, causes, 218
    and genetics, 75
    plasticity, 8, 152
    as a regulator, 62-63
    reinforcement, 7
    rigidity, 189
    and sensory acuity, 81
    sexual, 229-230
    and survival, 75
Behavioral load, 192
Behavioral theory of aging, 11
Bereavement, 284
Biographies, analyses of, 6
Biological age defined, 10
Biological clocks, 68
Biological theory of aging, 72-73
Blindness, 84, 94
Blood pressure:
    and age, 75-76
    and response speed, 184
Brain:
    anatomical changes, 265
    and behavior, 264
    circulatory disorders, 263-266

Brain (Cont.)
    damage and mental ability, 187-188
    deterioration, 265
    rat, aging of, 54
    syndromes, 262
    weight changes, 55
Buffered traits, 8

C

Car, driving skill, 139
Cardiovascular diseases, 68-69
Causes of death, 68
Cell death, causes, 52
Cell, post-mitotic in aging, 53
Centenarian, anatomy, 10
Cerebral arteriosclerosis, 263
Cerebral blood flow, 264
Cerebral damage, 188
Cerebral metabolic rate, 264
Cerebral vascular disease, 265
Champions, athletic, 143
Chemical turnover, 55
Chemistry discoveries (fig.), 208
Choice in behavior, 1, 2, 32
Choices, difficulties, 4
Chronic illness and socioeconomic status, 67
Circulatory disorders of the brain, 263-266
Class differences, 30-31
Clock analogy to aging, 68
Clocks:
    biological, 68
    compensated, 72
    dissipative process, 72
    types, 72
Cognitive changes near death, 280
Cognitive control of perception, 106
Cognitive strain, 192
Color vision, 88
Compensated clock, 72
Compensation:
    described, 132
    for sensory loss, 85
Concept formation, 177
Concrete nouns, 192
Concreteness in behavior, 191
Conditioned reflexes, 156
Conditioning, 154
Conditioning effects, 61
Conduction velocity of nerve, 117-118
Confidence, 190
Conflict, resolution, 276
Continuity awareness, 2
Counterpart theories of aging, 10, 73-74
Criteria of successful aging, 237-238
Criterion of intelligence, 180-182
Critical frequency of electrical phosphene (fig.), 95

Critical thinking ability, 173-174
Crime, 254-257
 and unemployment, 258
Cultural turnover, 13
Cumulation, concept, 8
Cyclical behavior, 12

D

"Dark glasses" effect, 86
Dark adaptation, 89-90
 and age (fig.), 91
 curves (fig.), 92
Deafness, 84
Death, 274
 accidental, 45
 fear, 247
 major causes, 68-69, (fig.), 69
 pedestrian, 137
 rates in widowhood, 236-237
 rates, white-nonwhite differences, 45
 reaction to, 5
 of spouse, costs, 44
 transmission of property, 279
Decline, terminal stages, 280
Decoding speed, 124
Deductive thinking, 174
Dementia, senile, 265
Department of Labor survey of training, 161-167
Depression:
 elements, 282
 and grief, 284-285
 and suicide, 258-259
Development and aging, 74
Developmental psychology, 3
Developmental tasks, 3
Dexterity, 134
Diagnosis, multiple in aged, 266
Difference threshold, 84
Digit-Symbol test, 186
 and response speed, 124
Disability:
 and income (table), 37
 days per person, 36
Discrimination learning in the rat, 156
Disease:
 and mental test performance, 183
 and socioeconomic status, 28
Disengagement, 6, 237-238
Disorganization and aging, 72
Dissipative process as a clock, 72
Divorce and remarriage, 35
Dizziness, 99
DNA in aging, 52
Doctor's fees, 43
Draft, military service data, 27-28
Drives, 7-8
Driver accidents, 137

Drivers over 65, 138
Driving skill, 139
Dying, task of, 280-282
Dynamics of the life cycle, 1, 21-22

E

Economic status and morale, 26
Education:
 books, and radio listening (table), 240
 correlation with mental tests (table), 178
 and employment, 200
Educational level and training, 162, 165-166
EEG and intelligence, 188
Ego, 238-239
Ego energy, 236
Electrical phosphene, critical frequency (fig.), 95
Employment:
 changes, 203
 and education, 200
 older workers, 200
 sex differences, 204
Endogenous depression, 283
Energy:
 changes, 6
 ego, 236
Environment, effects on life span (table), 60
Environmental influences and nervous system, 218
Ethnic diversity of population, 46
Evolutionary viewpoint of aging, 61
Excitation and speed, 120
Expectancy:
 in learning, 160-161
 to respond, 125
Expectation of life at birth (fig.), 20
Experience and worker output, 201
Extinction of eye blink, 155
Eye blink:
 conditioned, 154
 conditioning (fig.), 155
Eye, pathology in, 94

F

Falls:
 and age, 39 (fig.), 40
 and dizziness, 99
Family:
 cycle, (table), 19
 evolving relationships, 4
 income and age (table), 37
 life, duration, 18
 life, pre-industrial, 3

Subject Index

Family (Cont.)
  relations and the aged, 35
  three generations, 4
Fatigue:
  pupil, 96
  in rats, 119
Female sexuality, 230
Flexibility, 189-190
Flicker fusion, 94
Footwear workers, 201
Force of mortality, 67
Frustration, sources, 34
Functional disorders, 265
Furniture workers, 201
Futurity, 275

G

Galvanic skin response, conditioned, 154-155
Genetic control over longevity, 63
Genetic theories of aging, 10
Genetics, determined by behavior, 75
Geriatric psychiatry, 267
Gestalt Completion Tests, 105
Gifted children, achievements, 30
Glial cells, 54
Gottschaldt concealed figures, 105
Grief:
  definition, 282
  of dying, 280, 282-286
  and hostility, 285
Growth-expansion, need, 34

H

Hand withdrawal, conditioned, 154
Handwriting speed, 121-123
Health:
  and socioeconomic status, 26-27
  defined, 65
  insurance, costs, 42
  nonwhite, 36
  services, use, 27
Hearing:
  loss (fig.), 97
  sensitivity, 98
Heart muscle pigment and age (fig.), 54
Heredity and longevity, 59, 61
Heroes as standards, 7
Historical character of living things, 61
History of aging as a subject, 9
Honey bee, summer and winter differences, 62
Hopelessness, 282
Hospital:
  admissions, factors in, 266
  costs, 43
Hostility and grief, 285

Hours of free time (fig.), 216
Human development, described, 2
Hunger, 227-228
  food deprivation and activity (fig.), 228
Husband, age at family events, 19

I

Illiteracy and Selective Service, 28
Illness, costs, 43
Illumination and visibility, 93
Illusion, phantom limb, 146
Illusions, susceptibility to, 88
Impairment rates, 82
Incidental learning, 168
Income, 214
  and age (table), 37, (fig.), 215
  and disability, 36-37
  of families (fig.), 40
  and injury, 39
  median, 40
  sources (fig.), 41
Indian summer clarity, 275
Individual differences, 16, 57
Industrial training survey, 161-167
Infant mortality rates, regional differences, 45
Inflexibility in thinking, 174-175
Injuries:
  from accidents, 70
  regional differences in, 45
  by sex and age (fig.), 39
  by sex and family income (fig.), 38
  of workers (table), 140
Insurance, health, costs, 42
Intellectual superiority and social mobility, 31
Intelligence:
  criterion of adult, 180-181
  and EEG, 188
  and health, 183
  and maladjustment, 30
  and personality, 232
  test, German population retest (fig.), 185
  test scores, longitudinal (fig.), 281
Interest, 240
  changes in (fig.), 242
Interference in learning, 157-159
Irrelevant stimulus elements, 87
Irreversibility, concept of, 8

K

Kansas City Study of Adult Life, 235

L

Labor force:
  and age, 41

Labor force (*Cont.*)
  proportion over 65 (*fig.*), 42
Learning:
  and cell loss in the rat, 156
  defined, 152
  expectancy in, 160-161
  of incidental tasks, 168
  interference in, 157-159
  modifying conditions, 153
  of occupational skills, 161-167
  in oil refinery workers (*table*), 162-163
  in rats, 156-157
  in telephone operators, 164-167
  two-choice water maze (*fig.*), 157
Leisure:
  activities, 206, 240-241
  and values, 214
  time increase, 200
Life cycle:
  dynamics, 1, 21-22
  phases, 5
Life expectancy, 20
Life review, 273-275
  adaptive features, 278-279
  content, 276-279
Life satisfaction, 235
Life span:
  animals, differences, 57-59
  bee, differences, 62
  and environment (*table*), 60
  phases, 5
  similarity in twins, 54
Lifted weights, discrimination, 104
Light threshold of the eye, 91
Light-dark ratio and flicker frequency, 95
Lighting requirements, 94
Literary works (*fig.*), 212
Lipofuscin, 55
Load, cognitive, 192
Load-shedding, 193
Logical problem solving, 176
Longevity:
  and age of parents at birth, 65
  of cold blooded species (*table*), 58-59
  effects on (*table*), 60
  and heredity, 59, 61
  of mammals (*table*), 57
  summer-winter difference in bees, 62
Longitudinal studies of mental abilities, 187-188
Loss, reaction to, 283
Lower class values, 33

M

Maintenance biology, 12
Maladjustment, 254-260
  and intelligence, 30
  in late life, 268-269

Mammals, longevity (*table*), 57
Manifest age, 13
Marital status of those over 65 (*fig.*), 21
Marriage:
  age, 18
  and personality, 231-232
  roles in, 7
Married life, duration, 18
Maturation, 17
  earlier trend, 18
Mature type, 234
Maturity, criteria, 5
Matrices, progressive (*fig.*), 180
Meaning of work, 16
Medical care expenditures (*fig.*), 43
Medical discoveries, 209
Medical expenditures, 40
Medical expenses, 42
Memories, emergence, 278
Menarche, age at (*fig.*), 17
Mental abilities in one-egg twins, 185
Mental hospital admissions (*fig.*), 260
Mental illness:
  in aged, factors, 262
  and mobility, 29
  physical disability in, 267
  precipitating factors, 254
  and social class, 30
  types, 260-267
Mental-physical relations, 183
Mental test performance, 178-181, 183
Middle class:
  characteristics, 26
  home, 216
  values, 33
Midtown Mental Health Survey, 29
Military service data, draft, 27-28
Mirror vision, 145-146
  effects on learning, 159
Mixed tasks, speed of performance, 125
Mobility:
  correlates, 30-31
  and mental illness, 29
  and personal characteristics, 32
Morale:
  and economic status, 26
  and health and socioeconomic status (*table*), 27
Mortality rates, 67
  Negro, 36
  and type of job, 35
"Mother-in-law" (*fig.*), 106
Motivation, changes in, 8
Motivational changes, 239
Movement:
  control, 134
  time, 117-118
Muscular strength, 18

Musicians:
    creative productions, 209-210
    orchestral works (fig.), 211
Mutations in somatic cells, 52

N

Negro:
    income, 36
    mortality rates, 36
Nerve cells and aging, 53
Nerve conduction velocity, 117-118
Nervous system:
    changes, 55-56
    and environmental influences, 218
    as register of events, 25
    and slowness, 112
Neurons, brains of bees, 62
Neurosis:
    in late life, 267
    and social class, 30
Nonverbal intelligence, 180
Nonwhite:
    health, 36
    life expectation, 20
    suicide, 259
Nouns, concrete, 192
Nystagmus, 98

O

Obsolete social forms, 13
Occupation:
    noise, effects, 97
    skills, 140
    training, 161-167
Office automation, effects, 166
Office workers, output (fig.), 201
Oil refinery workers, training, 162-163
Olfaction, 100
One-egg twins:
    appearance, 14-15
    length of life, 59
    mental abilities, 185
Openness of behavior, 2
Orphans, 4
    Selective Service rejection, 66
Orgasm frequency, 229-230
Orientation in problem solving, 176
Oxygen lack, 56, 263

P

Pacing of tasks, 145
Pain, 100-101
Painting, best works (fig.), 211
Paired associates, learning, 159, (table), 160
Parental age and longevity, 65
Parental dependency, 35

Pedestrian deaths, 137
Perception, cognitive control, 106
Period, defined, 72
Periodic phenomena, 12
Personality:
    continuity, 231-232
    definitions, 223
    differentiation, 230-231
    and intelligence, 232-233
    and marriage, 231-232
    types, 224
Phantom limb illusion, 146
Phases of the life span (table), 5
Philosophical writings (fig.), 210
Philosophy, contributions, 209
Physical activity, dimensions, 66
Physical fitness, 66
Physical skills (table), 144
Physiological age, 60
Physiological and psychological correlations, 183-184
Pigment:
    and aging, 53
    in heart muscle with age (fig.), 54
    and oxygen lack, 56
Pilots, 141
Pitch discrimination, 97
Plaques in brain, senile, 55, 265
Plasticity of behavior, 8, 152
Play, 225
Poetry, 212
Postmortem studies, 264-265
Postural reflexes, 99
Potency, sexual, 239
Potential for senescence, 17
Practice and slowness, 112
Problem solving, 171-172
    orientation, 176
    and rigidity, 189
Productivity:
    and income, 214
    continuing, 217
    in chemistry, 208
    of workers, 201-202
    scientific, 206-207
Proverb interpretation, 175
Psychiatric illness and socioeconomic status, 29
Psychiatry of the aged, 267-268
Psychoanalytic psychology, 238
Psychoanalytical concepts of personality, 233
Psychological age defined, 10
Psychological losses, 284
Psychological and physiological correlations, 183-184
Psychology of aging (see also *Aging*):
    defined, 10
    history, 9

Psychomotor skills defined, 134
Psychopathology defined, 253
Psychosensory restitution, 96
Psychotic disorders and social class, 30
Pubescence, trend in, 17
Pupil size, 88-89
  and age (fig.), 89
  and flicker threshold, 94
Pupil:
  fatigue, 96
  response to light, 96
Pursuit rotor task (table), 146
Pyramidal system, 134

Q

Quantity-bounded relationship, 12

R

Radiant heat, pain sensitivity, 101
Radiation injury and aging, 52
Random somatic damage, 64
Rape, 255
Rat:
  activity (fig.), 226
  discrimination learning, 156
  fatigue, 119
  influences on longevity, 58
  learning, 156-157
  sex differences in speed, 119
  slowness of behavior, 54, 111
  startle reaction time, 116-117
Rate of aging, 16
Raven Progressive Matrices, 232-233
Reaction time:
  to auditory signals (fig.), 114
  practical implications, 127
  of rats, 117
  and set, 125
  stimulus complexity, 120
  to visual signals (fig.), 115
Reactive depression, 283
Reactivity and learning, 155
Recall, verbal material, 159-160
Reconciliation of life views, 274
Reflex time, 117, 119-120
Reflexes:
  conditioned, 156
  postural, 99
Regional differences in injuries, 45
Reinforcement of behavior, 7
Relationships, kinds, 12
Religious differences, 44-45
Remarriage after divorce, 35
Repetitive movement speed, 119
Research contributions, 207
Resolution of conflicts, 276
Response of pupil to light, 96

Retirement, adjustment, 205, 233
Rhythm of adult life, 6
Rigidity:
  cognition and, 106
  implications of, 13
  in behavior, 189
RNA in aging, 52
Role uncertainty, 7

S

Schizophrenic patients, 260-261
  aged, 267
Scientific achievement, 206
Scientific output and vigorous skills (fig.), 213
Seasonal variations:
  in accidents, 71
  in deaths, 68-69
Selection, high blood pressure, 75-76
Selective Service:
  data, 27-28
  rejection rate of orphans, 66
Self-haters, 235
Self-judgments of the aged, 247
Self repair of organisms, 51
Senescence, potential for, 17
Senile brain diseases, 263-265
Senile dementia, 265
Senile patients, 260-261
Senile plaques in brain, 55, 265
Sensitivity to pain, 101
Sensory acuity defined, 86
Sensory changes, implications of, 107
Sensory changes and mental illness, 267
Sensory impairments, 83
Sensory loss, compensation, 85
Sensory thresholds, defined, 83
Sequential phenomena, 12
Set:
  and learning, 160
  in problem solving, 172
  and reaction time, 125
Sex differences in:
  attitudes, 245
  crime, 256
  disability, 37
  employment, 204
  life expectation, 20
  mental tests, 188
  personality, 231-232
  suicide, 258
  swimming speed of rats, 119
  taste sensitivity, 99
Sex offenses (fig.), 255
Sexual behavior, 229-230
Sexual orgasms (fig.), 229
Sexual potency, importance, 239

Subject Index

Skills:
  and automation, 20
  characteristics, 135
  limitations, 136
  occupational, 140
  physical (table), 144
Slowness of behavior, rat, 54, 111
Slowness and the nervous system, 112
Smell, sensitivity for, 100
Social age defined, 10
Social class:
  and adverse environments, 36
  and aging, 25
  dynamics, 34
  and mobility, 32
  and morale, 26
  and psychiatric illness, 30
Social isolation, 27
Social role:
  activities, 235
  and personal adjustment, 33
Socioeconomic status:
  and chronic illness, 67
  and disease, 28
  effects on morale and health, 26
  and mental illness, 28-29
Speaking time, 124
Species differences, 16
  in longevity (tables), 57-59
Speech perception, 84
Speed:
  of behavior and condition of the organism, 126
  and blood pressure, 184
  and cardiovascular functions, 126
  and complexity of stimuli, 120
  decoding, 124
  and excitation, 120
  as a general factor, 121
  of handwriting, 121-123
  and intelligence, 233
  and irrelevant stimuli, 113
  and learning, 158
  repetitive movement, 119
  response, 124
  and set, 125
  in shift tasks, 190-191
  and stimulus complexity, 113
  of tapping, 180
  and timing, 112
Spontaneous activity in rats, 226
Sport championships and scientific output, 213
Sports, 144, 212-213
Startle reaction of the rat (fig.), 116
Stealing, arrests for, 255
Stereotypes about aged, 246
Stimulus complexity, 87, 120

Strain:
  behavioral, 193
  cognitive, 192
Streams of information, 34
Strength, maximum, 18
St. Petersburg and special facilities, 35
Subnormal aged, 270
Subsystems of the organism, 12
Successful aging, 237
Suicide:
  attempts, 267
  contributing factors, 258
  death rates for (fig.), 259
  mode, 259-260
  sex differences, 258-260
Survival:
  and mental test scores, 281
  and successful behavior, 75
Survivors and nonsurvivors, mental tests, 187
Swimming speed of rats, 119
Synaptic delay time, 120

T

Tapping time, 119, 180, 186
Taste:
  receptors, 100
  sensitivity, 99
  thresholds, 100
Terminal decline, 279-280
Terminal illness:
  changes, 282
  costs, 43
Telephone operator training (tables), 164-167
Television viewing (table), 241
Theories of aging, 10
  counterpart, 73-74
Thefts, 256
Thematic Apperception Test, 236
Thinking ability (table), 173
Thirst, 227
Three generation family, 46
Threshold:
  definition, 83
  difference, 84
Time-bounded relationship, 12
Time:
  direction, 11
  free after work, 216
  nature, 11
  pressure, 145
  uses, 205
Touch sensitivity, 101-102
Tree analogy to development, 1
Twins:
  age and appearance (fig.), 14-15

Twins (*Cont.*)
  intellectual correlations, 64
  similarity of life span, 54

U

Unemployment:
  characteristics, 204
  and crime, 258
  long term, 202
  rate (*fig.*), 203
Upward mobility, 32

V

Vascular changes and speed, 126
Vegetative centers, 56
Verbal learning, 159
Verbal tests, 177, 181-182
Vestibular apparatus, 98
Vibration:
  sense, 101-103, (*table*), 104
  thresholds (*fig.*), 103
Vice and conduct violations, arrests, (*fig.*), 257
Visibility and illumination (*fig.*), 93
Vision:
  color, 88
  defects, 94
Visual accommodation, 90
Visual acuity:
  correlation with age, 88
  defined, 88
Visual dark adaptation, 91
Visual discriminations, form, 105
Visual flicker, 94-95
Visual reaction time, 115
Vulnerability to crises, 33

W

WAIS:
  intercorrelations (*table*), 178

WAIS (*Cont.*)
  retest scores (*table*), 186
  scores, age and education (*fig.*), 179
  scores and health differences, 184
  subtests, 266
Water maze, learning of, 156-157
Watson and Glaser Critical Thinking Appraisal (*fig.*), 174
"Wear-and-tear" theories of aging, 10
Weber ratio, 86
Weigel figures, 191
Weight judgments, 104
White life expectation, 20
White suicide rates, 259
Widowhood:
  economics, 43
  financial status, 44
  social problems, 44
Widows, death rates for, 236-237
Wife, age at family events, 19
"Wife" (*fig.*), 106
Withdrawal:
  of affect, 284
  from life, 6
Word association, 192
  speed, 123-124
Work:
  and leisure, 205-207
  life, increase in, 199
  loss due to injuries (*fig.*), 38
  meaning, 16
  pattern, 217
Worker:
  age, 143
  injuries, 140
  output and experience, 201
  output (*fig.*), 202
Writers, productivity, 212
Writing:
  speed (*fig.*), 122
  time and effect of instructions (*fig.*), 123